Exploring Homemaking and Personal Living

Henrietta Fleck

Department of Home Economics and Nutrition
New York University

Louise Fernandez

Professor of Home Economics Education
Indiana University of Pennsylvania

Fourth Edition

Exploring Homemaking and Personal Living

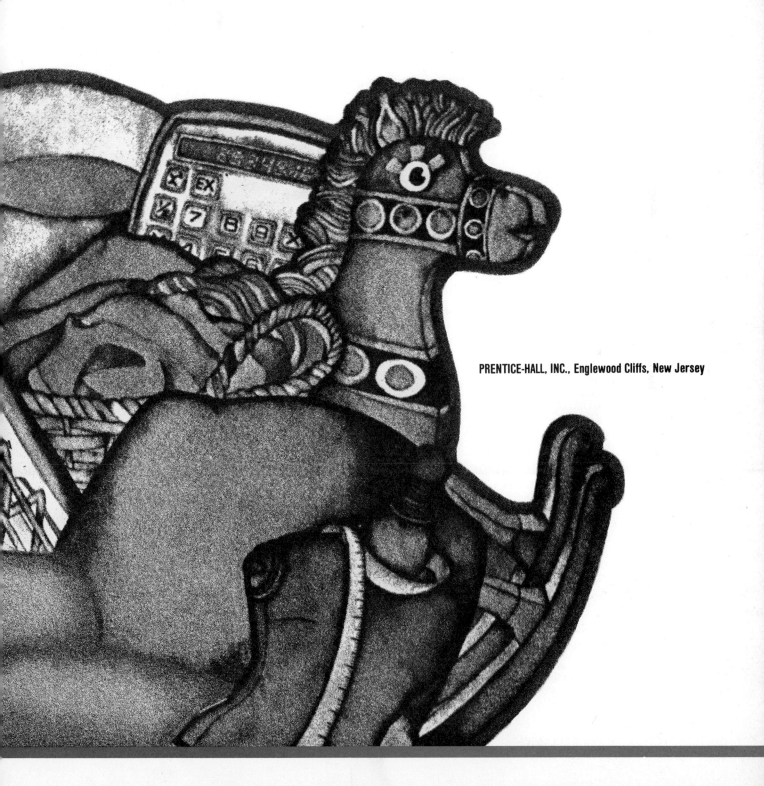

PRENTICE-HALL, INC., Englewood Cliffs, New Jersey

RELATED PRENTICE-HALL BOOKS

BUILDING A SUCCESSFUL MARRIAGE by Judson T. Landis and Mary G. Landis

CAREERS: EXPLORATION AND DECISION by Jack L. Rettig

CLOTHING—YOUR WAY by Jan Jones

FOOD AND YOUR FUTURE by Ruth Bennett White

HOME ECONOMICS CAREERS SERIES

CHILD CARE CAREERS by Xenia F. Fane

COSMETIC AND GROOMING CAREERS by Mari Friedrichs Messer

FASHION AND TEXTILES CAREERS by Martha S. Servian

FOOD CAREERS by Donna Newberry Creasy

HEALTH CARE CAREERS by James P. Sweeney

HOUSING CAREERS by Sidney Schwartz

INTERIOR DESIGN CAREERS by Rita Marie Schneider

MAKING HEALTH DECISIONS by Ben C. Gmur, John T. Fodor, L. H. Glass, and Joseph J. Langan

MAKING THE MOST OF MARRIAGE by Paul H. Landis

MARRIAGE, THE FAMILY, AND PERSONAL FULFILLMENT by David A. Schulz and Stanley F. Rodgers

PERSONAL ADJUSTMENT, MARRIAGE, AND FAMILY LIVING by Judson T. Landis and Mary G. Landis

REFLECTIONS ON RELATIONSHIPS: A STUDENT JOURNAL by Loni Kappler, Barbara Uittenbogaard, and Roger Uittenbogaard

THE FIRST THREE YEARS OF LIFE by Burton L. White

UNDERSTANDING AND GUIDING YOUNG CHILDREN by Katherine Reed Baker and Xenia F. Fane

YOU AND YOUR FOOD by Ruth Bennett White

EXPLORING HOMEMAKING AND PERSONAL LIVING, fourth edition
by Henrietta Fleck and Louise Fernandez
(previously entitled EXPLORING FAMILY LIFE, fourth edition)

Formerly EXPLORING HOME AND FAMILY LIVING, third edition
by Henrietta Fleck and Louise Fernandez
© 1971, 1965, 1959 by Prentice-Hall, Inc.,
Englewood Cliffs, N.J.

ISBN 0-13-297051-1   10 9 8 7 6 5 4

PRENTICE-HALL INTERNATIONAL, INC., London
PRENTICE-HALL OF AUSTRALIA, PTY. LTD., Sydney
PRENTICE-HALL OF CANADA, LTD., Toronto
PRENTICE-HALL OF INDIA PRIVATE LTD., New Delhi
PRENTICE-HALL OF JAPAN, INC., Tokyo
PRENTICE-HALL OF SOUTHEAST ASIA PTE. LTD., Singapore
WHITEHALL BOOKS LIMITED, Wellington, New Zealand

Designed by Celine Alvarez Brandes

Cover illustration by Bob Pepper

preface

You are at an important age. Physically, intellectually, and emotionally, you are growing. What you do now—the food you eat, the attitudes you develop, the daily habits you establish—can help you have a good life now and a full, rich life in the future.

EXPLORING HOMEMAKING AND PERSONAL LIVING is designed to help you achieve those goals, as an individual and as a member of a family. It is divided into eight areas, each representing an important aspect of your development.

Area 1, *Toward a Better You,* helps you become better acquainted with yourself and establish your goals for improved living.

Area 2, *You and Your Family,* explores your relations with other family members, and the importance of your heritage in forming your self-concept.

Area 3, *Child Development,* discusses characteristics of children at various stages, and how to attain mutually rewarding relationships both as an older sister or brother and as a baby sitter. This can help you later as a parent.

Area 4, *Food for Your Family and You,* considers the wise selection of food for optimum health, and the many influences that shape your food habits.

Area 5, *Helping with Family Meals,* emphasizes the planning, buying, and preparation of meals for your family and friends.

Area 6, *Your Clothes,* deals with the influence of clothes on self-image, and offers suggestions on how to become an intelligent clothes shopper. It also gives instructions on basic sewing.

Area 7, *Being a Good Manager,* offers many ideas on the efficient use of materials and money, handling of health emergencies, and improving the home environment.

Area 8, *Looking Ahead,* treats the influence of your present activities on your future career, and ways to make your life more interesting and pleasant.

Sections at the end of each chapter, "Thinking It Over" and "Things to Do," help make the text material more meaningful for you, your family, your friends, and your community. They challenge you to act—to question new ideas, think them through, investigate new ways of doing everyday things, and have other exciting and worthwhile experiences. The illustrations are planned to give you a better understanding of the content and to stimulate your thinking.

Many individuals have contributed to the preparation of this book. We are grateful to our professional colleagues, friends, and students for their excellent suggestions for the revision of the text. We are also grateful to our editors, Fanny S. Mach and Jane Standen, for their assistance in preparing this edition.

Henrietta Fleck wishes to express special appreciation to a number of her former students for their helpful suggestions: Lucy Beck, Carolee Nadel, Helen Pfaff, Andrea Roberts, Noreen Roach, Marilyn Vogel, Ann Wareham, and Margaret Westin. She is also grateful to her great-nieces Brenda and Diane Fleck, junior high school students in home economics in Gretna, Nebraska, for their valued insight and criticism in connection with selected chapters of the manuscript.

The authors are pleased with the encouraging comments and constructive suggestions that have been made by many teachers and students who have used earlier editions of this text. A number of their ideas have been incorporated into this revision.

Henrietta Fleck

Louise Fernandez

contents

area one

Toward a Better You

1 Personal development

INTRODUCTION

Probably one of the central questions you are asking yourself at this stage of your development is "Who am I?" Deciding who you are is not a passive exercise but a very basic question. It involves making a personal inventory, setting your own goals, and developing plans to achieve these goals.

When researchers asked people to write the answer to the question "Who are you?" more than 20 percent responded with terms that showed a limited idea of who they were. They often listed one role, such as *student* or *cook*, not their name. A person's name identifies him or her in all situations in a complete and individual sense.

Another significant area of development that probably concerns you is your social development. How can you increase your understanding of others? Are there things you can learn that would help you to achieve maturity in this area of development? Certain learning experiences have been found to be appropriate for different age levels. During your stage of development, training in personal and social adjustment are major tasks.

What does it mean to be a social person? A widely accepted definition indicates that it involves three processes. Every social group has its own standard for what is proper behavior. And the first thing one must do is learn to behave in an approved way. Generally, some variation in behavior is allowed by the group to fit an individual's own needs and desires. Second, you are expected to play approved roles. Again, every social group has its own recognized ways for people to behave. These involve different areas of life and approved roles for the two sexes. And finally, in order to be accepted as a group member, the individual must like people and social activities.

These are the main ideas that are explored in AREA ONE.

PERSONALITY DEVELOPMENT

What do we mean by the word *personality?* Your personality is you in all your human dimensions—body, mind, feelings, attitudes, and actions. The human personality changes and develops throughout life. It is generally accepted that our basic personalities are largely shaped in the early years of life. Our parents, families, and early environment set the pattern for the kind of persons we become. The environment includes all the people, places, things, and events that are part of your life. However, it is important to remember that we have also shaped our own lives to a great extent. And we can continue to change. The way you have reacted to all that has happened to you in your life has involved many choices and decisions. You expressed your own ideas of what you wanted to become in many ways. For example, have you ever noticed a small baby communicating that something was unacceptable? Observe small children. You will see that they show in many ways both the things they like to do and those they do not want to do. The many possibilities in life that exist for making choices, as well as each individual's drive toward self-determination means that *you can change if you want to.* In addition, you can develop those qualities that you like in yourself.

Personal Developmental Tasks

There are four major personal tasks you should learn to cope with at this stage of your development. These can provide a sound basis for your future success as an adult.

First, you must achieve satisfying relations with young people of your own age of both sexes. This involves
- Learning to work with others.
- Learning to be responsible in your relationships with others.
- Learning to relate to others unselfishly.
- Finding ways to get along with people who may be difficult to get along with.
- Learning to care seriously about others.
- Learning to give to and take from others.

The second task is to achieve a masculine or feminine social role. This task means that you must
- Learn to function as an adult male or female.
- Establish appropriate relationships with members of your own sex.
- Learn appropriate ways of relating to members of the opposite sex.
- Accept your own body with pride.

Third, you will need to learn how to handle your feelings and emotions. This means learning to
- Express your feelings in appropriate ways.
- Express anger so that the tension it causes can be reduced.
- Manage fear and insecurity.
- Express positive feelings of affection and approval.

How do you express anger, fear, or insecurity? How do you act when you are afraid? There are many ways to diminish tensions so that you will not act in ways that may be harmful to you. Sometimes strong feelings make us destructive. There are positive ways of handling such situations. One way is to become involved

You learn to work with others through sharing and cooperation.

Learn to function as an adult female or male.

Accept your own body with pride.

in physical activities. These may be sports, such as swimming or hiking, or work that involves muscular effort.

Lastly, you must achieve independence. To become an independent person you will need to

● Learn to do things as an individual with ideas of your own.
● Learn to think for yourself.
● Examine your values and standards.
● Give up childlike dependence on your parents or friends.

Establish appropriate relationships with members of your own sex.

Somewhere during this period you will discover that you no longer need to depend on parents and friends as you used to when you were younger. Making decisions on the basis of what friends think shows insecurity and lack of independence.

When each of these tasks is accomplished it will prepare you to function well as an adult.

"WHO AM I?"

The central question you need to answer in order to understand yourself and to make effective plans for your life is "Who am I?"

What has happened to you so far is only one part of who you are. More important than simply recognizing what has happened to you is how you have felt about what has occurred. Many people come from deprived backgrounds. They may be intellectually, emotionally, physically, or socially deprived. It is important for you to consider the fact that you may have lacked some advantages. But how you have reacted to any shortcomings is even more important. Some people seem to decide to live as victims of deprivation. Others decide to achieve all that it is possible for them to become despite their limitations. Many others, perhaps including you, come from privileged backgrounds. Opportunities for healthy growth and intellectual development have always been provided. What meaning do your past experiences have for you? That is the key question you should ask yourself.

Of course, you were born with certain potentials as well as limitations. We all were. But a very important fact for you to remember is that you are unique; there is no one exactly like you in the whole world. What do you consider your limitations? Can you see the possibilities for overcoming them? How can you use your shortcomings to your advantage? There are many possibilities. However, you must be realistic in evaluating those qualities that cannot be changed. For example, small stature, lack of athletic ability, and the like, are generally unchangeable to any significant degree. Look at your positive assets and capabilities. Focus on them when setting goals for your development. A realistic self-evaluation will form the basis for continued growth and achievement.

Self-Concept

In simple terms, self-concept refers to the mental picture you have of yourself. When you underestimate yourself, you are said to have a

Who am I?

low self-concept. You generally focus on your shortcomings and failures if you always have a low self-concept. Equally unrealistic is an exaggerated self-concept in which you overestimate yourself. The closer your self-concept comes to what you really are, the easier it is for you to become mature.

Having a strong self-concept involves

- Knowing your weaknesses.
- Recognizing your strengths.
- Thinking in terms of possibilities and potentials.
- Having a realistic, positive picture of yourself.
- Believing that you are a worthy person.
- Exploring as many options as possible to make wise decisions.

PREPARING FOR ADULT ROLES

During this stage of development, the experiences you have can help you develop the abilities you will need as an adult. As an adult you will function in many roles: as a worker, marriage partner, parent, citizen, or in other categories. Do you see yourself as an important person? Are you building friendly and cooperative relations with others? These are ways of preparing to take on the roles expected of adults.

During your period of development you are preparing for these adult roles by (1) developing positive attitudes toward family life, (2) studying and developing your intellectual skills, (3) think-

How do you relate to the opposite sex?

ing about and perhaps preparing for an occupation, and (4) developing your own system of values that will give deep personal meaning to your life.

Successful, satisfying family living is based on achieving a masculine or feminine identity. Positive attitudes toward family life are developed through many different kinds of experiences. How do you relate to the opposite sex? Some of this behavior may continue to be used when you are an adult and have a family of your own. You can gain insight and knowledge about families through the kinds of families you are closely associated with. Do you observe what other families are like? You probably have begun to establish in your own mind what you consider a rewarding family life experience to be. The families with which you are familiar will help you set up your own standards. The kind of family life you hope to have some day will be based, in part, on these family experiences you are having now.

To be an informed citizen in a democracy you need to develop your mental capacities. How can you make the important decisions a citizen is privileged to make if you have not learned to think for yourself? What facts and information do you need to make the choices you will have to make? You need to learn such basic skills as how to think creatively and how to express yourself clearly. You must acquire a fund of knowledge. You will also need to develop your sense of responsibility.

What do you plan to do as your life's work? You should examine your interests, talents, abilities, and inclinations. These will give you clues that will help you select the kind of work which will be most satisfying to you. Consider your hobbies and personal interests when you are trying to determine your future occupation. These frequently provide clues to your most absorbing interests. The decision about your life's work is generally the result of a long, gradual, and continuous process. Most young people change their minds a number of times before they definitely decide about the kind of work they want to do. Today, the rate of change in jobs is very rapid. New knowledge is increasing at such a pace that we can seldom say that you complete your education and go to work. Instead, successful men and women of the future must be able to change. They probably will be expected to learn continuously throughout life. For more job opportunities and successful career planning, you must be flexible, adaptable, and willing to learn. With these qualities you should be able to find satisfaction in any one of a large number of different careers. Whatever else you base your decision on, the career you choose should meet your own individual needs. It should be in keeping with your values. Whatever you decide to become, be the very best you can be. Take pride in the contribution you make.

Finally, you have your own way of looking at life. What you believe about your place in the world and what you feel is important in your life is your philosophy. The values and standards you live by express this pattern of beliefs. You will probably continue to live by them in pretty much the same way as an adult. When what you believe and what you consider worthy are in harmony, your life will have a deep inner, personal meaning.

COPING WITH CHANGE

How does personality develop? What factors have made you what you are? How many of your goals are you in the process of achieving?

Perhaps the most important concept that was presented in this chapter is that regardless of your past experiences or the shortcomings you may have to deal with, you can decide to change if you want to. Preparing for adult roles is a major task for young people. Your experiences and activities now will help you learn ways of coping with the roles you must assume as an adult.

THINKING IT OVER

1. Many people can help you in your personal and social adjustment. List ten people in your community who might be helpful, and in a small group of friends discuss the value of finding adults who can add to your personal maturity. Be specific in discussing the ways that the people you have thought of can help you.

2. Assume that you are trying to make an important decision about your future job or profession. What do you need to know about yourself? What factors will you need to discuss with your family? Are there elements you can find out for yourself? Do a thorough review of the process involved in making life-decisions.

3. Think of two or three typical decision-making situations or problems with which you were involved recently. Suggest how they could be resolved. Consider the possible long-range consequences of your choices.

THINGS TO DO

1. Observe infants or small children who refuse to eat or who have had enough to eat. How do they communicate this information? What message do they convey about their individuality by their behavior?

2. There are many ways to discover talents and special interests. To get some notion of your potential interests or talents, for 30 days clip all newspaper articles, cartoons, and magazine articles that appeal to you. Put them in a large envelope. At the end of this time, examine your collection. See if you can categorize or group the items together in some logical order in terms of topic, content, or activity. Then ask yourself why these items held a special appeal for you. It is very likely that they will reveal a tendency toward one or more areas of interest to you. Now, consider 10 ways you can increase your interest or develop your abilities in one or more of the areas you discovered.

2 Under-standing others

What processes must we learn and use in order to understand others? How do you feel toward others? How do you communicate? In what ways do people interact together? How do you respond emotionally to experiences and people? You will develop more effective ways of relating to others if you can answer these questions.

UNDERSTANDING AND COPING WITH EMOTIONS

Tensions and frustrations frequently are generated when people have to face a new situation or responsibility. Generally, people feel secure with what they know best. This is a basic principle of human relations. When you must go into unfamiliar territory it makes you feel anxious. Sometimes new knowledge and facts lead you to question what you believe. This can be extremely threatening. When experiences and events in your life seem to contradict your values and ideals, you will find that it makes you feel very uncomfortable. Sometimes people make you question your sense of worth. In situations of this kind, the decision you reach should be based on intellectual factors as well as how you feel about them. Try to separate facts and information from what you feel. Everyone has these internal reactions to new experiences. And they lead to tension and frustration.

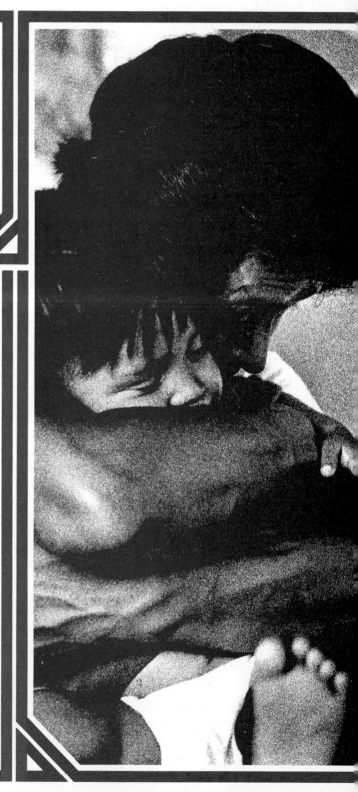

It is possible to find creative ways of relieving tension. A person can build inner strength and be better able to cope with frustration. There is no one best way for all people to learn. You can develop your skills by discovering options for yourself in everything you do. Studies tell us that we can develop our creative thinking skills with continued practice. Always try to see alternatives to problem situations by asking yourself a lot of "else" questions: How else? When else? Where else? Why else? Who else? What else? Also questions such as What can I take away or add? Can it be made smaller or larger? can help you develop your ability to see many possible solutions.

Another positive principle of human relations is based on the fact that if you provide options for *others* to use in coping with situations, you build mutual respect. This is a form of affirmation of others as unique human beings. An interesting result is that every time you find productive ways of meeting problems, you will discover that it becomes easier to think of more alternatives the next time you are faced with a problem.

Everyone has experienced negative emotions such as anger, fear, and jealousy. These feelings frequently get in the way of good communications with others. How can you handle these emotions effectively? They may interfere with your interaction with others. When you feel good about yourself you are more open and can deal with others on a positive level.

TENSION RELIEVERS

Some techniques that can help you relieve tension and reduce feelings of frustration include the following:

- Verbalize.
- Do something physical.
- Do something creative, inventive, out of the ordinary.
- Create chaos out of order, then reorder.

Ask yourself a lot of "else" questions.

- Do a visual search.
- Look at a common household item and describe its characteristics to find new uses for it.

In general, the simplest way to get rid of anger and tension is to talk about it. Discuss the problem with someone who is not involved in the situation. Often by the time you have explained it to someone else, a solution may suggest itself. Expressing your inner thoughts and feelings in a diary may help reduce tension. In this case you are "talking" to yourself and it may help you to find an answer.

Doing something physical uses pent-up energy and tends to make you feel more relaxed. Water has a beneficial value when one is upset. Keep your eyes closed and feel how the water goes over your hands and through your fingers. Listen to the sound of the running water. Did you know that hot and cold running water have very different sounds? Close your eyes and see whether you can tell which is which.

Look out the window for three minutes.

11

Thoughts and feelings written in a diary may help reduce tensions.

Look out the window to get away from your problems for a minute.

you may have to speak more loudly. You will also have to listen more carefully. Observe how the flow of ideas and the process of communication changes when you use the different group patterns.

Are you feeling tense and full of pent-up energy? Sometimes it is very satisfying to create chaos out of order and then put things right again. Dump a drawer full of things out on the counter or the floor. Then rearrange and put things back in a new order. Clean out a closet.

Have you ever tried a visual search to help you to feel more relaxed? Look through old magazines. Read the advertisements to find unusual word combinations. What new display ideas can you find? Look for attention-getting sketches or illustrations. Can you adapt your discoveries to a different purpose? Look through cookbooks. Find three new recipes that sound interesting to you. Try at least one of them.

Another creative exercise that can provide relief from tension is to "unlabel." This means that you simply take away the name usually used for an item. Then try to see it in a new way or used for another purpose. You mentally remove its common purpose and create different uses for it. For example, the minute someone says the word sheet, you know what it looks like and what it is used for. Now, unlabel it. Instead of naming it, describe its qualities. It is a large piece of fabric, is absorbent, may be colorful, has no seams, drapes well, is washable, and so on. You should have no difficulty in finding fifty new ways of using a sheet. Do this with other items, such as turkish towels or a potato peeler.

Focus on what ever seems restful, beautiful, calm, or different to you. Or try these: rearrange a closet, polish a mirror, scrub a tub, make something shine. Achieve order and a peaceful atmosphere in a small part of your surroundings. Fold towels or laundry; notice the texture, smell, and look of the clean items.

Are you feeling blue? Do something out of the ordinary. Write with a red or green pen. Sit on the floor to sew. Have a wheel discussion with six people in the group. Lie on the floor with heads close together in the center and facing the ceiling. This provides a wide view of your surroundings. It is easy to hear each other even if you are speaking softly. Or, reverse the wheel pattern by lying face down with feet in the center. This gives you a more restricted view and

Get rid of the blues. Do something out of the ordinary.

Try a visual search.

talk together as long as no human beings are present? Role-play inanimate objects. Assign roles such as an ashtray with a cigar stub in it, a lamp, and an empty glass on a coffee table with melting ice cubes in it. Indicate who the people are who have just left the living room where these inanimate objects are. Let the objects tell how they feel and what they think about the occupants and their life-style. What would happen to the role-playing if a person entered the room? What could you learn by just sitting there and listening and watching as inanimate objects do? What would some inanimate objects around you say if they could talk?

Another variation is to role-play a situation in twos. The two participants or a whole group of paired players sit back to back. They may be on chairs or on the floor. They will discuss the same problem. The communication would be like talking on the telephone. You cannot see the person you are talking to. Analyze to see how the communication process is limited because you cannot see the person who is talking. Could communication about a difficult problem be easier to handle sometimes if the speakers were separated like this? Why?

How can you express how and what you feel through nonverbal experiences? This is done through physical movements and actions or through creative activities. These procedures are based on the fact, which is seldom taken into account, that children learn most of their ways of responding emotionally at a very young age and before they can talk. Their knowledge of love, rejection, anger, and need comes through their physical senses, such as touch, hunger pangs, and flushed face during the preverbal period of development. As children learn to talk they learn words for things and actions, but generally not for feelings. They will say, "I am bad," instead of "I feel bad." Many young people have difficulty expressing how and what they feel.

How do you feel when you have a cold and ache all over? One youngster said she felt like a crooked stick. Can you show how it feels to be sleepy? hungry? strong? tired? sorry? You should try to demonstrate these feelings without using words.

YOU IN A GROUP

To be yourself in a group and think your own thoughts requires a certain degree of maturity. A genuine curiosity and a vivid imagination help to

Role-play in twos back to back.

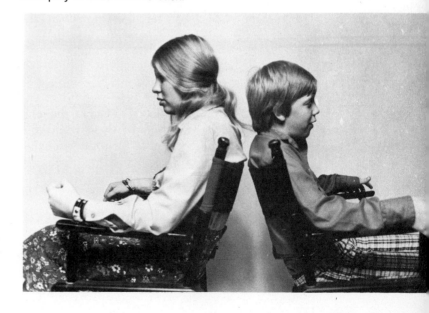

INTERACTION THROUGH ROLE-PLAYING

Two ways to help you clarify your feelings are through games and role-playing. These are also ways of testing how to express your feelings. Try some unusual role-playing procedures. For example, did you know that inanimate objects can

Be yourself in a group.

develop your capacity to think and reason. Learning to ask questions is a good way to develop your individuality and your social skills. It is told that when Dr. Jonas E. Salk was interviewed after his discovery of the polio vaccine, a reporter asked him how he became interested in research. Dr. Salk said that it was inevitable. From the first day he went to school and returned home in the afternoon, his mother did not ask him, "What did you learn in school today?" Instead she asked, "Did you ask any good questions today?" So that all through school and throughout his life, he learned the habit of making up good questions. Here is an important clue for you: It is never too late to learn to ask good questions.

CONCLUSION

Much of this chapter has focused on helping you understand how you and others feel, communicate, and interact together. An understanding of some of these factors should help you to be more satisfied with yourself. It should also help you be aware of the needs and feelings of others. As a consequence of studying this chapter, you should be able to get along better with yourself and others.

THINKING IT OVER

What do you mean by the phrase "The dignity and worth of individuals"? Consider how you would communicate with others and how you would behave in groups if you believed in individual worth and dignity. How would you expect others to treat you?

THINGS TO DO

1. Reread the story about Dr. Salk. Discuss: How would it influence a child's development, both intellectually and socially, if the parents always asked, "Did you ask any good questions today?"

2. Learn to develop your communication skills. Talk as little as possible for a whole day, if you ordinarily talk a lot. Listen to the meaning of the other person's words. What feelings are expressed by the person through facial expression and movement of the hands? How does sensitivity to the needs of others affect communication? If you are usually a quiet sort of person, try talking more. Become involved in conversations with others more often for a whole day. Note how you feel about your changed behavior. How do others respond?

3. Have you ever had a conversation with someone who made critical comments about you? What did you do? How did you feel? What should you do if you feel that the other person is mistaken or wrong? Is there a positive way of handling a situation where someone has an accusing attitude?

3 Coping with morals

Do you have the feeling that the world never fails to tell you what is right or wrong about your behavior? It may be your grandmother, the supermarket manager for whom you work part time, a student at school, or sometimes your best friend who tries to reform you. Has the time come for you to give this matter some thought? You may even admit that some of their advice has merit.

DEFINITION OF MORALS

The first thing to do is to decide what morals are. That is not easy. Some say they pertain to the "goodness" of a person. The interpretation of "goodness" will vary from person to person. You might start with some "good" characteristics that you believe are important to you at the moment. Such words as honest, loyal, responsible, considerate of others, or fair may come to mind. List as many "good" characteristics as you can. Talk with your friends about your ideas. Do they agree or disagree? Did they mention some traits that you had not considered but that are acceptable? Make up a new list—mentally or on paper—and group the traits into *Very Important, Important, Least Important*. Look at your list of "good" characteristics again. Do you feel that these traits belong to you?

ORIGIN

You may wish to examine your list of traits in other ways. How did your preference for these traits originate? Does your best friend think they are important? Has your grandfather made some suggestions? Was there a character in a story you admired who possessed these traits? Did someone at home, at school, in church or synagogue, or in your community influence you in the choices you made? Did the way you felt about these people seem important? Have you found certain moral standards workable—that is, they seemed right for you and gave you satisfaction, so you kept them? It may be impossible to trace the origin of some traits—they seem to have grown with you. This searching may lead to the conclusion that there are many influences on the kind of morals that you or any other person possesses. Which influences do you consider most important in your life?

IMPORTANCE

A discussion of morals is pointless unless this topic is important to you. You may feel morals are not important in your life, but you do have some kind of morals even if you have not thought about them or consciously planned for them. A family member or friend could quickly decide whether you are honest, thoughtful of others, violent, or nonviolent, or if you possess other moral qualities. Since you have morals anyway, wouldn't it be a good idea to get acquainted with them?

What are some tangible benefits from having some direction in your life as to what you feel is best for you and for others? Think of the persons with whom you have to associate who seem to lack moral direction. Is it easy to deal with someone who is careless about telling the truth, who has little respect for other persons' property, who is not dependable, and who is indifferent about the effect of actions on himself or herself, or on others?

EFFECT OF THE SITUATION

Does the situation have an influence on one's moral decisions? Take a look at a couple of situations and place yourself in the shoes of the leading character. What would you have done and why?

1-A friend of a friend of a friend tells Sam that an almost new tennis racquet can be purchased from a certain source, "dirt-cheap." Sam is tempted to buy because it is exactly the kind of tennis racquet that he would like to own. Some of his friends encourage him and others, plus family members, discourage him because of possible legal complications and other reasons. He wants that racquet badly. He does not buy it but wishes he had. A few days later Sam's prized baseball mitt is stolen from his back porch. He is upset and angry. "Why would

Are there boys and girls who try to sell you something at very low cost? What do you do if you suspect the goods have been stolen?

Telephone someone who can help you with a moral problem by referring to your "Hot Line for Help."

anyone steal my mitt? I worked so hard to earn enough money to buy it." His friend Frank points out to him that it is probably being sold cheaply to a friend of a friend of a friend.

2–Gale, a bright, competent, and popular student, is running for Student Council. Sarah and some friends are talking about the election and how they will vote. Sarah indicates that she will not vote for Gale, even though she would be good for the job. Sarah's reason: "Why should I vote for her? She has everything."

3–Bill is sauntering down the corridor to his locker one day when Hank, a student, approaches him and asks him if he would like to buy some marijuana.

4–Harriet watches a television program on the serious problem of the use of alcohol by youth. Statistics given indicate that the United States has a half million preteen and teen-age alcoholics, three out of every four youngsters beginning at age 9 or 10 do some drinking; and one in ten will become an alcoholic. In the light of these figures, Harriet wonders what the situation is in her own community.

Share your ideas with others. Can you draw any general conclusions from these situations?

DECISIONS AND VALUES

Experts tell us that decision making and values are important in dealing with moral problems. In making a decision, consider the consequences, gather adequate data to uphold your decision, and determine the effect of your decision on yourself and on others. Some consequences of your decision are immediate, others are delayed. Select one of the situations above and decide on possible immediate and delayed consequences. Which values of the main character were highlighted? How might they influence decisions?

SOME GUIDELINES

You may have decided by now that making moral decisions is not easy. No doubt at times you have made choices that you felt later were not the best. Making judgments, according to some authorities, requires experience. As mentioned previously, primary consideration must be focused on the consequences to you as a person and what results of a detrimental or satisfying nature, the decision may have on others.

Sometimes it is helpful to talk to someone about your decision and its moral aspects. This may be someone in your family, a neighbor, a friend, or others who respect your confidence in them and who have something to offer. You may find these individuals useful in varying situa-

tions. Why not consider them as a kind of personal "Hot Line for Help." There may be agencies or other organizations in your community that offer assistance that your friends have found valuable, and you may wish to give consideration to them. Can you suggest other resources?

HELPING OTHERS

It is possible that you are an individual who has sorted out moral values and ways of making decisions. In that event, you might be a great help to others, especially friends who have difficulties or who do not recognize the consequences of their acts. One way to help is to let such a person talk to you freely without critical reaction. Another procedure is to get the troubled person involved in activities in and out of school with individuals who are supportive, if behavioral change is a goal. This is not a suggestion that you become an amateur psychologist; but just being a good friend can be helpful. And the experience may provide insights for your own moral development.

Letting a friend talk to you may help her or him with a pressing moral problem.

THINKING IT OVER

1. Most of the emphasis in this chapter has been on personal morals. Are there morals of a national nature? Where do you stand on feeding the hungry, waging war, promoting honesty in government, protecting the consumer, helping the poor, controlling violence, and other problems with moral implications?

2. Has anyone served as a model in your moral development? If not, could you sketch one who might serve in this capacity?

3. What kind of moral traits would you like your children to have? How would you assist in their development?

THINGS TO DO

1. Analyze feelings associated with situations involving morals. Role-play an actual experience in which someone was dishonest with you. Try to share the feelings of other students as they describe their experiences. Were certain feelings held in common? Did you become better acquainted with other students as a result of this experience? If so, how?

2. Glance through your local newspaper and select some stories that depict moral situations. What were your reactions? What else would you like to know about the person or persons involved to clarify some questions or ideas you had?

3. Imagine you are the manager of a supermarket who is upset about the stealing of fruit, crackers, and other items or someone in the telephone company who has to cope with the many attempts of persons to make telephone calls from a telephone booth without paying for them. Dramatize how they might feel.

area two

You and Your Family

4 Family relationships

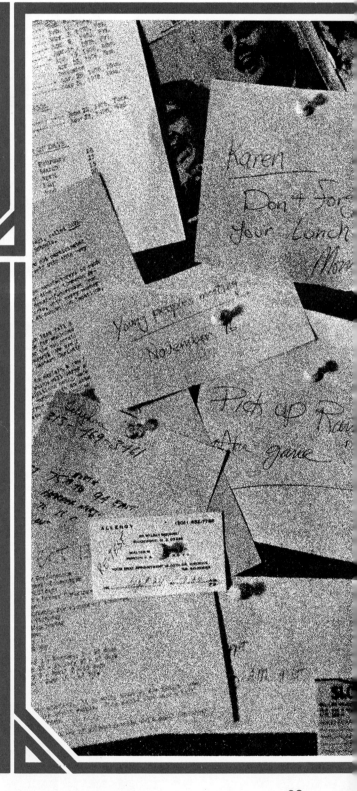

BASIC EMOTIONAL NEEDS

Cooperating and sharing provide the basis for happy relationships within your family and with people in general. Many young people ask, "What does my family do for me, anyhow?" Sometimes it is difficult to see the benefits you derive from being part of your family. Probably the most important way your family helps you is by meeting your basic emotional needs. All human beings have three basic emotional needs: (1) acceptance, (2) significance, and (3) safety.

Someone has got to like you.

You have to feel you amount to something.

You must feel safe and secure.

Family Acceptance

Since family members live so closely together and see one another under every sort of condition, adjustments and allowances must be made for everyone in the family. Regardless of whether you are at your best or at your worst, no matter what mistakes you make or how badly you behave, you can be sure that you are loved for yourself alone in your family.

Significance as a Person

In your family, you are given opportunities to achieve big and little successes, and to gain the recognition everyone needs. You develop a sense of pride in doing things well. And you find much pleasure in telling your family about the things you do in school, in sports, or in other activities.

Safety Through Your Family

A common problem which faces many young people is "How can I understand my family?" To get along well in any group you must understand the individuals who make up the group. Your first and most important experience with living in a group is in your family. You achieve a sense of belonging and a sense of security through your family. Your family is like a circle of safety where each one protects and supports the others.

Of course, you cannot see or touch any of these benefits, but you do feel them. When they are lacking, you also feel the loss. Your family helps you to develop into the kind of individual who understands others and who shares in the responsibilities and privileges involved in being a family member.

THE INDIVIDUAL WITHIN THE FAMILY
Family Members Are Different

No two people are exactly alike in the things they want, their attitudes, their temperaments, what they believe in, how they think, act, and feel—in countless ways. It is to be expected, then, that young people will have differences of opinion with their parents because of a difference of point of view.

For example, your attitude toward making decisions for yourself may be very different from the attitude of your parents. Even an older brother or younger sister might have different attitudes about decision making. Maybe you feel that you are grown up enough to decide what is best for you without asking advice from anyone. You may feel that you are dependable and able to make sound judgments. Your parents, on the

Your family is like a circle of safety where each one protects and supports the others.

other hand, may be reluctant to allow you this responsibility because you may have not had enough experience in making serious decisions. Each of you may resent the other's point of view, and conflict may result.

Adjusting to Differences

How you adjust to these different points of view depends largely on the kind of person you are and the kind of person you want to become. In order to gain the privileges that go with being grown-up, you must demonstrate that you have learned to handle the corresponding responsibilities. You must prove that you can take the consequences for your decisions and actions.

Learn to share and cooperate.

LEARNING TO SHARE AND COOPERATE

How do families learn to share and cooperate, to solve their problems, to get what they want and think best for everyone? There are three ways:

1–Do things together.
2–Talk things over and make cooperative decisions.
3–Give each member opportunities to try out new ideas.

Doing Things Together

Working and playing together builds family unity and happiness. You may not agree with your parents' ideas of fun. Why not come up with some suggestions of your own if the ones your family makes are not to your liking? Your busy parents would probably appreciate your suggesting an evening of fun for the family or your taking the initiative for planning a family visit to some place of interest. Your idea may get your family working and playing together. A student once said, "Initiative is the power of commencing." So let's get started.

Who Does What at Home?

Not too long ago, the mother of the family was expected to manage the home and do all the

Since we live so close to one another in the family we must make allowances and adjustments for everyone.

If the job must be done, it does not matter who does it.

work. But family life has changed. Today the successful home depends on the contributions of all of its members for its management and care. Boys and men share in the work of the home and the care of the children. Girls and women often help with work outside the home. A good motto for today's family might be "If a job needs to be done, it doesn't matter *who* does it." Family life will be more pleasant if everyone shares voluntarily. Sometimes families have conferences to plan who does what and to see that each one carries through assignments success-

24

Doing things together in the family promotes understanding and unity.

fully. There is no greater pleasure or greater reward than doing something for those you love.

If your family has assigned you certain household chores ever since you were a small child, it is likely that you find satisfaction in doing different, more grown-up kinds of work around home now. At first you were responsible only for simple tasks like emptying the wastebaskets and doing the easy dusting. Later you outgrew these jobs and learned more complicated ones, like making your bed and cleaning the bathroom. Now you may be doing the shopping, helping with the meals, polishing the silver, and doing dozens of other tasks. If you have always been taught to assume responsibility for those jobs around the house that were suitable for you as you grew, you probably have little difficulty cooperating with your family now. When each one of us does a part of the work it becomes easier for everyone.

A mother with six children and a large house to care for solved the problem of dividing the work (division of labor) by lining the six children up on Monday morning and assigning jobs for the week. "You wash dishes, you dry, you pack the lunches, you make the beds, you dust upstairs, you dust downstairs," and so on. The next Monday everyone moved up one position and she assigned jobs again, thereby rotating the chores. It made no difference whether the jobs fell to boys or girls. What was important was to get the work done, and she simply devised an interesting system to achieve her goal.

TALKING THINGS OVER

The way is being paved for unity and understanding when members of a family get together to talk things over. Some families meet once a week; others have discussions as problems arise. A family council need not be a formal affair; it can be a simple talk out where each one can have his or her say. Each one takes part in forming family decisions.

What are some of the problems that might be brought up at a family council? Sharing a room isn't easy. What can we do to cut down disputes? Can I get a raise in my allowance? Why can't I have a new dress? Why can't I stay out as late as Fred? Big or little, if the problem or question is important enough to cause worry, misunderstanding, or resentment, it is important enough to discuss in family council.

There are nine steps for putting a family council into practice:

1-The entire family is assembled. A parent or some other member may be asked to preside. (He or she just sees that everyone is heard.) Another member acts as secretary, taking notes and summarizing the ideas presented.

2-State the problem or subject for discussion.

3-Start with a problem that has a good chance of being easily solved.

4-Each person may make a statement, agree or disagree with what someone else has said, with *reasons* for agreement or disagreement, or raise a question related to the problem. No one may interrupt while another member is talking. If necessary, set a two-minute time limit.

5-Everyone should be heard and no idea should be discounted or ridiculed before all ideas are in or without an explanation, such as, it costs too much, would take too long, seems too difficult, and the like.

6-The secretary summarizes the ideas suggested.

7-Proposed solutions are offered.

8-A solution is selected either by majority vote (parents have veto power) or by general agreement or by volunteers taking on the responsibility.

9-The family works together on the agreed plan.

MAKING COOPERATIVE DECISIONS

The family council can be called by anyone in the family who has a decision to make or a problem to face. Listening to what others may have to say about something that concerns you personally will help you develop your powers of judgment by prompting you to look at all the evidence from every possible angle before you commit yourself to a course of action. Cooperative decisions arrived at in a democratic way have authority and value. Facing problems together, sharing time and money, and supporting one another's interests helps keep a family close and happy.

TRYING NEW IDEAS

Finally, as you grow and are ready to try something new, you will find it most satisfying and rewarding if your family lets you try your wings occasionally. When are you old enough to buy your own clothes or to go on a weekend camping trip? If you need a new shirt and want to shop for it by yourself and your family allows you to do as you wish, you are being told in effect, "We expect you to make the best choice you know how with the money you have. It's up to you." How grown-up you feel! In just such little ways do we gradually learn to take care of ourselves and to become truly mature.

The satisfactions we get from our families depend on adjusting, cooperating, and sharing both privileges and responsibilities. By doing things together, talking things over and making cooperative decisions, and giving each one a chance to try new ideas, we learn to understand our families. And it is this understanding that is the foundation of living happily together.

Some Pointers to Help You Get Your Point of View Across

1- Arguing is a form of communication. You and your parents argue because you *care* so much about one another.

2- Try to bring out into the open the real issues that are bothering you or your parents. Remember, it is very likely that your parents are not worried about the way you dress or the privileges you feel mature enough to handle, but they are concerned about *basic standards*.

3- Help your parents learn about the things you feel have changed since they were young. Share your world with them to the degree you can, in order to keep them informed about your expenses, social activities, and the like. It takes effort and ingenuity to bring your parents up to date.

4- Be reasonable in your demands. Balance your needs against those of the whole family in sharing family resources.

5- Timing is an important factor in making requests, You should not ask for expensive new clothes, for example, when family finances may be low right after Christmas.

6- Decisions based on compromise seldom satisfy everyone completely. But if you allow both sides of the issue to be aired, an agreement based on the joint facts may provide a satisfactory answer.

7- Listen to both the tone and the content of the discussion, and try to understand both what is being said and what is left unsaid.

8- You can increase the number of times your parents will approve of your requests by increasing their trust in you. You do not have to tell them *everything*, but casually and consistently sharing personal information with them is a way of showing respect and love. Demonstrate by your *actions* that you understand that freedom and responsibility go together.

9- No one is perfect. To achieve maturity you must learn to live with and tolerate the idiosyncrasies of others, including parents, with good humor.

THINKING IT OVER

1. Look up the everyday life of a culture other than your own. You may find a television program that shows what living in another part of the world among different people is like. Sometimes your librarian can suggest a good work of fiction or biography that portrays another culture accurately. How do they use time, materials, and other resources? How do they make a living

and secure their food, and what kinds of homes do they live in? What do they do for recreation? What are the relationships of parents to their children? Are the younger children and infants treated differently from the way older children are treated? Does the family's way of life have advantages over the kind of life-style your family has? Compare their ways of doing things to the way your family lives.

2. Have you ever thought of the obligations that children have toward their parents? Or do you believe they do not have any? How do your goals and values differ from those of your parents?

THINGS TO DO

1. Have a circle discussion (see page 55) on "Decisions and Consequences—Whose Responsibility?"

2. Have a debate on: "Should brothers help with cooking and dishes?"

3. Make a list of all the things you do in one day. Check those that required cooperating or sharing.

4. Plan and present a skit, "It's All in the Point of View," showing how differently grandmother, mother, father, you, and younger brother feel about the same problem or situation.

5. Develop a bulletin board display on "Family Fun Together"—at work, at play, through hobbies, on special occasions, picnics, and vacations.

6. Dramatize a family council in action.

7. Dramatize—with students sitting back to back—"Calling mother on the telephone to explain why you will be home from the basketball game later than you promised."

8. Prepare a Parents' Night at school. One idea is to plan a buffet or simple refreshments. Show parents what you are doing. Other ideas will occur to you.

9. Organize a panel of parents and students on "A plan for sharing home responsibilities vs. arguing about them every day."

10. Prepare and present a skit showing family cooperation or its lack.

11. Make chef's aprons (see pages 268 and 269) for your mother and father to wear when having a "backyard supper."

12. Use puppets to show a family discussing the use of the family car.

13. Make a class scrapbook on "Family Recreation," with descriptions of good radio and TV programs, games, hobbies, books, music, ideas for refreshments.

14. Make a list of problems about which you and your parents sometimes disagree. Arrange them in three groups: (a) problems you think you should be allowed to settle by yourself; (b) problems your parents should settle for you; and (c) problems that should be discussed and solved in a family council.

15. Conduct a community survey. Note recreational facilities, their cost, use, and so on. Get (or make) a large map of your locality and color in the recreation areas. Write a brief description of each area and its facilities.

PARTICIPATING IN THE COMMUNITY

Community groups like the "Y," PTA, and others may be able to use your services to answer the phone, pass out circulars, stuff envelopes, or take care of children while parents attend meetings.

5 Understanding parents

Ever since you can remember you have probably accepted your parents' ideas on almost everything as right and proper. They always seemed to know the answers to all your questions and you thought it was wonderful to have parents who knew so much. You decided that things were good or bad, right or wrong, largely according to the standards of your parents.

Lately, however, you find that what your friends think, say, and do quite often disagrees with what your parents believe is right. And because it is important to you to be liked and accepted by your friends, you want to do whatever they say. Unfortunately, you may have trouble with your parents because you may feel they do not understand how important your friends are to you. What should you do? If you conform to what your friends say, you may displease your parents. If you do as your parents suggest, you may not have any friends. Actually, the choice is not as final as it sounds, nor as bad for you.

WAYS OF UNDERSTANDING PARENTS

You must remember three things in order to understand parents:

1-Parents are interested in and want to know what you do because this is part of the responsibility they must assume in order to guide you.

2-Help your parents get to know you and your friends as young people on the road to maturity.

3-Get to know your parents as people. They have a life of their own; try to understand it.

Why Parents Act the Way They Do

Actually, most parents do not mean to pry nor do they enjoy restricting your activities. When you begin to feel that your parents are treating you like a child and keeping you too closely watched, just ask yourself whether you would prefer that they did not care at all where you were or what you were doing. They are concerned about you because they love you and because you are important to them. Besides, how can they guide you if they do not know anything about your interests and activities? In spite of the fact that you feel you are quite capable of taking care of yourself and of making your own decisions, this is one portion of your development in which it is wise to make haste slowly.

Privileges and Responsibilities

Part of the difficulty comes about because, to you, it seems that grown-ups can do as they please without anyone checking up on them or giving them orders. One of the lessons everyone learns is that with every privilege there are responsibilities. And it is easier for you to see the privileges adults have than to understand the responsibilities that go with them.

For example, you may not think it much fun to spend an evening with relatives, family friends, or neighbors when there are so many other exciting things to do. Why do your parents spend a quiet evening at home or visit with friends or relatives for recreation? Maybe it is because they cannot afford other kinds of entertainment after they have provided for the family's needs. They may choose activities that are free in order to give you and the family the things you want and need. Your parents would enjoy the luxury of going away to an expensive

It is important to be liked and accepted by your friends.

Friends enjoy one another's company.

resort or taking a long trip for their vacation, but the responsibilities they have toward you and the family do not give them the free choice you may think they have.

Life has its disappointments for all of us. Your attitude toward your parents and family when you do not get what you want or are not allowed to do as you please can tell a great deal about how mature you really are. If you sulk or pout, lose your temper, or behave in a childish way, it means you have not yet gained enough self-control to accept minor defeats gracefully. Of course, no one likes to be disappointed, but the manner in which you face setbacks is a measure of how mature you are.

Therefore, the first step in understanding parents is to realize the importance of guidance based on the love and responsibility parents have for you, and the danger of getting too much freedom too early in life. To help you grow into a mature, self-controlled adult, parents need to know

1-Who your friends are.
2-What interests you have.
3-How they can help you learn that privileges bring responsibilities.

Let Your Parents Know Your Friends

This brings us to the second step, which is finding ways of letting your parents know you and your friends as young people on the road to adulthood. If your mother thinks June is a bad influence on you (and June's mother probably thinks the same about you!), why not invite June over to your house for Saturday night supper and help your mother really get acquainted with her? Perhaps your mother will find that June is really as nice as you say she is. Or, your father may change his opinion of Robert if you arrange for them to get together in your father's workshop. Robert will be able to show how skillfully he can use his hands. Your father can show Robert some of his handiwork. This will give your father an appreciative audience, too.

Haven't you found that often you *think* you do not like someone simply because you do not know enough about that person, and that you feel close to those who have things in common with you? This is true of anyone, even parents. To help your parents accept your friends, use whatever ways you can to get them to know one another better. Whenever possible, have them do something together.

Parents Are People

What are your parents really like as individuals? What kind of personalities do they have? What are their interests, ideas, and attitudes? What are their hopes and dreams? What kind of people do they seem to like as friends? Parents have a way of seeming like the cozy living-room chair simply because they have been a part of your life for so long. You fail to see them as adults with lives of their own in addition to being your parents. If you have never thought about it in just this way before, you may discover some unusual facts about the kind of human beings they are. Try to look at your mother and father calmly and clearly as *individuals*. They have feelings, opinions, rights, and privileges like anybody else and these should be respected. You are on the road to a happy relationship with your mother and father when you can appreciate them as people.

Perhaps your mother is proud of her cooking and the meals she serves. But you think she fusses too much and you would enjoy hamburgers just as well. Or maybe your father enjoys puttering around in the garden and it seems silly to you. They work hard and these activities

RECOGNIZING HOW YOUR PARENTS FEEL

The next time you feel especially critical of your mother and father, try putting yourself in their shoes. Have you ever considered their feelings? Have you ever wondered what may be worrying them? Could there be some explanation for the times when they seem preoccupied? Maybe you have been concentrating too much on what you want to do and seeing only their faults and their apparent lack of consideration. How would you act if you were your parents? Could it be that you would also have faults and would not be tolerant enough? Could it be that you would be too demanding? Think about it honestly and you may be surprised at what you learn.

Building Good Will with Parents.

Showing appreciation and understanding and love has a spiral reaction. You may begin by showing a little genuine appreciation for something your mother has accomplished. Tell her how proud you are of things she makes, such as pizza or paper flowers. She will be pleased by your interest. You will feel very good and will pay her some sincere compliments for the delicious supper she prepared for the family. She will feel wonderful and will show it in her actions toward you, and so on. The more love and understanding and appreciation you show, the more are returned to you. It may begin with little things at the bottom of the spiral, but it will gradually build until it includes almost everything you think and do and feel.

When Andrew Carnegie's desk was on display recently, one of its pigeonholes bore the label, "Gratitude and Sweet Words." Practice finding the good in people, especially parents, and they will find the good in you. Generous praise for others will get them on your side. We all enjoy gratitude and sweet words; try giving them to your parents and watch the results.

The spiral can also work in reverse. Once grumbling and dissatisfaction are allowed to creep in, you will find that more and more things annoy you or make you angry. Your parents will feel less and less like being pleasant.

Watch those spirals. They go both ways. Try the upward spiral for a while and see what happens.

Understanding parents is no different from understanding other people. You can learn to know them as individuals with their own par-

Help your parents to know you and your friends.

are as important to them as your own activities are to you. It may be their way of being creative—just as your collection of sea-shells or airplane models may be satisfying to you. Showing them that you appreciate their activities and accomplishments will help them be more understanding of some of yours.

We all have different interests and tastes, capacities and needs. The important thing to remember is that we should make allowances for the ideas and quirks of our parents just as we do for those of our friends.

The more love, appreciation, and understanding you give to your family, the more are returned to you. This approach may begin with little things, but it will gradually build until it includes almost everything you think and do and feel.

ticular capacities, needs, interests, feelings, and ideas. You can learn to recognize that as parents they have certain responsibilities toward you and that in order to guide you they need to know what you do, where you go, what you like, and whom you know. And you can help your parents know your friends better by having them spend time doing things together.

THINKING IT OVER

As young people on the road to becoming adults, it may be helpful to you if alone and in groups you examine what the following ideas mean in terms of your relationships with your parents:

a. *Dependence.* In what areas of your life are you almost totally dependent for support and guidance from your parents? Somewhat dependent? Not dependent?

b. *Independence.* Does your need to stand on your own feet and to make your own decisions conflict with your desire to live up to and to be held to the standards of behavior in which your parents truly believe? Parents who care try to achieve the delicate balance between freedom and control for their teen-aged youngsters. Have you ever considered the fact that parents set limits because they care?

c. *Interdependence.* To what extent and in what phases of your living do you and your parents depend on and need one another?

d. What do the following mean? (1) *right* (2) *license* (3) *responsibility*

To achieve the kind of freedom and independence you want from parents and other adults, you should understand these ideas.

THINGS TO DO

1. Develop a "Code for Parents and Youth."

2. Have a parent-student panel discussion on "Things I wish my parents would not do, like choosing my clothes or being overprotective vs. Things parents wish young people would learn, like responsibility and better work habits."

3. Plan and promote a "Family Courtesy Week." Invite some parents to participate.

4. Plan and present a skit on one of the following topics: "Where are you going dear?"; "No sense of responsibility"; "I'm not a child anymore!"; "Gratitude and sweet words." To write a skit to initiate class discussion or for presentation in a PTA or Assembly program you will need the following:

   a. *The problem.* An example could be the problem of young people feeling resentful when their parents want to know where they are going, what they are going to do, and who will be with them; or jealousy in the family; or being treated like a child; and so on.

   b. *The situation.* Where will the action take place? At what time? Describe the scene.

   c. *The characters.* Try to make the people in the skit individuals whom you feel you could know. Give them names, tell how old they are, what their general dispositions are, how they feel toward one another, and how they fit into the problem and situation you have chosen for your skit.

5. Have a "Swap Session" in which parents and young people can get together and compare notes with others who have similar difficulties. Have a panel of experts to guide the discussion. It might include a doctor, a nurse, a Boy Scout leader, a Girl Scout leader, and others.

6 Cherish your heritage

There is a strong trend for Americans to take pride in their ethnic heritage. Many ethnic groups encourage this trend and have formed organizations like AIM (American Indian Movement) and circulated slogans, such as "Be Proud to be Polish" and "Black Is Beautiful." Broadly speaking, *ethnic* refers to a group of people sharing the same language and customs, including religion, nationality, and race.

KNOW YOUR ROOTS

It is good to understand your roots and to be proud of them. This understanding can make you feel better about yourself. Sharing ideas about your ethnic groups with one another will help build appreciation for each group. Mahatma Gandhi once said, "I want the winds of all cultures to blow freely about my house but not to be swept off my feet by any."

STUDY OTHER CULTURES

Your first desire may be to learn more about your own background. Later you may wish to learn about the backgrounds of many other people. For the latter, why not start thinking about the cultural backgrounds with which you are somewhat familiar? You may know a great deal about Spaniards, for example, but know little about the Chinese.

There are many ways to study a people, including your own. You might consider such factors as historical background, food, clothing, housing, festivals, family customs, value systems, home equipment, management of a home, markets, literature, prominent men and women, recreation, aesthetics, and others. In this chapter, a few topics have been selected and discussed briefly in order to help you and to encourage you to make further studies.

Food

Food gives meaning to life, according to the famous anthropologist Dorothy Lee. Family members prepare food and eat it in a manner that is typical of their culture. Americans, for example, use a knife and fork but hold and use them differently from the English, while the Orientals use chopsticks. Food is shared with guests. Eating as a group produces a togetherness that few other activities do.

Certain foods eaten by ethnic groups become identified with them. Although a food, such as rice and beans, may be common to many countries, the kind of beans and rice may vary from one region to another. The bread of an ethnic group usually creates a stronger attachment in an individual than any other food. Try to capture this feeling by sampling some of the breads of other peoples, such as the crisp crusted French and Italian bread; the *pita* or flat bread of the Middle East; the hard, thin, unleavened, crackerlike breads of the Scandinavian countries; the sour rye bread of the Germans; *matzoh*, the unleavened bread of the Jews; and the *tortillas* of the Mexicans. Try to imagine how these breads originated and how they are used with other foods of that culture.

Take a common food, such as carrot, ground meat, or custard and see how it differs from culture to culture. Consider the influences that have given a uniqueness to ethnic foods such as availability of food, climate, type of

A family reunion is a good time to ask questions of your relatives about your common heritage.

farming, soil, ease of distribution, and similar factors.

A culture attaches many meanings to foods. For example, in some parts of Africa, eggs and milk are evil and taboo. This is especially serious for growing children and for pregnant women. In some families, chicken soup is believed to cure almost any ailment. Orthodox Jews eat only kosher foods that have been prescribed by their religious dietary laws, for example, not eating milk dishes with meat dishes. In some homes, cooking and eating equipment for milk and meat are kept separate.

Although soul food is associated with black people, the food actually contains elements of American Indian foods, such as hominy, mush, popcorn, rabbit, catfish, yams, turtle, succotash, crabs, and other native foods. The hog, brought to this country by the early English colonists, also influenced the development of what became known as soul food, because black people used parts of the hog discarded by the plantation

A girl and her mother preparing tortillas—the Mexican bread.

SOUL FOOD

BAR-B-QUE SPARE RIBS	3.95
SMOKED HAM HOCKS	3.95
CHITTERLINGS	4.50
SMOTHERED PORK CHOPS	3.95
CHILI	3.25
SOUTHERN FRIED CHICKEN	3.95
PIGS FEET	3.95
BEEFBURGER	2.95
ROAST BEEF	3.95
LOBSTER TAILS	6.25
PRIME SIRLOIN STEAK	6.75

Served With CORN BREAD AND CHOICE OF TWO VEGETABLES

COLLARD GREENS BLACK EYE PEAS LIMA BEANS
CANDIED SWEETS BAKED MACARONI FRENCH FRIES
POTATO SALAD MUSTARD GREENS

DESSERTS

| SWEET POTATO PIE | .75 |
| APPLE or PEACH COBBLER | .75 |

| COFFEE | .50 | • | TEA | .50 |

Soul food has captured the interest of the public through restaurants.

owners. Among the dishes they created were chitterlings, made from the small intestines, thoroughly cleaned inside and out, dipped into batter, cut into pieces and fried; pig's feet and jowls used in many ways; and stomach lining for hog maws, and many other delicious dishes. Vegetables included eggplant, a wide variety of greens, turnips, okra, and peas. Cornmeal was used in breads, pancakes, grits, muffins, and cake. One of the basic seasonings was bacon or fatback. Many of the African spices and herbs were used for flavoring. Soul food gives identity, pleasure, and uniqueness to blacks.

To the Japanese, food must be tasty and beautiful—important qualities. Ingredients are as fresh as possible and of top quality. A great deal of time is spent in the careful chopping, slicing, sectioning, and cutting of food into bite-size pieces so it can be eaten with chopsticks. Food is cooked quickly because fuel is scarce. Additions to make the food tasty are soy sauce, ginger root, sesame seed, and sesame seed oil. The food is neatly and simply arranged to emphasize the natural beauty of the food. Some food is cooked at the table with the raw food attractively arranged on a platter.

Each ethnic group decides on the foods that are edible or inedible. For example, Americans are fond of corn but some cultures believe that corn is only for cattle. An old Jewish custom is to bring bread and salt to a new home because it means prosperity (that those living in the house may never be hungry—since bread is our greatest necessity and salt is the spice without which food has no flavor). Many also bring sugar, so that life in that home may be sweet. White bread is prized by many in preference to dark bread because many years ago only people who lived in castles had white bread so dark bread was associated with the lower classes. Another food often associated with the poor is dried beans. A wealthy man who had previously been poor said to a friend, "I don't eat beans anymore." Foods convey many meanings and it would be interesting to determine what meanings your culture attaches to various foods.

For purposes of health, it is sensible to determine the nutritive qualities of an ethnic diet. Use the Basic Four Food Groups (see Chapter 11) as a means of telling how adequate nutritionally a particular food pattern is. The Puerto Rican diet may be used as an illustration. The American Dietetic Association made some of the suggestions for testing the adequacy of this diet. You must realize that every Puerto Rican does not eat in exactly the same manner. Conclusions can only be general in nature.

Methods of food preparation for each culture must be examined in the evaluation of any cultural food patterns, to determine whether the best method was used to retain nutrients. Other points that might be considered in the study of these diets are kinds of food given to small children; food for the sick; available food served to all age groups; whether certain family members are given first choice of foods; and seasonal availability of food.

The service of food is another interesting area of investigation, as well as food for guests. What is eaten for snacks? In certain parts of Africa, for example, boys and girls pick wild fruit on their way home from school. This is not only a snack but it also improves the nutritive value of their diet.

Table 6-1

MILK GROUP:	Economic conditions prevent some Puerto Ricans from having sufficient milk. Some milk is consumed in a beverage, *cafe con leche*, that is a combination of milk and coffee. A native white cheese, like farmer cheese, is used in small quantities. Some American-type cheeses are also eaten. The diet usually does not have enough milk and might be improved if Puerto Ricans used evaporated or dried milk in their cooking.
MEAT GROUP:	Chicken is eaten frequently. Pork and beef cuts are usually fried. Salt codfish (imported) is a favorite but other fish are eaten in limited amounts. Ham butts and sausage are used for flavor. The intestine of the pig is eaten fried *(cuchifritos)* or stewed with vegetables and chick peas *(salcocho)*. Beans, such as chick peas, navy beans, and red kidney beans (a favorite) are eaten daily and combined with *sofrito*—a mixture of tomatoes, green peppers, onion, garlic, salt pork, lard, and cooking herbs—or eaten with rice. Eggs are used in cooking more than as a main dish. This food group appears adequate if sufficient amounts of these foods are eaten.
VEGETABLE AND FRUIT GROUP:	*Viandas* or starchy vegetables include green bananas and green plantain, served like potatoes with fish or meat. Carrots, green pepper, tomatoes, sweet potatoes and pumpkin (used to flavor and thicken foods) are especially liked. Head lettuce, tomatoes, cabbage, and onions are basic salad ingredients. Oranges, mangoes, papaya, bananas, and fresh pineapple are frequently eaten. Canned peaches and pears are commonly used. Fresh fruit and vegetables must be stressed in this diet because vegetables are often cooked for long periods and fruit may not be eaten in sufficient amounts.
BREAD AND CEREAL GROUP:	Bread is not consumed in large amounts. Plantain is often eaten in place of bread. French bread, rolls, and crackers are eaten. Noodles and spaghetti are included. Oatmeal and cornmeal are usually cooked in milk. Rice is often combined with the beans. More whole grain cereals would improve the diet.

The Japanese make a ritual of their tea service.

ideas. In addition, these garments are packable, can be made easily and quickly, and can be quite unique and eye-catching.

Boys and men can drape a long piece of fabric around their waists for lounging on the beach or for other leisure-time activity. If you are a boy you might like a West African vest made from a fabric of Nigerian design; a girl might like one, too. A loose African robe or *dashiki* can be adapted for both boys and girls and decorated in a personal manner. If you decide to make one of these garments have a "show and tell" to share your ideas with others.

This gaily printed headdress is called a **khanga.** Do you see any possibilities for adapting this head scarf for your own purposes?

African **dashikis** are hand decorated and may be worn by any member of the family.

Clothing

Clothing may reflect ethnic practices. You might enjoy studying the clothing worn by various ethnic groups, such as the headdress *(kaffiyeh)* of the Arabs, the Japanese *kimono,* or the *sari* worn by Indian women. The kind of fabrics used can be an interesting topic for research. Some costumes are worn on festival days or for special dances. Ask your relatives about this or talk to members of a senior citizens group who might have information about your ethnic group.

If you are a black student you may be interested in the fabrics and clothes of Africa. Often a length of fabric is wrapped or draped to make a garment—actually an art form with many possibilities. Nigerians make a billowy skirt called a *lappa* and combine it with a halter called a *bubba.* The Swahili version called *joho* is dressier and longer. Cottons with bold African designs are used for casual wear. Why not experiment whatever your skin color is—with no pattern and no sewing, just your own creative

Family

A study of the family life of an ethnic group can be exciting because you may be experiencing some of it in real life now. You can decide on the areas in which you are most interested but here are some suggestions: roles of various family members (does anyone have a preferred role or make most of the decisions?); the life-styles; a typical day; and family holidays. Are there special rituals at weddings and burials? Is the extended family emphasized, such as grandparents, aunts, uncles, and cousins living close and sharing in many activities? What are the important values, such as thrift, money, education, or happiness? As you study an ethnic family think about the characteristics you would like to continue or discontinue in your future family. Have stories or books that might give you additional information been written about the family life of this ethnic group?

Child Development

The rearing of children can give you insights into a cultural group. Find out about feeding practices; religious education, if any; play activities, clothing, role in the family; and discipline. A Folkway recording, *A Word in Your Ear*, in-

dicates the ways some cultures discipline their young. An English mother says, "Be good," a French mother says, "Be wise," a Scandinavian mother says, "Be friendly," a German mother says, "Be in line," and a Hopi Indian says, "That is not the Hopi way." Compare notes with others and select the ways of disciplining children that you approve of, and with which you can identify. Why is child rearing so important?

Note how this Tanzanian mother carries her child. Compare this with the ways that American children are carried.

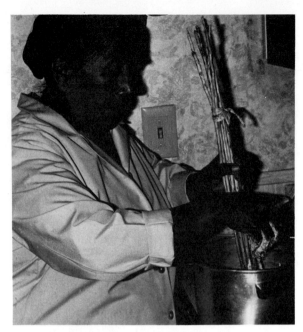

A Navajo Indian woman using traditional tools and pans.

are quite unique. Certain equipment or furnishings that were strictly cultural are now being adopted by other cultures. The Chinese *wok* for cooking is an example.

Language

Have you learned to speak the language of your ethnic group? Of course, some of you may have many ethnic groups in your background but you might like to select the one in which you have a special interest and learn to speak at least a few words of that language, or, better still, learn to speak adequately with members of your family who speak the language. Are there words or phrases that have special meanings not found in other languages?

Aesthetics

Learning about the literature, music, arts, and other areas of expression will give you even greater understanding of your background. Learn to sing the songs, dance the dances, look at the paintings, listen to the operas and other forms of music, and read the poetry and the great books. Try your hand at a simple craft to get the feel of it. Now share your findings with others, especially other members of your family, so that they, too, will appreciate the wonders of their heritage.

Equipment and Furnishings

The equipment associated with families can tell much about their way of life. What are the cooking utensils? How do they keep their homes clean? What are important pieces of furniture? Do they use any crafts to make their home efficient or decorative? Try to identify items that

Boys and girls enjoy an ethnic folk dance.

THINKING IT OVER

Someone has said that learning about your culture and becoming involved in ethnic activities may have a negative effect because people will have a stronger allegiance to their group than to being an American—that this experience will help to divide rather than unite us. What is your opinion?

THINGS TO DO

1. Make a study of a culture that is very different from your own or a group that lives in your community. What surprised you? Did your estimate of these people change as you learned to know them better? If so, how? Did any opportunities arise for you to continue having contacts with this group? Explain.

2. With the possible assistance of English and social studies students, you might like to compile bibliographies on sources of materials on various cultural backgrounds to help other students study their ethnic group. Discuss your project with your librarian for additions and possible purchase of other books or materials. If you are not familiar with the following books, you might like to read them or add them to your list:

Alford, Harold J., *The Proud Peoples: The Heritage and Culture of Spanish-Speaking Peoples in the United States*, New York: David McKay Co., Inc., 1972.

Harris, Middleton and others, *The Black Book*, New York: Random House, Inc., 1974. (A folk book of the black people)

Richard Siegel, Michael Strassfeld, and Sharon Strassfeld, *The Jewish Catalog*, Philadelphia: The Jewish Publication Society of America, 1973. (Resources for Jewish living)

Perhaps your librarian will help you plan an exhibit of materials for studying cultures.

3. Make a list of resources that are available in your community and that would broaden your horizons. In addition, you might attend a service of a religion that is different from your own. Try to eat a food of another culture every week for a period of time. Be friendly with someone from another ethnic background. Have a cultural night or fair. Bring some senior citizens to your class to talk about their childhood or youth. Have them prepare a favorite recipe or demonstrate a craft. Implement some ideas of your own to broaden your background.

area three

Child Develop- ment

7 What a young child is like

If you have a younger brother or sister of three to six, you have an opportunity to observe at first hand what children are like at this age. Perhaps you have played with young children in your neighborhood. Or you may have watched them while their parents went out. What are young children like?

CHARACTERISTICS OF YOUNG CHILDREN

Young children are of various sizes and shapes. Most human beings are. They have certain physical and mental characteristics that are developing. Children of this age are learning many of the skills they will need in order to become social persons. Their attitudes toward people and the social experiences they have come largely from their family during these years. Children should be given many opportunities to be with other children and with adults. When you observe young children you will note that they learn the proper ways of behaving in social situations by imitation and by direct instruction, usually from the parents and the immediate family. Do you know what to expect these children to be like? When you do, you will have a good basis for caring for them. Your own experiences will tell you that a three-year-old child is different from a six-year-old. They look and behave differently.

Who is a 3-year-old?

Characteristics of the Three-Year-Old

Three-year-olds still have an angelic baby look. However, they are not as helpless as they seem and are now capable of doing many things for themselves. At this stage of their physical development, they are learning to use the large muscles in their legs, arms, and bodies. Many of their play activities take the form of lifting, loading, pushing, pulling, sliding, and climbing. The development of the muscles that control the finer actions of the fingers and hands are not yet fully developed. So they may need occasional help in getting untangled from the rope attached to a pull-toy, for example.

They may need supervision while eating. They are usually not able to manipulate their hands and fingers very skillfully. They are just beginning to learn to use spoons and forks. Thus this is much too soon to insist on good table manners. They frequently need someone to suggest the next step or bring them back to something they had started to do. This is due to the fact that their attention span is short. While they are undressing you might suggest, "What should we take off next?" Or when they are putting toys away, you could say, "Will these all fit in the toy box?" Simple reminders that tell the direction of the next step of the task they are doing will often be enough to get them started again.

Social Development of Three-Year-Olds

At three, social and mental development are closely related. The child's first attempts to make friends may seem rather rough and direct. But three-year-olds are really just beginning to use their ability to talk as a means of making friends. In the beginning, they will often hit other children, grab playthings away from them, or push and shove them. What they are trying to say is,

"I like you and want to play with you." They lack experience in making social contacts so they use rather direct physical means instead. Adults who supervise children at play can teach them better ways of being friendly by direct suggestions. It is also helpful if the adult shows approval every time the child behaves in a desirable way. They need to know what is permitted. It is much more effective to let children know what they *may* do rather than to prohibit or punish those actions that are disapproved. Seldom, if ever, use the terms No, Don't, Stop, Get away from there!, You shouldn't, and the like. Only in cases of extreme and obvious danger should such terms be used. Phrase all requests, suggestions, directions, and comments of approval in positive terms. For example, "Good!" or "I knew you could do it by yourself" or "Wouldn't you like to try the swing now?" are very effective. It takes a long time to learn to use language to get along with others. Eventually, they will learn how to share things and ideas with others. But at this age, they do not understand the idea of sharing. They do not yet recognize that certain things belong to them and other things belong to others, so how can they understand what sharing means?

Children may need supervision while eating.

are doing as they play. This extensive verbal activity helps them develop their language skills. It also helps them enlarge their concepts of the world around them. They begin to understand a greater number of words. Also, when they are temporarily separated from their parents, a toy telephone provides them with an opportunity to talk out their feelings. It makes them feel close with the important people in their lives.

Three-year-olds like their social life to be strenuous and active. Toys and play materials and equipment are used in individual ways, since children of this age seldom play *with* other children but play *near* others. Occasionally they play with the same toys for brief periods of time. Generally, however, they seem to enjoy having other children around them, but play at their own individual games.

Language Development of Three-Year-Olds

Three-year-olds talk for the sheer joy of using words and hearing their own voices. Many carry on a running commentary about what they

Household Activities Are A Significant Source of Learning

Three-year-olds like to take part in all family activities—cooking, washing, cleaning, shopping, gardening, and so on. The shopping list that three-year-olds prepare may look like a lot of scribbles to you. But it makes them feel useful and part of the family to do the same kind of things that others are doing. Scribbled notes also enlarge their idea of what communication means. Young children learn that symbols have special meanings. It may encourage the child to want to learn to read and write. Not that three-year-olds should be formally taught to read and write! But the notion that these are other forms of transmitting information is a necessary basis

46

for the later development of the actual skills of reading, writing, and numbers.

Almost every child at this age wants to stand up on a chair so that whatever Mother or Father is doing can be seen. Much of the learning that occurs at this age is through observation, imitation, and participation. A child who is allowed to see and help with household tasks is learning to understand and do many activities which will be useful throughout life.

Three-year-olds can help make beds, empty wastebaskets, put soiled clothes in the hamper or throw them down the laundry chute, set the table, put groceries such as cereals away, if they are stored in the lower cabinets, start the dishwasher, and many similar activities. Try to provide as many opportunities for them to help and to do things for themselves as possible. With loving supervision, most three-year-olds are happy, learning, growing people. What other simple household tasks can a three-year-old do?

Physical Skills

Three-year-olds love to run, jump, climb, and go up and down stairs. They can balance themselves, and most can ride a tricycle. They enjoy a swing and a slide. Some communities have programs in which children are taught swimming and basic gymnastics. Usually, they can wash their hands, drink from a cup or glass, eat without much spilling, and take care of their undressing. It is easier for them to untie, unzip, unbutton, and take off their clothes than it is to put them on. Their ability and willingness to do things is uneven. Sometimes they may not learn any new steps in taking care of themselves while they are concentrating on developing their ability to talk and to learn new words. It seems as if they stand still in learning one thing while they focus on another. Basically, the extent to which they develop their skills and abilities for managing themselves depends on their mental alertness, curiosity, and social adjustment.

How They Grow

Each child's rate and pattern of physical growth is uniquely individual. A well-known specialist has compared this individual growth pattern to a number of trains, each leaving from the same starting point and each arriving at a similar destination. Each child's rate and pattern of growth is like a train that is going from New York to San Francisco. One may be like an express train moving at a fast, steady pace with

barely any stops in between. Another child may be compared to a train that goes express from New York to Pittsburgh, and then local to San Franciso, with many stops along the way. Another may proceed slowly like a local train to Denver and then grow very rapidly and be like a train going nonstop from Denver to the end of the journey. Each child has an individual, inherited way and speed of growing, even though they all go through the same stages of growth. Such factors as health, nourishment, and family influences may affect growth and development. Can you see why it is unrealistic to compare children in their physical growth except in a very general way? We should learn to observe and understand each child as a unique individual even though children of a given age have many characteristics in common.

What Are Three-Year-Olds Like?

They are very active most of the time and their play involves much physical movement. They are at the very beginning stage of learning how to make friends. When guiding or supervising them, the most effective technique is to use positive terms so that they will learn what is allowed. They are still too young to share and should not be expected to do so. Most three-year-olds are at a stage when they are rapidly expanding their vocabulary. They enjoy participating in homemaking activities. And all children have a unique rate and pattern of growth.

I am 4 years old!

Characteristics of the Four-Year-Old

By the time children are four, they can do all the things that three-year-olds can do, but with greater speed and accuracy. In addition, they have learned new skills. They move more confidently. They can manage their own clothes quite well. They go to the toilet when necessary. And generally, they eat the same food as the rest of the family. They need less help with the basic skills. However, they should have closer supervision. Since they are more independent and heedless, they do not foresee the consequences of their actions. An adult who is in charge of four-year-olds needs to be aware of the fact that this makes them susceptible to accidents. Therefore, adults should use preventive measures to protect them and yet allow them the freedom they need to explore and try new things.

There are three outstanding characteristics of four-year-olds that make them both delightful and frustrating to adults. They are (1) negative, (2) imaginative, and (3) talkative.

Reaction to Authority

The first thing one notices about four-year-olds is their high resistance to authority. This is just another way of saying that they say "No" and "I won't" much of the time when they are with adults. Most children go through a "No" stage between the ages of two and four. Younger children frequently say No simply to hear themselves talk. Then they follow through with whatever was requested. But four-year-olds resist more strongly and definitely. They are beginning to think and reason for themselves. They are starting to establish their individuality. In a sense, they are saying, "I am ME and I know what I want." Four-year-olds say No with their whole being. Have you ever seen four-year-olds who did not want to come in from play? Their No is loud and clear. They try to run away and if caught they pull away with all their might. Verbally, they often use strong language and name-calling. It is well to remember that this kind of behavior is just a stage of growth. Most children stop using negative behavior as soon as they feel important in their own eyes. Children of this age need much positive approval for what they accomplish. This builds up their self-esteem.

A four-year-old's "No" shows a high resistance to authority.

Four-Year-Olds' Imaginations

The second thing you will notice about four-year-olds is their vivid imaginations. They begin to play games with several other children. They often pretend that they are animals or other people or inanimate objects, like a boat, a car, or

This four-year-old boy is using his imagination to practice the role of an adult.

a plane. They use sound effects and whatever props they find around them in their play. To encourage their imaginative play provide them with old clothes, adult shoes, hats, handbags, pots and pans, empty cartons, and the like. An imaginative child is a learning child. They enlarge their understanding of the world around them. And they practice roles and learn how it feels to act in certain ways.

Talkative Fours

The third fact about children of this age is that they love to talk. They use their power of speech most effectively for a variety of purposes. They test new words by using them in sentences just for the sound of them and often not for meaning. They ask many questions. Sometimes they really want to know the answers. But very often they try to delay going to bed or doing some other routine activity by asking questions.

Once you understand that four-year-olds are very imaginative, often negative for reasons they cannot explain, and love to talk, you have the most important clues to establishing a happy relationship with them. Requests and directions should not be in the form of direct orders. Use your imagination and present them in a dramatic form or as enticing suggestions. A four-year-old will find it appealing if you pretend the

two of you are a train and you can follow the happy "engine," with sound effects, up the stairs. The *result* is what should concern you. If you can get a four-year-old to go upstairs without a fuss by playing a game of "Let's pretend," then by all means use your own ideas.

Nursery school teachers and many parents have developed what are almost standard methods for making routine activities more acceptable to both child and adult. By observing what children are like, they have devised ways of working with children that keep everybody happy. To quiet noisy, clumping feet, pretend to put on the "magic invisible velvet shoes." Or if they seem to need a period of very active movement to release pent-up energy, let them wear their noisy wooden shoes. When it is time to pick up toys, get the children to cooperate by "turning their switches on" and make them vacuum sweepers that collect everything in their path. Most children can be encouraged to do simple chores willingly if you realize the possibilities of "Let's pretend."

What Are Four-Year-Olds Like?

They are friendly, talkative, negative, questioning, curious, and imaginative. To anyone who has the responsibility of guiding and caring for them, their lively activity and alert, inventive, inquisitive minds can become annoying. But these are the very qualities that will help them develop their minds to their highest potential. So try to take advantage of these characteristics to guide and direct their growth and development with a sense of humor and imagination. They will thrive on it. And you will find them stimulating, enthusiastic, and charming.

49

What is a 5-year-old like?

programs are planned. Are the programs repetitious? Do they arouse the child's curiosity? Are the actions and routines lively? Do they encourage the children to participate and get directly involved? What standards of behavior do they portray and encourage? Are the children encouraged to ask questions and to seek answers for themselves? An analysis of these programs will reveal much information about what children are like.

Characteristics of the Five-Year-Old

With training, five-year-olds can dress and undress, including putting on their shoes. If low hooks or rods are provided, they can hang up their own clothes. They can get a drink and help themselves at the table. They can also be taught simple health habits, such as using their own towels, combs, and other personal belongings.

To live more happily with them you should be aware of three characteristics of five-year-olds. First, they are intensely curious about the world around them and are eager to experiment. Secondly, they love repetition in speech, actions, and routines. And third, they have uneven social behavior. Sometimes they have a grown-up attitude of sharing and cooperation. At other times a desire for attention makes them show off. Or they may act shy and self-conscious or ask embarrassing, direct, personal questions.

A curious child is a learning child. But anyone who is asked such questions as "Who? Why? What?" all day long may get tired of trying to answer them. Five-year-olds learn to speak better by repetition. As soon as you finish reading them a story the usual response is "Read it again." When you give an explanation, they often say, "Tell me again." They enjoy the same bedtime stories read to them night after night. These are the children who memorize and repeat singing commercials. But this constant questioning and repetition helps them understand their world. They learn to understand simple how and why relationships. And they develop a sense of security.

Successful children's educational programs on television, such as "Sesame Street" and "Mr. Rogers" are based on these factors of how children learn and grow. Watch these programs daily for several weeks and see if you can discover what the children are like for whom these

How to Manage Five-Year-Olds

A valuable clue to the handling of five-year-olds lies in the fact that they can begin to learn that certain consequences follow certain events or actions. Use positive statements that indicate both the action and the possible result. It is much better to say, "If you pull the dog's tail, he will growl and snap at you," than simply to make a negative statement like "Don't pull the dog's tail." Five-year-olds can understand that it hurts the dog, too. But if the consequences are stated in terms of what will happen directly to them, they will be learning a valuable lesson. When Mary or John comes crying and says, "Barbara hit me," your question should be "What did you do to Barbara just before she hit you?" Although there are children who occasionally strike or grab other children with little or no provocation, usually five-year-olds can understand that certain acts or behavior on their part brought on the consequence of being hit.

50

Getting Along with Others

Socially, five-year-olds get along quite well with other children. They like to play in groups. The contacts are less direct. Their play involves less use of grabbing and pushing than was typical at three, for example. However, they are experimenting with forms of social behavior that may seem annoying to others. Showing off takes the form of restlessness, doing stunts, and calling out in a loud voice. Often they get attention by going to the opposite extreme and being very shy.

With adults they are often very direct and personal. Their questions or comments may be embarrassing. Many of the funny stories we hear about children who upset their parents are quite likely true accounts involving five-year-olds. Because they are curious and really want to know, they often ask questions that may seem rude to adults. If someone asks them, "How old are you?" they will reply, "I'm five. How old are you?" Many people think this frank behavior of five-year-olds is impertinent, but actually the children are asking the same questions that the adults are asking them. Adults may interpret it as improper behavior, but in many cases it isn't. It is really the adults' attitude that they may ask what they wish, but children may not. How is a child supposed to know that adults resent questions of a personal nature, especially if those adults feel free to ask children such questions?

Family Business

Five-year-olds listen to everything that is said and repeat it when you least expect it. But they can be taught that matters discussed in the family are family business and should not be repeated to outsiders. It is fun to watch five-year-olds trying to learn this concept. For a while they may need to be reminded that whatever is under discussion is not to be mentioned away from home. Later, when they want to make certain whether something should be told or not, they may ask, "Is this family business?"

When five-year-olds are stopped from doing something they want to do or are frustrated, they are likely to sulk and withdraw. If toys or clothes are involved, they may try to throw them away. This is a childish way of trying to handle the situation. But it is appropriate for their level of development. They will also try to get their own way by refusing to comply with even ordinary requests. As they mature they will discover more grown-up ways of asserting themselves and of

meeting their needs and wants. Do you know people who behave at this five-year-old level when they cannot have their own way? What are more adult ways of getting results?

What Are Five-Year-Olds Like?

They are competent and able to take care of themselves in the routines of living, such as dressing, washing, and eating. They are intensely curious and want to try everything for themselves. They are developing a sense of security, sureness, and safety through repetition. And they are trying to discover more grown-up ways of behaving with other people.

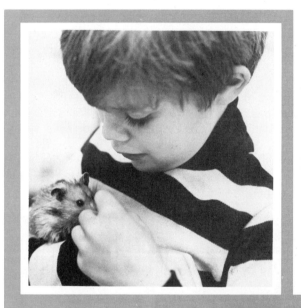

Five-year-olds are interested in pets and can learn to treat them kindly.

51

What's a 6-year-old like?

Characteristics of the Six-Year-Old

A six-year-old has established regular habits of eating, sleeping, and eliminating. The nervous system and glands have reached a stage of development that makes it possible for them to control these activities for themselves. They are competent in caring for their own simple needs, such as using a fork, carrying a tray, setting the table, drying dishes, wiping up spills, dressing and undressing, and going along familiar streets alone.

Six-year-olds are still very active in their play and enjoy strenuous physical activities. Since they have better coordination of eye and hand muscles, they can begin small-muscle activities. They can try simple craft work. Many still have difficulty in tying their shoelaces. Many six-year-olds learn to roller-skate quite well. Almost any game or activity that uses the large muscles and involves a lot of movement appeals to them.

Six-year-olds widen their range of neighborhood travel.

As with all stages of growth and development, it must be emphasized again that each child is an individual and different from every other child in many respects. You must know what these individual differences are as well as in what ways children of a given age are alike.

Effect of School

Because six-year-olds go to school and widen their range of neighborhood travel, their contacts become considerably wider. Adults in the neighborhood and in school become part of their world. Parents are no longer the center of the universe for them. The children they meet and live with daily give them a chance to learn ways of getting along with people. Some of the important skills in getting along with others that they learn include how to take the lead, how to follow, how to win approval, how to get permission, how to share and give, how to assume responsibility for the individual share of a group project, and how to wait for something they want and delay gratification of their wishes.

How to Lead Others

Some children seem to be natural leaders. They seem to know what to do to get along with other children their age. Usually, it is in school that six-year-olds get their first supervised experiences in leading others. They discover that to be a good leader they cannot shout commands at the others and expect them to follow for very long. They must learn to find jobs that appeal to the other children. They will discover that it is necessary to make others feel important as participants in the activity. They must be alert to the interests of others and come up with ideas for things to do when an activity begins to get boring. How many qualities of a good leader do you have?

It is equally necessary for six-year-olds to learn that there are times when others should direct the activities and when they must follow. Children get many opportunities to do both leading and following in school. What homemaking activities can you name that require you to be a leader? A follower?

How to Gain Approval

At six, children are learning to win approval with a much wider circle of people. Some of the skills for winning approval that they already have will work both at home and at school. Certain ways of behaving bring smiles from adults.

Certain ways of behaving bring smiles from adults.

Other ways bring disapproval and corrective measures from grown-ups. As one who is interested in the best possible ways of guiding children, you have a responsibility to show approval consistently for the kind of behavior that a six-year-old should continue to exhibit. A system of positive reinforcement will help children learn to do what is approved. This simply means that you always show approval for activities and behavior that you want the child to learn and to continue. Such activities as giving, sharing, and cooperating build good feelings.

Learning to wait for something you want is a difficult but necessary part of group living and growing up. At home and at school there are times when you cannot have what you want when you want it. Six-year-olds learn that they must ask for things, not demand them. They can express appreciation for help or favors. They learn that certain conditions determine if and when a request is granted. These conditions include the time, money, and amount of effort needed. Others who may be involved will have to

be consulted. Do these conditions often determine whether you do something when you want to or not?

Making Choices

An important clue to getting along well with six-year-olds is the fact that they like to choose for themselves. They want to decide for themselves what they will do. How can you use this fact to advantage with six-year-olds? One way is to find as many limited choices for them to make as you can. When you go for a walk around the block, does it really matter whether you go by the gas station first or come past it on your way back? If not, let the six-year-old decide. They also can make choices about the clothes they would like to wear and the food they want to eat. Often when you ask, "Do you want string beans or peas with your lunch?" it will encourage them to eat a vegetable rather than refuse to have one.

Whenever possible, then, provide six-year-olds with opportunities to choose and decide what should be done, or how or when to do it. This does not mean they will not need to be supervised. But it will reduce the number of times when they will feel frustrated. It will make them feel important and independent. It will also give them some real practice in making decisions. It may help them later on when the choices they must make are more complicated and difficult.

Six-year-olds want to decide for themselves what they will do.

A small caution: do not give them a choice if you cannot stick with the decision they will make. However, it is desirable to let them make choices, because it will help them develop judgment and learn to consider other possibilities.

To get along well with six-year-olds, you need tact, patience, energy, a sense of humor, and a willingness to let them decide, within limits, what they must do, and how, and when.

What Are Six-Year-Olds Like?

Six-year-olds are very active and have begun to have good coordination. They can master some skills involving the use of small muscles, but still enjoy rough-and-tumble games involving a great deal of movement. Since they go to school, they have begun to widen their contacts with other children and with adults other than their parents. They are learning to get along with people. They are also beginning to learn how to follow and how to lead others. They are mastering skills and behavior that will win them approval from others, and like to make choices for themselves. They should be given opportunities to make simple choices as often as possible. They are learning to be independent people.

CLUES FOR GETTING ALONG WITH CHILDREN

We have given a rather detailed picture of what preschool children are like at different age levels. It should always be remembered that most children of a given age are alike in many ways. But each child is also unique. Individual children should be observed and studied to discover their differentness, as well as their sameness. This will help you get a sound foundation for all you do with them and for them.

THINKING IT OVER

1. If you had a younger brother or sister who was four years old, how could you help him or her learn more? What role would the child's feeling of security play in his or her learning? Could the surroundings provide stimulation? How? What effect would talking or reading to the child have? How could you provide your brother or sister with the experiences needed for this purpose?

2. "Mothering" should be included for all young children and infants every day as part of their experience. What specific experiences could you provide that would give the child sensory, exploratory, manipulative, social, and emotional experiences to satisfy the need for mothering? The term *parenting* is often used to describe the behavior of parents toward their children, since both fathers and mothers are involved in taking care of their children. Why is *parenting* a better term?

THINGS TO DO

1. Find out from your family or friends funny true stories of embarrassing situations created by five-year-olds through their tendency to be direct and personal with grownups, and be prepared to share them with the class.

2. Collect cartoons featuring young children. From the activities and talk shown, guess the probable age of the children and give reasons for your choice.

3. Draw a chart showing the different methods human beings use to get what they want at different ages. What behavior does a baby use to let you know he or she is hungry, for instance? A child of two? Of three? Of four? Of five? A person your age? How does a three-year-old behave when he or she

wants to get something—a toy, for example—from someone else? A four-, five-, six-, and 13-year-old? Set up several situations and follow them through for different age levels.

4. Set up a similar chart illustrating the reactions at different age levels to being thwarted or stopped or forbidden to do something. What conclusion could you draw concerning grown-up or mature ways of reacting to each situation?

5. Make a list of limited choices suitable for young children who are ready for some independence and enjoy making their own decisions.

6. Play ball with preschool children of various ages and note the difference in their skills and coordination. Notice also their behavior and social reactions while they play. Report your observations to the class.

7. Tell how you would help a youngster who continuously asks, "Why?"

8. List the ways to handle the child between two and four whose natural response is always "No."

9. What are some ways of encouraging and some ways of controlling the use of imagination?

10. Collect examples of the questions a five-year-old asks. Have a circle discussion (see following) on how to answer them.

RULES FOR A CIRCLE DISCUSSION

1. Sit "round."
2. Select a leader and a timekeeper.
3. The leader starts the discussion by reading the question.
4. Each student, when his or her turn comes, comments or asks a further question.
5. Comments or questions or points of agreement with statements already made are limited to one minute each. Timekeeper calls "time" and the next student takes his or her turn.
6. Student may "pass."
7. No one may speak out of turn or interrupt—not even the leader.
8. When each one has had an opportunity to speak once around the circle, those who "passed" may like to make a contribution.
9. Leader summarizes and opens the question to free discussion, or states a new question.

8 Guiding young children

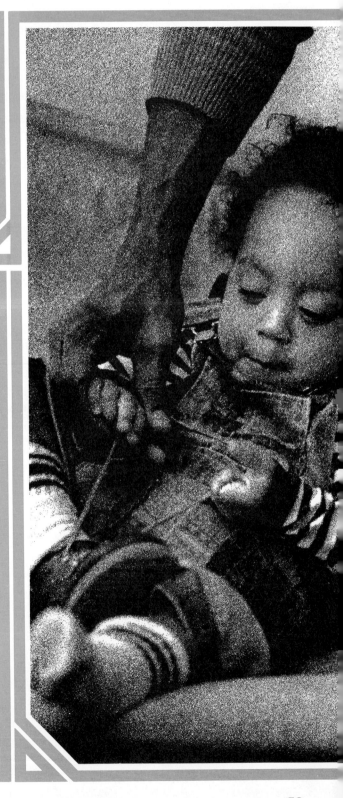

At each age and stage of development there are ways of behaving that are right *for that age.* A baby's life revolves around selfish needs, interests, activities, and point of view. A young child is guided through a period during which sharing and participating in the family's activities become important avenues of learning. With increasing age, the bigger world of neighborhood, school, and other community groups acquires significance. This process of growing up takes time and patience.

SIGNS OF READINESS

How much can we expect of children at various ages? What determines whether our expectations are fair and reasonable for the child? Very often we must wait until the proper physical development has taken place before we have a right to expect a child to achieve certain skills, abilities, and controls. A child must be ready before he or she can learn to walk, talk, undress and dress, climb, run, and so on. Before we should expect a child to do these things, the child must be physically and mentally capable of performing these tasks.

Learning to Dress

Very young children begin to learn how to dress when they cooperate by putting their hands through the sleeves or by pulling off their shoes while someone is undressing them. Later they will learn to unbutton garments or to open zippers by themselves. Eventually they will need no help in undressing and dressing. This is a series of steps of increasing difficulty which each child must master successfully before the next one can be learned. Have you observed that young children first learn to undress, open, unzip, snap open, untie, take off, before they can put on, button, zip, snap, and tie?

Self Feeding

In the same way, children learn to feed themselves and to take care of simple daily routines. Even very small babies begin to learn to feed themselves when they first hold the bottle without help. Can you think of all the steps that must be learned before a child is capable of handling a knife, fork, and spoon as expertly as you do?

Readiness to Learn

In each case, individual children give clues to their readiness to learn and should be encouraged to take as much responsibility as they are eager to have in doing things for themselves. They may button their coat wrong or spill food when they eat, but they must be given a chance to do things for themselves and to practice these developing skills if they are to become independent and self-reliant. If there is a young child in the family, the whole family may look for signs of readiness to do many things and guide and encourage his or her development.

Readiness Rates Differ

It has been found that children differ greatly in their readiness and ability to read and to do other tasks. There are a number of signs that show when a child is ready to read, for example. Maybe while you have been riding together a younger brother or sister has asked the meaning of words on billboards. Does he or she

pick out words in favorite books or in advertisements and want to know what they are? Does the child enjoy having you read to him or her and does he or she listen well? These are some of the signs for reading readiness. By encouraging word recognition and by answering questions about anything that is written, you can help a child who is ready to learn to read develop this very fundamental learning skill.

How can you determine readiness to learn other tasks? There are three clues to observe that are good indicators of readiness in a child:

1–The child seems interested in the task and wants to do it alone or wants to be shown how to do it.

2–There is a persistence in the child's determination to achieve some task even when obstacles or setbacks may occur. Frequent responses to an adult's attempt to help are "I will do it myself!" or "I can do it!"

3–There is improved performance with practice.

Close supervision helps keep a child safe, while he or she is learning simple skills.

LEARNING INDEPENDENCE

Probably the most important rule you can follow in order to help children learn to become independent is not to do things for them that they can do for themselves. Depriving them of the opportunity to learn to be independent and to take care of themselves may interfere with their optimal development, especially in intellectual and physical skills. Give positive reinforcement and approval when any task is accomplished successfully.

How can you help a child develop independence? The five keys to help you understand and guide a young child are

1–Expect only what is fair.
2–Set the stage for success.
3–Show approval for big and little achievements.
4–Respect each child for his or her individuality.
5–Give the young child unconditional affection.

Expect Only What Is Fair

You can learn to expect only what is fair and reasonable to the child if you remember what children are like at different ages. You must be aware of the mental and physical capabilities of the children at each age and stage of development if you are to be reasonable and fair in your expectations. However, all children benefit from stimulation and encouragement at any age.

Set the Stage for Success

In helping young children learn to take care of themselves be sure to give them gentle suggestions and plenty of time to try whatever they are trying to learn. One good rule to follow is: Make success fairly easy. Give them the minimum amount of help to succeed. For example, if they are learning to undress, sometimes they can learn faster if the clothes are bought with this self-help idea in mind. Zippers with large pull tabs, elastic waistbands, and simple knit pullovers make it easy to get into and out of clothes. If a child is learning to dress alone, you can make it easier by seeing that the clothes are arranged in the order in which they are to be put on. Generally, children will want to try new things if they can succeed fairly often.

When help is needed, give just enough assistance to solve the difficulty that the child seems unable to handle at the time. Sometimes toys get stuck or will not work. This can lead to a frustrating experience, if a little assistance is not offered. Occasionally, just a little help over a

Learning to eat by themselves is a basic task for young children.

rough spot will be sufficient. Or the child simply may not like to do a certain part of a job and will welcome a bit of help. As a rule, it is best to watch and wait and allow the child to figure out the solution. Sometimes simple verbal instructions will be all the help needed. But you need to size up the situation and decide whether you should delay or give immediate help.

Redirection

What should you do if a child is mishandling materials or hurting or endangering other children? Usually, you simply "switch the aim" to a more appropriate direction. This is called redirection. It has the added advantage of avoiding negative directions, such as "Don't do that!" or "No, no!" Grown-ups tend to use "No" and "Don't" much too often in guiding and directing children.

If Betty has a lump of clay in her hand and is evidently going to drop it with some force on Mary's head, what should you do? You might take the hand holding the clay and suggest, "Would you like to make a turtle out of that?" Or bring her over to a table, hand her a rolling pin, and suggest that she flatten out the clay and "make cookies." Young children are quick-change artists and have a short attention span, so you will find you can redirect them quite easily. They generally do not stick to any one thing very long. If you use your observation skills and your imagination you will get along very well with young children.

Show Approval

Probably one of the most effective principles of child guidance you can learn is that we tend to repeat the behavior and actions that are rewarded and approved. If you consistently approve the behavior and actions you want a child to learn, they will be continued, and the child will learn that those actions and that behavior are worthwhile. The key word in all this is consistency. It means that you recognize and reward the desired behavior every time. Conversely, it is generally true that behavior that is ignored or not recognized is frequently discontinued.

How can you make a child understand that you approve? You can smile or give a gentle pat. You can say, "That's right" or "Good" in a friendly tone of voice. Encouraging comments like "You almost did it that time" are better than "You can't do it." When you say, "You can do it! Try it. It's easy," you express confidence in the child's abilities. This can be a powerful motivation for learning.

Often youngsters can sense approval or disapproval of their actions. Even very young children have this general feeling. They understand the "secret messages" we all communicate without using language. Have you ever watched a young child perform for an audience of doting parents, brothers and sisters, and grandparents? The child clearly understands their pleasure and approval by their expressions and attention. Anyone who is observant when around young children also soon discovers that the approval given must be sincere and reflect true inner feelings, because children seem to be able to sense it if you do not really mean what you say and do.

Learning by Imitation

When you were little you learned to do what was expected of you by discovering which actions brought smiles to the faces of your family and which ones brought a harsh tone of voice. Another way you learned to do what was expected of you was by imitation. Children are great imitators. Therefore, if we expect them to be kind and considerate, we must provide them with constant examples of kindness and consideration to see and copy.

You also learned how it *feels* to be grown-up by play-acting. You pretended you were different people, invented situations, and experimented with different ways of behaving or reacting to them. Sometimes your dramatic play was so real to you that you literally became a cowboy, Indian, or movie actress. You gradually learned to repeat the things that brought approval from your family and stopped doing those you learned were undesirable.

You can teach young children to finish, to help, to be quick, to be careful, and so on by recognizing their big and little achievements and letting them know that you like what they are doing. Everyone needs a sense of achievement and approval. Be sure to provide for this need in the young children you care for.

How to Show Disapproval

How can you help children understand that what they are doing is not desirable? Sometimes, the best thing to do is to ignore it if in your judgment it is not harmful. In this way you will not make an issue of it and so it will not seem important to the child. Usually, the less concern you show, the less important it will seem to the child. Also, the child will find it easier to stop or change to acceptable activities if the negative behavior is not stressed.

But when there is an obvious risk or danger involved, you must take immediate steps to protect the child. Remember, you can foresee the consequences of children's actions because you have had more experience. So guard them at once if they seem to be heading for trouble.

Respect Each Child for His or Her Individuality

A fundamental respect for the child as an individual must be evident if you want to work well with young children. You want to build their feeling of self-respect and a feeling of adequacy. Children must be respected for what they *can* do now and for what they *may* achieve in the future. You should understand that there are certain limits beyond which it would be unreasonable to expect individual children to grow.

Children often accomplish rather surprising tasks because someone important to them expected them to do so. Has this ever happened to you? One way to encourage youngsters to try harder is to show them that you confidently expect them to do it.

Unconditional Affection

The basic and most important key to guiding children is to give them unconditional affection. This means that regardless of what they do or how they behave they are certain that you like them as persons. When John misbehaves, try saying, "I like *you* very much, but I don't like what you are doing." By separating the *action* you disapprove from the *person* you like, you are indicating that behavior can be changed without threatening the individuality of the person. Then by suggestion, direction, or explanation let the child know what action you do approve. As long as children can be sure that they are valued and loved as persons, they will try to behave in ways that will bring them approval and reward.

Each of the keys to guiding children is important. Usually several keys work together to help children learn to give and take. They need to learn this to get along with people. But if you want children to benefit from any of these techniques you must give them love and affection with no strings attached. You should not imply that you love them because they are good and conform to good standards of behavior, but that you love and respect them simply because they are the people they are. You can establish happy relationships with preschool children by giving them unconditional love, showing a sincere respect for the individual, approving big and little successes, setting the stage for success, and having reasonable expectations.

Children learn from one another
and at different rates.

THINKING IT OVER

1. Can you think of five times in the last week when someone used encouraging comments and approval to help you achieve some worthwhile goal? How did you feel? As you remember these instances, consider what might have happened if someone had not noticed and told you about it. Can you see why it is so important to use positive procedures with young children?

2. In this chapter, the word *discipline* is not used. However, the ultimate goal of discipline is for the child to become a self-directed, inner-controlled, independent thinker and decision maker. Can you determine the purpose of disciplining children after reading this chapter? Do further readings in this area to increase your understanding of this very important concept.

THINGS TO DO

1. Have a circle of ideas on different ways you can "Set the Stage for Success." Decide on a specific activity, like dressing. Tell how you would set the stage by laying out the clothes in the order in which the child will put them on. Assign a similar activity to each student and present your solutions to the group. Sit "round."

2. Plan and prepare a bulletin board to illustrate the circle of ideas you develop in Number 1.

3. Make a practice book for a young child. Use muslin. Include a zipper to open and close, buttons and buttonholes, shoelaces and holes to lace and tie, belt and buckle to close and open, ribbons to tie, snaps to snap, and so on.

4. Find out the difference between guidance and dominance and when the terms are used in reference to the care of children. Give examples of each.

5. Act out the part of a child eating lunch in a way *approved* by his or her parent. Show a child eating lunch with the parent disapproving of some of the actions. How does the *child* react to approval? To disapproval? How do *you* feel and what do you do when your parents show disapproval?

6. Make a list of 20 statements beginning with "Don't" that are commonly used in dealing with preschool children. Then match it with 20 statements saying the same thing in positive terms.

7. Have a contest called Accentuate the Positive. Select a leader. The rest of the class lines up. The leader reads a statement used with children, beginning with "Don't—." Each student in turn gives an acceptable "positive translation." If one misses, he or she drops out. Continue until the "top three positive experts" remain.

9 On the job as a baby sitter

Do you take care of young children? You may have taken care of your younger brother or sister often. Maybe you have become a regular sitter and take care of several small children in the neighborhood. You may even belong to a baby sitters club. Have you ever thought about what it means to be a good baby sitter?

GENERAL QUALIFICATIONS

There are some general qualifications parents have a right to expect from the baby sitters they employ. A list of these would include reliability, promptness, an ability to follow instructions, alertness, resourcefulness, and a cool head in emergencies. All these imply that the boy or girl who assumes responsibility for the care of a young child has some knowledge and understanding of what children are like. Baby-sitting is a serious responsibility and for the time being a child's life is in your hands.

A Baby Sitter Is Reliable

How would you describe a reliable person? A reliable person is someone who can be trusted to fulfill the obligations that have been assumed. When you agree to baby-sit, the parents can depend on you to give all your attention and energies to supervising the child or children left in your care. Their safety and well-being would be your chief concern. Of course, it will also be fun and usually you can earn some money by baby-sitting. Ordinarily, parents are careful to employ people who have demonstrated that they are reliable.

A Baby Sitter Is Prompt

Promptness is a desirable quality on any job. It is essential for the baby sitter to arrive on time. And you should arrange to stay as long as agreed upon. If an emergency arises or if you become ill or get a cold after you have made an appointment to baby-sit, you should call the parents well in advance so that they can make other arrangements.

A Baby Sitter Follows Instructions

The parents may leave specific instructions with regard to the care of their child, such as feeding, where supplies are located, any special activity to be allowed or not allowed, bedtime and prebedtime routines, and so on. These instructions must be followed carefully. Do not hesitate to ask questions if something is not clear to you. Have the parents describe to you in detail the procedures used at bedtime. Is the order supper, stories, prayers, and bed? Most children like their bedtime routines with no variations. Parents usually go through these activities so regularly that they are hardly conscious of established habits, such as giving their child a dilapidated stuffed elephant to sleep with.

Be sure to find out the family vocabulary for toilet needs. Each family seems to have its own code for such matters. Things will go more smoothly and safely if you know these things.

A Baby Sitter Is Alert

Another characteristic of a good baby sitter is alertness. You must keep awake and watchful to prevent accidents and to safeguard the child from dangers. Most children are careless and do not foresee the consequences of their actions. As

Give all your attention to the child left in your care.

a person in charge, you must use all your powers of observation to protect them from harm. It is wise to redirect children if they are heading for the stove, an open window, sharp equipment, medicine, the street, hot water, strange animals, and the like. At night when they are asleep you should check at least once every hour to see that all is well. You must keep your ear tuned in for any unusual noises or movements or for their call if they should awaken.

A Baby Sitter Is Resourceful

A baby sitter who is resourceful will use imagination and skill when faced with a temporary difficulty. For example, suppose you must prepare supper for the child. How can you provide a safe place for an inquisitive, active toddler for a short time? No playpen is available. What can you do? You can improvise a play area by placing four chairs on their sides and tying them together, if necessary. You must use your ingenuity in many ways when you are responsible for young children. If they find scribbling on the walls amusing, you could give them a large piece of wrapping paper, newspaper, or an opened out and flattened paper bag. Show them how to write or draw on any kind of paper, not on the walls. Whether you are playing with them, helping them to learn some new skill, or protecting them from hazards, the ability to see another way out of a difficulty is one you should use yourself and constantly coax them to acquire. It will be of real value to them.

Children need a lot of attention.

A Baby Sitter Keeps a Cool Head in Emergencies

The well-prepared baby sitter keeps a cool head in emergencies. You should not rely on memory but should WRITE DOWN all instructions and the names, addresses, and telephone numbers of anyone who might be needed in case of emergency. These include the parents, the doctor, fire department, police, and nearby friends or neighbors. Be sure you are familiar

Have the parents describe to you in detail the procedures used at bedtime.

Keep a cool head in emergencies.

If feeding the child is part of your duties, follow the parents' methods as closely as possible.

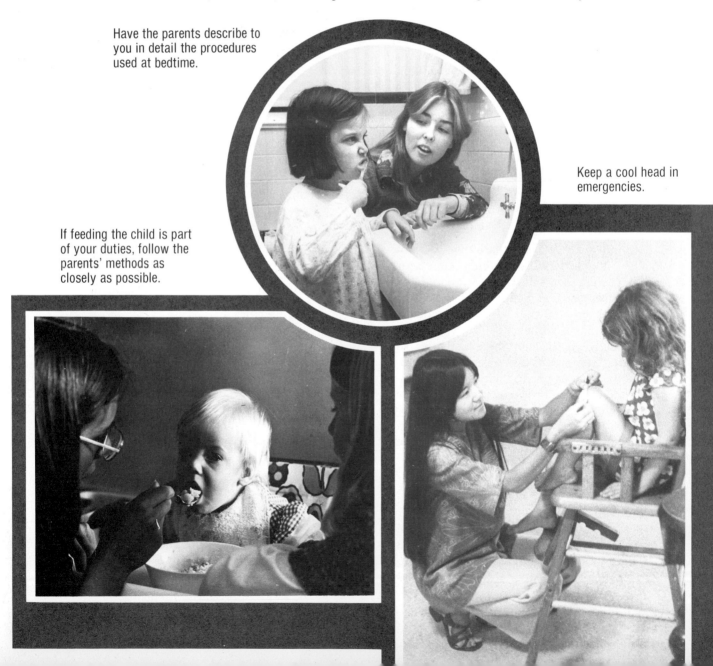

enough with the house to find light switches, the telephone, and the like. You must know how to lock the house if you are taking the child out. Is there another entrance besides the one you used? This would be important to know in case of fire and to protect you and the child against intruders. If you must put the child to bed, find out where the clothes are kept. You may need to know where the child's toys are kept, too.

FEEDING YOUNG CHILDREN

If you are to prepare food, be sure you know how the range or stove works and where the utensils and food are kept. Where is the can opener and how does it work? Children's food should be served not too hot and not too cold, but just right.

There are three important points to remember when supervising children while they eat. First, children need a lot of attention. Be casual, friendly, patient. Second, children need some babying. Maybe the very fact that a stranger is with them will make children a bit fussy. Smile and talk about pleasant things while they are eating. They will know that you like what they are doing. If a toddler stalls at mealtime, try a change of scene. Serve supper at a low table or on a tray in the living room. Add a quiet atmosphere: no fuss, hurry, or noise. Soft radio music sometimes has a soothing effect. Third, you should understand that children are likely to be messy at the table when they are learning to eat. Encourage their efforts to feed themselves. Be patient with their clumsiness. Do not scold, nag, or fuss. Above all, do not force them to eat. Respect their likes and dislikes, and whenever possible allow them to make choices.

Make the portions small. Make the servings so tiny that they will think, "Is that all I get?" instead of "Do I have to eat all that?" Allow a reasonable amount of time, at least half an hour, and then if the meal isn't eaten remove it casually with a friendly remark like "Guess you're not hungry." The child should not even suspect that it may upset you if the food you prepared is not eaten. Let your words and actions say, "What you eat is up to you."

If children are tired, bored, or upset, they may want to be helped even though they may know how to feed themselves quite well. It does no harm to encourage them by giving a little assistance.

HOW YOU LOOK AND BEHAVE ON THE JOB

Now a word about your appearance and behavior on the job. Arrive looking neat and clean. Wear simple washable garments. Since the safety and welfare of the child depends on you while parents are absent, keep telephone conversations to a minimum. It is rarely advisable to entertain your friends while you are on the job. Unless you are specifically invited to have some food, never raid your employer's refrigerator. Bring your own snack if you are accustomed to eating later in the evening. If the baby-sitting job is at night, bring some books and plan to study or read quietly when the child is asleep. You should know when your employer expects to return and how you will get home safely. Inform your own parents of these facts, as well as the name, address, and telephone number so that they can reach you should the need arise. Try bringing a medium-sized flashlight with you. It eliminates groping and fumbling in unfamiliar places—really puts light on the subject.

Construct a play kit to take when you go baby-sitting. Include toys, games, stories, and

Encourage children to try new activities.

65

pictures for variety. Be sure the toys are safe, sanitary, and inexpensive.

Your reputation as a baby sitter whom parents can rely on will depend on many things. You must be reliable, prompt, able to follow instructions, alert, resourceful, and cool in emergencies. Above all, use common sense and learn the "feel" of dealing with small children. The more confidence you develop, the better job of baby-sitting you can do.

YOU'RE ON YOUR OWN

You should arrive at the house early. This will give you a chance to watch the child and the parents. It will also give the child a chance to get used to having you there before the parents leave. Ask about pets. The youngster may be unable to go to sleep unless the dog is safely in the dog bed. There may be someone else living with the family. Find out if a family member or a roomer may be coming in around midnight. It would be both frightening and embarrassing if you thought it was a housebreaker.

Good nights have been said. The parents are gone and you are left alone with your charge. From now on, establishing a good relationship with a preschool youngster is up to you. *How* you say and do things is more important than *what* you say and do. Preschoolers may be a bit uneasy when they find themselves with a stranger. They may cry or hide in the bedroom. Or they may decide that this is the time to dump the toys from the chest in the middle of the living room floor. It is even possible that you will be bitten or kicked before you get them in bed. Suggest something to distract their attention. You may have to pretend that you are not particularly disturbed, but they should understand by your look and firm manner that you disapprove. They will test you by using bad language and talking back. If you are shocked or hurt, pretend you did not hear and go on with what you were doing. They are communicating distress and unhappiness at being left behind by their parents. As soon as you can, give them lots of loving attention and they should relax and enjoy being with you.

Even before the parents leave, take the child by the hand and say, "I'll read you a story." Act as if this is going to be a delightful treat for both of you. Any instructions or directions should be given gently but firmly—as if you were sure they were going to be carried out with pleasure. Help them to get started or to finish what they are doing if they seem to need some extra attention. Expect compliance.

What should you do if the parents told you bedtime is seven o'clock and the child refuses to go to bed? Or if the youngster seems overtired and whiny and it is only 6:30? Use your judgment. You should not expect to carry out instructions to the *minute*. Treat children of this age as equals. Let them show you how independent and helpful they can be. Ask them, "Which towel is yours?" and "Where are your pajamas?" Give them a chance to show you. Talk in your natural tone of voice, as you would to a friend. Answer questions as simply and directly as you can. When you finally get them to bed, say, "Good night" quietly and reassure them that you will be there if you are needed. They will probably call you or come out of bed several times to make sure you are minding them. Reassure them and say, "Good night" again quietly.

Use your common sense. Develop a calm, deliberate attitude. You should have few difficulties you cannot cope with when you take care of preschoolers.

THINKING IT OVER

1. A positive attitude toward working can be very helpful to your current and future jobs. How would your attitude affect your work? How would your employers tend to judge your work if you displayed a positive attitude? A negative one?

2. Assume that you are going to be interviewed for a summer job taking care of two young children five mornings a week. How would you prepare yourself for the interview? What facts or evidence could you present to the employer which might help you to get the job? What questions should you ask? What would you do about your personal appearance?

THINGS TO DO

1. Present a skit of a parent interviewing you for a job as a baby sitter. What evidence or examples can you present to show the parent that you are *reliable?*

2. Make a community survey on "What are the qualifications parents want in girls and boys who care for children?" Compile and analyze the information. Develop a Code for Baby Sitters on the basis of the survey information. As a class or club project, print a booklet with the Code and distribute it to parents of young children in the community. Members of the PTA in the elementary school would probably appreciate such a guide.

3. Develop a priorities scale. What should a baby sitter do first, second, and third in each of the following instances when responsible for a child?

In case of fire: In case of illness: In case of accident:
1.   1.   1.
2.   2.   2.
3.   3.   3.

4. Keep a diary of your experiences with children. Tell what you learned about them, what experiences you had with young children, if you agreed or disagreed with ideas you read or heard about children, and why, and what happened to children when you were observing them and why you think it happened. List any questions you may have about children that you want discussed or answered.

5. Devise a Baby Sitters Code of your own based on the letters BABY SITTERS CODE.

For example:

Be prompt in arriving for your job.
Alertness and vigilance will keep the child safe and away from harm.
Be cool and collected in emergencies.
You must use your imagination and be resourceful to keep the child happy.
Supplies and equipment should be where you can find them.
Information in writing is an aid with routines and in emergencies.
Take telephone messages carefully.
Telephone conversations with your friends should be avoided or short.
Every child needs understanding and loving guidance.
Reliability and dependability are important qualities of a baby sitter.
Safety and welfare of the child is your responsibility while parents are away.
Comfortable, happy children need someone they like and trust to look after them.
Obtain information such as time of your arrival and departure, and the address and phone number for your parents.
Dress neatly and be well-groomed.
Entertaining friends while baby sitting is not recommended.

COMMUNITY EXPERIENCES WITH YOUNG CHILDREN

1. Serve as a volunteer assistant to a playground supervisor.
2. Help keep children amused while parents attend PTA meetings, church, or when they vote.
3. Serve as an assistant at summer Bible school or church school.

10 Children's development through play

Children develop their social and motor skills through play. Children's play provides them with the kinds of experiences they need in order to learn how to relate to others. They also develop their physical and mental skills through play. So while play is generally considered as fun for them, it is also a source of very serious kinds of development and learning for young children.

FUN THROUGH PLAY

Having fun with children is just the same as having fun with anyone else. To have fun with children, you must share and participate, you must initiate, and you must appreciate the activities they are involved in. Sometimes it is pleasant to enter into the activities of others and participate. At other times you can add to the pleasure of others by suggesting some interesting ideas for new experiences or activities. And when others introduce suggestions or perform some activity, you add to the joy of the occasion if you can show your appreciation by your approval and active participation.

Children's play experiences are usually of three kinds: (1) free play, (2) supervised play, and (3) dramatized play. Regardless of the kind of play children are involved in, it is a means by which they learn. They also enjoy such experiences as storytelling, listening to records, and exploring their world through walks and excursions.

Free Play

Children do not have to be taught how to play. As curious, growing, learning beings, children generally find stimulation in the world around them. And because children learn from the moment of birth, they should be provided with a stimulating environment so that they can expand their learning and physical skills. Remember that environment as used here means all the people, places, things, and events in the child's world.

If you watch children at free play you can increase your understanding of individual children. You get clues to the child's personality and stage of development if you notice

★ The play materials selected.
★ How the materials are manipulated or used.
★ The way the child "talks" while playing.
★ The way success in what is attempted seems to affect the child.
★ The way failure in what is tried seems to affect the child.

This knowledge can help you establish a good relationship with most children. When space, materials, and equipment are provided, young children will find things to do that are suitable to their age and stage of development.

Supervised Play

Supervised play refers to those activities that are either watched over, initiated, or led by a grown-up. They may involve one or more children. When playtime is presided over by an older person, the child's freedom to choose materials, space, or activities may be limited. Often supervised play involves direct teaching. When you are in charge, you might help a child learn

an easier or safer way of doing something. For example, if the project is to build steps out of large blocks but the child forgets to build steps *down* the other side, you can teach that steps should go up and down for safety. Children enjoy learning simple circle games and often need help in remembering the rules. When a child runs out of ideas for things to do, you may have to suggest new activities or show how to use old materials in a new way.

Whether you supervise one child's play or a small group of children, your primary responsibility is to keep them safe. You must learn to keep your eye on your charges constantly. You should learn to keep your ear tuned in for unusual sounds and be ever alert. You will have to use your ingenuity to provide them with enjoyable experiences that are also safe.

Dramatic Play Has Many Possibilities

Dramatic play may be either spontaneous and free, or directed and supervised. In simple terms, whenever children say, "Let's pretend," they are using dramatic play. A ragbag with scraps of material, old clothes, hats, and shoes, empty cartons and boxes, and old pots and pans offers endless possibilities. Frames for eyeglasses (with lenses removed), neckties, and old curtains will be enjoyed. Many used and worn household and personal items are used by children as costumes and props for their dramatized play. The way they use these materials helps them understand the world in which they live.

You would be surprised at the many ways a child can use a sturdy cardboard box, for example. It can be a house, a garage for little cars, a dock for boats, a bed for the doll, and with a string attached, it has all the added uses of a pull-toy.

Children like being with grown-ups who have kept some of their ability to pretend. They enjoy being with you if you can enter into the situations they invent. They like people who have a sense of wonder and who find delightful discoveries in everyday things.

SPACE FOR PLAY

Children need to have a place to play. They should be free to do things without danger of hurting themselves or others, or of damaging the belongings of others. Ideally, they should have a room indoors so arranged that they can play in any part of it. It may be just a part of a room that is partitioned off for this purpose. But they should be allowed to handle and touch everything they can reach there. Outside, a fenced-in porch or part of the yard would be a good place for outdoor play. A sandy spot also offers fine possibilities for play and exploration.

Children enjoy being with grown-ups who can enter into the situations the children invent.

PLAY MATERIALS

Probably the most universally enjoyed play materials are blocks. Children play with them for years. They offer endless possibilities for creative play. They are used to build houses, barns, fences, roads. They become boats, trains, and trucks. Large smooth blocks of various sizes, colors, and shapes are best for the preschool child.

Crayons, paints, finger paints, and clay allow the child to explore colors, textures, shapes, and different "feels." Simple clay dough can be made at home.

HOMEMADE CLAY DOUGH

1 cup flour
½ cup salt
3 teaspoons alum
Enough water to hold ingredients together
Vegetable coloring

When not in use, store the clay in a covered container. To keep it in good condition, knead a small amount of water into it when the surface dries. Divide it into three or four parts and make each part a different color. Beet juice, grape juice, spinach water, and household bluing may also be used for coloring.

HOUSEHOLD ARTICLES MAKE GOOD TOYS

Many household articles, such as eggbeaters, lids, measuring spoons, wooden spoons, clothespins, and empty boxes and containers, are enjoyed by children. Things around the home that can be used in play activities include the following:

1—Spools—to roll, to be strung as beads, for tower building

2—Old dresses, shirts, hats, shoes, pocketbooks, wallets, scarves, gloves—for dress-up play

3—Cigar boxes or other small wooden boxes—to make cars, to form an engine with a tin can attached, for hollow blocks, for truck bodies

4—Lids (various sizes)—for wheels for pull-toys

5—Tin cans—to form a nesting toy of various sizes (remove the tops carefully, smooth the rough edges, and paint them)

6—Clothespins (paint them)—to use on the edges of cans, for hanging drawings on a clothesline to dry or display

7—Round cereal boxes—for a cradle for small dolls

8—Large crates and boxes (sand and paint them, if made of wood)—to make sinks, cupboards, stoves, tables; to provide storage space for a playhouse

9—Pieces of rope—for jumping, for pulling things

10—Old pots and pans—to use as playhouse utensils, for sandbox and water play

11—Old socks—to make dolls

12—Scrapbooks—to keep pictures from old magazines, cut and colored (old sample wallpaper books may be used to paste pictures in)

13—Pieces of cloth—to make hats, masks, and costumes for dramatic play; for dolls' clothes

14—Wrapping paper and bags—to put things in; to make hats and masks

15—Things to string—macaroni, dried seeds (such as corn, peas, winged maple seeds; melon, squash, and pumpkin seeds), seashells, popcorn, flowers, buttons, spools

16—Blunt-tipped scissors and paper and paste—to make paper chains, fold paper and cut out snowflakes, trace leaves on paper and cut them out

17—Tape measure—to measure everything in sight

18—Strainers—for sand play

19—Egg timer—to watch (fascinating for children of all ages)

20—Funnel—to pour things through

CHILDREN LIKE WATER PLAY

A small sand pile and a shallow pool, plus a few unbreakable cups, spoons, and pails in the backyard are exciting sources of pleasure for most youngsters. Water play is greatly enjoyed. If a shallow pool cannot be provided, give toddlers or preschoolers a pail of water and a small paintbrush. They will play contentedly for hours at "painting" the house or garage with water. Another form of water play that fascinates young children is blowing soap bubbles. Thick soapsuds in a bowl and a piece of spaghetti or a straw are all that is needed.

TOYS FOR CHILDREN OF DIFFERENT AGES

Although some toys are more suitable for a given age of preschoolers, children of the same age show great differences in their interests. Some toys that make a three-year-old happy may be equally interesting to a five-year-old and vice versa.

Toys for Three-Year-Olds

Three-year olds need toys they can

★ Push and pull.
★ Pile up.
★ Dump out.
★ Dig with.
★ Carry around.

Toys for Four-Year-Olds

Four-year-olds need toys they can use

★ In make-believe play.
★ To develop finger muscles.
★ To test their strength.
★ To learn how to balance.
★ To move fast.

These include such toys as baby dolls, doll carriages, swings, wagons, trestles made of planks, chinning rods, paper, crayon, chalk, easels, paints, thick brushes, jigsaw puzzles with a few large pieces, garden tools, sound toys, wheelbarrows, and simple musical instruments like tom-toms, triangles, cymbals, and drums.

★ Match and put together.
★ Handle, mold, and cuddle.

These include such toys as blocks, stuffed animals, rag dolls, wooden animals, doll beds, dishes, small trucks, pounding sets, pegboards, pull toys, sand toys, floating toys, beach balls, picture books, nesting cans, and carpet sweepers.

Toys for Five- and Six-Year-Olds

Five- and six-year-olds need toys

★ To do things with.
★ For mental and physical growth.
★ For construction.
★ For vigorous physical exercise.

These include a few woodworking tools that really work, boxes of soft-wood scraps, nails, boxes with clothing for dress-up play, household equipment like old irons and ironing boards, toy stoves and sinks, tea sets, xylophones, transportation toys, sleds, simple gymnasium equipment (like low bars, rings, climbing apparatus, slides, swings, and tumbling mats), beanbags, ladders, large packing-case playhouses, jump ropes, teeter-totters, and tree houses. Can you think of others?

Toy shelves that are open make both putting away toys and finding them to play with easier.

A PLACE TO KEEP TOYS

Open shelves are best for putting away toys. With shelves within easy reach, children will learn to keep their things in order more easily. You might enjoy designing and making a simple toy cabinet. Cardboard boxes can hold crayons, chalk, pencils, and other small articles. An egg carton will make a good container for beads and other things to string. A hook on the side of the cabinet is a handy place to keep the jump rope. A bushel basket makes a good storage place for blocks. The basket can be covered or painted to make it more attractive. Can you think of other ways you can make the toy shelves easy to keep orderly?

Table 10-1

SELECTING A GOOD TOY	Excellent	Good	Fair	Poor
1. Does it work?				
2. Is it safe?				
3. Is it sturdy and well-constructed?				
4. Is it easily cleaned?				
5. Is the color lasting and harmless?				
6. Can it be used in many different ways?				
7. Is it designed to meet specific needs of preschool children a. for active play?				
b. for creative or imaginative play?				
c. for dramatic play?				
8. Is the cost reasonable?				

CHOOSING TOYS

You should choose toys carefully. The right kind of toys include those that

★ Help the child learn by doing.
★ Give a child indoor and outdoor experiences.
★ Develop the child's large and small muscles.
★ Encourage creative play.
★ Help the child learn about shapes, feels, colors, and sounds.
★ Are durable and safe.

Table 10-1 should help you rate toys for children.

HOMEMADE TOYS

Nearly everyone enjoys planning and making toys out of materials found around the house. It is pleasant to talk about them at the supper table. Some toys can be made by the children themselves. They may not turn out as perfectly as those you could make, but they would give the children much satisfaction because they use and develop their skills. They also feel that they are participating in real work.

Make this simple wooden train for a three-year-old. The six-year-old can make it with your help.

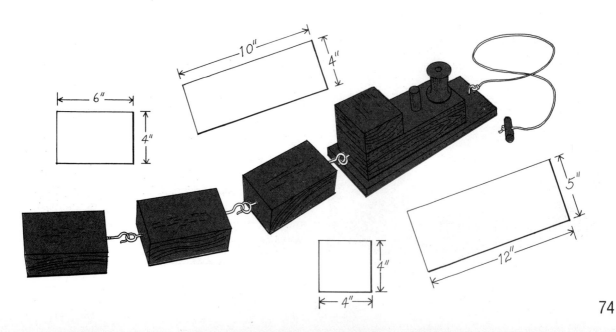

For cars:
Cut three blocks of wood 4″ x 6″ x 2″.
For the engine:
1-block 1″ thick, 4″ x 12″, with a rounded front end
1-block 2″ thick, 4″ x 10″
1-block 2″ thick, 4″ x 4″
For the front light:
½-small spool
For the funnel:
¾-large spool
For the whistle:
½-small spool
Glue blocks together and spools to blocks as shown in diagram.
To join the train together:
6-cup hooks

VALUE OF PLAY

What does play do for children? Freedom to try many activities by using a variety of materials has these benefits: (1) It helps them develop their ability to get along with others; (2) It aids in developing more skillful use of their muscles; (3) It helps them make countless discoveries about the nature of things around them; and (4) It helps them be more resourceful and exercise their imaginations.

TELLING STORIES

Storytelling has been a favorite way of amusing children for centuries. Can you remember a favorite story of yours when you were young? Have you ever read or told a story to a young child? How did you tell it? How did the child react to it? To be an expert storyteller, one that children will listen to and enjoy, you must consider the three important aspects of a well-told story: (1) Proper selection, (2) Effective delivery, and (3) Satisfactory reaction.

Because most preschool children like the same stories over and over again, they should be selected carefully or you will find yourself reading the kind of story that is no longer pleasant after repetition. A good story should include people, things, and events that are familiar to the child. Generally, children like activities they see in their own family and community. The story should be realistic and well-written. It should appeal to a child's imagination and should have plenty of action. And it should not frighten or disturb the young child.

A well-told or well-read story is a delightful experience for both teller and listener. To be a good storyteller, you should remember the four principles that are listed on the next page.

Table 10-2

DID YOU TELL A GOOD STORY?

YES	NO	
☐	☐	1. Did the story have familiar people, places, events?
☐	☐	2. Did it appeal to the child's imagination?
☐	☐	3. Did it have lots of action?
☐	☐	4. Did it frighten or upset the child?
☐	☐	5. Did you know the story well?
☐	☐	6. Did the child see you and hear you?
☐	☐	7. Did you dramatize people and events?
☐	☐	8. Did the listening experience seem pleasant to the child?
☐	☐	9. Was the child attentive?

1-Know the story so well that even if you are reading it you can look at the children instead of at the book most of the time.

2-Make sure that your listeners can see your face and hear you.

3-Dramatize wherever you can.

a. Change your voice for different characters.

b. Use facial expressions, especially those involving your eyes, smiles, frowns, and so on. Practice telling the story to yourself before a mirror and note appropriate expressions.

c. Move your hands and arms to show action.

d. Be enthusiastic.

e. Whenever possible let the children take part. Let them be characters in the story or have them show how certain actions or sounds are done.

f. Sometimes you can use simple props like a toy, small bells, a stick for rhythm, a telephone, a wastebasket for echoes, and other sound effects.

4-Answer questions as they arise. A good technique to use is to turn the question back to the children. For example, say, "Why do *you* think this happened?" or "What do *you* think will happen next?"

Finally, the success of your storytelling efforts depends on the children's reaction. Were they interested? Did they ask questions? Or did they seem restless and more interested in other things around them? Did they ask for more?

If you can answer YES to all the questions except Number 4 in Table 10-2, you are an expert storyteller.

Having fun with children provides an opportunity to learn a great deal about them.

WALKS AND EXCURSIONS

Because children are intensely curious about everything and everyone around them, you will find it rewarding to take them for a walk. It will give you a chance to observe at first hand how they see everything with a delightful freshness.

As always, when you are responsible for children you must keep them safe and happy. What questions do they ask? What things do they notice? What comments do they make? When you take them by the hand and set out for a stroll you will find it is a journey of discovery and exploration for them. If you have forgotten how to be observant and alert to your surroundings, a child can help you relearn.

LISTENING TO RECORDS

Another way children develop socially is by listening to records. Even very young children en-

joy "dancing." Some learn to operate a small record player and play their own records. Children's records should be chosen just as carefully as their books and stories. Look for simple rhythms, uncomplicated tunes, and easy words. Be sure you can stand the repetition. As with books and stories, children will play a favorite record over and over and unless it is selected with this repetitive factor in mind, it may turn out to be a source of annoyance to others in the family.

LEARNING ABOUT CHILDREN THROUGH PLAY

Having fun with children is a very individual experience. It provides an ideal opportunity to observe and encourage them in their social development. You can enjoy being with children and learn a great deal about children from your experiences if you remember these three points:

77

1- You must appreciate and enjoy their great capacity for learning through observation, imitation, and questioning.

2- You must be able to initiate and participate in their play activities and beginning social experiences.

3- You need to learn how to tell stories well and to supervise them in exploring their neighborhood, as well as with their beginning experiences in rhythm and music.

UNDERSTANDING PRESCHOOL CHILDREN

Preschool children need stimulation and assistance from others to develop and grow to their fullest potential. You can assist them by finding ways to help them develop self-respect, self-confidence, and self-control.

Young children learn very gradually to share and to take turns. You can help them by providing them with opportunities to take their turn on the slide at the playground, for example, and to share their toys. Be guided on their readiness for this phase of their development by their first efforts with you or others in the family before expecting them to share with other children.

Young children need to develop their vocabulary. This helps them develop both mentally and socially. Your example, the way you talk with them, gives them an opportunity to learn to talk and express themselves correctly. They need to learn to listen, too. Again, your example will be very valuable for them. Many toys and games provide both mental stimulation and social experiences. They are usually called educational toys and games. When you select a game for young children consider its potential value in helping them develop their minds and social abilities.

THINKING IT OVER

1. Think about the title of this chapter, "Children's Development Through Play." Consider the social values of all kinds of play.

2. Is play still important to you? What kinds of play do you enjoy? Why? What does it do for you? How do play and games affect you socially?

THINGS TO DO

1. Display a collection of household articles that children can enjoy as much as commercial toys.

2. List or collect pictures of household articles that are unsafe when used as toys.

3. Plan rainy-day activities for a four- or five-year-old child.

4. Teach a group of children a simple game. Be prepared to report to the class the method you used and how the children learned the rules.

5. Watch a boy or girl play with an empty carton. How many things does it become?

6. Give a child an old hat, clothes, high-heeled shoes, and a shopping bag. Observe what form of dramatic play evolves.

7. Watch children (boys and girls) at doll play. How do they behave when they pretend they are mothers and fathers?

8. Have a roundup of both commercial and homemade toys.

9. Construct a simple stuffed toy. Use old nylons or foam rubber stuffing.

10. Write an original story, poem, or nonsense rhyme for preschool children.

11. Take a child for a walk. What does the child observe that you would ignore? What questions are asked? What things seem to give the child pleasure? Be prepared to report to the class.

12. Make an illustrated booklet of "feel" pictures. Use velvet, felt, satin, rubber, and so on.

13. Have a "Hobo Picnic" for a group of youngsters. Children can come dressed in patched clothes, old hats, and so on. Each child can bring his or her own lunch in a bag on the end of a stick. Plan games, such as a treasure hunt or relay races with teams each choosing their own name, such as Rags, Tatters, and the like.

area four

Food For Your Family and You

11 Why we eat

"Does what I eat really make a difference?" is a question that keeps popping up in everyone's mind. You may find it difficult to believe that the food choices you make will influence your growth, physical development, personality, vigor, and the length and quality of life. They even affect your appearance and your schoolwork. Because your body can take a great deal of abuse, it is hard to realize that what you eat is affecting your life now as well as in the future and that you can profit by an improvement in food habits. You will have an attractive appearance, feel energetic, and be more alert and happy when you choose a balanced, nutritious diet. And you will probably have a longer, more active life.

WE ARE WHAT WE EAT

Every cell in your body was once food—your brains, your bones, your blood, and your muscles. How big you are, how strong you are, how healthy you are—each is affected by what you eat every day. Food has the building materials to make a sound body. And to attain your full growth potential and build the healthiest body possible you must have the right amount and the right kind of food. What you eat can be an asset or a liability. Which will it be for you?

Select Food Wisely

If you are careless about the food you eat, you may be tired, dull, cranky, or easily worried. In contrast, if you choose nutritious foods, you will look healthy, be peppy, and have shiny hair and clearer skin. You may consider yourself healthy because you are seldom sick. But you may not realize the great difference between a "so-so" and a "go-go" feeling.

Food gives you the energy necessary to carry on recreational activities, to do your school work, to take part in clubs and sports, and to help at home—in fact, all of life's activities. Even wiggling your little finger uses energy and therefore food. Calories give you energy, but other food substances are necessary for you to be a healthy, active person. Be sure you are satisfying hunger in the best way.

Select Food Wisely

WHAT IS NUTRITION?

Doctors, physiologists, chemists, physicists, and other scientists from the earliest days of medical science have thought about food and what happens to it in the body. Many of them performed experiments. From this work has come the science of nutrition as we know it today.

Nutrition may be defined as the process of everything that happens to food from the time it enters your mouth, is digested, and becomes a part of your body. Food may be used for growth, for maintaining life, for health, or for operating your body. You can see that food has some very important uses, especially in this period of your life when you are growing so rapidly. Build a habit of selecting nutritious foods every day so that all your body needs will be met.

HUNGER AND APPETITE

Hunger is your body's way of asking for food. Your body has many needs. Look around you and note that your friends and classmates grow at different rates. Not only does each of you

grow in height but your muscles and bones grow larger and longer. If you satisfy hunger with nutritious food, it will help you build a body that will function well all your life.

Appetite is the pleasant memory of foods you have eaten, such as those delicious hamburgers on your club picnic or that ice-cold watermelon you had after a hot day of shopping. In contrast, hunger is physiological, but appetite is mental. When you have many delightful memories associated with food, eating is a pleasure. You anticipate your meals with eagerness because you wish to repeat satisfying experiences.

THE NUTRIENTS

Although we speak in terms of foods, it is the nutrients within foods that are important. What are nutrients? They are substances that are essential for maintaining life, for growth, or for building your body, and for all the important functions of your body such as the beating of your heart, breathing, muscle action, and others. There are five groups of nutrients with which we are concerned: carbohydrates, fats, proteins, minerals, and vitamins. Some authorities include water and fiber or bulk as the sixth and seventh groups.

Requirements for Nutrients

How can you know how many of each of these nutrients you need each day? The Food and Nutrition Board of the National Research Council has examined available research studies and made recommendations. These are best estimates of the amount of essential nutrients that people of different ages might need. There are no recommendations for some nutrients, either because a deficiency in human nutrition has not been discovered or because we need so little of them that we seem to obtain enough. It is recognized that many factors—your rate of growth, age, sex, activity, and heritable influences—will affect your individual needs. For the recommendations of the Board see Table 11–5 on pages 92 and 93. Recommendations are stated in metric terms such as grams, milligrams, and micrograms. Some vitamin recommendations are in International Units.

All nutrients are equally important. Some individuals disregard this point and overemphasize protein or vitamins because they believe that these nutrients have special powers.

Calories express the amount of energy needed to perform tasks, as well as the energy value of foods.

CALORIES

Calories are a unit of measure, like pounds and inches. In nutrition and related sciences, calories express the amount of energy it takes to perform certain tasks. Calories also measure the energy value found in foods.

Needs for Energy

You need energy for three different operations, all taking place at the same time. First, you need energy to run your body processes—to breathe, to circulate blood, and so on. This energy is used no matter what else you do. Second, you need energy for each and every one of your activities. These include walking to school and sitting in class as well as riding a bicycle and playing ball. Third, you need energy in the growing process. It takes calories to lay down muscle tissue and to lengthen your bones. When you have attained your full growth and development, this final need will be satisfied.

Your Calorie Needs

How can you tell how many calories you need each day? The exact amount is difficult to

Table 11-1

CALORIE NEEDS OF BOYS AND GIRLS						
	Age Years	Weight (kg)	(lbs)	(cm)	Height (in)	Calories
Boys	11-14	44	97	158	63	2800
Girls	11-14	44	97	155	62	2400

determine, but some guides based on scientific experiments are available. The first need, to supply energy for normal body function, is called basal metabolism. Studies have shown that individuals will vary in the number of calories needed. Generally speaking, it has been found that a large person needs more calories to keep going than a small one and that boys need more than girls. There are also additional individual influences.

You need nutrients to carry on all your activities, such as clubs, sports, and social affairs.

Some studies have shown how many calories are required for various activities. For example, it takes more calories to ride a bicycle than to talk, to go upstairs than to go down, and so on. Studies of this kind are lengthy and expensive, and much more information is required. Table 11-1 shows the recommendations of the Food and Nutrition Board of the National Research Council for calorie needs of young people aged 11 to 14.

Caloric Content of Foods

Almost all foods contain calories. Some contain few, if any. It is the proteins, fats, and carbohydrates that supply calories. Proteins and carbohydrates provide four calories per gram and fats nine calories per gram.

There are several influences on the number of calories in a food. Because fat is concentrated and has more than twice as many calories as protein or carbohydrate, naturally the amount of fat in a food will make a difference—the more fat, the more calories. In contrast, water does not contain any calories, so watery foods like green leafy vegetables or fruit juices are low in calories. What you add to a food can increase the number of calories, such as butter or margarine on a slice of bread, mayonnaise on salad, or sour cream on a baked potato.

Table 11-2 shows the calories in some common snacks. Note the wide range in caloric value. Identify other nutrients found in each food. Some have few, if any, that will contribute to your diet. Some items, such as pancakes and waffles, have additions, usually of butter or margarine and syrup or preserves. Are you surprised at the few calories in some of the snacks?

Most American foods have been analyzed so that we can tell approximately how many calories each contains. Although calories are important, other nutrients in foods are also of interest.

Table 11-2

CALORIES IN SOME COMMON SNACKS	
Food	Calories
Apple, 1 medium	70
Banana, 1 medium	88
Brownie, 1 (made from mix)	85
Carrot, 1, 5½-in.	20
Celery, 1 stalk	5
Chocolate pudding, ½ c.	130
Chocolate malted milk, 1 c.	502
Corn, sweet, 1 ear, cooked	70
Cola-type beverage, 12 fl. oz.	145
Danish pastry, 1 oz.	120
Doughnut, 1 cake type	125
Frankfurter and roll	290
French-fried potatoes, 10 pieces	155
Pancake, 1, 4-in	60
Pizza, 5½-in. sector	185
Popcorn, with oil and salt, 1 c.	40
Popsicle, 1, 3 fl. oz.	20
Sherbet, ½ c.	130
Pretzel, Dutch, twisted	60
Spaghetti, with meatballs and tomato sauce, canned, 1 c.	260
Waffle, 1, 7-in. diameter	210

Excess calories are stored as fat. Only your doctor or the school nurse can tell if you are too heavy.

You may develop an appetite for high caloric foods that are sweet and rich.

WEIGHT

Two factors influence your weight—the number of calories that you eat every day and the number of calories you use in activities and exercise. If you eat many calories and lead an inactive life with much sitting, riding instead of walking, and having few activities, you will have more calories than you need and you will store the excess. This is known as adipose tissue or fat. If this storage of calories becomes large, you will be overweight, and if it continues, you will be excessively overweight or obese. This is undesirable, as you know.

On the other hand, if you eat fewer calories than you require and are extremely active, you are certain to be underweight. This state of weight is not only serious in itself but it probably means that you are short on other nutrients that you need for growth and body functioning.

Both underweight and overweight are medical problems. Your doctor should help you decide about the weight that is desirable for you. Do not try to make this decision yourself. The best plan for you is to have a nutritious diet with adequate calories and sufficient activity to keep you in good tone and to result in a weight that is healthy.

Table 11-3

FOODS HIGH IN CARBOHYDRATE VALUE

FOOD	PROTEIN g.	FAT g.	CARBO-HYDRATE g.	WATER %	CALORIES PER 100 g.
Sugar (white)	0	0	99.5	0.5	385
Maple syrup	0	0	74	25	286
Hard candy	0	0	99	1	383
Potato (raw)	2	0.1	19.1	77	83
Banana	1.2	0.2	23	74.8	88
White bread	8.2	3.3	52.3	34.5	276
Cake, plain	6.4	8.2	57	26.8	327
Pie, apple	2.1	9.5	39.5	47.8	246
Cereal (oatmeal)	2.3	1.2	11	84.8	63
Orange	0.9	0.2	11.2	87.2	45
Carrot	1.2	0.3	9.3	88	42

CARBOHYDRATE FOODS

Foods that are considered high in *carbohydrate value* are cereals, breads, and crackers, cakes and pastries, fruits and vegetables, legumes, and foods containing concentrated sweets, such as jam, sugar, and syrups. Some of these foods contain important vitamins and minerals as well as calories. These are the bread-cereal group, vegetables, legumes, and fruits. The other carbohydrate foods supply little else but calories. It is much wiser to obtain calories from sources that give extra dividends.

Table 11-3 shows the foods that are high in carbohydrate value.

FOODS CONTAINING FAT

Foods rich in fats are known to almost everyone. These include oils, butter, cream, and margarine. There are also "hidden" fats. These are foods containing fats that most people do not recognize. Examples of these are gravy, hard cheese, many sauces, meat and fish fat, and egg yolks. Perhaps you were aware of some of these

Table 11-4

FOODS HIGH IN FAT VALUE

FOOD	PROTEIN g.	FAT g.	CARBO-HYDRATE g.	WATER %	CALORIES PER 100 g.
Butter	0.6	81	0.4	15.5	716
Lard	0	100	0	0	902
Oil, vegetable	0	100	0	0	884
Bacon, raw	9.1	65	1.1	20	630
Steak, beef sirloin, raw	17.3	20	0	62	254
Avocado	1.7	26.4	5.1	65.4	245
Cream cheese	9	37	2	51	371
Cheddar cheese	25	32.2	2.1	37	398
Margarine	0.6	81	0.4	15.5	720

The number of calories you use in activities and exercise influences your weight.

sources of fats and high calories. Some fats contain important essential nutrients and so should be included in the diet. These will be pointed out later. A small amount of fat is needed in the diet to assist in the body's absorption of the fat-soluble vitamins A, D, and E and to supply an essential fatty acid.

Table 11–4 lists foods high in fat.

FOODS CONTAINING PROTEINS

Protein is one of the most important nutrients needed each day. As with calories, if you do not eat enough food containing protein, the amount lacking will have to be supplied from your own body. However, unlike calories, there are no stores of protein. The deficit will be drawn from tissue. It is especially essential that you obtain enough protein each day.

Purpose of Proteins

Proteins are important for the formation of all cells. As an ingredient of enzymes and hormones, they form part of the body's regulating system.

Proteins Have Amino Acids

Proteins themselves are composed of smaller units known as *amino acids*. Some of these can be manufactured in the body and others cannot. Thus it is important to eat foods that supply these essential amino acids. Animal proteins are a source of amino acids that the body cannot manufacture. Foods containing animal proteins are milk, meats, fish, poultry, and milk products, such as cheeses. Vegetable proteins, which are found in cereals, vegetables, legumes, and cereal products (bread, crackers, spaghetti), should be taken with animal proteins so that we can get the full value of the amino acids in the vegetable proteins. This is easily accomplished by serving such dishes as macaroni and cheese with a lettuce and tomato salad or cereal with milk.

Protein Requirements

Your need for protein is so great because of the unusual demands made for growth at your age. Thus it is especially important that you have a sufficient amount of a protein-rich food at each meal. Note carefully the food from both animal and vegetable sources just mentioned as supplying these necessary amino acids. The recommended daily dietary allowance for protein is 44 grams for boys and girls 11 to 14 years of age.

Animal proteins are a source of amino acids that the body cannot manufacture.

Sources of iron

NEED FOR MINERALS

The third group of nutrients necessary for physical fitness is minerals. Chief in this group are *iron, calcium, phosphorus, magnesium, zinc* and *iodine.* These nutrients are often found lacking in the food eaten by young people of your age. One mineral which is not listed in the requirements is fluorine. That is because we do not depend upon food for fluorine's source, but upon water, where it appears naturally or is added. This mineral is important for the prevention of cavities in the teeth.

Iron Is Lacking in the Diet of School Children

A lack of iron in the diet is America's most critical dietary deficiency. Several broad surveys have indicated that many school-age children do not get enough iron. This lack can result in the reduction of pep and vitality. You may have learned in science classes that iron is part of the red blood cell and that its chief function is to carry oxygen from the lungs to the cells, where iron participates in the release of energy. To insure a good supply of pep and energy, you should take care to include enough iron-rich foods in your diet. These foods are egg yolk, lean meat, liver, green leafy vegetables, dried apricots, and enriched bread and cereals.

Uses of Calcium

Almost everyone knows that calcium is "good for the bones." However, many do not realize that calcium is needed for numerous other important functions, among them clotting of blood and digestion of fats. Your needs for calcium are high during the time your bones are lengthening and strengthening.

The single best source for calcium is milk, so get your quota every day. Lesser amounts are found in citrus fruits, egg yolk, dark green vegetables, and oysters. Hard cheeses are a good source.

Phosphorus, Magnesium, and Zinc

Phosphorus and *magnesium* are closely related to calcium in functions, and all three minerals reinforce one another, but calcium and phosphorus often work together as a team. Foods rich in phosphorus are cheeses, meats, fish, eggs, and beans. Magnesium is found in

Iron is needed for pep and vitality.

89

Sources of calcium

eggs, nuts, beans, cereals, milk, and greens. These two minerals are found in more foods than is calcium. Zinc is necessary for growth and development. Food sources of zinc are oysters, tuna, sardines, meats, cereals, seeds, and nuts.

Iodine is Another Important Mineral

The lack of one other mineral, iodine, presented a serious problem to public health authorities in the past. It was found that those who lived in inland areas, away from sea water and sea-sprayed soil, were suffering from a deficiency of iodine and many developed a goiter. But now with improved transportation of foods (enabling us to eat foods grown in many sections of the country) and the use of iodized salt, the problem has been greatly reduced.

Minerals, then, are extremely important for your health and well-being. Lack of them can affect not only your physical growth and development but also your social activities. See Table 11–5 for the recommended daily dietary allowances for these minerals.

VITAMINS

One of the most exciting developments in the field of nutrition has been the gradual discovery of the many vitamins we know today. Vitamins function as regulators of body processes. Severe deficiency diseases have been discovered that were caused by a lack of vitamins. For example, scurvy is caused by a lack of vitamin C (ascorbic acid), beriberi by insufficient vitamin B_1 (thiamin).

Important Vitamins

The most important vitamins are vitamin A, the vitamin B complex (specifically thiamin, riboflavin, niacin, B_6, B_{12}, and folacin), vitamin C (ascorbic acid), vitamin D, and vitamin E. We know enough about these vitamins to be able to

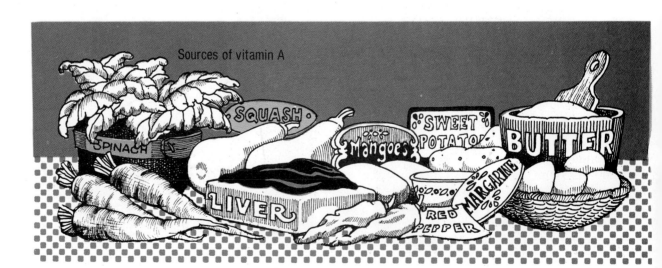

Sources of vitamin A

make recommendations about the desirable amount to include in the diet each day.

Purposes and Sources of Vitamin A

Vitamin A has been found beneficial for healthy skin, proper vision, and for tooth and bone formation. Important sources of this vitamin are liver, deep yellow and dark-green leafy vegetables, milk, butter, and egg yolk. Margarine is also usually fortified with vitamin A.

Thiamin, Riboflavin, and Niacin

These are three members of the B-complex which are related to many important body reactions, chief among them the utilization of calories. They also help digestion and are needed for steady nerves and an alert mind. No one food is a rich source of thiamin. Many foods, such as breads and cereals (enriched or whole grain), legumes, and pork, supply this elusive vitamin. Milk is a good source of riboflavin. Both riboflavin and niacin are found in liver, whole grain and enriched breads and cereals, and legumes. Diets are often low in these three vitamins.

Other B vitamins, such as folacin and B_{12}, are related to the prevention of anemia; B_6 is concerned with the body's use of carbohydrate and protein. Liver, organ meats, and other meats are the best sources of these vitamins. Dark-green leafy vegetables are a good source of folacin. Potatoes and vegetables are a lesser source of B_6. Vitamin B_{12} can be found only in animal sources of food.

Vitamin C

Among the many uses of Vitamin C in the body, the most important is its function as a ce-

Sources of vitamin C

ment holding cells together. It is also needed for strong teeth and bones, and helps in healing cuts or wounds. Everyone knows that oranges and grapefruit are good sources of vitamin C. But other fresh fruits and vegetables can supply sizable amounts. Broccoli, green leafy vegetables (properly cooked), cantaloupe, tomatoes, apples, and some types of potatoes are minor sources of vitamin C. Since this vitamin is easily destroyed by air and heat, the presence of vitamin C in your food will depend on proper storage and preparation of foods as well as choosing the right foods.

Sources of the B vitamins

91

Table 11-5

RECOMMENDED DAILY DIETARY ALLOWANCES, REVISED 1974

Designed for the maintenance of good nutrition of practically all healthy people in the U.S.A.

| | (YEARS) From up to | WEIGHT (kg) | (lbs) | HEIGHT (cm) | (in) | ENERGY (kcal)[2] | PROTEIN (g) | FAT-SOLUBLE VITAMINS | | |
								VITAMIN A (RE)[3]	VITAMIN A (IU)	VITAMIN D (IU)	VITAMIN E[5] (IU)
INFANTS	0.0–0.5	6	14	60	24	kg × 117	kg × 2.2	420[4]	1400	400	4
	0.5–1.0	9	20	71	28	kg × 108	kg × 2.0	400	2000	400	5
CHILDREN	1-3	13	28	86	34	1300	23	400	2000	400	7
	4-6	20	44	110	44	1800	30	500	2500	400	9
	7-10	30	66	135	54	2400	36	700	3300	400	10
MALES	11-14	44	97	158	63	2800	44	1000	5000	400	12
	15-18	61	134	172	69	3000	54	1000	5000	400	15
	19-22	67	147	172	69	3000	54	1000	5000	400	15
	23-50	70	154	172	69	2700	56	1000	5000	–	15
	51+	70	154	172	69	2400	56	1000	5000	–	15
FEMALES	11-14	44	97	155	62	2400	44	800	4000	400	12
	15-18	54	119	162	65	2100	48	800	4000	400	12
	19-22	58	128	162	65	2100	46	800	4000	400	12
	23-50	58	128	162	65	2000	46	800	4000	–	12
	51+	58	128	162	65	1800	46	800	4000	–	12
PREGNANT						+300	+30	1000	5000	400	15
LACTATING						+500	+20	1200	6000	400	15

[1] The allowances are intended to provide for individual variations among most normal persons as they live in the United States under usual environmental stresses. Diets should be based on a variety of common foods in order to provide other nutrients for which human requirements have been less well defined. See text for more-detailed discussion of allowances and of nutrients not tabulated.
[2] Kilojoules (kj) = 4.2 × kcal
[3] Retinol equivalents
[4] Assumed to be all as retinol in milk during the first six months of life. All subsequent intakes are assumed to be one-half as retinol and one-half as β-carotene when calculated from international units. As retinol equivalents, three-fourths are as retinol and one-fourth as β-carotene.

Vitamin D

Vitamin D is called the sunshine vitamin. This is because the sun's rays can change a substance under the human skin into vitamin D. Fog, smog, dust, clothing, and other factors may prevent vitamin D from forming in the skin. This vitamin is needed to regulate calcium and phosphorus in bone and tooth formation; it also governs the level of calcium in the blood. Very few foods contain vitamin D. It is found in fish-liver oil, herring, and fortified milk, and most fortified margarine. Some physicians prescribe vitamin D as a supplement to food for all young people as long as they are growing, that is, until they are about 21.

Vitamin E

This vitamin is important for healthy maintenance of cell membranes of the body and

Water-Soluble Vitamins							Minerals					
ASCORBIC ACID	FOLACIN[6]	NIACIN[7]	RIBOFLAVIN	THIAMIN	VITAMIN B$_6$	VITAMIN B$_{12}$	CALCIUM	PHOSPHORUS	IODINE	IRON	MAGNESIUM	ZINC
(mg)	(μg)	(mg)	(mg)	(mg)	(mg)	(μg)	(mg)	(mg)	(μg)	(mg)	(mg)	(mg)
35	50	5	0.4	0.3	0.3	0.3	360	240	35	10	60	3
35	50	8	0.6	0.5	0.4	0.3	540	400	45	15	70	5
40	100	9	0.8	0.7	0.6	1.0	800	800	60	15	150	10
40	200	12	1.1	0.9	0.9	1.5	800	800	80	10	200	10
40	300	16	1.2	1.2	1.2	2.0	800	800	110	10	250	10
45	400	18	1.5	1.4	1.6	3.0	1200	1200	130	18	350	15
45	400	20	1.8	1.5	2.0	3.0	1200	1200	150	18	400	15
45	400	20	1.8	1.5	2.0	3.0	800	800	140	10	350	15
45	400	18	1.6	1.4	2.0	3.0	800	800	130	10	350	15
45	400	16	1.5	1.2	2.0	3.0	800	800	110	10	350	15
45	400	16	1.3	1.2	1.6	3.0	1200	1200	115	18	300	15
45	400	14	1.4	1.1	2.0	3.0	1200	1200	115	18	300	15
45	400	14	1.4	1.1	2.0	3.0	800	800	100	18	300	15
45	400	13	1.2	1.0	2.0	3.0	800	800	100	18	300	15
45	400	12	1.1	1.0	2.0	3.0	800	800	80	10	300	15
60	800	+2	+0.3	+0.3	2.5	4.0	1200	1200	125	18+[8]	450	20
80	600	+4	+0.5	+0.3	2.5	4.0	1200	1200	150	18	450	25

[5]Total vitamin E activity, estimated to be 80 percent as α-tocopherol and 20 percent other to-copherols.

[6]The folacin allowances refer to dietary sources as determined by *Lactobacillus casei* assay. Pure forms of folacin may be effective in doses less than one-fourth of the RDA.

[7]Although allowances are expressed as niacin, it is recognized that on the average 1 mg of niacin is derived from each 60 mg of dietary tryptophan.

[8]This increased requirement cannot be met by ordinary diets; therefore, the use of supplemental iron is recommended.

probably for the synthesis of red blood cells and certain enzymes for body functioning. Common sources are oils, especially cottonseed, wheat germ, walnuts and peanuts, and green vegetables.

How to Get Vitamins in Your Diet

Can you get all the vitamins you need from foods or do you need to take pills as *supplements?* Most authorities feel that you should try to eat those foods that contain vitamins. If your physician believes you need to have your diet supplemented with preparations, he or she will prescribe them. There may still be some undiscovered factors in foods that are not included in pills. Thus it would be unwise to depend on preparations from your drug store as a sole source of vitamins. Recent research warns that an overdose of certain vitamins can cause serious consequences. The money spent on vitamins you do not need is a waste.

WATER IS NEEDED

Although water is not usually considered a nutrient, it is so important to the health of the individual that it should be mentioned briefly. Approximately 70 percent of body weight is water. Water is the basis for body secretions, and for blood, and is present in every cell. Your thirst regulates the amount of water you drink. However, many foods contain sizable amounts of water. It has been recommended that you drink from four to six glasses of water or fluid of similar content daily.

FIBER

Fiber or bulk is sometimes called the forgotten nutrient. Fiber is important for good intestinal tone and to discourage constipation. Including bulk in your diet may prevent certain diseases that occur in middle age, such as cancer of the colon, gallstones, and the formation of small balloonlike pockets along the intestinal wall that may become infected and cancerous. By developing now the good food habit of eating plenty of fruits and vegetables and whole-grain cereals, you may save yourself trouble later in life.

FOODS FOR YOUR DAILY DIET

What do all of these nutrients mean in terms of what you eat every day? How can you know which foods to eat so that you will have the right amounts of the essential nutrients? A kind of blueprint that is used widely in America is the Daily Food Guide, more commonly known as the Basic Four Food Groups, developed by nutritionists in the U.S. Department of Agriculture with the assistance of advisory persons and groups throughout the country. The Basic Four Food Groups are milk and milk products, fruits and vegetables, breads and cereals, and meat or meat alternates (fish, poultry, eggs, dried legumes, and nuts).

If the recommended amounts of each of these food groups is included in your daily diet, you can be reasonably certain of an adequate diet. Additional foods from the Basic Four or from other foods that you like may be included to supply sufficient calories and to ensure further adequate nutrients.

The following overview of each food group should be helpful in planning your daily food. The U.S. Department of Agriculture bulletin *Family Fare: A Guide to Good Nutrition* (Home and Garden Bulletin No. 1) also gives valuable information on the food groups.

Milk and Milk Products

Foods Included. **MILK**– fluid whole, evaporated, skim dry, buttermilk

CHEESE– cottage, cream, Cheddar type—natural or processed.

ICE CREAM

Amount Recommended. Some milk for everyone. Recommended amounts are given in terms of whole fluid milk:

	8-ounce cups	
		0348
		0349
Children under 9	2 to 3	0350
Children 9 to 12	3 or more	0351
Teenagers	4 or more	0352
Adults	2 or more	0353

Part or all of the milk may be fluid skim milk, buttermilk, evaporated milk, or dry milk.

Cheese or ice cream may replace part of the milk. Calcium equivalents below.

CALCIUM EQUIVALENTS

Ice Cream — 1/2 Cup

1/4 Cup — Milk

Cheese Cheddar - Type 1" Cube — 2/3 Cup

Cottage Cheese 1/2 Cup — 1/3 Cup

Cream Cheese 2 Tablespoons — 1 Tablespoon

Nutrient Contribution of Milk and Milk Products. Milk is the leading source of calcium. It is almost impossible to secure an adequate supply of calcium if milk is not included in the diet. This food group also contributes a good supply of phosphorus, magnesium, high-quality protein, vitamin B_6, and vitamin B_{12}. Milk and milk products are excellent sources of riboflavin.

Fruits and Vegetables

Foods Included. All vegetables and fruit. This guide emphasizes those that are valuable sources of vitamins C and A.

Amount Recommended. Choose four or more servings every day, including:

One serving of a good source of vitamin C or two servings of a fair source.

One serving, at least every other day, of a good source of vitamin A. If the food chosen for vitamin C is also a good source of vitamin A, the additional serving of vitamin A food may be omitted.

The remaining one to three or more servings may be of any vegetable or fruit, including those that are valuable for vitamin C and vitamin A.

Count as one serving: ½ cup of vegetable or fruit, or a portion as ordinarily served, such as one apple, banana, orange, or potato; half a medium grapefruit or cantaloupe; or the juice of one lemon.

Nutrient Contributions. Fruits and vegetables are relied on to furnish nearly all the vitamin C of the diet. Good sources of vitamin C are grapefruit or grapefruit juice, oranges or orange juice, cantaloupe, guava, mangoes, papaya, raw strawberries, broccoli, brussels sprouts, green peppers, and sweet red peppers. Fair sources are honeydew melons, lemons, tangerines or tangerine juice, watermelon, asparagus tips, raw cabbage, cauliflower, collards, garden cress, kale, kohlrabi, mustard greens, potatoes and sweet potatoes cooked in the jacket, rutabagas, spinach, tomatoes or tomato juice, and turnip greens.

This group furnishes more than one-half of the vitamin A that is needed in the diet. Vitamin A occurs only in animal foods, such as liver and milk, but many fruits and vegetables, particularly the dark-green and the deep-yellow ones, contain carotene that the body can change into vitamin A.

Contributions of calcium, phosphorus, riboflavin, and niacin of a fair nature are made by this group to the diet. A good contribution of iron, magnesium, and B_6 is made to the dietary allowances. Researchers are asking for added fiber in one's diet and fruits and vegetables are a good source.

Breads and Cereals

Foods Included. All breads and cereals that are whole grain, enriched, or restored. Check labels to be sure. Specifically, this group includes: breads, cooked cereals, ready-to-eat cereals, cornmeal, crackers, flour and grits, macaroni and spaghetti, noodles, rice, rolled oats, and quick breads and other baked goods, if made with whole grain or enriched flour. Parboiled rice and wheat may also be included in this group.

Amounts Recommended. Choose four servings or more daily, or if no cereals are chosen, have an extra serving of breads or baked goods. This will make five servings from this group daily.

Count as one serving: one slice of bread; 1 ounce of ready-to-eat cereal; ½ to ¾ cup cooked cereal, cornmeal grits, macaroni, noodles, rice, or spaghetti.

Nutrient Contributions. The major nutrient contributions of this group are to iron, thiamin, riboflavin, niacin, protein, phosphorus, magnesium, and caloric allowances. Some contribution is made to the B_6 allowance. Whole-grain cereals add fiber.

Table 11-6

HAVE YOU HAD YOUR BASIC FOUR TODAY?

TIME	Milk and Milk Products		Fruits and Vegetables		Breads and Cereals		Meats and Alternates	
	FOOD	AMT.	FOOD	AMT.	FOOD	AMT.	FOOD	AMT.
Morning			Orange juice	½ c.	Toast 1 slice, buttered		Boiled ham	1 oz.
Midmorning	Milk	1 c.			Danish 1			
Midday	Milk	1 c.	Mixed vegetable salad	½ c.	Bread 2 slices (for egg sandwich)		Egg,	1 chopped with mayonnaise
Midafternoon	Milk	1 c.	Apple	1				
Evening			Potato	1	roll 1, buttered		Minute steak	3 oz.
			String beans	½ c.				
			Tomato, sliced	½				
			Fruit bar	1				
Bedtime	Cocoa with ½ c. milk				Pop-up tart			

Meat or Alternates

Foods Included. Beef, veal, lamb, pork, variety meats such as liver, hearts, and kidneys.
Poultry and eggs
Fish and shellfish
As alternates– dry beans, dry peas, nuts, peanuts, peanut butter.

Amounts Recommended. Choose two or more servings every day.

Count as a serving: 2 to 3 ounces (not including bone weight) cooked lean meat, poultry, or fish

Count as alternates for ½ serving of meat, fish, or poultry: one egg; ½ cup of cooked dry beans, dry peas, or lentils; or 2 tablespoons peanut butter

Nutrient Contributions. The most valuable contribution of this food group is to the protein, niacin, vitamin B_6 and vitamin B_{12} allowances. Almost as valuable are the contributions to iron, phosphorus, thiamin, riboflavin, vitamin A and caloric allowances. A good contribution of magnesium is made.

USE OF THE BASIC FOUR

Now that you know more about the Basic Four Food Groups, your next step is to combine these foods to meet your individual or family nutritive needs. The table that follows may help you in planning and in checking whether you have the foods with the essential nutrients in your diet. Many factors will influence what you eat every day. The foods listed are not to be interpreted as typical. Rarely do two individuals in the same family eat exactly the same amount, kind, or preparation of food during a day and the differences widen outside the family. That is not serious if the basic four groups are fully represented.

Now plan your own day's diet. Take into consideration the foods you like to eat, availability of food in the markets, your facilities and your inclination about the amount of cooking to be done (or that of other family members if they take responsibility), the cost of food, your schedule, and whether you eat differently, such as being a vegetarian. You may not eat this frequently, but the American pattern appears to be going in this direction. If some food is eaten away from home, are you limited in the offerings? All of this may appear to be a great deal of work, but once you are organized you will establish habits of being conscious of your require-ments. It will be worth the effort, because you have to use your body for many years to come and what you eat now will make a difference.

RATING YOUR DAILY DIET

Check your diet frequently to see whether you are securing all the nutrients you need. Plan for a wide variety of foods because nutritionists tell us that then you are more likely to have an adequate diet. If you have a pocket calculator and wish to analyze your diet in terms of nutrients, use the table of Recommended Dietary Allowances to determine the allowances for your age group and with the help of a table of nutritive value in foods, you can judge whether your diet is adequate. The U.S. Department of Agriculture Home and Garden Bulletin Number 72, *Nutritive Value of Foods,* is a valuable source of nutrition information.

THINKING IT OVER

UNICEF reports that there are 400 to 500 million hungry and starving children in the world—more than twice the population of United States. What is being done, what needs to be done, and what can you do?

THINGS TO DO

Many students bring to school brown paper bags of snacks that they have brought from home or have purchased. You may call this junk food—candy bars, doughnuts, cookies, potato or corn chips, and similar foods. Do you follow this practice? If so, experiment with foods that are more nutritious, such as whole wheat crackers with peanut butter or cheese, fruit, carrot strips or other vegetables, milk, and the like. See if you feel better. Tabulate concrete evidence, such as your amount of endurance in sports, whether you feel energetic, and whether your skin is clear and healthy. And how about the cost in comparison to junk foods? Could you plan a snack revolution? Later, take a look at your breakfast habits.

12 When and where we eat

You may think you eat in the traditional three-meal-a-day pattern: breakfast, lunch, and dinner (or supper). But if you examined your food intake for a day or two, you would probably notice that you ate many times. You may miss a meal occasionally or frequently. Snacks may be more prominent in your eating habits than you realize. Keep track of the times you eat, every day for a week. In addition, you may note what you ate in terms of the Basic Four Food Groups to determine whether the time or times you ate affected the adequacy of your diet.

BREAKFASTS ARE NEGLECTED

Is breakfast skimpy, hurried, or omitted in your home? If so, have you ever thought about possible causes for this? The following are some of the reasons given for poor breakfasts: do not feel hungry after getting up; too sleepy to eat; no one in the family eats breakfast; do not wish to be late for school; went to bed late, so got up late; or both parents work and leave before the children are up. Can you add to this list?

You may be interested in some of the research done on breakfasts of schoolchildren. When the diets of children who had had little or no breakfast were analyzed, the results revealed that the nutrients in foods left out at breakfast were not made up in other meals.

Research also shows us that persons who eat a nutritious breakfast do better schoolwork and are more alert. This seems reasonable when you consider that you might go without food from a meal in the evening until a snack in mid-morning or lunch time.

BREAKFAST PATTERNS

What do we eat at breakfast? Americans have varied and interesting breakfasts, depending on the section of the country in which they live. Usually breakfast falls into the following pattern, with many variations within food groups:

FRUIT- fresh or juice, preferably citrus—orange, grapefruit, or tangerine; banana, strawberries, or melon

MAIN DISH- eggs, ham, codfish cakes, cheese combined with bread, or cereal and milk

BREAD- toast, pancakes, muffins, corn-bread, other hot breads, coffee cake, sweet breads

BEVERAGE- coffee, tea, cocoa, milk, or decaffeinated drinks

Breakfasts of endless varieties may be built from this pattern. It is especially important to have a citrus fruit and an animal protein food included in breakfast every day. Why skip breakfast when you have so many appetizing choices?

If you are a breakfast skipper, why not try a quickie, like a glass of orange juice plus a frozen waffle popped into a toaster and spread with soft cheese? A peanut butter sandwich and a milk-shake or a cheese sandwich and tomato juice are other possibilities. Soup and crackers are popular with some people. Or how about a Susan Jones Breakfast Shake that has an egg, graham or whole-wheat crackers, orange-juice concentrate, and milk—all whirled together in a blender? Or create your own instant breakfast to drink.

LUNCH PATTERNS

What you eat for lunch also depends on a number of things—whether you eat at home, carry your lunch, eat in the school cafeteria, or buy from an outside vendor. Even so, lunch, too, has a basic pattern with a number of variations:

MAIN DISH- sandwich with meat, fish, peanut butter, or cheese filling; meat, such as frankfurters, hamburgers, or spare-ribs; meat or fish casseroles; dishes with cheese, such as macaroni and cheese; or a thick soup with peas or beans and ham or other kind of meat

BREAD- in sandwich or alone, hot breads, and sweet breads

VEGETABLE- raw in salad, such as cole-slaw, tossed salad, or in pieces, like carrot strips

DESSERT- fresh fruit, dried fruit, ice cream, or plain cookie

BEVERAGE- milk, fruit or vegetable juices, cocoa, soda, and the like

What you eat for lunch depends upon a number of factors.

Lack of planning frequently results in skipped breakfasts.

You should have about a third of your day's calories and nutrients for breakfast.

Lunch Problems

For good nutrition, you need to have approximately one-third of your day's calories and nutrients at lunch. This may be difficult to do without careful planning. Many problems may have to be overcome. You may not have much time for lunch. You may be in a rut and not pack a variety of foods in your lunch box. You may have little choice in the places where you eat, and, also, you or your mother may not have time to pack as much as you would like for lunch. These problems and possibly many others can be solved by a little careful thinking. Again, the important thing is to be sure to have one of the protein foods at each lunch.

DINNER IS THE MAIN MEAL OF THE DAY

The surveys mentioned earlier also found that dinner is usually the one ample meal of the day. In many homes, it is the only time when the family eats together. A number of combinations may

Don't be in a rut in choosing foods for lunch. You can have great variety in sandwiches.

be served at this meal. You and your family will want variety in your main meal. Having the same foods too often is not recommended.

The following list of foods will indicate some of the possible variations within food groups:

APPETIZER– soup, fruit or vegetable juices, or hot hors d'oeuvres

MAIN DISH– meat: roasted, broiled, or pan-fried; casserole dishes with meat; fish; stew; meat loaf; beef, ham, veal, or lamb; cheese dishes, like soufflé or rarebit; eggs, like omelets

STARCHES– potatoes, prepared in many ways; hominy, macaroni, spaghetti, rice, or noodles

VEGETABLES– all varieties, cooked in many ways, or raw in salads

BREAD– breads, such as Italian, rye, or whole-wheat, rolls, hot breads, or bread-sticks

DESSERT– fruit: fresh, canned, or stewed; puddings, ice cream, plain cake, sherbet, or ices

BEVERAGES– milk, tea, coffee, or cocoa

MISCELLANEOUS– butter or margarine

Of course, items from all these food groups are seldom included in the same meal. Each family has its own distinctive pattern. Some of the factors that influence this pattern will be discussed later (see page 104). Follow the same rule that was applied to breakfast and lunch, namely, that each food should be selected from the viewpoint of the nutrients it can offer.

Dinner is often the main meal.

After-school snacks can be nutritious yet easy to prepare.

FOOD BETWEEN MEALS

Even though you have three large meals of nutritious foods each day, you may find that you are hungry between meals. This is because you either are entering or are in the midst of a period of rapid growth and development. Therefore, the food you eat between meals must also help to provide necessary nutrients.

All too often, food taken between meals contributes mostly calories and is lacking in other nutrients. Fruit, milk, small sandwiches, and cookies fortified with nutrients (raisins, dry skim milk, and cereals) all make good snacks.

ADJUSTMENTS NECESSARY FOR MEALS

You may find that your meals have to be adjusted from day to day for various reasons. Sometimes, because of these interruptions in your daily schedule, you may tend to skimp a little here and there. You may not eat as much or you may miss a meal entirely. This is not a good practice. It is wiser to see to it that radical changes in your meals from day to day do not alter your total day's food. Perhaps your family might get together to discuss what everyone will be doing during the week. This way, you can plan ahead for these changes in your meals.

Influences on Meals

Your whole way of living changes when school starts in the fall, and your food pattern is probably different from what it was in the summer months. In schools that have two sessions, a student's food pattern may be entirely different from that of the rest of the family. If the weather is bad, you may decide to have lunch at school instead of going home. Perhaps both your father and mother are working or you yourself have taken a part-time job. Maybe you made the basketball team or are in the one-act play and have to practice until dinner time. What happens to that after-school snack? Sometimes bus routes change and you have a longer ride. Does this hurry your breakfast? All these factors, and many others, may bring about a change in your food patterns. If you are aware of these influencing factors, you can guard against any deficiencies in the nutritive content of your meals. Then eating won't be just hit or miss.

Where you eat often determines what you eat. Is this true in your case? Can you name the

Where you eat often determines what you eat.

Table 12-1

DISCOVER YOUR EATING PATTERNS		
Check the following on a separate piece of paper:	Yes	No
1. Do you eat breakfast with your family?	☐	☐
2. Do you omit breakfast more than twice a week?	☐	☐
3. Do you sleep so late in the morning that you have to rush to get to school?	☐	☐
4. Do you have enough time for lunch?	☐	☐
5. Are you hungry in the morning while you are in school?	☐	☐
6. Do you include a protein food in your lunch menu?	☐	☐
7. Do you ever omit lunch?	☐	☐
8. Do you like to eat between meals?	☐	☐
9. Do you have time for a snack after school?	☐	☐
10. Are you a vegetarian?	☐	☐
11. Do you ever omit supper?	☐	☐

different places you ate in last week? Does each place have its own special food?

Where You Eat Will Influence What You Eat

Every group of friends has its own particular hangout. And, depending on its location, each place is a "natural" for certain foods. If you gather at a drugstore, your choice of snacks is probably different from that offered at a candy or corner store. In some places you have no choice and everybody has the same thing, like a pizza, a carbonated drink, or "pop." Vitamin and mineral content is not considered; you eat or drink only because it is the thing to do.

During a normal day, you might eat at the kitchen table, in front of the television set, at a school function, such as a basketball or football game, in the cafeteria, or even walking along. One boy may eat a bag of pretzels on his way to school, while another may eat an apple. Can you see the difference in the nutrients that each one gains?

Your family may often eat at fast-food restaurants that have specialties like hamburgers, pizza, hot dogs, fish and chips, tacos, or bagels and lox. Although the food is good, cheap, and served quickly, the choices for adequate servings of all the Basic Four Food Groups may be limited. Fruit, for example, is seldom served and if you drink soda instead of milk, that food group will be missing. This is not serious if you make definite plans to have these lacking foods at home or elsewhere later.

When you eat dinner on a tray in front of the television set you may not have as complete a meal as you would if you were sitting at the family table. If your school serves candy and soft drinks at ball games, you will not get the same nutrients that you would if hot dogs and hamburgers were served. Where you eat strongly influences what you eat.

Keep Nutrition in Mind

Of course, you may not want to go against the crowd and choose a different drink or food just because it is good for you. At times, however, you may have a wider choice when you are out with friends. Perhaps then you can keep the nutritive value of foods in mind and take those that will give you the most for your money. Don't forget, everything you eat adds to your total nutritive intake. Cut down on the foods that are mostly calories.

THINKING IT OVER

Review your eating patterns for the past week. What happened that facilitated the eating of enjoyable and nutritious food in pleasant circumstances? What factors, if any, prevented you from having such experiences? What are your conclusions? Now look at the week again and dig a little deeper for reasons. Do you need to improve your life in some ways? Do other people have to change, too?

THINGS TO DO

1. Analyze your checks in the section "Discover Your Eating Patterns." Would you make any changes? If so, why?

2. Conduct a survey of breakfast habits in your class. Summarize the results in categories you consider important. Suggested categories are number of students omitting breakfast, adequacy of breakfasts consumed, and possible reasons for these situations. Think about some action plans, such as clever posters highlighting the results of your survey, an exhibit of ideas for quick breakfasts, or a bulletin board display that all students may see.

3. How many times has your eating pattern been disrupted this past week? Did you plan for these changes and still have as nutritious a meal as you would have had otherwise?

13 What we eat

Did you ever look at your dinner plate and wonder why that particular food was there? How did your mother happen to cook beefsteak instead of bear steak? Why do you have French dressing on your salad and your sister mayonnaise on hers? Why do you drink milk and your parents coffee? Many factors influence our food patterns. Let's see why you like certain foods more than others.

REASONS FOR EATING CERTAIN FOODS
Geographical Location

Geographical location has something to do with selection of food. In some sections of our country, potatoes are served at each meal; in others, grits are a favorite. Baked beans are a traditional New England dish. In the West, salad is eaten at the beginning of the meal, while elsewhere it may be eaten with the main course or following it. Or salad may not be served at all. People living in the coastal regions like certain fish that are found nearby. A thousand miles away such food is unknown.

These are a few of the many examples of regional influences. Today, because of increased transportation and communication, you will find that geographical food patterns are not as marked as they were 100 years ago. Yet they still have some effect on most diets.

Background

America has often been called the melting pot. Our different backgrounds tend to influence our food habits and this is reflected in family diets. Perhaps your family cooks with olive oil, lard, or butter. Maybe you know someone who prefers cheese or yogurt to milk. Recipes for food from other countries have been handed down from one generation to another. Holidays or special occasions usually call for certain dishes that are family traditions.

Religion

Many of our food choices may also be dictated by religious beliefs. In your home you may have fast and feast days according to your faith. Some religions forbid certain foods, such as pork by the Jews and Moslems. You may feel good if you follow these laws and guilty if you ignore them.

Life-Styles

The variety of life-styles in this country is increasing. Your life-style will have an effect on your nutrition. Each life-style stresses values considered important, such as family, friendships, job, money or income, religion, health, politics, and many others. A life-style selects certain values and rejects others. A thumbnail sketch of a few life-styles is given here.

Your family may live on a dairy farm in a rural area, in a crowded tenement in a large city, in a large industrial center, or in a commune on a farm with other families who have a common philosophy of life and who are interested in a "back-to-nature" way of life. Your family may be migrants who travel wherever they can find work. Or you may live in a wealthy suburb with a father who commutes and is worried about foods containing cholesterol and a mother who constantly tries to lose weight. Do you know anyone with a life-style like any of the above?

There are many possibilities. You might be giving serious consideration to becoming a vege-tarian, because your best friends are vegetarians. You might be part of a middle-class community surrounded by people who are interested in health foods. Your family might be in professional sports, such as baseball or tennis, and there might be great emphasis on health and food that will build muscle and stamina. Look at each of these life-styles and try to see how their activities and values will affect how and what the people eat.

Can you think of other life-styles that have not been mentioned here? What about one-parent families, being poor, or living with your grandparents where there is a great gap between your ages? What about living in an isolated area such as the northern woods or Alaska? Suppose you were an Indian living on a reservation? Your actual life-style may have characteristics of several described here. Furthermore, you may have moved from one life-style to another several times. How do you describe your life-style at present and how is it affecting what you eat?

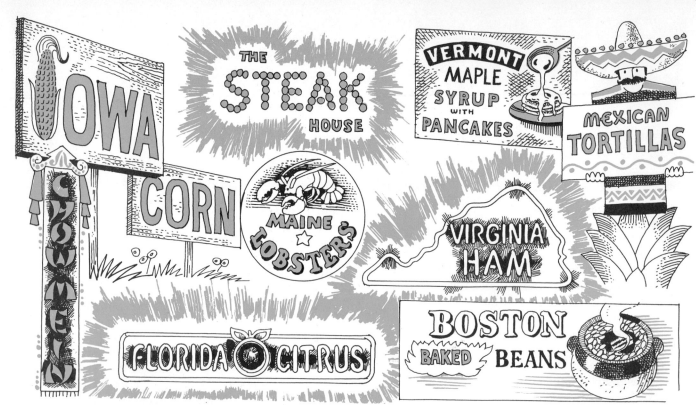

You eat certain foods because of the section of the country you live in.

Vegetarianism

This life-style has become popular in this country, especially among the young, because many believe in the sacredness of animal life and feel it is wrong to kill animals and eat them. Another reason is that it takes less than an acre of land to produce food for a vegetarian but twice that much for a meat-eating person, an important consideration when so many in the world are hungry. Spiritual values is another mo-

A small grocery store may specialize in food of a particular ethnic group.

tive. Research has shown that adults can live on a vegetarian diet, but there is little evidence of its effect on individuals who are growing.

There are three general types of vegetarian diet—*lacto-ovo vegetarian* (eggs and milk and milk products may be included), *lacto-vegetarian* (milk and milk products may be added), and *strict vegetarianism*, in which all foods of animal origin are forbidden. There is considerable assurance of an adequate diet if milk or milk and eggs may be included, but a strict vegetable diet has serious limitations.

Vitamin B_{12}, for example, is found only in animal sources, such as meat and milk. A supplement of this vitamin, or food fortified with it, is important in avoiding anemia. A lack of calcium is equally critical, because you would not be drinking milk on a strict vegetarian diet. This shortage can be partially relieved by the consumption of large quantities of dark-green vegetables, such as collards, dandelion greens, kale, and mustard or turnip greens. One cup or 200 grams of broccoli will give you 206 milligrams of calcium, but you need 1200 milligrams every day! Riboflavin may be another lack. Some may be obtained from green leafy vegetables, but the amount you would have to eat might overwhelm you. Milk, you may recall, is one of the best sources of riboflavin, and that is not included in a strict vegetable diet. Vegetable protein does not rate as high as animal protein because the essential amino acids may be lacking or, if present, are not in sufficient amount for your need. For a person of your age, this type of diet can be a hazard, because you will not receive adequate nutrients for growth and vitality.

"Health," "Organic," and "Natural" Foods

Among your friends or neighbors, or in your own family, there may be a strong interest in "back-to-nature" foods. "Organic" foods are to be grown under special conditions. For example, chemical fertilizers are taboo and are replaced by manure or garbage compost. Pesticide sprays and dusts are not allowed. The crops are harvested at the peak of ripeness. Their flavor is considered better than that of supermarket purchases, but the fruit may be wormy.

One decided advantage of this method of producing food is that the air and water are not polluted by chemicals. One disadvantage is that these methods are difficult to apply to large-scale production of food, which is so necessary for a hungry world. Garbage compost, for example, can supply nitrogen to the soil at a cost of $12 per pound, dried cow manure at $5 per pound, and commercial chemical fertilizer at 7½ cents per pound, approximately. Likewise, many consumers pay twice as much for these "health" foods as for the same nonorganic foods in the supermarket.

Authorities condemn the use of the words "health" or "healthful" in the sale of these foods. Such use is considered misbranding by the Food and Drug Administration, because the words imply health-giving or curative properties. Sometimes "health-food" merchants and others give the impression that "health" foods are absolutely necessary for the maintenance of health and life. The American Medical Association has issued a statement deploring the use of these terms in relation to food, indicating that "the claims are vague, misinformative, and misleading." Essential nutrients are only one factor in providing health. No scientific evidence is available to demonstrate that "health," "organic," or "natural" foods are more nutritious than the ordinary foods purchased in the market.

Many exaggerated claims have been made for these foods, such as long life, beauty, and a cure for certain diseases. What claims have you heard? Users of "health" foods do not always combine these foods in such a way that they will result in an adequate diet. Eating "health" foods is not a guarantee that all the nutrients will be consumed in adequate amounts. So a "health," "organic," or "natural" food eater must be informed about nutrition as well as everyone else. Have you ever observed what a "health" enthusiast eats? How might you judge the adequacy of such a diet?

On the positive side, the concern about "health" foods has increased interest in the wholesomeness of the food we eat. Many individuals have become gardeners. Has this idea occurred to you? Large amounts of fresh fruits and vegetables, nuts, dried fruits, seeds (such as sunflower seeds), legumes (soy beans are popular), vegetable oils, cultured milks, granola and other cereal combinations, and herbs have been added to the diet of many. Has your family reflected any of these eating changes?

Foods of other cultures, such as Chinese bean curd and fermented bean paste, millet used by people in the Far East, seaweed of the Japanese, alfalfa and bean sprouts, and yogurt are some foods adopted in the diet of many people. Have you tried to prepare any of these foods?

Food usually is more expensive in a health food store than elsewhere. Apples may be wormy because pesticides are not used. Vitamin and mineral preparations, plus items such as alfalfa tea, are usually not needed if you eat a nutritious diet.

How you eat may be the difference between winning and losing.

Food for Athletes

Your diet can be greatly influenced at present because you may wish to excel in some sport. You may have received so much advice that you are uncertain about what to eat. Research findings conclude that an adequate diet and adequate water intake appear to be the critical nutritional factors in maximal athletic performance. In other words, a high-protein diet, excessive vitamins, or overemphasis on any one nutrient is undesirable. If carbohydrate has been adequately stored in the body, an athlete in action can perform longer. It is important for the athlete's diet to provide this carbohydrate. Milk has sometimes been prohibited because of "cotton mouth." This condition is caused by the rate of saliva flow, the amount of perspiration, and the reduction of water content in the body, and not the milk in the diet. In fact, dehydration is one of the most serious problems of athletes. Many coaches are now permitting individuals in a game to drink water as required. The practice of consuming quick-energy foods such as dextrose, honey, sugar, and other sweets can be detrimental, because water is drawn from the gastrointestinal tract or other parts of the body. If sweating is profuse in these instances, dehydration can occur. Unless water is replaced promptly, performance will suffer.

The pregame meal should be eaten not less than three hours before a game. Some athletes have found that a liquid meal rich in nutrients is helpful because digestion may be delayed with an ordinary meal, if the player is nervous. Most athletes have worked out a meal that is satisfactory for them. Check any "miracle" or "winning" diet for nutritional adequacy before trying it. And be wary of special vitamin preparations or specially prepared beverages for athletes.

OTHER INFLUENCES ON OUR FOOD CHOICES

These influences, geographic, cultural, and religious, are usually mixed and combined with our American customs, like turkey on Thanksgiving, chicken every Sunday, and apple pie and ice cream. Your diet will have "a little bit of this and a little bit of that."

The Home

We must not forget, too, that your family situation determines, to some extent, what appears on the dinner table. Your parents have decided how much money they are going to spend for food. They may consider it wiser to serve less expensive (but equally good) foods and have more money for the family vacation.

The kind of equipment you have at home affects the food prepared. If food were cooked on an open fireplace, as in pioneer days, you would eat different foods from those prepared on the modern range. If your family has a garden, a freezer, a waffle iron, or other such aids, your food pattern will reflect this.

Family Favorite Foods

Sometimes your family eats favorite foods—popcorn on Sunday evening, hot biscuits on Saturday night, or gelatin desserts. You might not be eating these if you were a member of the family next door. Instead, you would be eating their favorite foods. Foods that are among your favorites may never have been tasted by some of your classmates. And foods that are very familiar to them may be unknown to you.

Certain Foods Disliked

In spite of all this, there are foods that others in your family like that you can't stand. Why is it that we like some foods and dislike others? Did you ever try to figure out why you turn up your nose at turnips? There are many reasons for disliking foods. A food may have been scorched or may have had an unpleasant flavor the first time you ate it. Other possible reasons are the "feel," odor, or appearance or unfamiliarity. Whatever our reasons for disliking some foods, we can all agree on why we like most foods: they taste good.

Chili con carne may be one of your family's favorite foods and may be served regularly.

Fresh home-baked bread has a special aroma and flavor that appeal to young and old alike.

The Taste of Foods

Most foods are preferred for their taste. There are four kinds of taste sensations: sweet, sour, bitter, and salty. Many foods are a combination of taste and aroma. Without knowing exactly why, we know we like foods that have a taste that is pleasant to us. And our tastes differ.

Sometimes we want to eat something because it reminds us of something pleasant. One girl remembered that the first time she tasted Sloppy Joes was at a party, and she has liked them ever since. A food such as a dessert or a piece of candy often seems like a reward. How many times have you heard this remark: "If you eat all your vegetables you can have a big piece of cake?" Doesn't that make you want cake?

Different Reasons for Eating Food

There may be many things at the back of your mind when you tell your mother what you'd like to have for dinner. You may prefer plain foods. Maybe you're suspicious of those big casseroles containing mixes of you-don't-know-what. You might like to have the same foods each day: cornflakes for breakfast, lettuce and tomato salad for lunch, and so on. Some people just don't like to change their food patterns. Perhaps you heard on radio or TV that gelatin would build muscles. Or you may become interested in eating a certain cereal be-

Don't be afraid to try new foods.

your cold"? Isn't it safer to ask your doctor than to prescribe your own treatment?

Sometimes Foods Are Refused

Again, you might refuse a food because it has a strong flavor or is rough, slick, or lumpy. Some things take too long to eat, such as a sandwich that won't stay together, meat that takes extra chewing, or chicken eaten from the bone. Perhaps you feel you don't have time for a big breakfast, or you have only an hour at noon time to rush home and back. All these reasons determine personal likes and dislikes.

Unpleasant Experiences with Foods

Once in a while you might refuse some food because you've been urged to eat it—it's "good for you." Have you ever burnt your mouth on a dish that was too hot? Weren't you wary about choosing it again? Sometimes you think a food is "only for babies," like cereal or milk, or for "people without teeth," like chopped meat. Maybe that's the real reason you shook your head at dinner last night.

cause you were told it would help you grow, make you attractive, or keep you healthy.

Do you believe that certain foods make you sleepy, that combinations of foods (like milk and cherries) are harmful, that fish is a brain food, or that cucumbers are cooling? Are there other beliefs about food that you hold or with which you are familiar? Have you ever tried to prove these ideas scientifically? No food has any of these qualities, according to research. These fallacies may have been handed down from someone in your past.

Are you inclined to follow the latest reducing fad or eat a certain food because "it will cure

You Are Reflected in Your Food Preferences

Most of us never think about the foods we eat and what they represent. We don't realize that they stand for us as individuals. Your cafeteria tray reflects your own preferences which, in turn, may tell the section of the country you live in, your family patterns, your religious beliefs, and your knowledge of foods for health. Why do you think you eat the foods you do?

THINKING IT OVER

1. Think about the food that is strongly typical of your region, your nationality, or your life-style. Are these foods that you would like to serve someday in your own home to your children? If so, why?

2. What would it be like if everyone in your community had to eat the same foods every day? Is your reaction shocking and unpleasant? Describe the feelings that this idea generates?

THINGS TO DO

1. Make a list of your five favorite foods in the order in which you like them best. Now do the same for the five foods that you dislike the most. Can you give any reasons for these food preferences? Compare your list with those of your friends. Are there any similarities? What was the most liked

food? the least liked? Now look at your list again. What about the nutritive value of the foods you listed? Does this make a difference in the adequacy of your diet?

2. Visit a "health-food" store, if there is one in your neighborhood. Which foods did you note that were new to you? How did the cost of some common foods compare with the prices where you usually shop? What kind of health claims were made?

3. Select a life-style that is different from yours and interview someone living in that way about his or her food patterns. Were the foods different from your own diet? Did methods of preparation and service differ? Was there anything about the way of eating that you would like to try?

14 How we eat

Eating together is a pleasant social experience. There are many occasions for sociability and food. Among these are after school, at basketball or football games, at the harvest festival or the school bazaar, and many others. When you are with friends, you do not worry about your manners or how you will eat certain foods. But have you ever been invited to a party or to someone's home where you hardly knew anyone and the food was strange? You may wish you had more know-how.

MANNERS ARE SENSIBLE

Table manners are based on experience and common sense. Courtesy to your friends and pleasure are additional factors. Many changes have come about through the years and informal service is prevalent today. Although the modern trend is toward leniency and informality, it is not lax.

Good manners should be practiced at home at every meal. Then they are no longer troublesome rules but normal behavior. You truly will have that envied confidence and social ease the French call *savoir faire* (and the Americans call know-how).

Good manners begin before you reach the table. You enter the room quietly and allow your mother to be seated first. After, in the following order, the other members of the family should take their place: the girls, the father, and the boys.

Wherever you eat, at home or away, eating is an enjoyable occasion. Both in your actions and your conversation you should bear this in mind. Bickering, requests for new clothes or a bigger allowance, or scoldings are out of place. Since your mother is the hostess, she indicates when to begin to eat and when you may be excused from the table.

How to Handle Implements

Some people grasp the knife and fork as if they were going to run away. Ideally you should be so familiar with these implements that they become extensions of your hands.

The knife and fork should be placed near the right (or left if you are left-handed) outer rim of the plate when you are not using them. Never place them in gangplank fashion, from the table to the plate. When you have finished, lay your knife and fork side by side near the center of the plate. The fork prongs should be up and the cutting blade of the knife turned toward the center.

When you have finished, don't place your knife and fork gangplank fashion.

Do's and Don'ts of Table Manners

You probably have many questions about the proper way to serve and to eat foods. Here are some pointers that might be helpful.

Be sure to—

- Eat slowly and quietly.

- Use your spoon for fruit, soft desserts, soft-cooked eggs, occasionally for vegetables.

- Use your fingers to eat such foods as nuts, pizzas, sandwiches, doughnuts, cookies, potato chips, candy, corn on the cob.

- Help pass dishes and see that everyone else is served before you begin to eat.

- Taste your food before you add additional seasoning.

Touch your lips lightly with your napkin before taking a drink of water so food and grease marks are not left on the glass.

Cut a sandwich or hamburger in two or more pieces and use one hand to convey them to your mouth.

- Open your napkin in half and lay it across your lap.
- Be careful in taking your first taste of foods that are apt to be very hot.
- Let foods that are too hot cool naturally.
- Start from the outside implement and work in when choosing the right silver.
- Discover new foods. Taste everything.

Be sure *not* to—

- Talk while your mouth is full.
- Chew with your mouth open.
- Reach across the table or in front of others.
- Blow on food to cool it.
- Cut up all of food before beginning to eat. Only cut each bite as you eat it.
- Serve yourself with your own silver. Use serving pieces provided for this.
- Butter a whole slice of bread at once. Break off and butter one small section at a time.

- Only take on your fork bite-size portions that can be easily chewed.
- Ask to be excused before leaving the table.

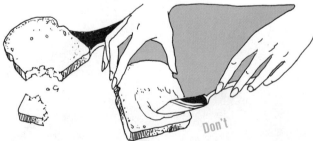

- Fuss with your appearance, such as combing hair or using powder compact at table.

- Spit out seeds from fruit, such as watermelon. Remove them from your mouth with a spoon.

- Crush or crumple your napkin when you have finished.

- Hand food, such as a roll, to someone else. Pass the serving plate.

Don't "worry your foods with your fork." When dishes are served that are combinations of different foods, such as stews and casseroles, eat everything.

Pardon Me!

Did you ever knock over the water glass? Drop food or silver on the floor? Perhaps some elusive food, such as peas, wandered off your plate or the crumbs just flew when you broke that roll. These are embarrassing situations that could and do happen to anyone.

If your particular nightmare is knocking over the water or milk glass, first of all be calm about it, because it is an accident. Quickly and sincerely apologize to your mother or to your hostess if you are visiting. If you are at home,

perhaps you can get a cloth and quickly do whatever is necessary to make the table neat again. If you are a guest, your hostess will take care of it. Once the damage has been repaired, dismiss it from the table conversation—but not from your mind. Remember that it was actually carelessness on your part that caused this mishap. Be sure that quick, unguarded movements don't bring about a repeat performance.

Solutions to the other problems are simple. Food or silver on the floor should remain there until the meal is over, unless they will be a hazard to serving. If this is so, whoever is responsible will take care of it. In any case, never pick up food or silver from the floor and place it on the table. But you may quietly place food on your plate if it has wandered to the table. Crumbs are best left there.

The "rule of thumb" in any embarrassing situation is to be as inconspicuous as possible. If an accident happens, apologize once, repair the damage (if that is your responsibility), and do not mention it again.

SIMPLE STANDARDS OF TABLE SERVICE

Does the salad go to the right or to the left? Just where should I put the milk glass? Do questions like these come to mind as you set the table? There are rules about table service that are known and accepted everywhere. Naturally

An attractive table setting. What contributes to its attractiveness?

there are a few variations which may be true in your particular community. But it is wisest to learn the general custom and then become aware of local deviations. In that way you will be at ease anywhere you go.

Attractiveness of the table and meal, convenience, and efficiency are basic to all table service. The ease and comparative inconspicuousness of serving food is the result of careful planning. When you know that all is going smoothly, you can relax and enjoy your meal, whether it be breakfast at home or your birthday party.

TABLE APPOINTMENTS

Study the table setting on this page. What do you think is the reason for its attractiveness? The keynote is harmony. This means harmony in color, harmony in the texture of linen, the kind of chinaware, the type of silver, and also the harmony of the table itself with its surroundings. For example, it would be out of tune to use your mother's fine, delicate china to serve your friends an after-school snack in the kitchen. Nor would you use rough-textured ceramic pottery dishes with a damask tablecloth.

Table Linen

There is wide variation in the kinds of table appointments. Table linen may be informal mats of plastic, cork, or the more formal woven cotton and fine linen. Cotton and linen cloths in a number of colors and designs may be used to suit the occasion. Easy-care materials for table linens are simple to launder and come in attractive colors and patterns.

Silverware for the Table

Silverware includes the flatware (eating implements) and holloware, which includes the tea and coffee services, platters, and other serving dishes. These may be in sterling silver or silver plate. In addition, many of these pieces are made in attractive patterns of stainless steel. The cost, the amount of entertaining done, upkeep, and durability determine the selection in each family. The cost and upkeep of silver holloware have limited its use in many homes. Perhaps you have a silver teapot or coffeepot that belonged to your grandmother or a great-aunt and that you like because it represents something from your family's past.

Silverware includes flatware in silverplate, sterling silver, or stainless steel, and holloware, such as serving dishes and coffee and tea services.

China for the Table

There are three general types of chinaware: vitrified china (porcelain ware), semivitreous ware (or earthenware), and pottery. China is usu-

China of good quality and pleasing color and design is important to a table setting.

ally represented in a family's "best dishes." These are fine and delicate and the patterns may be traditional or modern. Today's informal living has suggested earthenware or pottery as the choice of many families. All three types of chinaware offer a wide choice in quality, color, and beauty of design. An increasing number of plastic dishes that rival pottery in attractiveness and design are being made for informal table settings.

Table Decorations

An appropriate centerpiece or table decoration is needed to complete an attractive table setting. It does not necessarily have to be expensive flowers or silver candelabra. A bowl of fruit, a little snowman, gourds grown in your window box, and many other simple seasonal ideas will add interest and variety to your table. Other suggestions are a single flower floating in a bowl, balls of colored string or yarn in an attractive container, flowers or leaves that you have dried, or an interesting assortment of candle holders made from spools or gelatin molds. Candle holders are not only attractive, but they are also practical, because candlelight will save some electricity. Tucking a calendar in your centerpiece in a clever way may be helpful to family members especially if a future event is being discussed at the meal.

You may be accustomed to the idea of a table decoration for a party or when you have guests. Did you ever try your hand at devising an eye-catcher for your family brunch table?

When you plan your table decoration, keep these pointers in mind:

1–It should be low, no more than ten inches in height.
2–It should not cover more than one-third of the table space.
3–It should not be top-heavy or unsteady.
4–If you like flowers, the container should be large enough to contain the necessary amount of water to keep your flowers fresh.

Guides for Table Decorations. Simplicity, season, and economy should be your guides in planning attractive table decorations. Look around you for challenging ideas. These might be the calendar your young sister made in kindergarten as a focal point for a New Year's decoration, or your family activities portrayed by pipe-cleaner men. It can be a family game to see who can create the most appropriate and interesting table decoration.

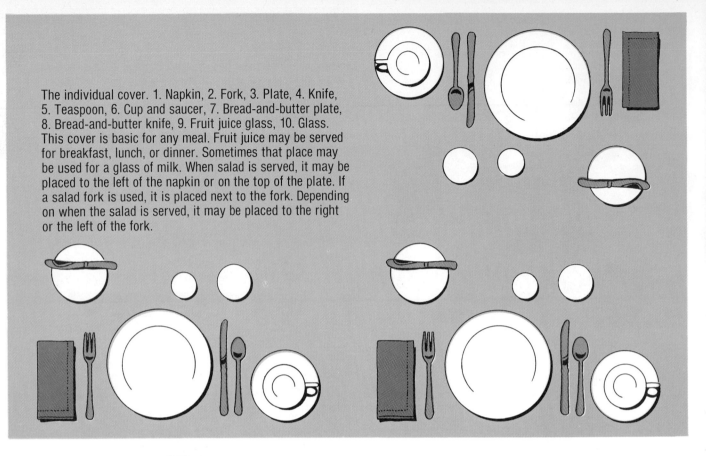

The individual cover. 1. Napkin, 2. Fork, 3. Plate, 4. Knife, 5. Teaspoon, 6. Cup and saucer, 7. Bread-and-butter plate, 8. Bread-and-butter knife, 9. Fruit juice glass, 10. Glass. This cover is basic for any meal. Fruit juice may be served for breakfast, lunch, or dinner. Sometimes that place may be used for a glass of milk. When salad is served, it may be placed to the left of the napkin or on the top of the plate. If a salad fork is used, it is placed next to the fork. Depending on when the salad is served, it may be placed to the right or the left of the fork.

THE INDIVIDUAL COVER

Were you ever so crowded at the table that you wondered just how much room each person needed? Probably your mother has learned by trial and error just how many people she can seat at the table without putting in an extra leaf. It is suggested that each person requires from 20 to 24 inches. This space, which contains the silver, glassware, china, and napkin, is called the cover. Here is the accepted way to set the cover for each individual.

RULES FOR SETTING THE TABLE

In setting the table, all flat silver should be one inch from the edge of the table. Forks are placed with the tines up. The meat knife is laid with the cutting edge toward the plate. If the dessert is one that is eaten with a fork, the dessert fork is placed next to the plate. If soup is served, the soup spoon is laid at the extreme right. In general, the silver is placed so that the rule "from the outside in" may be followed. There are a few deviations, as you can see by studying the diagram.

Just before the meal is served, butter or margarine and the roll or slice of bread are placed on the bread-and-butter plate. Water glasses are filled and milk is poured and placed just to the right of the water glass. Salad is usually served at luncheon or dinner. Salad plates, which are part of the cover, are placed at the left of the napkin. If pickles, relishes, gravy, a tray of bread, and so on are included in the menu, you need to consider them as you arrange the table. The type of meal and the kind of menu determine the way a table will be set.

Before the meal is served, a quick and careful mental check will ensure a smooth table service.

IDEAS FOR ATTRACTIVE MEALS

The effect of the table setting should be one of overall attractiveness. Ways to achieve this have been discussed. Harmony reflected in good taste is basic. Dishes, silverware, and linen should be sparkling and shining. The table should have an air of careful, not haphazard, arrangement. It should seem uncrowded and uncluttered.

Color Is Important in Foods

Thoughtful menu-planning will add to the attractiveness of meals. Color combinations should be pleasant and provide contrast. Baked pork chop, candied sweet potatoes, and French-style string beans will offer a pleasing color combination. Contrast this with boiled cod, mashed potatoes, and cauliflower. Neither should colors be harsh. A vegetable salad plate with sliced tomatoes and pickled beets is not as tempting as sliced tomatoes with sliced cucumbers.

Texture Must Be Considered

A contrast in texture of foods is desirable in menu-planning. For example, a smooth-textured food, such as creamed chicken, should be served with a crisp vegetable, such as raw carrots or sliced tomatoes. A fibrous meat, such as a pot roast, is combined with a "soft" food like mashed potatoes. The third food may be an "in between" such as cooked carrots.

Flavor Should Be Considered

Flavors in food should blend, rather than clash. If you were serving a strongly or characteristically flavored vegetable, such as broccoli, it would taste better with a dish such as tunafish casserole instead of a strongly flavored meat like corned beef.

Foods Should Be Well Fixed

For meals to be attractive, foods must be properly prepared. Vegetables should not be cooked until they lose all color and become limp. Neither should they be so undercooked that they are difficult to chew. (Ways of preparing foods are discussed in Area 5.) Foods should be seasoned while cooking even though more salt and pepper may be added later.

Little things may add much to the attractiveness of the meal. Garnishes, like radish roses, a sprig of parsley, or broiled apricots may perk up a dish. Warm dinner plates and chilled dessert plates (if the menu dictates) will help keep food at the proper temperature while it is being eaten. An old rule, "Hot foods hot and cold foods cold," governs table service. A final, but by no means unimportant, point is that the correct dish for the particular food should be used. For example, a baked apple served on a small plate would be enjoyed much more if it were placed in a fruit dish or saucer.

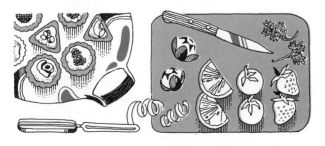

Where you eat will help to determine how formal or informal the arrangements should be.

Adapt the Service to the Menu

Menus should be planned with an eye to the service. For example, if you are thinking of eating on a tray while you watch a special television program, you will want a simple menu. Finger foods and those that are cut with a fork are in order. Your beverage should be placed on a side table to prevent accidents. Plan to use a minimum of dishes so that the tray is not heavy.

FAMILY TABLE SERVICE

In today's informal living, most Americans emphasize simplicity. Usually the whole family participates in serving meals. Mealtime should be a pleasant, uninterrupted family gathering. "I forgot the salt" or "We need more milk" and so on can only create a jumping-jack, hurry-up atmosphere. A simple, well-coordinated system makes for a relaxed, dignified mealtime when the proper standards of table etiquette and table service are observed.

The Family Helps Serve Meals

The family meal service should be conducted in a spirit of cooperation. The duties should be divided and rotated. Although mothers and daughters traditionally were responsible for the preparation of meals and setting the table, there is a strong trend for these responsibilities to be unisex in nature—that is, everyone in the family helps in all areas. This is to be encouraged, because it is valuable for men to have these skills, too, and mealtime becomes a truly family affair. In many homes, because of busy schedules or for other reasons, whoever comes home first starts the meal.

When dinner is ready, the water, milk, bread and butter, and first course should be ready. If the menu omits a first course, the main course may be on the table. Often the first course, which may be a fruit or vegetable juice, can be served in the living room.

The actual service of a meal is a family tradition that varies from family to family. In some families, the father serves the main course. In others, the father may serve the meat, but a son or daughter (and sometimes the mother) may serve the vegetables. These are variations that reflect family tradition. One person, usually one of the children, should be appointed to replace any items needed during the main course. Others should remain seated.

Again, one member should be appointed to clear the table. This may be a son or a daughter. The meat and vegetable dishes should be removed first and then the plates and other dishes used for the main course. Even though it may save time, the dishes should not be scraped and stacked at the table. This is reserved for the kitchen. Salt and pepper, butter, relishes, and other accompaniments are removed also. If

Meals can be more interesting when a father or sons help with the meal preparation.

there are any crumbs on the table, they are brushed into a small tray or plate.

The dessert plates and the cups and saucers, if a hot beverage is on the menu, are brought in. Cream and sugar are placed on the table. Often the mother will serve dessert and beverage, and they are brought to her at this time. After the meal, the family leaves the table and the member appointed to clear the table and wash the dishes assumes this responsibility. Most family meal service is dictated by common sense. But you need to keep in mind that a relaxed, unhurried, pleasant atmosphere is desirable. You should plan with this in mind.

Family Meal Service May Differ

Although there are general rules for the service of meals, your family will have to adapt its service to specific family needs. For example, your father may work at an extra job two nights a week and has to eat early. Your brother may work after school and comes home later. Your mother may work and sometimes her hours are uncertain. Differences in the schedules of family members are quite common among families so on these evenings, service may have to be simplified. One way is to have a one-dish meal prepared in an electric skillet that can be easily reheated as members come home. A bowl of tossed salad or a dish of raw vegetable relishes

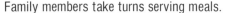

Family members take turns serving meals.

can be kept in the refrigerator as well as ice cream or pudding for dessert. Sometimes dessert may mean helping oneself from a fruit bowl on the table. In this way each family member can pick up his or her own food and sit in the breakfast nook or at the kitchen table. If the meal has to be eaten alone, some music, listening to the radio, or reading the evening paper may help to make a pleasant and relaxing time as well as encouraging leisurely eating.

On those evenings when all the family is at home or on weekends and holidays. it can become an occasion for setting the table and having a happy family-get-together. Several services are available. By the use of cookware that can be brought to the table, various family members can do the serving. Your mother or father may serve the main dish and a son or daughter serve the vegetables. Sometimes the food is of such a nature that it is easier for several family members to "dish up" in the kitchen and bring the filled plates to the table.

Another possibility for serving is to place the food into serving dishes that can be easily handled at the table. The food is passed around and each person serves himself or herself. One advantage to this method is that each person takes the size serving desired and less food is wasted. Second servings are simplified. Why not share family meal services among classmates and out of it may come a number of ways to make your service easier and more pleasant.

Using cookware for serving food is efficient.

Meal service may be more formal when dinner is a special occasion.

There may be occasions when a more formal service is desired, such as a birthday dinner, an anniversary, or some other reason for celebration. The meal may be served in courses with family members taking turns in being responsible for the service of a course. For example, the first course may be fruit cup, fruit or vegetable juice, antipasto, chopped liver, or a seafood combination. At the end of the course the dishes should be removed and the hot food served. Your father or your brother may wish to carve the roast chicken or turkey, baked ham, or whatever the meat may be. Your mother or you may serve the vegetables on the same plate as the meat. At the end of this course, the table is cleared again. If a salad was not served with the dinner, it may be served as a separate course. When the salad plates are removed, if served as a separate course, the dessert is served. Dessert may be served in separate dishes and placed before each family member. If the dessert is cake or pie, your mother or one of the children may want to cut and serve it. Sometimes the coffee is served with the dessert but in some homes it is preferred separate. Some family members like to drink coffee or whatever beverage is served and linger at the table to tell family stories of interest. This is a lengthy and somewhat formal service but it gives a special feeling of enjoyment.

Family meals should not be taken lightly. The food you have at your family table will provide many memories in the years to come. When family meals are humdrum and "so-so" they become routine, almost like brushing your teeth. Do not let that happen because eating with your family is an important part of your life.

Meals in today's families are not limited to the dining table. In fact, the trend is to eat "all around the house." Dinner may be in the living room, on the porch, out on the terrace or patio, on the beach, in the recreation room, or most anywhere. Changes in eating patterns are fun and add spice to the table.

But this does not mean that you can become careless about either your table etiquette or table service. Your family's meals should be pleasant and uninterrupted whether they be in the basement or the dining room. Even more careful planning is needed for a smooth meal service when you break the routine.

Did you ever decide to surprise your parents and eat Sunday night supper in the living room only to find yourself making many hurried trips to the kitchen for forgotten silver or salt? Lack of planning can turn an eating adventure into a misadventure.

Plan for Unusual Meals

The next time you plan to serve a meal away from the usual place, take time to write down your menu. Then, list all the items you will need for service. This would include silverware, dishes, napkins, and salt and pepper. You will need to think of extra things, too, like trivets for hot dishes, pot holders, and barbecue forks. Plan how each detail of the menu will be served and eaten. Will the salad be a relish plate of celery curls, carrot sticks, or will it be a tossed salad that calls for a second set of plates and silver? Questions like these answered ahead of time will guarantee a pleasant time.

Be informal, but don't relax your standards of service. Rather, changes in surroundings give you an opportunity to see if you know what to do away from "home base."

BUFFET SERVICE

You will have many more opportunities for parties and other social events as you grow older. Many occasions suggest a get-together. One of the easiest and most relaxed ways to entertain your friends is a buffet supper. Or you may try your hand at a buffet Sunday night supper for your family.

If you are entertaining, one of the advantages of a buffet is that all the preparation is done before your guests arrive. Apart from your duties as host or hostess, you are free to enjoy yourself. A buffet is "self-service" because the guests help themselves. Careful thought and preplanning will make everything go smoothly.

Entertain your crowd with a well-arranged buffet.

Foods Appropriate for Buffet Service

When planning the menu, you must remember that all foods should be easy to eat, either with fingers or with a fork and spoon. A sample menu pattern might be a hot dish, a salad or raw vegetable, bread, dessert, and beverage. One suggested menu might include baked beans and frankfurters, cole slaw, brown bread, Indian pudding, and a milk punch. Another suggested menu might include a casserole dish, such as Spanish rice or creamed tunafish, a tossed green salad, apple pie, hot buttered biscuits, and fruit punch.

Perhaps instead of a hot main dish, your friends might prefer hearty sandwiches, or do-it-yourself "Dagwoods." In that case you could have all the "fixings" for sandwiches, including a variety of relishes. A vegetable tray with carrot sticks, celery curls, green pepper rings, and cauliflower flowerettes, and cherry pie for dessert would complete the menu. The possibilities for a buffet supper menu are only as limited as your imagination.

Table Settings for a Buffet

The table arrangement depends upon your menu and the number of guests you expect. Sometimes an easier service is obtained if the table is pushed against the wall. The most important thing to remember is that everything should be accessible to all your guests. A colorful tablecloth or the bare table is equally acceptable. Your centerpiece should reflect the occasion. A miniature Christmas tree, a football, school colors, or any other motif can set the tone for your party. The centerpiece on a buffet table may be higher than the usual ten inches.

Before you set the table, you should mentally follow the path your guests will take. Once you have done this, you can decide on the best place for the various dishes. Usually the main dish is at one end of the table. Beside it is a stack of plates and the serving spoon. Salad and rolls, with the necessary serving implements, are set at intervals along the table. The silverware and napkins, arranged in rows, may be placed either at the beginning of the table or at the end. Many prefer the latter for easier service. The beverage may be picked up at the buffet table or served in the living room after the guest has been seated. Dessert may be obtained later from a side table or it may be served individually in the living room.

Role of Host and Hostess for a Buffet

What do you, as host or hostess, have to do during the buffet supper? Just before the guests are due to arrive, place the food in the designated places. Then you are free to greet your guests. When about half have come, suggest that they come to the buffet table. You may need to help some of your friends select food or you may have to invite one or two to help themselves. You may make suggestions about their seating when they have returned to the living room.

It will be necessary to check the table to see if more food has to be brought in. Perhaps your mother, sister, or a friend can assume this responsibility. You may suggest that your guests return to the table for second helpings. When they have finished, you may direct them to place their plates on a side table or you may take the plates yourself. Then you must see about the service of dessert. As host or hostess, you want each guest to enjoy himself. You should be able to circulate freely and visit with your friends.

Use Buffet Service in Many Ways

A buffet supper does not have to be held in the house. As indicated earlier, it can be an outside affair, on the porch or out on the patio. A tailgate picnic in which the tailgate of your station wagon or pick-up truck serves as a table for food is fun. This is a good plan if a number of your friends plan to go to the county fair or a football game, or on a similar outing.

Each home has many possibilities for entertaining in this simple, informal fashion. And you

A picnic can be fun when careful planning assures that nothing will be left behind.

need not wait for a party occasion to have a buffet. A Saturday brunch, a Fourth of July supper, and many other holiday meals are good times for family buffets.

Basic to all table service is a simple, unhurried atmosphere. There should be an opportu-

When you are a guest in a friend's home, be sure to express your thanks to his or her parents before you leave.

nity to practice accepted table manners at every meal. In this way, correct etiquette will become a way of life, not "company manners," and you will be at ease wherever you go.

COMPANY FOR MEALS

It is always fun when your parents allow friends of yours to stay for supper. But your responsibility doesn't end with the invitation. Even though they may be your best friends and you tell them to make themselves right at home, there are still many little things you can do to make sure they enjoy themselves.

Manners for a Host or Hostess

Provide your guests with towels and washcloths so they can freshen up for dinner. Be sure they know everyone. Don't take it for granted that just because they're your best friends they have met your older sister or your father. Warn them in an inconspicuous way about family traditions that might catch them unawares, such as saying grace.

Remember that you and your parents are sharing the host and hostess roles. Watch your friends' plates and be sure they have enough to eat. Suggest that they have a second helping, but if they refuse, don't urge them. If they refuse food or leave some on their plates, don't call attention to it.

To really enjoy themselves, your guests should be included in the conversation. If your sister is asking for a new dress for the prom or your brother is monopolizing the air waves talking about his model airplane, try to change the subject. However, it would be rude for you and your friends to carry on a private conversation.

Having company for meals will give you a chance to practice for the more formal occasions when you will have a number of guests. Even though you know your guests as well as you do any member of your family, they will appreciate your thoughtfulness. They will enjoy themselves because you will have made every effort to make them comfortable and at ease.

Being a Guest

Apart from the general discussion on table etiquette, there are a few special pointers that may put you at ease when you are visiting at mealtime. If you are aware of the accepted table manners and meal service, you will have no difficulty.

When you are a guest, however, you want to enjoy yourself thoroughly. In order to do this, you should cooperate with all suggestions (even though they may be things you would rather not do). If you just *hate* chopped beef and a meat loaf is served, you should eat it with a grin and a willing spirit.

If it is an informal occasion, offer to help in setting the table, washing the dishes, and so forth. If your friend's mother says she will serve in five minutes, be prompt. Avoid all disagreeable topics while eating. These would include such things as illness, accidents, your diet, and foods that you dislike or that disagree with you. You should contribute your share of pleasant conversation. If you have any question about which fork or spoon to use or how to eat a particular food, follow the leader, your hostess. She will indicate the way it should be done.

When you leave, thank your friend and his or her mother for a wonderful evening and a delicious dinner. If you attend a more formal gathering, you should send a note of appreciation to your hostess when you reach home.

"Actions speak louder than words," is an old saying. These little courtesies will assure your hostess that you enjoyed your visit and appreciated her thoughtfulness.

THINKING IT OVER

1. The next time you eat out, take a look at the table setting. Could you improve it? Was the food served in the most appropriate dishes? What changes would you make in the service and table setting and why?

2. Recall when you were six or seven years old. What do you remember about your family meals? Your classmates might relate their memories and you can share ideas about the role of family meals in your life.

THINGS TO DO

1. Your class might plan a lacto-ovo-vegetarian buffet supper as a demonstration of less expensive entertaining and in keeping with efforts to help the hungry world. Read about vegetarianism, a diet with an interesting history. Famous men such as Pythagoras, Tolstoy, and Shaw were vegetarians. Can you name others? Your entertainment might highlight interesting facets about this diet.

2. Plan some table decorations from "throw-aways." Make an exhibit and share your creative efforts.

area five

Helping with Family Meals

15 Before you cook

It is "the thing" these days for both boys and girls to be able to cook. Maybe you do a great deal of cooking now but are not too sure you are using the right methods. Your cooking experience may be limited to helping a little here and a little there, but more competent cooks in the family usually take over. Perhaps you have been too busy doing other things besides cooking.

Whatever your experience, it might be well to think about some rules that will guide you in becoming a good cook. Rules are important and serve as a blueprint of the best way to do things. And rules can be fun.

READING RECIPES

First, you will need to know how to read recipes. A recipe consists of a list of ingredients with detailed directions for preparing them. Each ingredient is important, and so is each step. Look at the following recipe for banana milkshake. Notice that there is a list of ingredients at the top, with an amount for each. This is followed by a list of directions. The first step in preparing a recipe is to study the recipe. Next you must put out the ingredients listed in the recipe. Then you will be ready to prepare the recipe. Do you have any questions about recipes?

Banana Milkshake

1 medium ripe banana
1 cup of milk

1. Peel the banana.
2. Slice the banana into thin slices (about 20) into a bowl.
3. Beat the banana with an eggbeater until it is smooth and creamy-looking.
4. Pour the cold milk over the banana.
5. Beat very slowly with the eggbeater at first, being careful not to spatter.
6. Beat until foamy and the banana and milk are well blended.
7. Pour into a tall glass and drink it.

Some Extra Ideas: You may use any kind of milk—whole, skim, low-fat, dried (whole or skim), or evaporated (whole or skim). Add a teaspoon of vanilla for flavor or a spoonful of ice cream for something special.

COOKING TERMS

Now look at other recipes in home or school cookbooks. Do you notice words that you do not understand? Perhaps this list will help you.

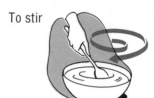

To stir

To keep the ingredients moving in a circle, by the use of a spoon or fork.

To beat

To stir with a quick, repetitive, over-and-under motion, or to stir very rapidly.

To sift

To place dry ingredients in a sifter and shake into a bowl or onto waxed paper.

To boil

To cook in water, causing bubbles to rise to the surface.

To combine

To mix two or more ingredients together while stirring.

To melt

To turn a solid substance into liquid by heating.

To bake

To cook in an oven.

To blend

To combine several ingredients until they are well mixed.

To cream

To soften butter, margarine, or shortening with the back of a wooden or mixing spoon.

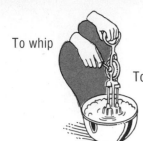
To whip
To beat with
an eggbeater.

To pan-fry

To cook in a small amount of
shortening in a frying pan.

To slice
To cut across
into flat pieces.

To cut and fold

To cut down the center of the batter
with a spoon or whip and gently bring
mixture up and over. Repeat until well
blended. Usually done when adding
beaten egg white.

To roll

To roll a rolling pin over dough
in all directions.

EQUIPMENT FOR COOKING

Certain equipment is necessary if we are to be successful in our
cooking. Place a sheet of paper over the names of these implements and see how many you can identify by their uses. Can
you think of other uses—perhaps special uses that you yourself
have found for the implements?

Pastry blender

To mix flour and fat for muffins, biscuits,
and piecrusts.

Dry measuring cups:
1, ½, ⅓, ¼ cups.

To measure
flour, sugar, cereal, and other ingredients.

Mixing bowls

To mix ingredients in a recipe.

Rubber scraper
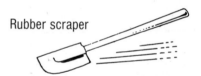

To clean batter from sides of a bowl.

Measuring spoons:

1 tablespoon
1 teaspoon
½ teaspoon
¼ teaspoon

To measure fat, sugar, flour, and the like.

Wooden spoon

To stir hot foods that are cooking, and
for other stirring.

Baking sheet
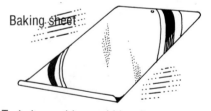

To bake cookies and biscuits.

Spatula

To remove cake and cookies from a pan;
to level flour, sugar, and the like when
measuring.

Fork

To stir
coarse cereals; to pick up vegetables and
fruit; to test whether vegetables are
done.

Liquid
measuring cups:
1 cup, 2 cups

To measure milk, water, vegetable or
fruit juices, and other liquids.

Paring knife

To peel fruits and vegetables.

Grater

To shred food.

130

Biscuit and cookie cutter

To cut biscuit and cookie dough into different shapes.

Oblong pan

To bake bread, cakes, and coffee cakes.

Casserole

To bake mixtures of meat and vegetables and a sauce.

Electric blender

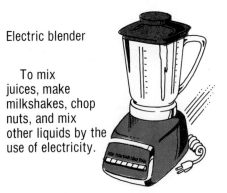

To mix juices, make milkshakes, chop nuts, and mix other liquids by the use of electricity.

Wire rack

To cool cake, cookies, and pies when they come from the oven.

Pastry brush

To brush melted butter on rolls.

Vegetable brush

To clean vegetables and some fruits.

Frying pan

To pan-fry meat or vegetables.

Cake pan

To bake cakes.

Muffin pan

To bake muffins and cupcakes.

Eggbeater

To beat eggs and make milkshakes.

Flour sifter

To sift flour.

Kitchen scissors

To cut poultry and raw vegetables into pieces.

Thermometer

To test temperature of oven and cooked candy and meat.

Rolling pin and bread board

To roll biscuits and pie crust; to crush crackers or toast for crumbs.

Pie pan

To bake pie and coffee cake.

Saucepan

To cook meat, fruit, or vegetables in water.

Electric mixer

To mix batter and dough, and make icings.

Pancake turner

To turn pancakes and meat patties.

Double boiler

To cook over water food that requires a low temperature, such as milk puddings.

When you think you can understand the terms used in recipes and are familiar with the equipment you will use in cooking, the next rule concerns measuring. In reading a recipe you notice that it may call for a certain amount of flour, sugar, tomatoes, salt, or other ingredients. Through careful experimentation experts have discovered the best ways to measure, and it is well to follow their advice if you want to avoid failures when you prepare your favorite dishes. A little too much salt or not enough flour may ruin your plans to surprise your friends with an after-school snack.

Study the following illustrations carefully. Then practice measuring flour, sugar, salt, and other ingredients.

Flour—Sift flour through the sifter once onto a plate or waxed paper. Then put flour into a measuring cup with a spoon. (Don't shake the cup or pack the flour!) Fill the cup heaping full and level off with knife. Now you have measured one cup of flour.

White sugar—Sift if lumpy. Spoon it into a cup heaping full and level off with knife. You have measured one cup of white sugar.

Milk, juice, syrup—see marker lines on liquid measuring cup. To measure, place on table and fill to proper line. Stoop to see at eye level.

Brown sugar—Pack brown sugar into the cup and level off with knife. Sugar will hold its shape when removed from cup.

Vanilla or other flavoring—Use measuring spoons. If recipe calls for 1 teaspoon of vanilla, pour vanilla into spoon until full.

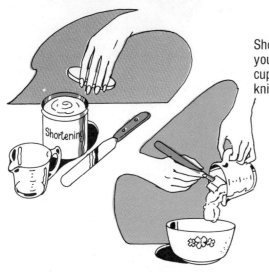

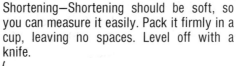
Shortening—Shortening should be soft, so you can measure it easily. Pack it firmly in a cup, leaving no spaces. Level off with a knife.

While looking through cookbooks you may have noticed a number of abbreviations. Here are some of the common ones:

T or tbsp = tablespoon
t or tsp = teaspoon
c = cup
fg = few grains, usually in connection with salt or sugar

Another help in cooking is a familiarity with what are known as equivalents. Below are examples.

Some cookbooks have recipes with metric measurements now. When metric measurements become more prevalent, we will have to be ready with metric know-how. A table of metric measurements may be found on page 164. A Spanish recipe with metric measurements is included in Chapter 21. Begin to think metric.

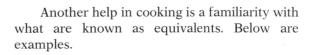

3 teaspoons = 1 tablespoon

4 tablespoons = ¼ cup

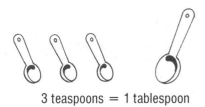
2 cups = 1 pint

4 cups = 1 quart

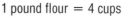
1 pound flour = 4 cups

1 pound sugar = 2 cups

¼ pound shortening = ½ cup

TABLE OF EQUIVALENTS

16 tablespoons	=	1 cup
8–10 egg whites	=	1 cup
1 tablespoon flour	=	¾ tbsp. cornstarch
	=	1 tbsp. granular tapioca
	=	2 tablespoons granular cereals
1 cup flour	=	⅞ cup corn meal
	=	1 cup graham flour
	=	1 cup rye flour
	=	1½ cups bran
	=	1½ cups bread crumbs
	=	1 cup rolled oats
Juice of 1 lemon	=	3 tablespoons, approximately

Now you may feel that you are ready to go into the classroom or into your kitchen at home and cook. But there are some other rules that must be observed. These rules directly concern *you*.

HOW TO DRESS FOR COOKING

The way you dress for cooking is important. In class you will discuss the best kind of clothes to wear. Some kind of wash clothes is best. At home it is advisable to wear some kind of play clothes or something that will wash easily. Girls and boys should pin back their hair or tie it. Boys might like to wear a chef's cap.

Scrub your hands and nails until they are very clean. Wipe them dry so that bowls and other utensils will not slip out of your hands. You will make a better cook if you are neat and clean.

SAFETY RULES FOR COOKING

There are a few safety rules that are well to bear in mind. They are listed below with reasons for following them. Find other good reasons that each is important.

Are there other safety rules that are important?

CLEANING UP

Maybe your mother complains whenever you cook because the kitchen is a shambles when you finish. Cleaning up is something that should be done as you work and not left to the end. On the next page are a few good rules to remember so your mother will be pleased to have you in the kitchen and your teacher will praise you in the laboratory. All good cooks practice these rules.

Table 15–1

COOKING SAFETY RULES

Rule	Why It Is Followed
1. Use a potholder to pick up hot dishes.	So you won't burn your hands.
2. Keep your hair out of your eyes.	So you can see and won't have accidents. Also, so you won't touch your hair with your hands.
3. Put hot pans on a heat-resistant surface.	So table tops will not be marked.
4. Stir hot foods with a wooden spoon.	Metal spoons get hot and burn you.
5. Cut away from you.	So you will avoid accidents.
6. Wipe up things that spill on the floor, like fat or water.	So you won't slip and fall.
7. Keep apron strings or ruffles away from flames.	So your clothing won't catch fire.
8. Turn handles of saucepans away from the edge of the range.	So you won't knock them off and scald yourself.
9. Wash knives separately from other dishes.	So you won't cut yourself.
10. Don't use aprons or towels for potholders.	Very dangerous: they are too thin and you'll burn yourself.
11. Keep cupboard doors closed.	So you won't bump your head.

Code For A Good Cook

1–A good cook is clean.

a. Always wash your hands upon entering the kitchen. Wash your hands whenever necessary.

b. Nails should be especially clean. Inspect them before preparing food.

c. When coughing or sneezing, turn head away from food.

d. Whenever a handkerchief or tissue is used,  your hands should be washed carefully with soap and water.

e. Soak dishes before washing them. Put egg, milk, and flour dishes into cold water, and dishes with grease or sugar into hot water.

f. Return all containers to their proper places with the lids tight.

g. Keep the table, sink, cupboard counters, and other working space free from clutter, crumbs, and spills.

h. Keep a sponge or damp cloth handy to wipe your working space.

i. A good cook leaves a clean kitchen.

◀ **2–A good cook uses a tasting spoon.**

a. Use a special spoon for tasting which is never placed in the bowl, pan, or container holding food. Use the mixing spoon to put food onto the tasting spoon. Do not touch the tasting spoon while transferring food from the mixing spoon or allow the spoons to touch each other.

3–A good cook knows equipment.

a. Three points are important: know the purpose of each piece, know how to use equipment, and where to find it. ▶

◀ 4–A good cook measures all ingredients accurately.
5–A good cook remembers simple measurements and equivalents.

6–A good cook uses tested recipes.

   a. Sources of tested recipes and reliable cookbooks are known to a good cook.

7–A good cook works efficiently.

   a. A plan is made for work.

   b. A tray is used to carry ingredients or equipment.

   c. All ingredients and equipment are assembled before cooking.

8–A good cook uses safety measures in the kitchen.

Here are additional reminders. Read your recipe carefully and if you are puzzled about anything, ask for help. Collect all the necessary ingredients and equipment before you start. If you plan to bake something, turn on your oven before you start your recipe. Reread all the rules given here. Watch the clock carefully if time is mentioned in your directions. Correct timing means the difference between undercooking and overcooking. Don't skip any of the directions.

THINKING IT OVER

   1. Take another look at the information and directions given in this chapter. Would you omit some? Add a few? Change the wording so that points are clearer?

   2. Do you know that an American woman named Fannie Farmer was the first person to stress the importance of accurate measurements in cooking? Have you had the experience of adding more salt or sugar to food than was necessary, or being careless about measuring the milk for a quick pudding? It can be disastrous! Taking just a bit more time and being certain that measurements are accurate and what the recipe calls for pay dividends.

   We are fortunate in America because we have so many good cookbooks. In some countries the recipe will have a direction like "a spoon of sugar." You do not know if it is a teaspoon, a cereal spoon, or a tablespoon. So you guess. This means you do not have a standard recipe, and results will vary from time to time. If you find such a recipe, the best thing to do is to experiment until you develop a corrected and accurate recipe.

Examine cookbooks at school and at home. Did recipes in which you were interested always give you the information about the number and size of servings, length of time to cook or bake, list of ingredients and measure of each, and clear directions? What kind of reputation does a cookbook have. Get opinions from persons who have used cookbooks. Are there points to consider in checking the reliability of a cookbook?

THINGS TO DO

1. Watch someone who is a very good cook while he or she is preparing food. If the cook is willing, ask questions. Now, if possible, observe other cooks. What did you learn that might help you in your own cooking? Could you have given them some advice?

2. Make a game out of seeing how many kinds of kitchen equipment you can identify in a classroom or at home.

16 Cooking the basics

Now that you have studied nutrition and the things you have to consider before cooking, you are ready to step into the kitchen or laboratory at school with extra know-how. Who knows, you may become one of the best cooks in your neighborhood!

The word *basics* has several meanings in this chapter. You will be trying and experimenting with recipes that are typical of everyday foods you eat. Secondly, each section represents foods in the Basic Four, so that you can be assured of a nutritious diet. Lastly, it is well to remember that many recipes that may appear complicated are actually adaptations of these basic recipes or combinations of these fundamental types.

KEEP THE NUTRIENTS IN

There are some general points to consider in the preparation of the milk, fruit-vegetable, meat and alternates, and cereal-food groups.

1– Do not drown a food in water during cooking, because water-soluble vitamins and some of the protein may be lost, as well as other nutrients. Use only that amount of water that will be necessary to cook the food.

2– Watch the temperature at which a food is cooked. High temperatures make protein foods tough and stringy, vitamins are lost, and the final product is not the best. Use a thermometer whenever you can, to be certain. And of course unnecessary high temperatures are a waste of energy.

3-The temperature at which foods are stored before or after cooking has an effect on their food value. Too high temperatures and too long storage are likely to result in the loss of valuable nutrients and taste. Try to eat food while it is fresh or as soon as possible after it is purchased or brought into the house from the garden.

MILK

Milk should be cooked at low temperatures to avoid a loss of nutrients. Keep it stored in the refrigerator and do not keep it for more than three days. Consider the possibilities of different kinds of milk, such as fresh, evaporated, or dried. Become familiar with the many kinds of cheeses on the market. Consider other dairy products, such as yogurt and sour cream. Milk is often neglected in the American diet. Use your ingenuity to serve milk often.

Milk in Every Meal

Milk is such an important food that you will want to include it in every meal you can. At breakfast, you will use it on your cereal and perhaps drink some. A creamed dish will add more milk. Some people like hot creamed soups for breakfast.

Skimmed dry milk solids will make a dish more nutritious. You can add several tablespoons to a glass of whole milk for greater food value. If you use vegetable juices (like tomato juice), fruit juices (like orange juice), or soft drinks (like root beer) instead of water to dissolve the milk, you will have a very tasty beverage. The fruit juices and soft drinks make it very foamy, so that your beverages will look like an ice cream soda. The juices make a pretty colored drink.

There are many interesting desserts with a milk base. You'll find it fun to eat something so

delicious knowing that you are also improving your diet. Creamed vegetables give variety to the menu. You can use a medium white sauce or cream of celery or cream of mushroom soup undiluted. Vegetables that are especially good with soup as a sauce are chopped spinach (frozen, fresh, or canned), carrots, broccoli, or cauliflower.

A few milk recipes are offered here. The tomato rabbit can be served for lunch or a light supper. You might like it for breakfast or as a hearty snack. Homemade yogurt offers an opportunity for you to experiment as well as to save money. The Pink Chiffon Pudding is an attractive, low-calorie, but highly nutritious dessert and so easy to prepare. Think of ways to vary these recipes so that they may be marked with your personal stamp.

A brother and sister are helping to prepare foods for a holiday dinner. Some of the food was frozen ahead of time.

Tasty milk beverages are an easy way to meet your milk quota.

MAIN DISHES WITH MILK

Tomato Rabbit

SERVINGS - 4, ½ cup each

1 cup Cheddar cheese, shredded or cut up
     in small pieces
1 can condensed tomato soup with ½ can
     water
⅛ teaspoon dry mustard
Crackers or toast

1. Place the cheese in the top of a double boiler.
2. Add the tomato soup and water.
3. Cook over hot water until the cheese is melted and the mixture is smooth.
4. Add the dry mustard. Mix well.
5. Serve over crackers or toast.

Experiment with different types of cheese, such as Swiss or processed cheese. Try other kinds of condensed soup, such as cream of celery, cream of shrimp, cream of chicken or pea soup. Vary the seasonings, such as dillweed, thyme, basil, chopped parsley, or chopped green pepper. Think of other bases for serving, such as corn chips, potato chips, bite-size Shredded Wheat, or other unsweetened cereals.

Homemade Yogurt

Yield: 1 quart

1 quart fresh or reconstituted nonfat dry
     milk solids (1 cup dried milk and 3¾
     cups cold water)
2 tablespoons plain yogurt (buy from the
     supermarket and use as a
     starter—should not be more
     than 3–6 days old)

1. Place the liquid milk in the top of a double boiler or a heavy saucepan (watch the temperature so that the milk does not boil) and heat it until the thermometer reaches 180°F (82°C).
2. Cool the milk mixture to 110°F (82°C) or lukewarm.
3. Mix a little of the warm milk with the yogurt and then stir it into the milk. Mix well.
4. Pour the mixture into a wide-mouthed sterile jar or into individual containers, such as cups or custard cups. Keep it well covered with plastic or foil.
5. Place it in a warm place, such as in a pan of warm water placed over the pilot light of a range or in an unheated oven. A warmed thermos bottle is another possibility. Some wrap the jar in several layers of newspaper or a clean bath towel or a piece of a blanket.
6. An important point is that the yogurt mixture *must not be disturbed* or the whey will come to the surface or separate.
7. The time of incubation of the culture depends upon the amount of starter and the maintenance of a proper temperature. Time varies but the average time is about five hours.
8. The yogurt maker and all the utensils must be kept scrupulously clean, because undesirable bacteria and germs can also grow in this warm atmosphere.
9. Refrigerate the yogurt for several hours before eating it.
10. Yogurt may be eaten plain or served with maple syrup, honey, preserves, or fresh or canned fruit. It is also delicious spooned over cereal, vegetables, meats, cooked eggs, and other foods. Added to salad dressing is another use.

Making your own yogurt can be done like a science experiment.

Yogurt should have a custardlike consistency and a slightly acid flavor. If a thick yogurt is desired, the addition of 4 tablespoons of nonfat dry milk solids to the milk mixture is helpful. This addition makes the yogurt more nutritious. There a number of opportunities for experimentation with this recipe by varying the amount of starter, the kind of milk you might use, and the ways to keep the yogurt mixture warm for incubation. Shortening the incubation period is a challenge.

DESSERTS WITH MILK

1- Experiment with instant puddings using milk. Garnish with fruit, chopped nuts, or coconut.

2- Make fancy eggnogs to serve as beverages or desserts.

3- Make puddings of crackers, bread, cake, or broken cookies covered with a custard.

4- Try gelatin desserts with custard. You may put the custard over the gelatin or the gelatin on top of the custard.

5- Prepare tapioca cream and cornstarch pudding.

6- Try fruit whips made with dried skim milk solids or evaporated milk.

Pink Chiffon Pudding

SERVINGS – 4

1 package fruit-flavored gelatin—
        strawberry, raspberry, or cherry
1 small can evaporated milk
1 teaspoon lemon juice
1 cup boiling water

1. Pour the evaporated milk into an ice-cube tray to cool.

2. Put the gelatin into a bowl. Pour the boiling water over it. Stir until dissolved. Cool.

3. When the gelatin is syrupy and beginning to set, it is time to whip the evaporated milk.

4. Place the evaporated milk in a bowl. Whip until slightly stiff. Add the lemon juice. Continue to whip until stiff.

5. Whip the gelatin with a beater until light-colored and frothy.

6. Fold in the evaporated milk. Pour into cups or molds.

7. Serve with fruit, or cold milk. This attractive dessert might also be used as a snack with an oatmeal cookie. Another variation is to use the pudding as a pie filling with a graham cracker crust.

Can You Identify These Vegetables?

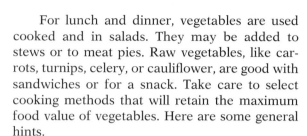

FRUITS AND VEGETABLES

These foods are important for their vitamins and minerals, as well as their fiber or bulk. From a nutritional viewpoint, it pays to include a wide variety from this group in your diet. Here are a few points to bear in mind in their preparation.

1– When fruits or vegetables are cut into small pieces, a great deal of surface is exposed and the vitamin loss will be great, unless they are used immediately. This is important to remember in preparing vegetables to cook and in cutting fruit or vegetables for salad.
2– The same can be said for shredding or grating a fruit or vegetable. Cabbage and carrots are often prepared in this way. They should be served as soon as possible.
3– Vegetables should be cooked in a small amount of water. If they are cooked in a large amount of water, many nutrients, especially vitamins, will be lost. If possible, always use the cooking water of vegetables in sauces, soups, or gravies.

How to Get Vegetables into Your Daily Meals

You may think you eat enough vegetables, but do you really? Would it be possible to make them one of your favorite foods? There are a number of ways of introducing vegetables into your meals. Vegetables are not eaten for breakfast very often, with the exception of tomato or mixed vegetable juice as a substitute for fruit juice. Remember that you need three times as much tomato juice as orange juice to get the same amount of vitamin C.

For lunch and dinner, vegetables are used cooked and in salads. They may be added to stews or to meat pies. Raw vegetables, like carrots, turnips, celery, or cauliflower, are good with sandwiches or for a snack. Take care to select cooking methods that will retain the maximum food value of vegetables. Here are some general hints.

Cooking Vegetables

1– Boil green vegetables in lightly salted water—½ teaspoon salt to 1 cup of water. The amount of water depends on the cooking time. Bring the water to a boil. Add the vegetables and cover the pan. When the water begins to boil again, reduce the heat and start to count the time. Table 16-1 is a guide on cooking time for vegetables.
2– With spinach, beet greens, and other tender leaves, the water from the last washing is sufficient. Place the leaves in the pan. Sprinkle salt over the layers. When the pan begins to steam, turn the heat low, and cook slowly so that the vegetable will not stick to the pan.
3– The tips of vegetables like asparagus and broccoli need less cooking than the stems. Stand the vegetables in a deep pan so the stems will boil in the water and the tips in the steam. Splitting stalks of broccoli will reduce cooking time and improve the appearance of the vegetable.
4– It is unnecessary to thaw frozen vegetables first. Separating into small pieces hastens the cooking. Nor is it necessary to boil the water first. Water from the tap is satisfactory. Frozen vegetables take less time than fresh vegetables, so guard against overcooking.
5– Heat canned vegetables in their own liquid.
6– Serve vegetables promptly. They lose flavor upon standing.

7–The flavor of vegetables is improved with a seasoning of butter, margarine, bacon drippings (for greens), meat drippings, or salad oil. Lemon juice is good with broccoli. A little vinegar and sugar heated together goes well with cabbage or string beans.

8–Sauces add variety to vegetables. Use about 1 cup of sauce to 4 servings of vegetable. Cheese, cream, or mustard sauce is delicious.

9–Vegetables may be baked in the oven in casseroles with sauces for a change in the menu. Lima beans and tomatoes with seasonings also make a good dish.

Here is a list of vegetables. How many do you know? In how many ways might they be prepared? With what other foods might they be served?

List of Vegetables

Artichokes	Celery	Parsnips
Asparagus	Cucumbers	Peas
Avocado	Dandelion greens	Potatoes sweet, white
Beans, green	Eggplant	Radishes
Beans, lima	Endive	Squash, winter
Beans, wax	Escarole	Squash, summer
Beets	Green peppers	Spinach
Broccoli	Lettuce	Tomatoes
Brussels sprouts	Kale	Turnips, yellow
Cabbage	Kohlrabi	Turnips, white
Carrots	Onions	Water cress
Cauliflower	Parsley	Zucchini

Table 16–1

GUIDE TO BOILING TIME FOR VEGETABLES

Vegetable	Approximate time to allow after water returns to boil	
	FRESH minutes	FROZEN minutes
Asparagus	10 to 20	5 to 10
Beans, green lima	20 to 30	6 to 10
Beans, snap	15 to 30	12 to 18
Beets	15 to 30	
Broccoli (stalks split)	10 to 20	5 to 8
Brussels sprouts	10 to 20	4 to 9
Cabbage: shredded	3 to 10	
quartered	10 to 15	
Carrots	8 to 10	3 to 6
Cauliflower	6 to 10	3 to 6
Chard	10 to 20	8 to 10
Collards	10 to 20	
Greens: beet	5 to 15	6 to 12
dandelion	10 to 20	
mustard	20 to 30	8 to 15
turnip	10 to 30	8 to 12
Kale	10 to 25	8 to 12
Okra	10 to 20	
Potatoes, small whole	15 to 20	
Peas	8 to 20	5 to 10
Spinach	3 to 10	4 to 6
Turnips, white or yellow	12 to 15	
Zucchini (Italian squash)	15 to 20	

SOURCE: Home and Garden Bulletin No. 41, U. S. Department of Agriculture

NOTE: When using a pressure saucepan for cooking green vegetables, follow the timetable that came with it.

A tasty dish can be prepared by combining a fruit with a vegetable. Here is an example:

Carrots and Apples

SERVINGS – 4

2 large carrots or 3 medium carrots
2 large cooking apples
¼ teaspoon salt
1 tablespoon butter or margarine

1. Wash and scrape the carrots. Cut them into slices, matchstick pieces, or other forms. Place them in a saucepan.
2. Barely cover the carrots with boiling water and boil.
3. While the carrots are boiling prepare the apples by washing, coring, and cutting them into rings, slices, or cubes. Peel or not as preferred but the peel does add extra fiber. Apples cook more quickly than carrots and for that reason can be added later. Add to carrots.
4. Complete cooking time from moment carrots start to boil should be about 8 to 10 minutes.
5. Test for doneness with a fork for tenderness.
6. Drain (save the water), add the butter or margarine, and serve promptly. Experiment with other combinations, such as pineapple or slices of orange instead of the apples. Try shredded cabbage or beets instead of carrots.

VEGETABLES IN SALADS

Another pleasant way to increase the use of vegetables in your diet is to include salads in your daily meals.

Points in Preparing Salads

1- All ingredients for salads should be well-chilled except for hot salads, such as hot potato salad.
2- In individual salads, do not have greens hanging over the edge of the plate.
3- Drain canned fruit and vegetables so that your salad will not be soupy.
4- Work for a simple arrangement in your salad plate. Avoid clutter.
5- Prepare salads just before serving to give them a fresh look and taste.
6- If possible, make just enough salad; leavings cannot be kept very well until the next meal.

Salads as Main Dishes

Salads may accompany a main meal, as they most often do, or may themselves be a main dish at lunch or supper.

If a salad is the main dish, be sure also to include in the meal something hot, such as soup or a hot beverage.

Dinner salads have chilled greens as their base. Greens are whatever is available on the market. Try to experiment. Don't think of lettuce as the only salad green. Fresh spinach mixed with lettuce is very green and rich-looking as well as tasty. The greens can be used alone in a

You may increase the use of vegetables in your diet by including salads in your daily meals.

To give your salads a fresh look and a fresh taste prepare them just before serving.

The nutritive value of food can be lost in many ways.

tossed salad. Tomatoes, cucumbers, radishes, celery, carrots, small pieces of cauliflower, and other vegetables are very good. A simple dressing is best because it does not hide the good vegetable flavors.

Main Dish Salads. A hearty salad for lunch may have a tossed salad as its base with such foods as slivers of chicken, ham, bologna, cold cuts, cheese, or sliced egg added. Which are your favorite salads? Have you tried a new salad lately?

Fruit is Important in Daily Meals

We have said much about the role of fruit in your meals. Indeed, fruit may be served at any meal. At breakfast, it comes to your table as fresh or canned juice, cooked, or on cereal. For lunch, fruit may be in a big salad as the main dish or as a dessert. For dinner, fruit is generally used as an appetizer or as dessert.

You probably think of fruit as something you eat from the tree in your backyard or as a snack at just about any time of the day. Fruit makes the best bedtime snack and may be used in your home in that way. How often do you eat fruit? How many kinds of fruit do you know? Do you have any new ideas for using fruit in the diet?

MEAT AND ALTERNATES

This group includes a wide range of foods. Meat, such as all cuts of fresh beef, pork, lamb, and veal; poultry, such as chicken, turkey, duck, goose, and game; and cold cuts, sausages, and canned meat are typical. Other animal sources of protein are fish, eggs, and cheese. Vegetable sources of protein are beans, peas, and nuts.

Vegetable sources of protein often lack essential amino acids. Soy beans contain more high-quality protein than other sources and are incorporated into many foods, such as meats, to stretch the food without substantially reducing the high-quality protein, and made into foods, such as soybean curd and cheese. Certain foods if eaten together *at the same time* will tend to supplement protein deficiencies. For example, rice and beans, popular in the Caribbean, in Mexico, and in Latin America, supplement each other's protein. Rice is deficient in leucine and isoleucine but beans are abundantly supplied with these essential amino acids. Wheat or corn and beans are other good combinations. Brazil nuts and sesame seeds when eaten with green vegetables make a better protein contribution than if eaten alone. A small amount of animal sources of proteins such as meat, fish, eggs, milk, and cheese will enhance the vegetable proteins.

America may have to give attention to vegetable sources of protein in the diet in light of the hungry world. More research is required to determine the amino acid content of vegetable proteins and the proportion and amounts of various foods required in supplementation. You may wish to build a file on this important subject.

A few recipes are suggested here for this food group.

Steps in preparing a skillet meal.

Meal-in-a-skillet Dinner

SERVINGS - 6

6 slices bacon
2 tablespoons reserved bacon drippings
5 frankfurters
¾ cup thinly sliced celery
¼ cup slivered green pepper
1 tablespoon flour
2 tablespoons dehydrated minced onion
½ teaspoon salt
¼ teaspoon seasoned pepper
¼ cup water
1⅔ cups undiluted evaporated milk (a large can)
1½ cups frozen green beans
1½ cups frozen corn niblets
½ cup chopped peanuts

1. Fry the bacon at low temperature, pouring off the fat as it accumulates, until the bacon is crisp. Drain it on a paper towel. Save 2 tablespoons of the fat. Crumble the bacon.
2. Slice the frankfurters into thin slices about ¼-inch thick.
3. Place the bacon drippings into the skillet in which the bacon was cooked.
4. Add the frankfurters, green pepper, and celery, and sauté until the celery is tender.
5. Add the flour, onion, seasoned pepper, and salt.
6. Gradually stir in the water and evaporated milk.
7. Add the bacon and the frozen beans and corn and simmer for about 10 minutes.
8. Add the chopped peanuts and serve when heated.

This recipe is excellent for those evenings when the family is especially hungry and does not wish to wait for a more elaborate meal to be cooked. A tossed salad and a dessert can complete the meal. There are many possible variations to this skillet meal. Omit the bacon and frankfurters and use brown-and-serve sausages. Instead of the corn, a can of macaroni and cheese may be added. Tuna is another possibility. Other vegetables may be used. Which basic four food groups are included in the original recipe? Quite nutritious, isn't it? Do some brainstorming with the family for other suggestions for a skillet meal.

Hi-pro Salad Toss

¼ cup vegetable oil
2 tablespoons vinegar
¾ teaspoon garlic salt
⅛ teaspoon chili powder
⅛ teaspoon ground black pepper
1 (20-ounce) can chick peas (drained)
1 medium green pepper, cut into thin strips
1 4-ounce can sliced pimientoes, drained
4 cups, approximately, of salad greens—
                raw spinach,
                romaine, garden
                lettuce, etc.
1 (7-ounce) can tuna
4 ounces Cheddar cheese, shredded
1 cup corn chips

1. Combine the oil, vinegar, salt, chili powder, and pepper.
2. Arrange the chick peas, green pepper, and pimientoes in a shallow dish.
3. Pour dressing over these ingredients.
4. Cover and chill for several hours or overnight. Drain. Save the dressing.
5. Before serving, place the shredded salad greens in a salad bowl.
6. Scatter the crushed corn chips over the salad greens.
7. Place the tuna and corn chips in the center of the salad greens.
8. Arrange the chick peas, green pepper, and pimientoes in circles around the edge of the bowl and toward the center.
9. Pour the salad dressing over the salad.
10. Sprinkle the cheese over the tuna.
11. Toss the salad just before serving.

A nutritious salad that can be a main protein dish at lunch or dinner.

nutrients like iron (if fortified) and the B vitamins that are difficult to find in some of the other groups.

A few suggestions for recipes are offered here.

Identify the foods in this salad that would contribute to your day's allowance of protein. Are there certain ingredients whose protein supplements that found in other ingredients? Think of variations of this salad. Other types of beans, such as pinto or kidney beans, might replace the chick peas. Canned salmon, mackerel, or sardines may replace the tuna.

BREADS AND CEREALS

Yeast breads, quick breads, crackers, cooked cereals, ready-to-eat cereals, and macaroni, spaghetti, and other types of pasta are among the foods included in this group. These foods carry

My Granola

YIELD - 7 cups

2½ cups rolled oats
1 cup shredded coconut
½ cup nuts (almonds, filberts, pecans, walnuts, or others)
½ cup sesame seeds
½ cup wheat germ
⅓ cup cooking oil
½ cup chopped dried apricots
½ cup chopped dates
½ cup raisins
2 tablespoons vanilla

1. In a large bowl mix the rolled oats, coconut, nuts, and wheat germ.
2. Stir the oil into the mixture.
3. Spread evenly in a shallow pan, 13x9x2 inches.

4. Bake in a 325 degree oven for 45–50 minutes, stirring every 15 minutes.
5. Remove from the oven and mix in the dried fruit and the vanilla.
6. Place in another pan to cool, stirring occasionally to prevent lumping.
7. When cool, store in tightly covered jars or in plastic bags.
8. Granola will keep for two weeks and if total amount will not be consumed by that time, freeze some for later use.

Granola can be used as a breakfast cereal, as a snack, for stuffing poultry, as an ingredient in candy, cakes, and breads, and in countless other ways. What do you suggest? Consider possible adaptations of this recipe. Look at the ingredients on a package of granola in the store. Any ideas for your own recipe? How does the cost of the package compare with that of your recipe?

French Toast

SERVINGS - 6-8

3 eggs, beaten slightly
½ teaspoon salt
1 teaspoon sugar
1 cup milk
6-8 slices bread (2–3 days old)
1 tablespoon fat for frying

1. Combine the eggs, salt, sugar, and milk in a shallow dish.
2. Dip the bread into the egg mixture to moisten it.
3. Brown it on one side on a well-greased griddle or frying pan. Turn and brown it on the other side. Add extra fat to keep it from sticking, if necessary.

Serve this with syrup, jam, honey, confectioner's sugar, or sliced fresh, frozen, or canned fruit. For variation spread two thin slices of bread with cranberry jelly, cheese spread, or deviled ham before dipping the bread into the egg mixture. Brown it as in the recipe. The cranberry jelly French toast goes well with creamed chicken or creamed ham.

Cooking can be fun when you learn to prepare tasty foods that are also nutritious.

THINKING IT OVER

Think about your resources for becoming a good cook, such as available equipment, encouragement of others, sources for recipes, and the like. What is the status of your resources? What can you do about it?

THINGS TO DO

1. Make an analysis of your food likes and dislikes within the Basic Four Food Groups. Could you find and prepare some recipes of a group or groups of food that you are neglecting that might improve your rating?

2. Would you be interested in encouraging someone younger to cook? What might be some beginning recipes? How would you teach? What should be emphasized? How would you check on your degree of success?

3. Look at labels for soybean additions, such as labels on ground-meat products, imitation bacon, and packages of soybean extender. Try extender in an experiment. Prepare your meat loaf recipe in the usual way. Divide into two equal parts. Add the correct amount of soybean extender to one part. Place it in same pan side by side with the other part and bake. Now have your family taste-test at the table when you give them a sample of each type. Set up criteria for judging, such as appearance, flavor, juiciness, and other characteristics. Does the soybean extender make a difference in your cost and number of servings?

17 Becoming a meal planning expert

Now that you are cooking more and more, you are ready to put all your best recipes into a meal. You will become a meal planner. Doesn't that sound businesslike? And actually it is business. A meal can be costly unless you plan well. If you plan nutritious meals, health may be improved and doctor bills saved. More and more people are eating at home rather than eating out because it costs less. So your services as a meal planner are needed.

Here are some ideas to consider in the preliminary steps of your planning.

POINTS IN PLANNING MEALS

1–Use of recipes

a. Consider the number of servings, length of time for preparation, kind of ingredients, equipment needed, changes to be made in the recipe, and best ways to follow the directions.

2–Type of food to be prepared

a. Will mixes and ready-prepared food be used or will food be prepared at home?

3–Characteristics of your family

a. What they like and dislike in foods

b. Religious and national background

c. Amount of money you have to spend on food

d. Where you live
4–Effect of season of the year
5–Menu
  a. Avoid repetition.
  b. Pay attention to color, texture, and shape.
  c. Serve foods that are simple but well prepared.
  d. Use foods in season.

PREPARING LUNCH ON SATURDAY

Suppose we start with lunch on Saturday. There are many things you will have to think about before you start to cook. For instance, is Saturday lunch a hearty meal because the family has been busy all morning? Perhaps everyone in your family has been doing chores such as cleaning house, working in the garden, or doing some repair work on the house or in the apartment. On the other hand, Saturday may be a lazy day at your house. Everyone may sleep late and not be very hungry when lunchtime arrives. Your Saturdays may vary from busy to lazy days and you will want to plan accordingly.

If it is a day when everyone will be very hungry, plan for a meal with plenty of food. You might plan a number of menus using the following patterns as a guide. Check on nutritional factors to consider in planning meals, as given in Chapter 11.

Menu

1–Main dish, such as baked beans and franks, hamburgers and casserole dishes
2–A cooked vegetable and a salad, or a large salad, especially if the main dish includes vegetables in the recipe
3–Some kind of bread or roll
4–Some kind of dessert, such as fruit, a simple pudding, or ice cream from your freezer
5–Some kind of beverage, like milk, fruit or vegetable juice, or tea or coffee for your parents

Menu

For a lighter meal, the following plan might be adapted:
1–Main dish, which might be a sandwich or a salad. The salad might be fruit or vegetable, in which case crackers and cheese or a fish or meat sandwich might be served with it. If the salad has meat, fish, or cheese in it, plain toast or crackers might be served.
2–A beverage such as a milkshake or iced tea will be served.
3–Dessert is optional.

Planning Menus

Suppose we plan a menu and follow through the necessary steps in preparing this lunch. Here is a simple meal that would be easy to prepare:

MENU
TUNA-NUT CASSEROLE
FRENCH BREAD OR ROLLS
CABBAGE AND CARROT SALAD
SLICED BANANAS AND BROWN SUGAR
MILK

This hearty meal may be eaten indoors or outdoors.

A light lunch.

Get Your Recipes

The first step is to collect your recipes. Since you will buy the bread and the bananas, you will need recipes for the casserole and salad. Following are the recipes.

Tuna-Nut Casserole

SERVINGS – 6 small or 4 large
TEMPERATURE – 325 degrees F
BAKING TIME – 30 minutes

1 cup dry cereal, corn or wheat flakes
1 can condensed cream of mushroom
        soup, undiluted
1 can chunk-size tuna (1 cup)
1/2 cup peanuts, salted or unsalted
1 cup diced celery
1/4 cup minced onion or 1 tbsp. onion
        flakes
1/2 tsp. salt, if nuts not salted
Dash of pepper

1. Collect all the ingredients and equipment needed.
2. Heat the oven.
3. Set aside ½ cup of the dry cereal for the topping.
4. Place a layer of cereal in a well-buttered casserole.
5. Alternate layers of tuna, celery, nuts, and soup with the cereal.
6. Cover with remaining cereal and bake.

This casserole may be prepared in individual casserole dishes and baked for 20 minutes. Canned salmon or other cooked fish may be substituted for tuna.

Cabbage and Carrot Salad

SERVINGS – 6

2 cups cabbage, shredded
1 cup carrots, shredded
1/3 cup mayonnaise
1 tablespoon lemon juice or vinegar
1/2 teaspoon sugar
Dash celery salt, if desired

1. Shred the cabbage and carrots on a grater into a bowl. You might use the coarse plate on a food grinder and grind the cabbage and carrots. The vegetables are more attractive when grated, but the food chopper saves time.
2. Combine the mayonnaise, lemon juice, and celery salt.
3. Mix with the carrots and cabbage until well combined.
4. Serve on lettuce or other salad green for individual salads. If you wish to save on dishes, place the salad in a large bowl and let the family serve themselves.
5. Sprinkling paprika or chopped parsley on the salad before serving will make it look more attractive.

Check Your Supplies

After you have become familiar with your recipes, check on your supplies. For this menu you will need the following list:

dry cereal	lemon juice or
tuna	vinegar
peanuts	lettuce or salad
celery	greens
onion or onion flakes	bananas
salt and pepper	brown sugar
cabbage	milk
carrots	French bread
mayonnaise	butter or margarine

Look in the cupboard and other places where you keep supplies. Place a check after the supplies you have on hand. Then see what is left. Those items will have to be purchased.

Make Out Your Market Order

A good way to make up your market list is to group together articles that will be found in the same area in the grocery store. Here is what the market order for this meal might be like:

> 1 package salted peanuts
> 2 quarts milk
> 1 loaf French bread
> 6 bananas

A Schedule Is Important

Any job worth doing requires a schedule. This should include plans for marketing, preparation, serving, and clean-up. Here is a suggested form. See if you can improve on this idea.

Steps in Planning a Meal

1. Plan your menu.

2. Get your recipes.

3. Check your supplies.

4. Make market list and shop.

5. Plan your service.

6. Make a schedule for preparation.

7. Serve the meal.

8. Clean up.

9. Rate yourself.

153

Cornbread on top of chili makes a good meat pie.

My Time Plan

For Marketing

1- Get to the store early.
2- Bring the groceries home; put the milk into the refrigerator.

For Preparation

TIME - 1 hour

1- Get out all the supplies and equipment needed for cooking. Look at the recipes for clues.
2- Light the oven.
3- Prepare the casserole. Read the recipe carefully.
4- Prepare the salad and put it into the refrigerator.
5- Set the table with napkins, place mats, dishes, and silver.
6- Place the French bread in the oven to heat.
7- Slice the bananas. Sprinkle them with brown sugar. Place them in the refrigerator.
8- Pour the water.
9- Pour the milk.
10- Place the casserole and the salad on the table.
11- Take the bread from the oven and cut into slices. Serve.
12- Call the family for lunch.

As you prepare the lunch, keep track of your time by jotting down how long it takes you to do each job. This will help you when planning such jobs in the future. Were you able to prepare this meal within an hour or longer? What would you do differently next time?

How to Serve Lunch

The service of the meal will need consideration. Answer these questions:

1- How will the casserole be served at the table? Since it is a very hot dish, it would not be wise to pass it around. Should Mother or Father serve? Since you prepared it maybe you would like to serve it on the plates. There may be times when your sister or brother might like to have the privilege of serving. You will have to decide this with your family.
2- As was suggested in the recipe, the salad may be placed in a large bowl, or in individual plates or bowls. How will you serve it? You might like to serve it on plates at the table.
3- Will you put the bananas at each place at the beginning of the meal, in keeping with its informality, or will you clear the table of the main course and then serve the bananas? Some of your family might like to have milk or cream on the bananas. You must plan for this.

A help-yourself salad meal is always good. Make combinations of salad ingredients and serve with a variety of breads.

4-What will you do about the glasses of milk? Will you pour them ahead of time and place them on the table or provide a pitcher and let everyone pour his or her own? A pitcher is a good idea because your older brother might like to have seconds.

It will be helpful to listen to the comments of your family. Did they like the meal? Although your family may be proud of the lunch you have prepared, they are not interested in any fancy service. They may have other things to do and want to eat as fast as they can. You may have to adjust your service to these needs.

Cleaning Up After a Meal

Members of your family may be willing to help you clean up. If everyone gives a hand and takes food and dishes from the table, it will save you many steps.

Planning Other Lunches

Once you have established a routine you will be able to plan and prepare other meals for your family. Some suggestions for the main dish follow.

Beans and Franks

SERVINGS - 4
TEMPERATURE - 350 degrees F
TIME - 20 minutes

1 one-lb. can baked beans in tomato sauce
1 lb. franks
1/4 tsp. dry mustard or 1 tsp. prepared mustard

1. Start heating the oven to 350 degrees F.
2. Combine the beans and mustard in a 1½-qt. casserole.
3. Arrange the franks on top, putting some of them under the beans.
4. Bake for 20 minutes.

A nice variation is to sprinkle with sharp cheese before putting in the oven.

With this main dish you might serve a tossed salad, cinnamon buns, and milk.

Another interesting main dish is made with hamburger. Here is the recipe.

Hamburger Corn Bake

SERVINGS - 6
TEMPERATURE - 350 degrees F
TIME - 25 minutes

11/2 lbs. ground chuck
2 tablespoons oil or bacon fat
1 No. 2 can whole corn
1/2 cup chopped green pepper
1 No. 2 can tomatoes
1/3 cup chopped onion
1 teaspoon salt
1 package corn muffin mix

1. Heat the oven to 350 degrees F.
2. Place the oil or fat in a skillet which can be placed in the oven later.
3. Brown the ground chuck in the hot fat. Stir well.
4. Add the green pepper, tomatoes, corn, onion, and salt.
5. Prepare the corn muffin mix according to the directions for cornbread on the box.
6. Pour the batter over the meat and vegetable mixture.
7. Put in the oven and bake for 25 minutes.
8. Serve the hamburger in pie-shaped wedges.

With this main dish serve a plate of carrot strips, celery curls, pieces of raw cauliflower, or whatever raw vegetable you have on hand. A milk frostie (see page 338) is good with this meal, serving as both beverage and dessert.

Ideas for Menus

The following suggestions are offered to help you in planning interesting lunches on other days for your family. You may make any combinations you desire.

Keep your eyes and ears open for luncheon ideas. The cookbooks at home will stimulate you. You might like to try some of the dishes served in the school cafeteria. Exchange recipes with your friends.

Table 17-1

Table 17-1

IDEAS FOR LUNCH OR LIGHT SUPPER MENUS

MAIN DISH	SALAD	DESSERT	BEVERAGE
Leftover ham heated in cream of mushroom soup	Fruit salad	–	Ginger ale
Spaghetti and meatballs	Lettuce salad	Cookies	Milk
Spanish rice	Lettuce-cottage cheese salad	Sherbet	Coffee and milk
Hamburgers, potato chips	Apple-cabbage salad	Cup cakes	Milkshake
Thick vegetable soup with cheese, crackers	Tomato salad	Ice cream float	–
Toasted cheese sandwiches	Sliced orange-banana salad	Brownies	Milk
Tuna fish salad on crisp rolls, cream of celery soup	–	Sliced peaches	Hot cocoa
Cold meat loaf sandwich	Lettuce-tomato	Fresh fruit	Milk
Peanut butter and cottage cheese sandwich	Pickled beets	Grapes	Buttermilk

SUNDAY BREAKFAST OR BRUNCH

Another meal that is equal to your abilities is Sunday breakfast or brunch. Again, the type of meal varies with the habits of your family. If you are early risers, you prefer to have breakfast; if you like to sleep late, you probably have brunch. Brunch is a word coined from combining breakfast and lunch. The differences between breakfast and brunch are slight. For instance, fruit is sometimes served for dessert at brunch instead of at the beginning of the meal. Dishes that are suitable for lunch may be served for brunch. Suppose we take a simple menu pattern and see how you might change it from a breakfast menu to a brunch menu.

For fruit juice you might use fresh, frozen, or canned orange, tomato, grapefruit, or tangerine juice. For variety you might combine some of the fruit juices, such as orange and grapefruit juices. Sliced banana with orange juice poured over it is also a pleasant change. Fresh fruits in season, such as sliced peaches,

Breakfast Menu

**FRUIT IN SEASON OR FRUIT JUICE
DRY CEREAL IF FAMILY SO DESIRES
EGG OR MEAT DISH
BREAKFAST BREADS
COFFEE FOR YOUR PARENTS
MILK FOR YOU**

strawberries, or other types of berries, and different kinds of melon are very popular. Your family may have other preferences.

For bread you might use toast, rolls baked by your mother and put in the freezer, cinnamon buns, or hot biscuits or muffins. Some members

Waffles may be served with a variety of toppings.

Fruit added to dry cereal improves the taste and also adds to the nutritional value.

A Simple Breakfast Menu. With this pattern in mind, let us plan a simple breakfast menu that your family might enjoy. Here is a suggestion for you.

Breakfast Menu

GRAPEFRUIT AND PINEAPPLE JUICES
ASSORTED DRY CEREALS
SCRAMBLED EGGS
COFFEECAKE
COFFEE AND MILK

Look over your menu and decide whether you can do any preparation the night before. You might choose the cereals you will serve. The mats you plan to use on the table might be selected. Check to see that the fruit juice is placed in the refrigerator.

The next morning you will heat the coffee-cake in the oven and place the cereals on the table. Do not cook the eggs until your family is ready to eat. The eggs can be cooked while the juice and cereal are being eaten. If it is family custom to have everyone sitting at the table during breakfast, you might cook the eggs last and then put them in a covered vegetable dish or casserole to keep them hot. Your mother might make the coffee for you this time, but you will want to learn so that you can prepare it for your family the next time.

If your family likes to have brunch, the menu may be the same or you might like to make some changes. Some family members are not interested in cereal for brunch. Often the family will drink the fruit juice first or have a dish of fresh fruit at the close of the meal. To make the scrambled eggs more substantial and tastier, you might add grated cheese, diced bologna, or bits of bacon or ham. Serving the scrambled eggs over hot split frankfurters or with sausage will also make them more appealing.

of your family might like jam, marmalade, or some other type of spread with their bread. Honey is also very tasty.

There are many main dishes from which you may choose. Eggs in some form are eaten in most homes. Eggs can be fried, soft-cooked, hard-cooked, poached, scrambled, baked, or made into an omelet. If hard-cooked, they may be sliced or diced and served in a sauce. Undiluted canned soup or a white sauce may be used. Which kind of eggs does your family like best?

The most common beverage for breakfast is coffee, although tea is served in many homes. Hot milk or cocoa are served occasionally.

Scrambled Eggs

SERVINGS – 4

6 eggs
4 tablespoons milk
1/2 teaspoon salt
1/2 tablespoon butter or margarine

1. Break the eggs into a mixing bowl.
2. Beat the eggs with a fork until the whites and yolks are well mixed.
3. Add milk and salt. Then stir very well.
4. Place the butter or margarine in a skillet and melt it.
5. When the butter or margarine is melted, pour in the eggs you have just stirred.
6. Keep stirring with a wooden spoon. Keep scraping the bottom and sides of the skillet.
7. The eggs are done when they are firm, but still fairly soft and creamy. Don't let them get hard and watery: then they are too well done.
8. Divide the eggs into four servings. Put them on warm plates. Serve at once—nobody likes cold eggs!

Some ways to serve eggs for brunch.

SERVING AT ALL HOURS

In some families members arise at different hours. This may mean serving breakfast at different times. It would be helpful of you to offer to take over this responsibility whenever other family members ask to be relieved. In such circumstances, you would have to cook each one's eggs when that person is ready for them. Perhaps some other type of preparation, such as soft-cooking, frying, or hard-cooking would be more suitable.

During vacations you might be responsible for the family breakfast during the week. The same may be true for lunches. By helping at first, you will be able to take on more and more responsibility.

THINKING IT OVER

1. Think about ways in which breakfast can be a good starter for the day. Think not only of the food you eat but also of your attitudes about eating breakfast, and the kind of person you are early in the morning.

2. Think of the different ages of the members of your family. How does age influence what a person eats? Plan some breakfast menus that might be adapted to different ages.

THINGS TO DO

1. Plan food you can carry easily for an early morning hike. How will you take into account ease of preparation, toting, and the amount of food needed for a healthy appetite? Adapt the menu to the fact that no cooking will take place.

2. Plan breakfast menus that vary in cost from very inexpensive to very costly. Which foods make a breakfast expensive?

18 Buying food

Do you ever wonder how you might help your family during those periods when money is tight? You might be able to make suggestions as to ways to save on feeding the family. Lightening the family food budget from some of its stress and strain will be welcomed. Because food is purchased so often, the benefits of savings are quickly evident. So help to recognize bargains that are really bargains. It can be fun to be a sleuth in the supermarket!

INFLUENCES ON YOUR SHOPPING

Before you make out your shopping list you must come to grips with certain facts. How much money is there to spend? This will vary from family to family, not only on an income basis but on the basis of your family food preferences. Is your family of the gourmet food type? You would have to run around to specialty shops buying unusual foods and those of exceptionally high quality. Obviously, you would spend considerable money. Maybe your family uses food stamps and you have to plan carefully to have enough food to eat. Your family may be insistent on only one type of food. For example, your father or some other member of your family may want expensive cuts of meat like steaks, chops, and roasts. Someone else may eat only the bread from a special bakery. Your family may be the type that eats a wide variety of foods and is quite flexible about making changes, if necessary.

Another factor is the size of your family. If your family is small you may have difficulty in getting packages with the right number of servings. If your family is large, you will wish to look at large containers and other possibilities of buying in larger quantities.

Age is important. Is there a baby in your family that requires baby foods? Does one of your grandparents live with you and has special food requirements? Is someone in your family on a modified diet and cannot have salt or sugar, or has other limitations because of allergies to certain foods? All these points must be considered.

The activities of your family will determine amounts of food. If you and other members of the family are involved in sports you will need more food because of the exercise. You and others are growing and need plenty of nutritious food. The work of family members is a consideration. If members of the family eat at different hours, you may have to buy food that will hold up for long dinner hours, or you may have to pack lunches. If your family entertains a great deal, refreshments will have to be added to the shopping list or extra foods for meals. What are other influences, particularly for your family?

Advertising

Have you ever thought about the number of food advertisements to which you are exposed every day? You see them in the newspaper and the magazines you read, see them on television, hear them on the radio, and see them in the windows of supermarkets or when you ride on the bus. How do they affect you? Have you ever bought something because you saw the advertisement? Advertising can be helpful in comparing prices among stores, in learning about new foods, and in getting information about specials that stores may have. Sometimes advertisements in newspapers or magazines offer free booklets on recipes and cooking tips, as well as

Think about the ways in which advertisements reach you.

nutrition information. Are there other ways in which advertising can be helpful to you? Of course, you pay for the advertising of products you buy.

There may be some adverse effects of advertising. Perhaps your younger sister or brother insists on a certain cereal because it was advertised on television. The cereal may not be the best nutritionally and it may not be the best buy for the family food budget. Advertising makes foods very attractive and may encourage you to buy when it is not to your advantage. Has this happened to you?

Labeling

One of the important parts of shopping is reading the label. You will wish to be informed about the information you can expect on a label before you start to shop. Mandatory information

Make a list of what you plan to buy before shopping.

on any label includes the name of the food, ingredients, net contents in common units of measure by weight or volume, and name and address of packer, manufacturer, or distributor. If meat or poultry is shipped across state lines, the product must have the circular mark of inspection of the U.S. Department of Agriculture.

There are aspects of label protection for the consumer. The label must be easily read and un-

Here are a few of the influences you need to consider in making a grocery list.

derstood. Imitations must be prominently marked. Ingredients must be listed in the order of predominance. If water is listed first on a can of stew, there is more water than any other ingredient. If the ingredients of a food are not listed, the product meets the standard of identity (that is, it contains standard ingredients regardless of brand, as established by the Food and Drug Administration) and listing is not required. This may be true, for example, of a loaf of white bread. The container must not be misleading, such as looking larger than it is. Any type of enrichment must be definitely stated in terms of units, milligrams, or appropriate measure for the nutrient and it is inadequate to state "meets one-third of the daily dietary requirements."

Are you buying chicken and vegetables or vegetables and chicken?

Nutritional Labeling

In addition to the above information, many cans or packages will have nutritional labeling. This labeling is voluntary for most foods but if a nutrient is added to any product, even to replace those lost in processing, or if a nutritional claim is made about a food in the labeling or in an advertisement, that product's label must have nutritional labeling. For example, if any reference is made to calories, protein, fat, carbohydrate, vitamins, minerals, or use in dieting, the label must contain complete nutrition information. Foods that are sold as "enriched" or "fortified" must contain complete information about nutrition.

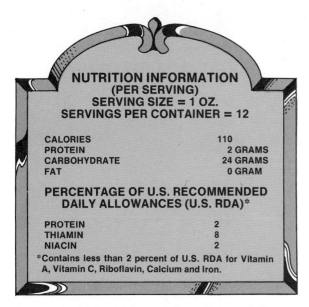

NUTRITION INFORMATION
(PER SERVING)
SERVING SIZE = 1 OZ.
SERVINGS PER CONTAINER = 12

CALORIES	110
PROTEIN	2 GRAMS
CARBOHYDRATE	24 GRAMS
FAT	0 GRAM

PERCENTAGE OF U.S. RECOMMENDED
DAILY ALLOWANCES (U.S. RDA)*

PROTEIN	2
THIAMIN	8
NIACIN	2

*Contains less than 2 percent of U.S. RDA for Vitamin A, Vitamin C, Riboflavin, Calcium and Iron.

An example of the minimum information a nutrition label must have.

Regulations for nutrition labeling by the Food and Drug Administration include following this standard format: serving size or portion, for example, 1 ounce dry cereal or 1 cup milk; servings per container, such as 4 servings for 1 quart of milk; caloric content or calories; protein, carbohydrate, and fat to the nearest gram and the percentage of U.S. Recommended Dietary Allowances (U.S. RDA).

To understand nutritional labeling fully, you will have to wade into the metric system. Grams are a smaller unit of measurement than ounces. Many food components are present in small amounts, and others will demand even smaller units of measurement.

The metric system is a base-10 or decimal system of weights and measures. The base unit for weight or mass is the gram. Certain prefixes must be identified. *Milli-* is 0.0001 or 1/1000, so a milligram is 1/1000th of a gram. *Kilo-* is 1000, so a kilogram is equivalent to 1000 grams. On the next page are a metric table and an equivalency table that will be helpful in reading nutritional labels.

U.S. RDA

The U.S. RDA are based on the 1968 Recommended Daily Dietary Allowances of the Food and Nutrition Board of the National Research Council. The lower part of the nutrition panel gives the percentage of the U.S. RDA of the mandatory nutrients: protein, vitamin A, vitamin C, thiamin, riboflavin, niacin, and iron. Other nutrients are optional. Listing of nutrients that appear naturally in a food is optional, but it is mandatory if they have been added to the food. Other optional listings include the amount of sodium, fatty acids, or cholesterol. This information is helpful if any members of your family have to restrict these substances on a physician's advice.

The differences between U.S. RDA and RDA must be clarified. The U.S. RDA (Table 18-3) is a set of standards proposed by the Food and Drug Administration for use in the regulation of nutritional labeling. The RDA provide standards that "encourage the development of food habits by the population of United States that will allow for maximum dividends in the maintenance and promotion of health." This is the goal stated by the Food and Nutrition Board of the National Research Council, which establishes these standards approximately every five years. See Table 11-5 for a table of the RDA.

The U.S. RDA are derived from the 1968 Recommended Daily Dietary Allowances, based however on broad age groups from children over 4 years of age through female and male adults but not including RDA for pregnancy and lactation. For most nutrients the highest RDA for any sex-age category was selected to be the U.S. RDA for each nutrient. Thus, a diet meeting the U.S. RDA would also meet the RDA for most persons in a family or in the population. The U.S.

A label may include optional listings for cholesterol, fats, and sodium.

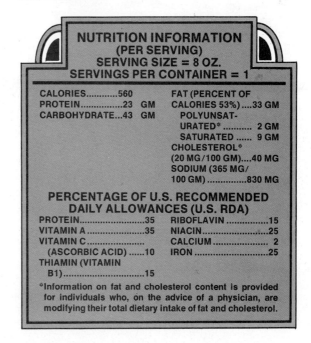

NUTRITION INFORMATION
(PER SERVING)
SERVING SIZE = 8 OZ.
SERVINGS PER CONTAINER = 1

CALORIES............560		
PROTEIN............23 GM	FAT (PERCENT OF	
CARBOHYDRATE...43 GM	CALORIES 53%)....33 GM	
	POLYUNSAT-	
	URATED* .... 2 GM	
	SATURATED ...... 9 GM	
	CHOLESTEROL*	
	(20 MG/100 GM)....40 MG	
	SODIUM (365 MG/	
	100 GM) ....830 MG	

PERCENTAGE OF U.S. RECOMMENDED
DAILY ALLOWANCES (U.S. RDA)

PROTEIN........................35	RIBOFLAVIN 15
VITAMIN A 35	NIACIN.......................25
VITAMIN C....................	CALCIUM 2
(ASCORBIC ACID) 10	IRON 25
THIAMIN (VITAMIN	
B1)..............................15	

*Information on fat and cholesterol content is provided for individuals who, on the advice of a physician, are modifying their total dietary intake of fat and cholesterol.

The Metric System

length

temperature

volume

mass

Table 18-1

METRIC TABLE

1 kilogram (kg)	= 1000 grams (g)
1 gram (g)	= 1000 milligrams (mg)
1 milligram (mg)	= 1000 micrograms (μ)
1 liter (l)	= 1000 cubic centimeters (cc or c³) or 1000 milliliters (ml)

Table 18-2

EQUIVALENCY TABLE

1 pound (lb)	= 454 grams (g) or 0.45 kilogram (kg)
1 ounce (oz)	= 28 grams (g)
1 quart (qt)	= 0.95 liter (l)
1 cup (c)	= ¼ liter (l) or 250 milliliters (ml)
1 tablespoon (T)	= 14.8 milliliters (ml)
1 teaspoon (t)	= 4.9 milliliters (ml)

Vitamins are generally measured in international units (IU), micrograms (μg), or milligrams (mg)

RDA on nutritional labels are mandatory for those nutrients indicated previously. The reason for these limitations is that it would be impossible to list all the RDA's for both sexes at all age levels on the label of most food packages. Compare the nutrients listed in the RDA table 11-5 and the U.S. RDA table 18-3. Now look at the illustration of a food label and note the placing of U.S. RDA on it. Having this information can be quite helpful in your buying of food.

The Food and Drug Administration has established other regulations that will be helpful to you in your shopping. The basic nature of the food or its characterizing properties or its ingredients must be stated in accurate, simple, and direct terms. This affects, among others, seafood cocktail, in which ingredients must be identified; crabmeat in which the species of crab must be indicated; and diluted orange beverages in which the content of orange juice to the nearest 5 percent must be stated and the name must indicate dilution of orange juice.

Another confusing area that has been clarified is the content of "heat and serve" dinners. There must be one or more sources of protein, to be derived from meat, fish, poultry, cheese or eggs. These sources, exclusive of gravy or sauce, must supply 70 percent of the total protein in the dinner. Secondly, one or more vegetables or vegetable mixtures, other than potatoes, rice, or cereal-based product, must be included. The third requirement is that the dinner contain rice, potatoes, or cereal-based product. You might check labels to determine whether these rules have been followed.

Nutritional labeling is very helpful but you must remember that certain nutrients, such as phosphorus and zinc, have not been included in the U.S. RDA, although they are considered in the Recommended Daily Dietary Allowances (see Table 11–5). Everyone is urged to eat a wide variety of foods including generous amounts of whole foods, such as milk, fruits, vegetables, eggs, whole-grain cereals, and some meat, to be certain of meeting all nutrient essentials. A high proportion of refined and imitation foods may lack nutrients. It will take some practice to identify all the information on a label, but if you want to know what you are eating, this is the only way.

FOOD SAFETY

There are a number of factors that affect the safety of the food we eat. Many people are sus-

Table 18-3

U. S. RECOMMENDED DAILY ALLOWANCES (U.S.RDA)*

(for use in nutrition labeling of foods, including foods that also are vitamin and mineral supplements)

	Adults and Children Over 4 yrs	Infants and Children Under 4 yrs of age
Protein	65 g[a]	28 g[a]
Vitamin A	5,000 IU	2,500 IU
Vitamin C	60 mg	40 mg
Thiamin	1.5 mg	0.7 mg
Riboflavin	1.7 mg	0.8 mg
Niacin	20 mg	9.0 mg
Calcium	1.0 g	0.8 g
Iron	18 mg	10 mg
Vitamin D	400 IU	400 IU
Vitamin E	30 IU	10 IU
Vitamin B_6	2.0 mg	0.7 mg
Folacin	0.4 mg	0.2 mg
Vitamin B_{12}	6 mcg	3 mcg
Phosphorus	1.0 g	0.8 g
Iodine	150 mcg	70 mcg
Magnesium	400 mg	200 mg
Zinc	15 mg	8.0 mg
Copper	2 mg	1.0 mg
Biotin	0.3 mg	0.15 mg
Pantothenic Acid	10 mg	5 mg

[a] If protein efficiency ratio of protein is equal to or better than that of casein, U.S.RDA is 45 g for adults and 20 g for infants.

*This table lists the U.S. RDA's for vitamins and minerals in the order in which they appear on nutrition labels.

SOURCE: FDA Consumer Memo, DHEW Publication No. (FDA) 73-2042, Public Health Service, Food and Drug Administration, Rockville, Md., 1973, p.2.

Check any purchase of a heat-and-serve dinner to be certain that it contains an adequate amount of a protein food, a vegetable or vegetables, and a starch food, such as potatoes, rice, or a cereal-based food.

picious of food additives. Many food additives actually improve a food. Think of the many foods that would be less tasty if no salt had been added. Sodium and calcium propionate are used in bread and wrapped cheese to prevent mold. If we made these products at home, this addition would be unnecessary, but food has to be transported and shelved. Lecithin is a vegetable emulsifier manufactured from soybeans that is used to make foods smoother and creamier. Other additives are used to improve color, flavor, texture, and keeping qualities. Many of our packaged foods could not be produced without additives. Artificial sweeteners, added bulk, or nonnutritive ingredients must be declared on the label.

The Food and Drug Administration is charged with the responsibility of determining whether an additive is harmful. The tests are long and tedious, and usually consist of animal experiments. It is not always the additives that are deliberately added to foods, many of which are harmless, but rather the residue from fertilizers, pesticides, and other additions made in the processing that may be dangerous. One question

that has been raised recently is the safety of the water added to so many of our foods. When you buy food in a store you must remember that the food has passed through many hands and possibly machines. Considering the complex system required to feed our nation, it must be admitted that we have not suffered from broad national epidemics or illnesses. That does not mean that we should relax—consumers must always be vigilant about food and its safety.

KINDS OF STORES

Where do you buy your food? This will reveal to a large extent how much you spend for food. If you buy at a small neighborhood store because they speak a foreign language or because you know the owners well or because they deliver, the food will be more expensive. They may offer special services but your family and you may ask yourselves if you can really afford them. You may buy from specialty shops, such as a bakery, a fruit and vegetable store, a meat market, or a fish shop. Again, it is well to compare prices to determine how much you are paying for the food. Sometimes you buy at a store that has the foods of your ethnic group. Some food of that nature may be important psychologically but perhaps you can buy staples in a less expensive place. If there is a delicatessen counter in your supermarket or a "deli" in your neighborhood where you can buy many prepared foods, such as potato salad, cold cuts, and other personal preferences, the cost may be higher. There may be emergencies when this service is helpful, but ask yourself what is to be given up if the prices are much higher for this service.

BEFORE YOU SHOP

There are some jobs that have to be done before you go shopping—in other words, more homework. This means reading all the food ads in your newspaper. Listen to shopping advice on television and radio. Sometimes relatives and friends will tell you about good buys.

A shopping list is a "must" because it helps you to stay within your budget and balance costly foods against less costly foods. Counting the foods you have at home on shelves and in the refrigerator or freezer and what you have on the list, how well are the Basic Four Food Groups represented? Have you indicated the amounts to be purchased? Sometimes more is

If you were to read the ingredients in a sugar-cured ham, the list would be a very long one with not a synthetic chemical in the lot. But the list is frightening when you read it. That is because you do not know the meaning of the words. Of course there are some additives in foods about which there is a question, but you will be reading about them and can identify them quickly.

If your family is Italian, you may buy some of your food in a store that has Italian foods. Are these foods more expensive than the ones you buy in a supermarket?

purchased than is needed. With perishable goods, this can mean a loss of money. Dinners are usually planned around the meat or protein dish. so consider what else is to be served. Plan for alternatives for all of them in the event that they are not available. If possible, arrange your list according to the departments in the store to save steps. Place dairy products, frozen foods, meats, and other perishable foods at the bottom of the list to buy last.

WHAT TO DO IN THE SUPERMARKET

Stick to your list to avoid impulse buying. Use the cost per serving as a buying guide. Compare prices of established brand names with supermarket labels. Compare package sizes by weight. Determine whether convenience foods are worth the cost and saving of time. Read the labels. Do not let a stock display fool you. The item may not be on sale. Keep in mind prices of food from week to week to determine whether prices are higher or lower.

Buying Meat, Fish, Poultry, and Other Sources of Protein

Record prices for these foods make it imperative to select carefully. Because of the cost, older members of the family may assume this responsibility, but shop with them and learn how they make decisions. At times you may have some suggestions to offer. Do not be fooled by low prices. Think about the cost per serving. A boneless cut, ground meat, or variety meats (liver, heart, kidneys) serve from 3 to 4 persons. Inexpensive, less tender cuts of meat are just as nutritious as tender cuts but must be stewed or braised or cooked by other, longer methods. Canned luncheon meats may be a good buy and are easy to prepare.

In buying fish compare the cost of the fresh and frozen. Frozen fish is often less expensive. Sometimes it is cheaper to buy unbreaded fish and do your own breading. Less expensive canned mackerel may be substituted for tuna. Use chunk or flaked tuna in sandwiches where color is less important. Do you have any suggestions to add?

Whole chicken or turkey is generally cheaper than parts. A larger turkey or chicken has more meat and less bone in proporton to younger birds. You need ⅓ to ½ pound of poultry per serving.

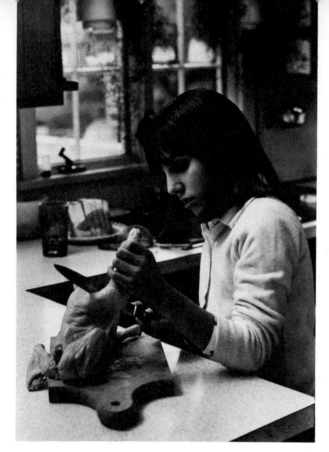

It is usually cheaper to buy a whole chicken and then cut it into parts just before you prepare it.

Lentils, dried beans and peas, or peanuts may be used in thick soups or casseroles as good sources of protein. They are even more nutritious if small amounts of meat or cheese are added. Supplementing the dried legumes with green vegetables, cereals, and nuts increases their nutritive value.

Buying Fruits and Vegetables

Fruits and vegetables should be selected for their vitamin A, vitamin C, and iron content. Review Chapter 11 for the best sources of these nutrients. Plan to have some fresh fruit and vegetables in your diet every day.

Buy fruits and vegetables in season when the price is the lowest for these fresh foods. Compare the cost of the fresh or frozen, because they are comparable in nutritive value. In buying fresh vegetables and fruits, bear in mind that size is not a criterion of quality or nutritive value. Select for the purposes intended. If celery is to be used in soup, it need not be as attractive as celery used for relishes. For cooking choose fruit and vegetables of somewhat the same size so that the cooking time will be the same. Color is

indicative of nutritive value, especially for the dark green and deep yellow vegetables. Shape should be good because forked, rough, cracked, and uneven surfaces are difficult to peel and are wasteful. However, russet-colored oranges and grapefruit are often good buys and the color does not affect flavor or nutritive value. The redness of an apple does not relate to nutritive value and sometimes the redness affects the price.

Consider the number of servings per pound in calculating the cost. The waste in fresh lima beans and fresh pineapple is considerable. In oranges and grapefruit, heaviness denotes juiciness, so lift them and compare. Dried fruits are graded according to size and the larger ones are more expensive. The edible part of small prunes is about 10 percent less than that of the larger sizes, but the cost may be 30 to 40 percent less. Whole fruit and vegetables when canned are more costly than halves, quarters, diced, sliced or other cut styles. When buying canned fruit remember that the heavy syrup which contains sugar adds calories without adding nutrients.

Fruits and vegetables are cheapest at the height of their season. Some fruits, such as fresh figs, loganberries, and kumquats, have a limited season and growing area, so they are more expensive than most fruits. In buying fruit juice, check to see whether there are additives, and compare the prices of fresh and frozen.

Review all the points to consider in buying fruits because you may become bewildered when you look at the displays of many kinds of fruits and vegetables.

You want to make the best buy of some cheese for grilled sandwiches. What is your best selection?

Some sherbets do. The addition of nuts, chocolates, and fruit in ice cream dilutes the milk value. This does not mean to avoid these additions, but to realize that the milk equivalency value has been reduced.

Buying Cereal and Cereal Products

This group includes hot and cold cereals, breads, rice, macaroni, spaghetti, and other pasta, and crackers. Cakes, cookies, and other baked products are other possibilities. Compare the cost per ounce or per serving of bread. Raisin, nut, and health breads are usually more expensive. Day-old bread can be used satisfactorily for toast, puddings, and sandwiches and is much cheaper.

In comparing the cost of cooked cereals, remember the increase in volume in cooking. Whole grains such as rice increase four times, flaked cereal such as rolled oats doubles in volume, and granular cereal like wheatena increases five to six times. Among the cold cereals, puffed varieties and sugar coated cereals are usually more expensive. Many of the cold cereals have considerable sugar, honey, maple syrup, or other sugars added. This dilutes the nutrients in cereals, because only calories are added. In

Buying Milk and Milk Products

Compare the cost of the various types of milk such as fresh, evaporated, and dried. Dried milk is usually the cheapest but your family and you may prefer fluid milk to drink. Use the dried milk in cooking and save. Dry milk and evaporated milk can be whipped and used as a base for desserts and mock sour cream—quite a saving over whipped cream, and much more nutritious.

In buying cheese, compare the prices of domestic versus imported cheeses and sliced, cubed, grated, and shredded cheese with cheese in a wedge or chunk. Determine whether the cheese is made from whole milk or skim milk, and whether fat or other ingredients have been added. When pimientoes and chopped olives, for example, are added to cheese, the milk values are diluted. Fancy packages and soft cheese in a jar are usually more expensive.

Compare the cost of ice cream in various size containers and purchase the size most suitable for your purpose. Ices do not contain milk.

What does the label on a cereal box tell you about the nutrients it contains, the amount of sugar, and the presence of whole grains?

other words, calories have increased, but protein, minerals, and vitamins are the same, so proportionately you have fewer nutrients in relation to amount of calories. An instant cereal costs more than a quick cereal and a quick cereal costs more than a regular cooked cereal. Time may be a factor in your planning, but keep these points in mind. Cereals as a group are the least expensive of foods yet are the most neglected foods. Think of ways in which you can get more cereal into your diet or at least get the required amount.

Some General Points

Storage space must be considered in buying food. Is there adequate space and are foods kept at the right temperature? Try to keep foods moving. Why keep a can of baked beans on your shelf for months and months? Foods do deteriorate if kept too long. The same is true of foods in your freezer. Date them for reminders. The size of containers can be a problem if they do not fit the place you have for them.

Learn to be flexible in making purchases. If you have fresh grapefruit on your list and it is not available, why not choose canned grapefruit juice without sugar? When you have a green vegetable in mind, do not make your choice until you see what is the best buy for the day.

Remember that you have to pay for the services connected with a food. If you buy a frozen dinner, for example, it is usually more expensive than one you prepare yourself. Making your own bread crumbs, baking your own cookies, and cooking your cereal are only a few examples of ways to cut the food budget.

You may feel as though you are a walking encyclopedia of information as an expert shopper, but you must continuously update this information. Read the newspapers and magazines

If your family is fond of apple pie, why not make it and save?

about changes and new products, and for other assistance. Government bulletins are an excellent source of help. Your state or county extension service will send you one free copy of materials on buying food. Look for changes in laws and labeling, too. Remember that you will be buying food for the rest of your life and you might as well become an expert while you are young.

THINKING IT OVER

1. Think about all the factors that enter into the cost of food. Who gets the food dollar, for example? Do you know all the costs of putting a box of cereal into your kitchen, for example? Have you ever considered the cost of damaged goods—for example, a customer helping himself or herself to some cookies and putting the damaged box back on the shelf? What about the customer who pilfers, putting a small jar of preserves or a package of gum in a tote bag or pocket and not paying for it? This practice is reported to be common among shoppers, regardless of income level.

2. Do the poor pay more for groceries? Your class might undertake a project and compare prices in various stores according to the income level of the families who live there. Take some common food items, such as fresh milk, a loaf of white bread, a pound of margarine, or a package of rice. All prices must be surveyed on the same day. What were the conclusions? What about provisions for securing food stamps or commodity or donated foods of the U.S. Department of Agriculture programs? Are there any plans in your community to assist the needy elderly with their shopping for food? Have a rap session about all the ideas that have occurred to you.

THINGS TO DO

1. Remember that all your food is not purchased in the supermarket. Your family and you eat out. Have you ever made a survey of the cheapest and best places to eat? If not, why not now?

2. Maybe you are a calorie-conscious person. Have you ever compared the cost of buying foods in which the calories have been removed with the cost of buying foods of low calorie content in their natural state, such as fresh fruits and vegetables, lean meats, and the like?

3. Experiment and be a gourmet cook with inexpensive foods. Try substituting less expensive food items for the expensive ones listed in your recipe—for example, whipped evaporated milk for whipped cream, or evaporated milk that is undiluted in recipes calling for half and half. Your family will love you for this activity.

4. Clip ideas from newspapers or flyers from the grocery store about food bargains and put them on the family bulletin board. Buying food may not be as exciting as a football game, but it does have its dramatic moments when you are the winner!

19 Snacks and fun foods

Snacks and fun foods are eaten all over the world. In Egypt you might buy licorice water from a vendor, in Russia you might be served hot tea in a glass, and in Japan in the wintertime you might buy hot noodles at a noodle shop.

Snacks are not new. In the early history of our country, note was made of the Indian runners who carried bags of corn for munching. Today our most noted snacking time is the coffee break.

Fun foods, although often of the snack variety, are usually associated with occasions when you and your friends gather together after school, after a game, or for a rap session. Informal parties may be in this category. Another possibility is when a few of you bicycle through the park or elsewhere and stop to share the contents of the brown bags you have with you. Eating food together is an intimate experience. Talking and sharing personal problems and interests are easier during and after the sharing of food. These values are important to consider in connection with these foods.

PURPOSE OF SNACKS

In our rush to find something good to eat, we may overlook the reason for having a snack. As explained in the chapter on nutrition, you are hungry because you are growing rapidly and need additional food. Sometimes the previous meal has been rather light and you feel the need for something extra. A snack is right, too, when you are very hungry long before the next meal. Snacks should carry you to the next meal. You should never eat so much that you are not hungry at the next meal or feel that the edge has been taken off your appetite. Do not become interested in snacking as a way of eating all your food.

Let us think about some general rules about snacks.

Rules for Snacks

1-Good snacks include milk, fruit, raw vegetables, and cereals.
2-Snacks can be expensive. Consider cost when planning them.
3-Consider nutritious snacks for your family as well as yourself.

Your Background Influences Your Snacks

In many instances the kind of snack served reflects the family's national background. Your parents may have coffee in the middle of the afternoon and Sue's parents may have tea. The kind of bread, cookies, and other food served may also be significant. If your family lives on a farm or in a large city, this will affect what is eaten between meals. What influences the snacks in your house?

SNACKS AT HOME

If you are sitting around the fireplace in the house or an open fire in the backyard, it is an added pleasure to have something to munch. You can roast nuts by putting them uncracked into a corn popper and holding them over the coals until they are a delicate brown. Cool them slightly. Shell them. Add butter or margarine and salt.

If your home is like many homes and does not have a fireplace, you can toast nuts in a skillet. Put two tablespoons of butter, margarine, or salad oil in a skillet. Add two cups of shelled nuts. Toast the nuts over a low flame. When they are a light brown, remove them from the flame. You may add salt or, for a change, you may use celery salt.

Popcorn is liked by almost everyone. You can pop it yourself in a skillet, an electric popper, or a wire popper. If you use a skillet, be certain that you have the lid on tight so that you will not lose your popcorn. You can butter and salt it in the usual manner or sprinkle it with grated cheese. The salt in the popcorn and nuts will make you thirsty, so you will want to have some kind of beverage nearby. On the next page are some suggestions for snack beverages.

Fun food and bicycling are a great combination.

173

Ideas for Snack Beverages

The preparation of an interesting beverage to go with your snacks is a good test for your imagination. Listed here are some suggestions.

Orange Apricot Cooler

SERVINGS - 6

1 cup frozen, fresh, or canned orange juice
2 cups apricot nectar
1/4 cup lemon juice
1 teaspoon sugar
2 cups ginger ale

1. Add the sugar to the orange juice and mix well.
2. Combine this mixture with the other juices and the ginger ale.
3. Pour the cooler over cracked ice and serve it immediately.

Purple Cow

SERVING -

3/4 cup cold milk
2–3 tablespoons concentrated grape juice

Gradually add the grape juice to the cold milk. Stir briskly and constantly. Always pour the juice into the milk. Serve immediately.

Molasses Smoothie

SERVING - 1

1 cup cold milk
1 tablespoon molasses

Stir the molasses into the cold milk until dissolved. Serve at once. If desired, add a scoop of ice cream and 1 drop of peppermint flavoring.

These milk drinks are easily prepared and the ingredients are usually on hand at home. Your friends will enjoy them very much. With these cold drinks you might like to serve bread and butter, crackers, or cookies.

Dips

Something your entire family might enjoy is a dip for dunking crackers, pretzels, sticks of raw vegetables, or potato chips. Listed here are some quick and inexpensive dips.

Pink Cheese Dip

1 cup cottage cheese
2 tablespoons chili sauce or catsup
2 tablespoons chopped peanuts or other nuts

Mix all the ingredients well and serve the dip in a small bowl. Very good for spreading on crackers.

Pimento Cheese Dip

1/2 cup pimento cheese
1/3 package onion soup mix
1 tablespoon salad dressing
1/4 cup milk or thin cream

Mix all the ingredients until they are well blended. If the dip seems a little thick, add a little more milk. It should be thin enough to dip potato chips in easily without breaking them.

Ham Dip

1 small can deviled ham
1 three-ounce package cream cheese
1 eight-ounce can tomato sauce
1/8 teaspoon celery salt
1/8 teaspoon onion or garlic salt
1 teaspoon barbecue sauce

Mix all the ingredients until smooth and creamy. If you have an electric blender, you can mix the ingredients quickly. Serve with toast or crackers.

HAVE YOUR OWN SODA FOUNTAIN

One way to impress your friends is to serve them sodas you make at home. In addition to serving them as refreshments, your family might like to have them for dessert at lunch or dinner. Here are some ideas to start you thinking about homemade sodas.

Orange Soda

SERVING - 1

1/2 cup undiluted frozen orange juice, thawed
1 tablespoon light cream
1 cup soda water (approximately)
2 scoops vanilla ice cream
1 scoop orange sherbet

1. Pour the orange juice and cream into a 12-ounce glass. Mix well.
2. Add ¼ cup of the soda water and stir.
3. Alternate the vanilla ice cream with the orange sherbet.
4. Fill the glass with soda water and serve at once.

Chocolate Soda

SERVING - 1

3 tablespoons chocolate syrup
2 scoops chocolate ice cream
1 scoop vanilla cream
1 cup soda or sparkling water (approximately)

1. Place the chocolate syrup in a 12-ounce glass.
2. Add the ice cream, alternating the chocolate with the vanilla.
3. Add soda water and stir until the mixture is foamy. Serve at once. Chocolate chip or mint chocolate ice cream might be used.

Soups Make Good Snacks

Have you ever come home on a cold day and had a cup of hot soup? In warm weather you might like to try cold soup, although hot soup is good any time. Maybe you have thought about soup only at mealtime.

SNACKS FOR FRIENDS

When friends stop by to see you, refreshments of some kind seem necessary, even if it means munching on a bag of potato chips and having a glass of milk. It is especially nice to have something to nibble on when you are watching television or talking to your friends about the latest school happenings. Sometimes you help your mother prepare the food when friends of your parents come to visit.

Surprise Your Friends with Pizzas

One of America's most popular snacks is pizza. You might like to ask your Italian friends about the way pizzas are made. They may describe different types, such as baked or fried, depending upon the section of Italy where their ancestors lived. Since you and your friends may be hungry and in a hurry for food, a number of suggestions will be given here for making pizzas quickly. You will need some kind of bread base for the pizza. Here are some good ideas:

1-English muffins, cut in two.
2-Unbaked refrigerator biscuits, rolled very thin.
3-Brown-and-serve clover leaf rolls, rolled so that they will be thinner.
4-Buns, split in two.
5-Biscuit dough that your mother or you have prepared from a recipe in a cookbook. A biscuit mix might be used. Cut the dough in circles and roll it thin.

Toppings for Pizzas. Place whatever you use as a bread base on a baking sheet or in a flat pan. Leave about one inch of space between each. Then put the topping on. Here are some ideas for making toppings that will be different:

1-Spread with pimento or other cheese spread. Top with a tablespoon of tomato paste and slices of stuffed olives.
2-Cut a circle of American or Swiss cheese. Add a spoonful of tomato paste and top with slices or buttons of mushrooms.
3-Use cheese spread, tomato paste, and little sausage balls.
4-Spread with deviled ham. Add a spoonful of catsup and top with slices of pickle or small pickles.
5-Use a circle of cheese, add a slice of tomato, and top with a tiny Vienna sausage.
6-Spread with peanut butter. Top with cooked bacon curl and green pepper rings.
7-Spread with cheese, add a spoon of catsup, and top with anchovies.

You will want to experiment with other combinations for toppings.

After you have the pizzas arranged, place the pan under a broiler or in an oven at 350 degrees F for five minutes. Cut each pizza evenly into pie-shaped pieces. Serve hot. Cold tomato juice or vegetable juice would be a good beverage to have with your pizzas. Lemonade is also good.

Waffles for Snacks

Another quickie when you are hungry and would like to serve something tasty to your friends is waffles. They will take the place of a sandwich. Here are possibilities for making waffles:

1-Make waffles from a recipe in a cookbook.
2-Use a pancake mix in making the waffle batter. This will save time in mixing. Follow the directions on the package.
3-Use waffles that have been frozen and stored in your freezer. Your mother or you could make these ahead of time and freeze them. When you are ready to use them, put them into the toaster.
4-Buy frozen waffles and put them into the toaster.

Toppings for Waffles. There are a number of ways to make interesting toppings for waffles. Here are a few:

1-Spread waffles with a soft cheese and serve with a sliced tomato.
2-Cover the waffle with canned chili con carne, chicken a la king, or meatballs in tomato sauce.
3-Place a dipper of ice cream on the waffle.
4-Cover the waffle with sliced peaches or other sliced fresh, frozen, or canned fruit.

With waffles you will want a beverage, of course. Milk, orange or pineapple juice, or hot cocoa would be good.

Nibbles

Sometimes you are hungry because you have had a light lunch. Or you have been doing some kind of exercise and have the urge to nibble on something. Here are some suggestions that are good both when you are alone and when you have guests:

1-Sprinkle cheese over potato chips and heat them quickly in the oven. Sprinkling paprika over the chips will make them a pretty pink.
2-Crackers and cheese are filling.
3-Graham crackers and peanut butter go well together.
4-Carrot or celery strips are nutritious.

Fruit Between Meals

A piece of fruit is good to eat when you are hungry between meals, because it is not so likely to spoil your appetite for the next meal. If you want to serve something especially nice to friends, you can serve frozen or canned pineapple chunks on toothpicks on a pretty plate. A bowl of fruit in season is attractive. You might take the responsibility of keeping a bowl of apples or other fruit handy so that the family can help themselves.

Any one of these fruits will make a good snack.

Raw vegetables are good for nibbling.

BUYING SNACKS

When you stop somewhere for refreshments after school, after a movie, or on a Sunday ride with your family, what do you usually order? Keeping in mind that food eaten between meals can be nourishing, what would be a good choice? Something with milk or fruit should be high on the list. If you have a sandwich, choose whole-grain breads. Vegetable juices like tomato are nutritious and refreshing.

If you are buying these snacks from your allowance, you will give some thought to cost. Which selections from the menu are the least expensive and the most nourishing? Look at the menu carefully. Compare prices of similar types of foods, such as beverages; hamburgers, pizza, hot dogs, fish and chips, and French fries; or sweet foods, such as ice cream, cake, pie, and cookies. You may wish to eat the same food as your friends. Your wallet may be rather flat. These and other points need to be considered. Of course, you will not wish to make a major problem of your decision, so find shortcuts to good answers.

Cost is also important to consider if you are being treated by a friend. It then becomes impolite to order the most expensive things on the menu.

FUN FOODS

These foods are, as the name indicates, refreshments consumed when you are having a good time. To define that occasion might stretch the imagination, because so many happenings can be fun. Examples are get-togethers for a holiday such as Halloween, during Christmas vacation or other vacation periods; engaging in some sport such as tennis, volleyball, or softball, and eating afterwards to discuss the game; or going to a professional baseball or hockey game and buying food there. Eating is casual, and all the foods described in this chapter are appropriate, plus others that your creative mind has concocted.

Informal parties might be included in this category, and here are some suggestions for food. One of the best parts of your party will be the refreshments. If it is a small party, you might sit at the table. This will give you an opportunity to decorate the table. You might have a help-yourself plan. Here the table is set up and guests serve themselves. Sometimes it is nice to serve a plate to everyone. If possible, have seconds so that everyone will have enough to eat. The time of day will to some extent determine the type of refreshments.

If the food is cold, sandwiches, a beverage, and some kind of sweet like doughnuts, cookies, cake, or ice cream are acceptable. Sometimes the food is limited to a dessert type of dish, such as ice cream with some nutritious cereal cookies and a beverage. This type of refreshment is especially suited to informal parties. If you live in a section of the country where the climate changes with the seasons, a cool drink like lemonade or a fruit punch might be served in warm weather and a hot drink such as cocoa in the wintertime. If the party is at meal time, a regular meal is served. Food can have a number of interesting garnishes. For example, at a patriotic party, cupcakes can have little flags stuck in them. Doing something different to food makes it more interesting to your guests.

THINKING IT OVER

1. What kind of food was served between meals in grandmother's day? What were the reasons for serving this kind of food?

2. Think of the feelings you have when you eat with someone. Does eating together make you feel more friendly? Does it help you talk more easily with others? What are some of the advantages of eating together between meals?

THINGS TO DO

1. You may decide to serve pizzas to your friends. You look in the cupboard and the refrigerator and see English muffins, catsup, olives, some meatballs left from lunch, a jar of pickles, and a package of sliced cheese. What kind of pizzas might you plan?

2. Think of all the occasions when snacks are served in your home. Are there good reasons for them? Are snacks planned? What conclusions would you draw? Would you suggest any changes?

3. Make a survey of menus from places where you and your friends stop to have snacks. What are the least expensive and the most nourishing dishes you can order?

4. What would you suggest for a snack shelf in the cupboard and in the refrigerator? Why have you made these choices?

20 Packing a lunch

In many families packing a lunch may be a way of life for several reasons. It may be the only way to get something to eat because you cannot buy lunch where you expect to be. The family may be saving to buy something for your home, the car, or a vacation, or for other reasons. It may be a serious financial situation because of national economic conditions and after a family brainstorming session on ways to make ends meet, carrying lunch has a prominent place on the list. What may be other reasons for carrying lunch?

Packing these lunches day after day may become quite a chore. Let's see if we can't make the packing easier and the lunch a delight for you to eat as well.

STANDARDS FOR LUNCHES

The first point is to establish some standards for lunches. It is not a matter of packing anything you can find and doing it in a hurry. Let's start with the idea that you are packing your own lunch—the kind of lunch you would like to have. The food should have interesting flavors, textures, and colors. Avoid sameness. You want enough to eat but you don't want to pack so much that food will be wasted. And you want a package that is easy to carry.

Supplies for Packing Lunches

Before you think about what you will have for lunch, it might be a good idea to think about the place where you will fix your lunch and the equipment you need. Is there some nook in the kitchen where you can put all your supplies so you won't have to look everywhere for the wax paper or the aluminum foil? Maybe there is a shelf that could be arranged for you. Here are the things that you will want to have handy:

1–Wrapping materials, such as wax paper, aluminum foil, or plastic paper.
2–Plenty of paper napkins.
3–Paper cups with tight-fitting lids and plastic forks and spoons.
4–If there isn't room on the shelf, you will want to keep nearby a breadboard for cutting and spreading sandwiches, a spreading knife, and a cutting knife.
5–A saltshaker should be handy for seasoning.
6–An egg slicer is also helpful.

Keep Everything Clean

If there is ever a need to keep everything clean it is when you prepare a lunch. Wash your hands well before preparing the lunch. Wash very carefully all the fruit or vegetables you are going to use. Do not use any of your wrappings again. Clean the lunch box and the thermos bottle thoroughly. Washing with hot water and soda or with hot suds is necessary. Airing helps them keep a sweet odor. All containers for food must be clean. It is important to have everything clean so that your lunch will be free from undesirable odors and flavors. A well-packed lunch can quickly lose all its attraction if these precautions aren't taken. Furthermore, cleanliness will discourage bacteria from growing or even being present. Bacteria can cause food spoilage or make you ill. Every step in preparing lunch should be done carefully, to be sure everything is clean and wholesome. Food will look better, taste better, and be better for you.

Carrying a lunch to school may be one way to help the family budget.

FOOD TO HAVE FOR LUNCHES

As with any other meal, you can plan your lunch from a menu pattern. A good lunch will have a main dish that is protein in nature, unless proteins are provided elsewhere in the meal. Excepting when you have cottage cheese or a thick soup with meat in your thermos, this is seldom the case. Sandwiches are generally the main dish, since they are easy to carry. The filling should be of egg, meat, fish, cheese, or other protein food. Peanut butter or beans in sandwich fillings will meet the protein allowance, if at least a cup of milk is drunk with the lunch.

Some kind of fruit or raw vegetable and a sweet will complete the lunch. If you cannot buy a beverage, it may be necessary to include that in your lunch box as well. This should be milk, if the lunch is for you.

Following are some suggestions to help you plan your lunch.

Supplies for making lunches should be kept together.

3– Keep the crusts on. The sandwich will keep its shape better and will not break and crumble so easily.

4– The fillings should be moist but not runny.

5– Spread the filling to the edge—but not over the edge—of the slice of bread.

6– The filling should be well-seasoned. It is a good idea to taste the filling before spreading it.

7– Wrap lettuce, tomato, and other sandwich additions separately. They will taste much better and the sandwich will not become soggy.

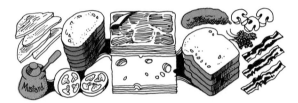

8– Meat sandwich fillings:

a. Combine slices of ham with Swiss cheese. Provide mustard in a separate container.

b. Combine chopped ham and chopped dill pickle, and moisten the mixture with salad dressing.

c. Combine chopped chicken, chopped celery, and minced parsley moistened with salad dressing.

d. Combine sliced chicken and crisp bacon, with tomato added later.

e. Combine mashed liverwurst, chopped mushrooms, and relish, with salad dressing to moisten.

Sandwich Suggestions

1– Use a variety of breads, such as whole wheat, rye, raisin, oatmeal, corn and molasses, cracked wheat, fruit, or nut.

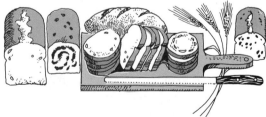

2– Spread both slices of bread, preferably with butter or margarine, since mayonnaise will soak the bread.

9– Fish sandwiches:

a. Combine flaked tuna, chopped cucumbers, lemon juice, and salad dressing.

b. Combine flaked salmon, grated carrot, onion salt, and salad dressing.

c. Combine chopped shrimp, Worcestershire sauce, and chopped pickle with mayonnaise.

d. Combine flaked crab meat, shredded cabbage, and cream salad dressing.

e. Combine salmon and chopped egg, and moisten with catsup.

10—Cheese sandwiches:

a. Combine cheese spread and chopped salted peanuts moistened with salad dressing.

b. Combine cottage cheese, peanut butter and catsup.

c. Combine cream cheese and strained apricots.

d. Combine cottage cheese, chopped dates and nuts, and salad dressing.

e. Combine grated American cheese and marmalade.

11—Egg sandwiches (see other suggestions on page 112):

a. Mix chopped hard-cooked egg with chili sauce.

b. Combine hard-cooked egg, chopped ripe olives, and salad dressing.

c. Mix cold scrambled eggs, crumbled crisp bacon, and celery salt.

d. Combine hard-cooked egg, chopped celery, and salad dressing.

e. Combine chopped hard-cooked egg, mashed sardines, and salad dressing.

12—Other sandwich fillings:

a. Peanut butter mixed with mashed banana and honey.

b. Mashed baked beans, combined with chopped celery and salad dressing.

c. Peanut butter, mixed with jelly, and salad dressing.

d. Prune pulp with bacon. Watch the lunch for a protein food such as egg, cheese, or meat.

e. Corned beef hash with crushed pineapple.

Increased Vitamins

Fruit or raw vegetables may be included in the lunch box as something fresh and to increase vitamins. The best fruits for this purpose are apples, oranges, bananas, plums, grapes, and fresh berries placed in a paper container. For the raw vegetable, carrot strips, pieces of celery, cauliflower flowerettes, rings of green pepper, pieces of lettuce, watercress, and other salad greens are good. A few sprigs of parsley will go well with your sandwich. They may be alternated with slices of cucumber, radishes, or strips of white or yellow turnip.

Add Variety to a Package Lunch

For a sweet, some kind of cookie packs best. Recipes for two types of easily prepared cookies follow. They pack easily. You may use them on many other occasions. Brownies are a good luncheon cookie. Stuffing dates or prunes with peanut butter or other fillings makes an interesting change.

Brownies and milk may be served as a delicious after-school snack.

Cinnamon Bites

SERVINGS: – 32 pieces

1/2 Cup sugar
1   teaspoon cinnamon
1/2 cup melted butter or margarine
3   cups junior-size shredded wheat
1/2 cup finely chopped nuts

1. Mix the sugar, nuts, and cinnamon.
2. Melt the butter and dip each shredded wheat biscuit in the butter.
3. Roll each biscuit at once in the cinnamon, nut, and sugar mixture.
4. Place the biscuits on waxed paper for an hour and let them dry.

Chocolate Cereal Bars

SERVINGS: – 18 cookies

1   6-ounce package semisweet chocolate pieces
1   cup miniature marshmallows
1/4 cup chopped nuts
1   cup puffed cereal, small shredded wheat biscuits, or other ready-to-eat cereal.

1. Line a 9" x 4" loaf pan with waxed paper.
2. Melt the chocolate over hot water.
3. Add the marshmallows and nuts.
4. Add the cereal to the chocolate mixture. Mix well.
5. Pack the mixture into prepared pan. Chill until firm.
6. Remove from pan. Peel off paper. Cut into bars.

These cookies are also good with a glass of milk after you have played ball or had a session of folk dancing.

Instant puddings, cookies, frozen fruit, and other desserts may be packed in paper cups with lids. Glass jars with tight-fitting lids are also good but make the lunch box that much heavier.

Baked beans, whole canned tomatoes, potato salad, jellied salads or desserts, and macaroni salad may be packed in paper cups with lids or in glass jars. If you use your imagination, you can think of many kinds of food that will add variety to a package lunch.

If you have a thermos bottle, you can make other interesting additions, such as milk, cocoa, fruit drinks, vegetable juices, hot soups in cold weather, a thin stew with small pieces of meat, or other liquid dishes.

A PACKAGE LUNCH REQUIRES PLANNING

The lunch should be prepared just before you leave the house so it will be as fresh as possible. Since this is usually a very busy time, you will have to plan the lunch carefully and allow time for packing it. Some of the preparation can be done the night before. The fruit can be washed and put into the refrigerator. The sandwich fillings can be made and also placed in the refrigerator. Check all the supplies so you won't omit some necessary food. You might become the family lunch expert and work out short cuts to preparing tasty lunches.

A biking picnic is a good way to be with friends.

PACKING THE LUNCH

Every item in the lunch box should be wrapped separately. This will prevent the transmitting of odors and flavors from one food to another. Do not slice sandwiches into small pieces or they will dry out. Arrange the food so that it will fit well and not be jostled about. This will prevent crushing, too. Pack the lunch in an order just the reverse of that in which it will be eaten, putting the dessert in first. Thus, when you open the box, the food you will eat first will be on top. Place at least two napkins in the box—one for you to use and one to spread your lunch on. A light plastic lunch box is good for packing. If you do not wish to carry anything home and can buy a hot dish, such as soup or stew in the cafeteria, you might pack your lunch in a paper bag.

PICNICS
A Biking or Hiking Picnic

Other possibilities for packing a lunch are for a biking or a hiking picnic.* A beautiful Saturday morning in the fall or spring is an especially good time. Your friends and you will probably pack your lunch in a backpack or knapsack. Each of you may pack your own lunch and, if you like, put it together when you are ready to eat. Another way is to divide foods on your menu and have each person make and bring one item for everyone.

Keep your lunch simple. Stick to packable and easy-to-eat foods. Here are some basic suggestions that you may vary: meat, cheese, raw

*Ideas from Gale Steves

vegetables, bread, and fruit. Some suitable beverage must be carried with you.

For the meats, select small whole salamis, beef jerky, or smoked or garlic sausage. Presliced meat or cheese tends to stick together on a hot day, but is satisfactory if the temperature is right. Sharp Cheddar or smooth-tasting Gouda are good if your choice of fruit happens to be apples. Experiment with other types of cheese. A jar of peanut butter is good and may be appreciated by your vegetarian friends. Breads may be hard rolls, crusty but seedless Italian or French bread, or Swedish rye wafers. They do not crush easily in your knapsack.

Apples and pears, washed and well chilled before packing, are good because there is little refuse and they are delicious with other foods. Crisp chilled raw vegetables, such as celery, carrots, zucchini sticks, and radishes will add crunch.

Some kind of canned beverage will be refreshing. The large amount of water in the fruit and vegetables will help quench your thirst to some degree. The cans may be wrapped in towels, so that you won't have to listen to the clinking of the cans as you ride and they will also be kept cooler. The towels may be used to place the food on for serving.

Keep utensils to a minimum. A small cutting board, a jacknife, paper cups and plates, and napkins are possible items to take. Most beverage containers are self-openers, but an opener will be necessary if your favorite beverage does not come in that type of container. Some paper towels are good for wiping sticky fingers.

A biking picnic may be good for family fun. In these days of saving energy, bicycles are popular with the entire family. It might be a friendly gesture to ask the elderly man who lives next door to join you on his trike (adult tricycle) if you do not go too far for him to travel. It would be so enjoyable for him.

Older people enjoy biking picnics.

Other Picnics

A picnic will require some planning. Have you ever been on a picnic when it was discovered that the salt or something else important had been forgotten? You will have to decide whether you will cook or prepare food at home beforehand. A picnic will require the following steps:

1- Plan your menu. Select foods that can be easily handled and that your family will like.
2- Select foods that carry easily. A cream pie, for example, is difficult to pack.
3- Plan for more than you usually eat because everyone eats more on a picnic.
4- Consider equipment you will need. Will you use paper dishes? What kind of serving or cooking equipment will be necessary?
5- If the weather is hot, special consideration must be given to food that spoils easily. Keep food cold. Illness results quickly from food that is spoiled.
6- Plan how you will serve the food. Try to keep it as simple as possible.
7- If there are no facilities for cleaning up, include "moist towelettes" for washing your hands.
8- The kind of transportation will influence the kind of picnic you will have. If you live in the city and must go by bus to your picnic spot, avoid heavy items.
9- What will you wear to the picnic? Comfortable wash clothes will be best.
10- Take a first-aid kit with you for cuts or other injuries.

Picnic Foods. There are many foods that are appropriate for picnics. If you plan to cook out, you will begin planning your meal with the main dish. This could be frankfurters, hamburgers, steaks, fish or fish cakes, or eggs with bacon or ham. If it is to be a backyard picnic, you might have barbecued meats of various types.

For vegetables, you might have a potato salad, a tossed salad, a bowl of mixed vegetables (such as sliced tomatoes, cucumbers, celery, or carrot strips), corn on the cob, or frozen French fries, which can be heated quickly. For dessert, melon of all kinds (especially watermelon), ice cream, cake, cookies, or fresh fruit are fine.

Think about other ways in which a packed lunch would be appropriate. Perhaps you can help other members of the family pack a basket of food for a sick relative. Perhaps your father takes on a night job and must take his lunch. What kind of food would you suggest for a midnight lunch?

THINKING IT OVER

1. What do you do while you are eating a lunch you have brought from home? Do some of your friends eat with you? Do you buy milk or a cup of soup to go with your lunch? What do you talk about while you are eating? How are your manners? Have you ever thought about how your eating looks to others? Do you rush through your lunch so you can do something else? What are some ways in which you might make eating your lunch a more pleasant experience?

THINGS TO DO

1. Plan a week's interesting menus for your lunch box. What kind of grocery list would you need?

2. Suppose you were packing a lunch for your father or your older brother. What might be some interesting surprises you could tuck into the lunch?

3. Suppose you had to pack a lunch for someone on a holiday, like Washington's Birthday. What kind of lunch might you plan?

4. Suppose you were tired of eating a lunch brought from home every day. What might you do to regain your interest? Would you look at your menu to see if you could try some different foods? Could the lunch be packed better? Share your ideas with others.

21 Sharing our ethnic foods

Now that you are interested in your ethnic background as well as those of your friends and classmates, why not give ethnic foods some attention? Think about the students in your class. Which backgrounds are represented? Now think about the people living in your community. Any additions? What about your own family? Maybe your mother had Irish, French, or Polish ancestors. Your father's family may have been Italian, Mexican, English, or Brazilian. Perhaps you know someone with an American Indian heritage.

Why not share recipes as well as learning something about the foods that are common to a certain heritage? This may lead to better understanding among individuals of various heritages. When you learn about their foods you learn about their family life and when you eat their foods a common bond is established.

A few ethnic recipes are given here to arouse your interest in ethnic foods.

A MEXICAN DISH

Hot seasonings and beans are two characteristics of Mexican food. Here they are combined in chili con carne.

Chili con Carne

SERVINGS: – 4

    2 tablespoons fat
    1 medium onion, chopped
    1 pound ground chuck
    1/2 teaspoon black pepper
    1/4 teaspoon cayenne pepper
    1 teaspoon salt
    1/2 teaspoon chili powder
    1 tablespoon paprika
    1 No. 2 can of stewed tomatoes
    1 No. 2 can of kidney beans

1. Melt the fat in a skillet
2. Add the chopped onion and cook until slightly glazed but not brown.
3. Add the ground chuck and brown well.
4. Add the pepper—black and cayenne, chili powder, salt and paprika. Toss and stir until well mixed.
5. Add the tomatoes and kidney beans and cook slowly for about 20 minutes.
6. Serve in bowls. A little chopped green or red pepper on top of the chili con carne is an attractive garnish and adds extra flavor and nutrients. May be served on rice.

A JAPANESE DISH

A delightful dish from Japan is Sukiyaki. This is another one-dish meal. Fuel is very scarce in Japan, so that is one reason for cooking everything together. This dish is nourishing, too. You might be interested in a story about the origin of the name Sukiyaki. Suki means plow and yaki means roasted. For over a century the eating of beef was forbidden in Japan. As the story goes, a farmer slaughtered a steer in secret on a lonely mountainside and then cooked it. He used a part of his plow as a grill over the fire. So the term "plow-roasted" came into being.

If you do not have all these ingredients, try to find substitutes. It will not taste the same as the recipe but you will get some idea of the dish. For example, if you do not have round steak, perhaps you can use some other meat. Be certain that the slices are paper-thin. Frozen spinach might be used for fresh spinach. If you do

Sukiyaki

SERVINGS: – 4–6

    11/2 pounds round steak cut across grain
         into paper-thin slices
       1 bunch scallions, tops and all cut into
         2-inch pieces
     1/4 pound mushrooms, sliced thin
       1 large white onion, sliced thin
     1/2 medium head Chinese cabbage,
         shredded
     1/2 pound fresh spinach, washed thor-
         oughly
       1 can sliced or diced bamboo shoots
     1/4 cup soy sauce
       2 tablespoons sugar
     1/2 teaspoon monosodium glutamate

1. Place a little beef suet, butter, or margarine in a large skillet before putting in the steak.
2. Brown the steak.
3. Add all other ingredients. Cook covered for 5 minutes. Remove the cover. Cook another 5 minutes. Vegetables will still be crisp.

A JEWISH FESTIVAL DISH

Hanukkah is known as the Festival of Lights in the Jewish religion. It celebrates a victorious battle and the rededication of the Temple, when only one jar of oil with a single day's supply for the Eternal Light miraculously burned for eight days. At this festival, the custom is to light one candle and then add a candle each night for a total of eight nights.

Gifts are often exchanged, and family and community celebrations are held. Potato pancakes *(latkes)* are a traditional dish served on this holiday, together with other festive foods. A recipe for potato pancakes is included here.

not have Chinese cabbage available, use another type of cabbage. The flavor will not be so delicate, however.

The vegetables in this dish will have a chewy texture and a pleasing flavor. Also, the short cooking period of the vegetables assures the retention of much of their food value. This dish may be served with rice or fried noodles. Since you already have vegetables in Sukiyaki, you may decide to skip a salad. Can you think of a dessert that would go well with this meal? A fruit dessert would be one possibility. How about canned mandarin oranges? They would add to the nutritional value of the meal.

Jewish Potato Pancakes

SERVINGS: - 6

6 medium potatoes
1 small onion, grated
2 tablespoons flour
2 beaten eggs
1 1/2 teaspoons salt
1/4 teaspoon pepper
2 tablespoons chopped parsley (optional)
1/4 cup oil

1. Coarsely grate the potatoes.
2. Squeeze out the water and drain the potatoes well.
3. Add the onion, flour, salt, pepper, eggs, and parsley. Blend well.
4. Heat the oil in a skillet.
5. Drop the batter by heaping tablespoons into the hot oil, leaving a small space between pancakes. Flatten each pancake with the back of the pancake turner.
6. When the pancakes are golden brown, turn them over.
7. Brown the other side.
8. Drain them on a paper towel. Keep warm while other pancakes are baking.
9. Serve with sour cream or applesauce.

A DISH FROM INDIA

India sends us curried dishes. These dishes use a wide variety of foods in their preparation and provide a good way to use leftovers. If you have not eaten curried dishes, it is wise to select a mild curry for seasoning. There are over 200 varieties of imported and domestic curry powders in this country, so explore those varieties available in your area.

This curried meat may be served with rice. Fresh fruit makes a nice dessert. Relishes of raw vegetables and pickles are good with the curry. This is still another idea for a meal for your family. You will want to encourage them to try foods of other countries.

A PUERTO RICAN DISH

In Puerto Rico a dish that is prepared often is Guineos al Horno, baked bananas. This might be used as a dessert or to accompany baked ham. You might prepare it for your family's dessert some day and if they like it you might do it again when your mother plans baked ham for a company dinner.

Curried Meat

SERVINGS: - 4-6

- 1 1/2 pounds of beef, veal, lamb, or pork shoulder cut into 2-inch squares
- 2 tablespoons flour
- 1/2 cup butter or margarine
- 1 clove garlic, minced
- 2 large onions, sliced
- 2 small apples, cored, peeled, and chopped
- 2 tablespoons curry powder
- 2 tablespoons brown sugar
- 2 tablespoons raisins
- 1 tablespoon Worcestershire sauce
- 1 lemon, sliced
- 2 tablespoons shredded coconut
- 2 cups water
- 1/3 cup broken walnut meats
- 1/4 teaspoon grated lemon rind
- 1 1/2 teaspoons salt

1. Sprinkle the flour over the meat.
2. Melt the butter in a large saucepan.
3. Add the meat, onion, and garlic. Brown lightly. Stir well.
4. Add apples and curry powder and cook for 5 minutes.
5. Add the water and remaining ingredients.
6. Simmer over low heat for about an hour or until the meat is done.

Guineos al Horno

SERVINGS: - 6
TEMPERATURE: - 425 degrees F
TIME: - 10 minutes

- 6 ripe bananas, peeled
- 1/2 cup lemon juice
- 1/4 teaspoon vanilla
- 3 tablespoons brown sugar
- 1/4 teaspoon nutmeg or cinnamon

1. Place the peeled bananas in a baking pan.
2. Cover each banana with lemon juice and vanilla.
3. Sprinkle each banana with brown sugar and spice.
4. Bake 7 minutes until bananas are tender and easily pierced with a fork.
5. Serve hot as a vegetable or as a dessert.

A SOUL FOOD DISH

One of the favorite soul foods is sweet potato pie. Here is an interesting example of a vegetable made into a dessert. Refresh your memory about soul foods by rereading pages 35–36.

Sweet Potato Pie

YIELD: - 1-nine-inch pie

Pie Crust
11/2 cups flour
1/4 teaspoon salt
1/2 cup shortening
1/4 cup (about) cold water

1. Measure the sifted flour and salt. Sift together into a bowl.
2. Measure the cold shortening.
3. Cut the shortening into the flour mixture with a fork, two knives scissors style, or a pastry blender, until the mixture looks like cornmeal.
4. Add a small amount of cold water at a time by sprinkling it on a dry place each time. Mix lightly with a fork, bringing the dampened particles together with dry ones. Run the fork along the bottom of the bowl and bring the dry particles to the surface. Push aside dampened parts. Continue adding water until the mixture is sufficiently dampened and not crumbly. Avoid stickiness because that means that you have added too much water.
5. Form the dough into a ball but handle lightly and as little as possible. Chill well.
6. Place the dough on a lightly floured board. Roll it lightly in all directions with a rolling pin, keeping the dough round. Loosen the dough occasionally with a spatula if the dough sticks. Flour the board slightly. Roll the pastry to ⅛-inch thickness and at least two inches larger than the pie pan.
7. Prick the dough generously with a fork to prevent the crust from bubbling when it starts to bake. Fold the dough lightly into a semicircle and transfer it to the piepan. Lift back the semicircle and fit the crust gently to the pan. Do not grease the pan. Let the dough rest for 5 minutes so that it can settle in the pan. Press out any air under the piecrust.
8. With a scissors cut the piecrust ½ inch larger than the pan. Fold the dough so that it has an upright edge. Flute the crust with your fingers.

Filling
3 large sweet potatoes, cooked and mashed through a sieve
4 tablespoons butter or margarine
1/4 teaspoon salt
1/2 cup sugar
1 cup half and half (milk and cream)
3 eggs, separated
1/4 teaspoon cinnamon
1/2 teaspoon nutmeg (optional)

1. Cream the margarine or butter until soft and creamy.
2. Add the sugar, salt, and cinnamon and nutmeg (if used) and stir until well blended.
3. Add the mashed potatoes to the sugar mixture and mix well.
4. Add the half and half to the beaten egg yolks.
5. Combine milk and eggs with the potato and sugar mixture. Mix well.
6. Beat the egg whites until they are stiff and fold them into the potato mixture.
7. Pour the mixture into the piecrust.
8. Bake in a preheated oven at 425 degrees for 30 to 35 minutes.
9. The pie is done when a silver knife inserted into the center of the pie comes out clean.
10. Remove the pie from the oven and place it on a rack.
11. Serve it hot or chilled. Cut it into 5 or 6 wedges.

Undiluted evaporated milk may be substituted for the half and half. Cost will be cut.

You may find different versions of these recipes, because some have changed with family usage or depending upon the supplies that are available. Try different versions of them and make your own recipe by combining the best features of each.

A CHINESE DISH

The Chinese are noted for their use and combinations of fruit. Here is a quick and delicious dessert that might be served with Chinese fortune cookies and tea. Your family or guests will enjoy reading and sharing their fortunes.

Chinese Fruit Compote

SERVINGS: – 4

   2 cups pineapple, canned chunks in juice
1/2 cup canned mandarin oranges

1. Chill the pineapple and oranges.
2. Serve promptly after removing the fruit from the refrigerator.

Ingredients for a Chinese meal may be purchased in a Chinese grocery store.

A SPANISH DISH

During your study of ethnic foods you may find recipes in cookbooks of other countries that have their ingredients in metric measurements. If you have access to a metric scale, you might try this Spanish recipe.

Rich Biscuit

500 grams flour
  5 grams salt
125 grams butter or margarine
1/4 liter milk
  1 egg, slightly beaten

1. Sift flour, baking powder, and salt.
2. Add the butter and cut into the flour mixture with a pastry blender, a fork, with two knives used like a pair of scissors, or work with your clean hands.
3. Add the milk a little at a time, and mix only enough to moisten the ingredients well.
4. Pat out on a lightly floured board to a thickness of 2 centimeters.
5. Cut with a round cutter, place on a baking sheet, and brush each biscuit lightly with beaten egg.
6. Bake at 220° C (400° F) for 10-15 minutes, depending on size of biscuit.
7. Remove and cool.
8. Spaniards split the biscuits, spread with marmalade and top with whipped cream. You might like to use the biscuit as a base for strawberry or other fruit shortcake.

Ethnic food recipes may be found in your grandmother's cookbook, in publications, and by writing to relatives.

USING INTERNATIONAL RECIPES

When you have prepared international recipes so that you have confidence you might think of ways of sharing your know-how. You might prepare some for gifts to friends and relatives with a little history about the recipe. If their response is encouraging, you might take orders for the recipe you like to prepare best and sell the food. Your classmates and you might have a food fair. You might prepare some of the food and ask individuals of different backgrounds in the community to donate a favorite food. All of it might be sold and the money contributed to a worthy community cause. In some schools students have prepared cookbooks of their recipes and distributed some of them among the neighboring public libraries so that many people could enjoy them. In one school that had a printing class the books were printed and sold, and the funds given to an important school cause. Many persons may share your interest in ethnic foods.

THINKING IT OVER

1. Think about the times when you have eaten foods you considered very strange. Did the recipe come from another country? Did you start eating with the idea that you would probably not like the food? Were your conclusions always right? If you disliked it, did you analyze why—was it due to texture, flavor, or was the combination of foods different from what you usually eat? What might you do to make eating these new foods a pleasant experience?

2. Many families have interesting food traditions. Maybe your favorite bread is rye, your eggs are usually fried, or you have waffles for breakfast on Sundays. Some of these family food traditions may have originated in your mother's or your father's family and kept right on going in your family. Maybe you think this is trivial, but someday you may be transferring some family eating ways into your own house, starting your own family tradition. Many families have to move often. Keeping to the same family food habits might make the adjustment to new ways easier.

THINGS TO DO

1. See how many prepared foods from other countries are found in your grocery store. If you live in or near a large city you might visit a food specialty shop and see how many varieties you can find.

2. Consider different kinds of family holidays and the foods served with them. Are there nationality influences?

3. In class, plan a simple meal consisting of dishes of other countries. Invite students from elementary grades who may have been learning about these countries in social studies. Share information about the people of these countries.

4. Bring from home a small serving of a food that you believe represents a foreign influence. Organize a tasting party and share your ideas with other members of the class.

5. Have a class discussion about ways in which interesting foods of other countries might be introduced into our daily meals.

6. Visit a restaurant that serves food typical of an ethnic group and talk to the owner. Read the menu carefully. If possible, have each student order a different dish and share the different foods for tasting.

7. If you have a background of many ethnic groups, analyze your food patterns and determine which ethnic food group or groups seem to dominate. How would moving to another country influence what you eat?

area six

Your Clothes

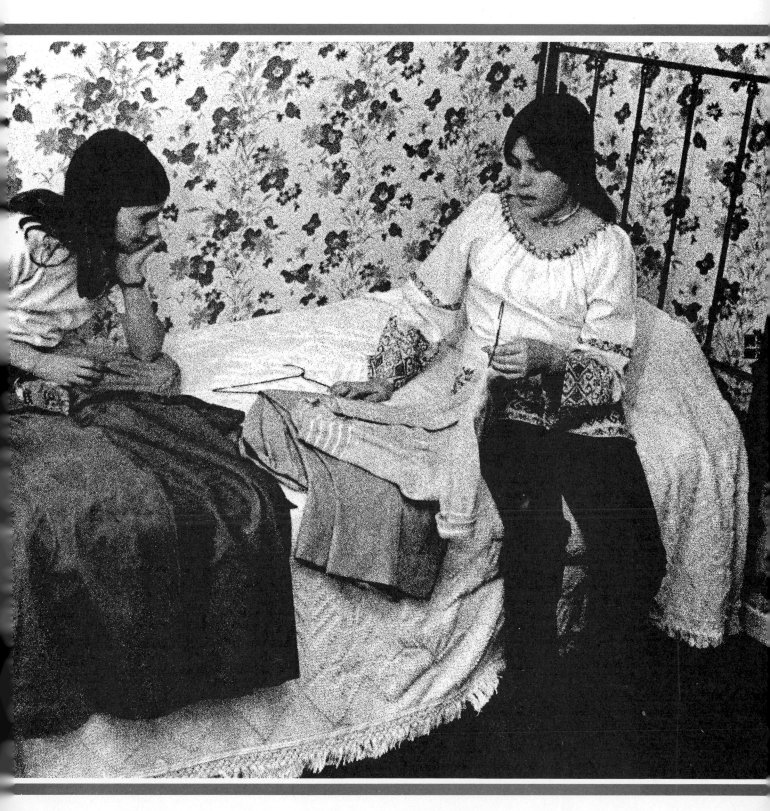

22 The language of your clothes

Your clothes are your closest environment; intimate, next to you, and part of you. Some authorities in the clothing field refer to clothes as your second skin or your clothes companion. Clothes protect you, give you pleasure, but also speak for you. Clothes are an extension of your personality. All in all, clothes are an important factor in your life.

MEANING OF CLOTHES

Psychologists tell us that clothes reflect ourselves. How you feel about yourself may be shown in the clothes you wear. Your garments are among your most personal belongings. Maybe your brother or your sister objects when you borrow a sweater. When you look well in your clothes and someone compliments you, it gives you a good feeling. When you want to impress someone, you may take special care in selecting the clothes you will wear for meeting this person.

Clothes have an image meaning. Do you dress the same for washing a car as for going to church? Why the difference? Clothes, then, have a meaning associated with a purpose. How may personal characteristics be reflected in an individual's clothes—such as being neat, artistic, thorough, careless, or indifferent? How may clothes identify a group (headband or headdress, jewelry, jacket, or pin), a community, or a region? (Do the clothes of inhabitants of California differ from those of Maine?) Have you ever seen a girl wearing a boy's shoes or a boy wearing a scarf that he knitted himself? What are your reactions?

At one time clothes communicated a message of modesty, but that seems less important now. Nationality is indicated by the Indian *sari* or the Japanese *kimono*. What are some meanings that you attach to clothes? What are your clothes telling others about you?

How the World Looks at Your Clothes

Clothes help identify you in certain ways to the people who see you. For example, policemen or policewomen in their uniforms tell everyone quickly who they are. Other uniforms help people recognize the job of the person wearing them, such as a nurse or a gas station attendant. You may be attending a school that requires a uniform.

The climate in which you live is revealed by the clothes people wear. If you are wearing a heavy coat, muffler or scarf, mittens, and boots, you are obviously dressed for cold weather. What clothing adjustments do you make for climate? Do members of your family agree on what is suitable for various types of weather? How do you resolve these problems?

The world further judges how well you select your clothes for the occasion or activity. Are you guilty of wearing a party dress or suit to work, for example? What kind of clothes are considered appropriate for attending sports events, participating in specific sports, or for work? Sometimes a community will impose certain dress codes. For example, a church has a sign "No halters permitted" and a restaurant displays another "Bare feet are not allowed." Why such signs? What are your reactions? In addition, the world notices overdressing, such as an unusual display of expensive fabrics, leather, or fur.

If your crowd or community approves of certain types of clothes and if you dress very dif-ferently, you may become less acceptable, or you may stand out as being too "different." This may result in a feeling of not belonging. You may have a strong personality, be unusually talented, or have status with your friends that causes them to overlook your clothes. There is a tendency for people to conform in certain ways to the kind of clothes approved by your community.

Your Clothing Image

Your clothes definitely affect the image or picture you present to others. You can send the message, even to people who do not know you, that you are drab, lively, sporty, neat or messy, fashion-conscious or old-fashioned, arty, sophisticated, or classic, or even have a sense of humor by making a belt of tape measures or wearing a necklace made from safety pins or paper clips. You may let others know about your concern about a social problem such as pollution by wearing a pin with a message.

Your clothes are an extension of your personality.

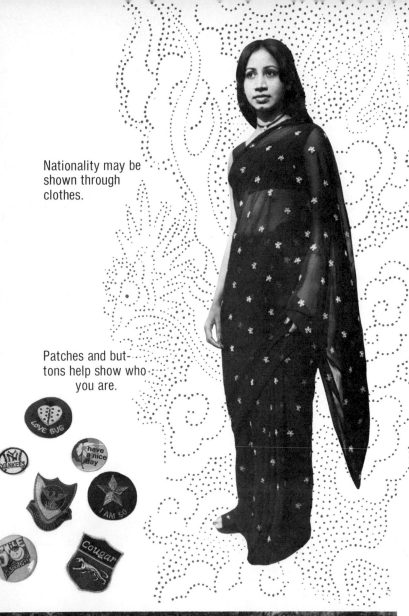

Nationality may be shown through clothes.

Patches and buttons help show who you are.

If you take part in a sport, you usually wear special clothes.

You have the power to transmit the kind of meaning you desire. The impression you make depends on the choice you make. Your appearance leans on what you do with what you have—body build, cleanliness, cosmetics, and clothes.

Your body build and facial characteristics are mostly inherited and not easily changed. You cannot change the color of your eyes unless you wear contact lenses. You can change your weight if it is compatible with health and your doctor's advice. You are in your growing years and must be certain to have adequate nutrients for growth. Cleanliness and cosmetics are discussed in Chapter 23. What you can do about clothes is discussed throughout this Area. Put it all together and if you have been realistic about the image you can attain, you should see a change for the better.

Most of the characteristics of your body build are inherited.

COLOR IS IMPORTANT

Color Adds Meaning

Color plays a vital role in our lives and the color of our clothes is an important factor. Which colors seem to be happy colors to you? Which ones appear to express serious moods? You may say that Sally is green with envy or that Joe is blue because he did not make the team. Have you ever remarked that your father was in a brown study or that a friend of yours had a purple passion for pizza? How about the cowardly character on television who is referred to as yellow and the man down the street who sees red every time you run across his lawn? Do you wear a bright raincoat on rainy and dreary days to help you have a happier outlook? Think about the effect that various colors have upon you.

Colors are used for safety. Yellow slickers are recommended for children on rainy days. Iridescent stickers may be helpful. "Day-glo" colors—orange, red, and bright yellow—are suggested for improved safety at night. Wearing something white at night is suggested for bicycle riders. Snow skiers are warned against wearing all white. Strong colors help skiers see one another in the snow.

At one time color was associated with season—bright or pastel colors for spring and summer, and dark colors for winter and fall. Today the emphasis is on fashion colors. Seasons may be identified with primary colors, earth colors, pastels or heathers, and other favorites. This

Color coordinate your wardrobe

does not mean that you must discard all your clothes each season. A girl can update her image by buying a skirt, a scarf, or a necklace that will give your appearance the new look. Boys may add a different touch to their clothes by a new belt, tie, T-shirt, jacket, hat or cap, or scarf. Experiment with coordinating or blending colors with each other. Color can be the most exciting part of your wardrobe.

Color combinations you might enjoy are unlimited. Look around for color combinations. They can be found in nature, works of art, or even on fruit and vegetable stands. Many clothes designers work around the color, proportions, and combinations found in the works of famous painters. They may refer to their clothes as the Picasso line, for example. By studying different painters it was discovered that colors could be blended if chosen carefully. You can do the same with your clothes.

Color Can Enhance Appearance

Keep in mind that you should choose clothes that will flatter you. Becoming colors can do a great deal to enhance your appearance. You have already formed ideas about the colors that are best for you. But perhaps there are many you have never attempted to wear that would be equally flattering.

Learn Your Colors

You may have studied the following fundamental color theories in other classes. But a brief review will help you understand the reasons for picking certain colors for your clothes.

A color wheel is a device by which are shown the primary, secondary, and intermediate colors. The *primary* colors are those not made from mixing other colors. These are yellow, blue, and red. The *secondary* colors are a mixture of two primary ones. These are green (yellow and blue), purple (blue and red), and orange (yellow and red). The *intermediate* colors are a mixture of primary and secondary colors. These are yellow-green, blue-green, blue-violet, red-violet, red-orange, and yellow-orange. Then there are *neutral* colors. These are black, white, and gray. You must understand these color classifications in order to decide what combinations will be best in your wardrobe.

Yellow, orange, and red are warm colors, while blue and green are cool colors. Colors also vary in intensity, each having a range of value from very, very light to very, very dark. Examples are shades like a pale, pale blue and a deep navy blue. The color value also may vary with different kinds of textures. Certain fabrics seem to absorb colors, such as a heather-colored wool sweater. A navy blue sweater has a different depth of color from a navy blue silk dress. Perhaps you have had a green sweater or a red shirt that was not becoming. That does not necessarily mean that green and red should be omitted from your wardrobe. You might be able to wear these colors in a different shade and even in a different fabric.

How to Choose Colors for You

Good detective work takes time, and finding the most becoming colors is no exception. You need to turn to your trusty mirror and analyze yourself again. Decide about your hair color, skin tones, and the shade of your eyes. Then decide whether there are any features that you want to highlight. By repeating the same color, certain shades of blue will emphasize blue eyes. Or perhaps there are features you would like to minimize. If your skin has yellow tones you will want to avoid wearing shades of yellow.

A color try-on session can be fun. All you need are samples of as many kinds of fabric in as many colors as you can find. Then sit in front of a mirror and place the swatches on your shoulder one at a time. Be sure that the fabric is

A color try-on session can be fun—and helpful.

against your skin and under your chin so that the full effect of the color on your hair, eyes, and skin tones can be seen. The colors that make your skin look clear and healthy will be the best for you. You should exercise special care when selecting them.

If the color experimenting session is not possible, you can find some hints that will help you in the Color Selection Chart that follows. These are only suggestions but you can keep them in mind and experiment yourself the next time you are shopping.

Colors will be becoming if they either contrast or harmonize with your own coloring. For example, navy blue is an attractive shade for blondes and beige or white is equally effective for brunettes. Warm tones of brown go well with brown hair and eyes, and rust and copper shades flatter redheads. Be sure not to make the contrast too harsh or the colors so harmonious that you appear dull.

Always look at colors in the clear light of day. Then you can be certain which are becoming.

Table 22-1

COLOR SELECTION CHART		
Hair	Skin	Becoming Colors
Blonde	Fair	Dark colors and a pastel contrast, navy blue, white, gray, greens *Try* red, yellow, tangerine, golden browns.
Blonde	Dark	Green, blue (most shades), beige with bright colors, pink, rose *Try* gray-blue.
Mid-brown (most numerous)	Fair to dark	Yellow (all), green (all), blue (all), clear red, beige, and gray with bright colors *Try* violet.
Brunette	Fair	Pastels, pale pink and blue, navy blue, deep green, bright green, red, wine *Try* tangerine, brown.
Brunette	Dark	Tangerine tones, red, bright green, blue (most shades), beige, maroon (dark red) *Try* warm brown, blue-green.
Red-head	Fair to dark	Pink (some shades), blue (all shades), green (all shades), white (for fair skin occasionally), dark brown *Try* beige, greyed yellow.

Combining Colors

You would hardly wear an outfit of all one color. Even a uniform, such as worn by a person in the armed forces or a flight attendant, is usually a combination of colors. Usually one predominates and one or two others are used in smaller amounts. The predominating color is best if it is in a dull shade. There are several different color combinations that are pleasing.

Good Color Combinations. Gray trousers worn with a white turtleneck sweater and a gray, white, and black sport coat would be a *neutral* color harmony. A white dress with black buttons and belt is another example of this combination. The simplest harmony is that of two or more neutral colors.

If you were to wear charcoal gray trousers, a white shirt, and a red tie, you would have a combination called *accented neutral*. Another example is a charcoal gray shirt or slacks and a red sweater. By adding a dash of color to a neutral shade, you will get an accented neutral combination.

Another simple combination, called *monochromatic*, is made up of various shades of the same color. Brown trousers with a tan shirt and a brown-and-tan striped tie is an example. Dark

Look at color in the light of day to determine if it is becoming. For clothes worn in the evening look at color in artificial light.

blue jeans, a Levi shirt in pale blue, and a medium blue sweater is another example.

Analogous color harmony is more exciting. Look at the color wheel and choose two or three colors that are next to one another. They should be colors that include only one primary color. For example, a combination of blue with touches of blue-violet can be interesting. This principle is often used in planning designs of ties and sports clothes.

A green dress with a touch of red or a navy blue school or team sweater with orange lettering combines colors that are opposite each other on the color wheel. This is known as a *contrasting* or *complementary* combination. These color combinations should be softened so that they will blend in a pleasing manner. By using one color in a different value from the other colors, you should get the desired results.

Color Combinations for You. How can you determine which combinations will be best for you? A person should try on different shades when buying a dress, slacks, jeans, or a suit. One advantage of shopping in a department store is that you can buy everything at the same time. The new suit has shirts and ties that go well together. The new coat blends with both the school skirt and the new wool dress. Salespeople can offer good pointers on clothing selection.

Although girls have many more opportunities to wear a variety of colors, boys have a choice of many colors in ties and scarfs, sports clothes, and sweaters. Sweaters, jackets, and shirts, as well as ties and scarfs, should be of a suitable color. The same rules of color selection and combination apply to both boys and girls. If the skirt or slacks have a bold pattern, it is a good idea to wear a solid shirt in one of the colors of the skirt or slacks.

You may choose a color for reasons other than that of attractiveness. You may have a liking for a particular shade. That is all well and good if the shade becomes you. But if, for example, red is just not for you, is there any way you can wear this shade? Perhaps little touches can be used as an accent, such as a red flower or pin on a navy dress. Or red can be worn as part of a tie pattern. You could buy only red pencils or your school-bag could be red plaid. One could buy a pocketbook with a red lining. You might even wear red pajamas or use a red bedspread. There are many ways of introducing color into your daily life.

Sometimes it is difficult to find the color you desire while shopping for clothes.

Now take a look at your clothes. Which colors are present? How did they get there—by plan or accident? Does your wardrobe reflect a color scheme? If not, are you convinced that you might work toward one? Are you willing to accept new colors? One drawback is that often you find a shirt or sweater that has the style and fit for you but the color is wrong, or in contrast the color is right but the garment does not fit. This means that additional shopping may be necessary to find the best colors for you.

TEXTURES IN CLOTHES

You will have to consider the texture of a material when you are deciding about its attractiveness and color effect. Different textures will affect color. You will have to decide about combining textures.

Textures may be rough, like bulky tweed, or smooth, like silk. They may be shiny, like satin, or dull, like corduroy. They may be heavy, like leather jackets, or light, like a silk scarf. Or they may be soft, like fur, or stiff, like vinyl. A combination of textures, such as a cotton dress or shirt with a wool sweater, may add richness, style, or individuality.

Occasions Influence Type of Textures Suitable

Experience, common sense, and advice from your parents and older sisters and brothers will help you develop an understanding of how to choose interesting texture combinations.

There is considerable flexibility about combinations of textures. The choice will depend on you. For example, a sweater may be over or under a sheer blouse or shirt. A body suit may be worn under a loose V-neck dress. Weather, current trends, and other influences may affect your choice of texture combinations. Experiment. Develop your own look.

Texture adds interest to a garment. Think about the textures in your wardrobe. Do you have an interesting variety? Do you have any favorites? Why? Do textures have special meanings for you? Is it possible to have an overabundance of textures?

This helps you introduce several textures in an outfit.

How do these girls' outfits reflect good taste?

Top an old dress with a sheer jacket made from an old dress or from a remnant for a money-saving new look that is tasteful.

THE LANGUAGE OF TASTE

Taste may be an old-fashioned word, but in relation to clothes it means putting everything together so that the overall effect is attractive and pleasing and shows your ability to make good selections. You may vary in your awareness of basic art elements for a pleasing picture. For example, you may or may not have "color sense." Yet with a feeling for balance or harmony among colors, lines, shapes, and textures, you can develop a pleasing appearance.

Most of us like the familiar—in a broad sense, what most other people are wearing. We may be shocked at extremes or at something new that is very different. After it has been around awhile, we may become accustomed to it, but sometimes it doesn't "take."

You experience with clothes can make a difference in your taste. Browse through clothing departments and specialty shops with your eyes open. Look at displays in store windows. Observe what others are wearing. Notice interesting designs and colors, new color combinations, and even new ways to tie a scarf. The art of tying scarfs in various ways is sometimes called scarfology. Be observant and you will have some basis for developing your taste. Leafing through magazines and experimenting with your own clothes are other experiences that are helpful. Selecting someone as a model of good taste and listening to what this person says about clothes can be enlightening.

Your values or what you think is important is reflected in your clothes. When money for clothes is scarce, clothes can be recycled in ways that still show good taste. (See Chapter 26 for suggestions on recycling clothes.) The casual life-style of most people today is expressed in their garments, but good taste need not be and is not discarded. Tastes do change and are a reflection of the society in which we live. It is not only the community that sets standards, but choice of certain clothes is universal. Jeans, for example, are found in many parts of the world. Clothes have so many meanings.

THINKING IT OVER

1. Give serious consideration to the message that your clothes give to a stranger. Do you ever gain a clue about what others think? Would you want to change this message? How would you dress differently? Have you ever analyzed what your friends tell you about your clothes? Can you put this all together for meaning?

2. Look at the members of your class. How would you select those who are best dressed for school? What criteria would you establish for judging good student dress? Do class members agree on the criteria? Could guides be developed incorporating ideas from your discussion?

THINGS TO DO

1. From a mail-order catalogue develop a wardrobe for an imaginative boy and girl. Include all the basics for a particular season, such as winter or summer. Try to have each wardrobe well coordinated and versatile. Figure the cost and compare the two wardrobes. How could you save money if you actually purchased all or part of one of the wardrobes?

2. Make a survey of your community and determine all the various ways that color is used for safety and for directions and identification on doors, sidewalks, streets, and highways, and in parking lots and other places.

3. Interview individuals in your school or in your community about the clothes someone would wear who is considered popular, sporty, intelligent, lazy, and so on. Make your own list. After the interviews, interpret your answers and try to reach some conclusions.

23 Looking your best

Have you ever noticed that you usually look the way you feel? You look good because you feel good. This, in turn, gives you self-confidence and poise. Everyone wants to look his or her best at all times. Very few people whom we consider beautiful or handsome are really as good-looking as we think. Usually their secret lies in the fact that they are well-groomed. They know the right clothes to wear; they have chosen clothes that are becoming to them. You can do many things to make yourself more attractive. That is the purpose of personal grooming.

PLAN TO LOOK YOUR BEST

Of course, looking your best doesn't just happen. It is the result of planning—planning what to do and when. After all, looking your best should come naturally. It need not be a chore. An attractive appearance is the result of working out a daily routine that answers your needs and can easily be followed.

Each person grows at a different rate of speed. One year you may be the shortest one in your class and the next year you may be the tallest. And your rate of development varies. As you grow and develop, your interest in yourself and what you can do to improve your personal appearance increases. Personal grooming is a combination of many things: bathing, care of your hair, your hands, your skin, your teeth, your clothes—all the things that go to make up YOU. How can you, as a committee of one, go about improving your appearance? This is a kind of "do-it-yourself" project.

What do you do to look your best? What are some pointers of good grooming? Score yourself in the accompanying chart (Table 23-1) to determine just what you need to do to put your best foot forward.

Can you name two ideas that might be considered the twin points of good grooming? Cleanliness and good general health are mentioned as the foundation of an attractive appearance. Neither the most glamorous clothes nor the best haircut can disguise the need for these two basic ingredients.

Cleanliness refers to your clothes as well as to your body. Easy ways to be sure that everything is really clean will be discussed later. There is, of course, no substitute for good health. Without it, it is impossible to have shining hair, a clear skin, and pep and vitality. These twins will be the starting point, the important must, of every grooming habit: cleanliness and good general health.

TIME TO CHANGE YOUR HABITS

Once you have decided that good grooming is important, when can you expect to see the results of new habits? In some cases a difference will be noted right away. First of all, if you know that your clothes are becoming, clean, and neat, your hair is styled becomingly, and your nails are neat and well cared for, you will begin to feel self-confident because you are sure that these improvements will be noticed by everyone.

However, some problems may take longer to solve than others. For example, a blemished complexion won't clear up overnight. But you may notice an improvement in a week or so. So don't waste any more time worrying about your complexion. Get right to work on it and be patient. Your thought, time, and effort will be rewarded and the results will be sure to please you.

You look the way you feel—well-groomed and attractive.

DAILY BATHING IS IMPORTANT

Years ago it was the custom to bathe once or twice a year. Both men and women lavishly used perfumes to disguise body odor. Even a generation ago, Saturday night was known as the traditional bath night. Scholars tell us that people of some cultures were sewn into their clothes and would bathe only as the seasons and their costumes changed.

Times are different. Today "one a day" is recognized as a basic rule in regard to bathing. Sometimes, on hot days, or when you have been especially busy and there is a special event coming up for which you want to look your best, you may want to take a second bath. But the basic minimum is at least a "once-over" every day.

Growth and development vary with age.

Purpose of a Bath

Why do you think this is such an important rule to follow in personal grooming? First of all, a bath gives one that scrubbed look that is the very foundation of attractiveness. Then there are health reasons. You may not realize that waste products are excreted daily through the pores of the skin. Unless these deposits are washed away, the pores become clogged. When this happens, your body cannot take care of itself efficiently. Also, stale perspiration needs to be washed away so that the odor may be removed. Bathing does not prevent perspiration, but it can help prevent an offending odor.

Other Bath Benefits

Bathing can also be a real health and beauty treatment. A bath stimulates circulation, improves the texture of the skin, massages muscles, relaxes you when you're all wound up, and peps you up. A quick shower can make you feel cool on a hot day. Did you realize you got all these benefits from bathing?

Ways to Bathe

There are three ways to clean yourself from head to toe: a shower, a tub bath, a sponge bath. Each can be equally effective. The important point to remember is that bathing is serious business; it takes time and effort.

It makes little difference which method of bathing you choose for your own routine. A sponge bath may be necessary on a camping trip or where bathing facilities are not available. Fill a basin with warm soapy water. Take one half of a large washcloth or small towel, dip it in the water, and scrub vigorously over your entire body. Dip the dry part in clear water and go over the body again. Rub down with a dry towel. No matter what the technique, there are six steps to proper bathing. But first, you can't do a really good job unless you have the right equipment. See how many of the items listed on page 212 you use for your daily bath.

To look your best it is necessary to plan and keep a schedule.

Table 23-1

GOOD GROOMING CHART

	Take a clear look at yourself. If this column describes *you*, give yourself . . . 5	When you seem to fit into this category, give yourself . . . 3	You're falling down in your grooming routine if this describes you. You get a mere . . . 1
General appearance	Alert, full of vim; eyes bright, step light	A bit tired, look bored, feel hungry, dread going from place to place	Listless, droopy, feet drag, circles under eyes
Standing posture	Erect and easy	Tend to slouch and lean against anything handy	Rubber legs and sway or curved back; shoulder sag
Sitting posture	Erect, sit well back in chair, both feet on floor	Forward slump, feet curled under or around anything handy; "corkscrew" look	Pronounced slouch, ungraceful pose
Hands	Clean, nails clean and trim	Dirty or stained; nails either untrimmed or dirty	Very soiled nails; bitten or broken, untrimmed
Hair	Clean, glossy and shining; neat and arranged becomingly	Oily; needs a shampoo; should be combed; rearranging would help; needs restyling	Dull and straggly; careless arrangement
Face	Clean and clear, free from blemishes	Needs washing, some blemishes	Oily, blemished look; unhealthily pale
Neck and ears	Really clean	Need washing, generally have a gray look	"High water mark"; could stand a thorough scrubbing
Teeth	Clean, white, no cavities; no "bad breath"	Teeth need brushing; should see dentist about cavities	Badly stained or damaged; unpleasant breath
Clothes	Clean, pressed, need no repairs	Mussed or dirty; button missing or minor repair needed	Soiled and badly wrinkled; need mending; safety pins instead of buttons
Color and style of clothes	Harmonious colors and appropriate style, design becoming, appropriate for school; feel comfortable; fit right	Maybe one false note: colors do not go together; too dressy for school; flashy; too tight, wish you could change	Too fussy, unsuitable for school; color and design haphazard; feel self-conscious
Shoes	Comfortable, clean, and appropriate.	Scuffed and need a good polish; no heels or heels too high; shoe laces need attention	In a bad way: could use heels, soles, a good shine; careless walking habit causes excessive wear and tear

If you score:

45 to 50____ This is tops; keep up the good work.

40 to 45____ With attention to a few minor details you should achieve that well-groomed, confident look.

30 to 40____ Check those weak spots which drag your score down. Develop a plan and work on improving these areas.

20 to 30____ Take your grooming schedule in for major repairs. Here's where that willpower you're so proud of can come in handy. Fix one major item each day; in no time you will be proud of yourself and your accomplishments. Also, don't be afraid to ask for help. Your key thought is "Plan a definite time for your grooming routines and stick to it!"

Shower, tub bath, or sponge bath are equally effective.

Essential
1-Pure soap
2-Washcloth
3-Bath-sized towel
4-Shower cap

Nice but Not Necessary
1-Long-handled bath brush
2-Hand brush
3-Talcum

What are the six steps mentioned above? Here they are in their proper order:
1-Rinse yourself thoroughly.
2-Lather up.
3-Scrub and scrub.
4-Rinse and double rinse.
5-Dry thoroughly.
6-Apply an antiperspirant and a deodorant.

You might ask, "Why do we need to discuss all this? Everyone knows that this is the way to take a bath." That's true. But many don't take the time to follow each of these steps carefully, and are therefore only half-washed—and half-clean.

Additional Steps

Two extra steps may be added. If you want to use talcum or bath powder, it is best applied after you are thoroughly dry. A second step is a shortcut to hand and toe care. After your bath, while the cuticle is still soft, push it back with your towel. (Consult the section on nail care for a complete description of how to do this.)

CARE OF YOUR SKIN

What is the first thing you notice when you greet someone? His or her face. All would agree that a glowing, unblemished complexion is important in making a good impression. Don't forget that your face is unprotected from the elements. Because it is exposed, it attracts grime and bacteria. So to keep the good clear skin that you have, or to help clear up your complexion, it is necessary to establish a routine of logical skin care.

Believe it or not, many skin problems are caused by the breaking of age-old health rules. You have heard of these rules for years. Sometimes they are called the inner guard. Yet many people can trace facial blemishes to their breaking the ancient rule against eating too many rich foods. Some of the worst offenders are chocolates, sweets, greasy fried foods, and gravies. Foods that are good for the complexion are discussed in Chapter 11. But briefly they are fruits, vegetables, milk, meats, and foods that are simply prepared.

Health Rules Are Important

Other health rules necessary to a clear complexion are plenty of sleep and rest, proper elimination, regular exercise and fresh air, and—perhaps the most difficult—no worry or tension. Be relaxed and happy. Unless these basic health rules are followed, other things you may do will have no effect on your total appearance.

Cleanliness Affects Your Appearance

Then there is the outer guard—the things that you can do directly to improve the appearance of your skin. Again, cleanliness is behind that glowing look. Don't be a slacker and consider a few quick splashes in the morning with a quick once-over before bedtime the kind of cleansing that will prevent a blemished skin. You should allow time for two good washes a day plus a long careful cleansing at bedtime.

How to Clean Your Face

Very little equipment is needed to produce a clean face. It takes only (1) a pure bland soap, (2) a washcloth, (3) a soft towel, and (4) a hair band or scarf.

The technique is simple. Be sure to tie back your hair or use a headband. After washing your face and neck thoroughly, rinse carefully with warm water to remove the soap. Then rinse again and again, gradually lowering the temperature of the water until the last rinse is cold wa-

Use age-old health rules to prevent skin problems.

ter. Such complete rinsing will help prevent skin blemishes. Warm sudsy water is necessary to open pores and remove dirt lodged therein. Rinsing chases away soap and cool water rinsing will close pores so that fresh dirt won't readily find a stopping place.

Time for Cleansing the Skin

When are the best times for this cleansing routine? You start it off upon arising in the morning. Then, what about after school, when you come home for that snack and to change to play clothes? Naturally, you must be sure to give your face and neck a good cleansing at bedtime.

Blemishes can be a plague at your age, but being healthy and clean are helpful safeguards.

Skin Blemishes

In spite of your best efforts, blemishes are apt to occur. They seem to be a plague of the teens. Some teen-agers don't get them. But the old saying, "An ounce of prevention is worth a pound of cure," is probably true. Actually there are three types of blemishes that may appear: blackheads, pimples, and acne. If you can't seem to prevent them with the health and cleanliness routine, you may need to see a skin specialist.

Treatment for Blemishes. What can you do about blemishes? First of all, you can start on a concentrated program to be clean. Wash your face and neck thoroughly several times each day.

Pointers for a Good Complexion.

Check yourself on the following:
★ Be faithful to your cleaning routine.
★ Keep your washcloth fresh and clean.
★ Refuse to share towels, powder puffs, and the like.
★ Remember trouble spots—behind the ears, the neck, and around the chin and nose—you need extra rubbing here.
★ Never pick at blemishes.

CARE OF YOUR HAIR

To look your best, why not start at the top? Your hair is probably your most distinctive feature. This is fortunate. With effort, you can make the changes you desire.

General Information

Your ancestors are an important factor in determining the kind of hair you have. Thus your genes help to determine whether your hair is straight or curly, or whether it will turn gray at an early age. You may have red-headed genes in your family. Have you studied your family as to hair types? Can you identify other family members who have hair similar to yours?

Construction of Hair. There are three layers in each strand. The inner core is the medula. The middle core is the cortex, which contains melanin, the coloring matter. Only two basic pigments are found in hair—brown and red. The combination of these two intensities accounts for all the different hair colors in the world. The outer layer is the cuticle, which consists of translucent overlapping cells. Have you ever looked at a hair under the microscope?

Kinds of Hair. Everyone possesses a unique kind of hair. No two heads of hair are exactly the same. Your hair helps identify you.

Certain hair characteristics may be placed on a kind of scale for purposes of description. For example, there is *straight to curly hair* with many variations from very straight to very curly. Curly hair may vary from a slight wave, to many ringlets, to frizzy hair, or to a crisp, tightly curled type. Other characteristics with wide ranges are *fine to coarse; in color* from white to blonde to brown to black, *dry to oily, thin to thick,* or *short to long.* Can you name other characteristics of hair? The way you care for or style your hair will be influenced by the kind of hair you have.

Health Habits and Hair

In order to have healthy-looking hair, you need to practice health habits. An adequate diet, plenty of exercise in the fresh air, enough rest, and freedom from worry are good rules. If your hair seems lifeless, colorless, and dull, take a look at your basic health customs and plan needed improvements.

Brushing your hair stimulates your scalp.

Your hair should be soft, gleaming, well-groomed, and becomingly styled.

Daily Care. Do you picture your hair as clean, shiny, and easy to handle? What you do to your hair every day will or will not reflect these characteristics.

Along with other morning chores, you will brush, comb, and arrange your hair so that it will look well. During the day, you may wish to comb your hair occasionally to give it a fresh appearance. That means you have to carry a comb or perhaps a small brush. Habits have to be established so that you will not forget about how your hair looks.

Another daily responsibility is brushing your hair. This may be done in the evening. Brush strokes should be carried from the scalp to the very ends of your hair with a long sweeping motion. Brush the top and back of your hair up and the sides out. Boys need to brush their hair as well as girls.

Grandmother's 100 brush strokes a day are not in as strong favor as formerly, because the scalp may become overstimulated by too much brushing and make your hair oily. Dry hair can take more brushing than oily hair. Brush thin or fine hair gently with a brush that has soft bristles. An oval brush is best for long, thick hair. For medium-textured hair of shoulder length, a round or half-round brush is recommended. A flair-style brush is suggested for wavy or curly hair.

Massaging the scalp stimulates the circulation and encourages healthy hair. Use the balls of the fingertips of both hands and massage in a rotating motion over the entire scalp. Do this every day.

Brushes and Combs

The brush you use on your hair every day requires consideration. Handle the brush so that the bristles are used evenly. In this way, parts of your brush will not be worn unevenly.

In selecting a brush, there are a number of points to bear in mind. Natural bristles from the backs of wild boars are more expensive but absorb hair dirt and grime and distribute natural oils better than other types of bristles. Nylon bristles last longer and are easier to clean. In buying a nylon brush, check for rounded edges and ends for improved brushing. Tufts of nylon bristles should be of uneven length. The longer bristles clean and shine the hair.

Nylon bristles slide through the hair more easily than the boar bristles and are easier to handle while styling your hair. Brushes with both types of bristles are available. One brush combines the purposes of cleaning and styling.

Note the pad into which the bristles are embedded. Rubber has the advantage of greater flexibility. Metal and wood are other satisfactory materials for bristle pads.

Combs are usually made of plastic, hard rubber, or nylon. Heavier combs are more durable. A comb with large teeth is good for combing out snarls in wet or dry hair.

A lifting comb, sometimes called an African pick, is helpful in reviving an Afro hairdo. For delicate hair, heavy-duty picks with rounded edges are used to prevent snags. Metal, wood, or plastic are the materials used for a pick comb.

Other tools for hair care are a hair dryer and blowers, a sharp scissors for cutting or trimming hair at home, rollers of various sizes, and clips for pin curls.

Shampooing

Regular shampooing is a must in hair care. How often you shampoo depends on your type of hair and other influences. Oily hair, in general, requires more shampoos than dry or normal hair. If you are active in sports, or physically active in other ways, your hair will have to be shampooed more frequently. If you live in an environment in which there is considerable soot, dust, or smog in the atmosphere, the number of shampoos will have to be increased. Fewer shampoos, in contrast, may be required in a dry, clean climate. If you have dandruff, you will have to shampoo more frequently and use a medicated shampoo to treat the condition.

Select your shampoo carefully. Experiment for a type that does the most for your particular type of hair. Compare prices among shampoos that seem equally effective for you. A mild shampoo that tends to be neutral is preferred to one that may be acid or alkaline in nature.

Your activities will affect your shampoo schedule.

Here are some pointers for various hair types. A regular creme rinse will help smooth the hair, remove the tangles, and reduce frizziness and static electricity. The hair of black people absorbs moisture more readily during shampooing and thus takes longer to dry. For them, a shampoo with an oil base or conditioner is recommended for shine and control. A creme rinse is helpful for adding oil and making it easier to comb the hair. If the hair is especially dry, it may be necessary to apply an oil conditioner after shampooing.

Certain steps in shampooing are suggested. First, brush your hair and scalp briskly. Next, wet the hair thoroughly with warm water. Avoid hot water. Apply the shampoo to your hands or directly to your scalp and work up a good lather. Rub the scalp vigorously with the balls of your fingertips. Rinse thoroughly. Apply the shampoo a second time and repeat lathering and rubbing the scalp. Rinse thoroughly in warm water until all of the shampoo has been removed. Give yourself a final rinse of cold water. If your hair is dry, you may add a small amount of olive or other oil, a teaspoon or less, to the last rinse. Experiment to determine the best amount of oil to use. If your hair is long, do not shampoo the ends as much as the scalp because essential oils may be removed and hair will split more readily. A lemon and water or vinegar and water rinse tends to remove curds of soap. After shampooing, rub your hair gently with a clean towel and then style it. Clean your brushes and combs in warm, sudsy water after each shampoo. Rinse thoroughly in clear, running water. Dry the brushes with their bristles down.

Where you wash your hair may be a problem. The easiest place is the shower. If that is not possible, consider washing under the bathtub faucet, or in the bathroom or kitchen sink. A spray is handy for rinsing. A small bowl may be used for pouring rinse water over the hair.

Styling

Select a hair style that is currently in fashion and yet reflects your way of life, personality, and taste. Avoid a style that is demanding and constantly requires refixing. The size and shape of your face must be considered. Long hair may not be the best choice if you are very short. Exotic or unusual styles may not be comfortable for the shy person. If some of your features are dominant, very short hair may accentuate them. Remember that hair has a softening effect if it frames the face.

A hair stylist can give you suggestions about highlighting your most desirable features and playing down less desirable ones. The texture of your hair and the line of growth must be considered so that your hair will be more manageable.

Experiment with your own hair and with the hair of your friends. It can be fun. Molding your hair into possible styles while wet or with lather can give you some notion of how you will look with a certain style.

Another consideration is to begin your styling with a good haircut. This is true for long or short hair. A good operator usually relies on sharp scissors, not a razor or thinning scissors. Wavy hair requires less cutting but must be shortened occasionally. Long hair needs the ends trimmed to remove split ends and to give a

Which hairstyle says you?

Which hairstyle says you?

bouncy look. Generally hair is cut while wet. Hair should be cut about once a month. Long hair may be cut every six weeks. Much will depend on the rate your hair grows and cutting will be done accordingly. Hair grows from ½ inch to 1 inch per month.

Whether you should cut your hair at home is debatable. Many books and magazines give step-by-step procedures for cutting hair. If you have the right kind of sharp scissors and feel that you have a knack for hair cutting, you may experiment. But remember you will have to live with a disaster until your hair grows out. It is especially difficult to cut your own hair. It may be possible for friends to share haircutting.

Some people prefer a blow-dried look. Superfine, thin hair may be dried with a blower, but the hair should be constantly lifted with a brush or comb for body. For short, uncurled hair, style the hair with a hand dryer that has a brush or comb attachment. For slightly longer, curlier hair, dry the hair with a blower in one hand and a round brush in the other to turn the hair back. Keep the dryer on a low setting for short or fine hair. You will have to experiment to find the best way to blow-dry your hair.

If you use rollers, remember that jumbo rollers make loose waves, large rollers make deep waves, and small rollers give tight curls or ringlets. Pin curls make soft curls like corkscrews. If you prize curly hair and yours is straight, a permanent may be the answer for you. On the other hand, you may have curly hair and want straight hair. Remember that your hair structure is weakened from the chemicals in permanents or straightening products.

If you have curly hair, the natural Afro is easy to handle, although part of the hair may be less curly and may not stand up as you desire. You may require a permanent in that part of your hair. The Afro style can suit different facial shapes and can be adapted for an oval face, asymmetrical for a square face, or fuller at the top or sides to meet your needs. Bangs can soften angles. Braiding has many variations. Cornrowing is an ancient African hair style that Cicely Tyson, the talented actress, has encouraged as an art form. The entire head of hair is braided into neat rows. What are some good ideas that you have discovered?

Special Hair Care Needs

If you live where the sun shines all year round, your hair will demand extra attention. Most people need to moderate the amount of sunshine they get. Sunshine will make light hair lighter and may remove some of the oil, which must be replaced by conditioners. When you swim in the ocean or in a pool, always rinse your hair with clear water after swimming. If you comb your hair wet at the beach, do so gently to avoid breaking the hair. Braid long hair before swimming to reduce tangles. A shampoo with a conditioner is recommended for sun lovers.

Hair is affected in other ways. Do not take medicines that you do not need or that have not been prescribed for you. Drugs can impair the health of hair.

Hair problems can be transmitted easily. Do not borrow a brush or comb. Always use your own clean brush and comb.

With all the electrical hair gadgets on the market, you may wonder about the energy cost. Actually the cost is low. But if there are many users, considerable energy will be needed. So consider ways to reduce the use of these gadgets. Partially drying your hair with a towel before using an electrical dryer or blower is advised. What ideas do you have for saving energy?

HAND CARE

Look at your hands. Do you like the way they look? When you open a door, hand someone change, or shake hands are you proud of their appearance?

Once a day a good hand wash is desirable. The use of a nail brush or an old toothbrush that is set aside for this purpose is desirable. Have a nail file or clippers near the washbowl to smooth any torn or broken nails. Some people keep a nail file in their pocket, backpack, or tote bag for emergencies.

There is a technique for washing your hands thoroughly. It is simple, but effective. A nail-brush or handbrush is necessary equipment. Use lukewarm water and work up suds with the brush. Scrub every last bit of your hands and nails gently but firmly. Be sure to scrub the back of your hands and your nails. Then rinse in lukewarm water. Dry thoroughly, and then push back the cuticles. Easy? Yes, but it will give your hands an appearance that will stand the closest inspection.

You should wash your hands whenever they need it, of course. But be especially certain to wash them before each meal, after using the bathroom, and at bedtime. These are good times to give your elbows a scrubbing. If they are

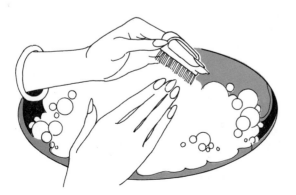

rough, rub them with a little baby oil or lanolin. This will also reduce their tendency to become dirt catchers. Each night, too, you can check for rough nails. Unless you track these down, you can easily snag your favorite sweater.

You may feel that you are "all thumbs" when it comes to trying your first real manicure. Perhaps you think that cutting your nails with the kitchen scissors every once in a while will do. But this is not so. A weekly manicure is a must for neat nails and trim cuticles. You'll need little equipment: an emery board or metal nail file, cuticle or olive oil, a nail scissors, and a cuticle stick.

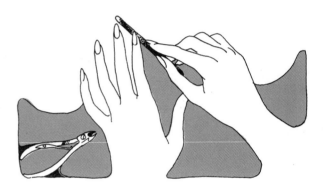

Method of Manicuring

The best time to do your nails is after your weekly shampoo. Then your cuticle is soft and your nails will file easily. First, using either the emery board or metal nail file (and be sure that it is a good one), file your nails. Follow the natural shape of your fingers so that the nails will have rounded curves. Be careful not to make them too deep at the corners. Since you lead such an active life, your nails should not be long and clawlike; rather, they should be short enough to allow you to use your hands easily. After filing, rub cuticle oil on the cuticle. With an orange stick, gently push back the cuticle. You will not need to cut the cuticle if you are faithful about your weekly manicure. Each night, after bathing, you can push back the cuticle. Also, don't wait for your weekly manicure to take care of broken nails. Include this in your daily once-over.

Use of Nail Polish

To polish or not to polish nails is a question that puzzles many girls. Most decide that school is not the place for colored polish, though some will use a natural or colorless finish. Some believe that a little polish protects your nails. If you do wear nail polish, apply a base coat and then

218

one coat of the polish. Allow plenty of time for each application to dry before adding the second one. Remove chipped polish. Remember that polish is only a finishing and somewhat unnecessary touch. Hands that are clean and manicured are well-groomed without any polish.

You will notice that you get results—fast. Everyone notices dirty hands, broken nails, and ragged cuticles. You hands can look their best with only a few minutes of regular attention.

Do Check Yourself for Attractive Hands and Nails

1—Wash regularly.
2—Keep relaxed. Do not play with your hands, touch your hands to your face, or use your hands excessively while talking. Use your hands naturally.
3—Remember that your hands are not can openers, screwdrivers, or scissors.
4—Protect hands from extremes of temperatures and strong cleaning solutions.
5—Avoid extremely hot or cold water for washing.
6—Dry your hands thoroughly.
7—Avoid biting your nails.
8—Keep your nails well manicured.

Keep these points in mind and your hands will give away the secret—that you care about your appearance.

POSTURE IS ALSO IMPORTANT

Unless you stand and sit straight with your shoulders back, all your efforts with grooming and clothes will be ineffective. Take the lessons you have learned about posture to heart and you will be amazed at how much better your clothes look on you.

THERE ARE RULES ABOUT MAKEUP

Some girls your age—it depends on their school, their friends, and their parents—are beginning to use a little makeup. Others never think of using it. But if makeup is worn, there are a few general rules that should be followed and a few hints about how it should be done that one may find helpful.

The basic rule is that makeup should never look obvious. It should only enhance one's face and appearance. That is as it should be since a clear, healthy skin has its own coloring and seldom needs any help.

The natural look is the most acceptable. A very subtle feminine or masculine cologne or toilet water may make one feel more grown-up. For girls lip gloss is the first step and may be followed by a very pale shade of lipstick especially if one has attractive lips and wishes to highlight them. For many girls your age lipstick will be worn only for a party. Makeup is a very personal aspect of grooming and practices vary from place to place. What is done in your community? What about the cost of these cosmetics, if used? Girls should take some colored snapshots of themselves with and without makeup. What is your reaction?

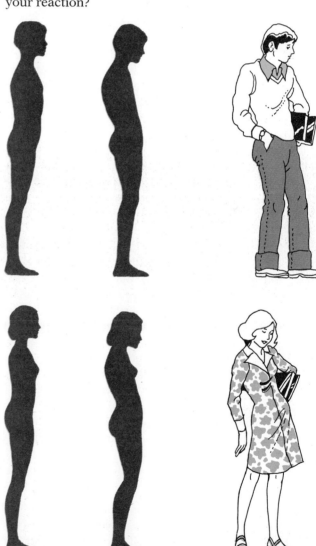

Poor posture can waste all your efforts in self-grooming.

Your teeth can add to or detract from your smile.

CARE OF TEETH

Every time you laugh or speak, your teeth are noticeable and can add to or detract from your appearance. Healthy teeth are necessary for chewing your food and must last as long as you live.

Teeth should be brushed after food has been eaten. If you are not at home, eating a carrot, an apple, or raw fruit is good, if available. Rising your mouth with water is helpful. Gums should be exercised with your finger and dental floss used to dislodge particles between your teeth if your dentist so advises. Some families use a water spray to clean their mouths in addition to brushing. Visit your dentist twice a year to remove the dental film or plaque that builds up and is destructive if not removed periodically. Your dentist will check on the condition of your gums, too, because they are the structure that holds your teeth in place and consequently are most important. You will probably be advised to limit sugar consumption to a minimum because eating large amounts of candy and other sweets, according to authorities, may lead to cavities. Resistance to cavities varies among individuals.

CLOTHES GROOMING

Not only is self grooming of importance but good care must be given to your clothes. They will look better and so will you. The basics are the same—soap and water. If you keep your clothes clean they will last longer.

Basics for Clean Clothes

Dirt makes clothes wear out faster and weakens the fibers. The appearance of dirty clothes is undesirable. There are three basic ingredients required for washing clothes. *Soap or detergent* is important. Detergent is preferred for most clothes because of its greater ability to wet your clothes and to pull out the dirt. Soap is sometimes preferred for delicate fabrics. Cold water soap is used for wools that will shrink in warm or hot water. Most wools will shrink if allowed to soak. Cold water detergent may be used where hot water is not available. *Water* is necessary to dissolve the dirt in the clothes. Most clothes are cleaner if washed in hot water. More suds are created that get between the fibers of the clothes and the dirt adheres to these suds and is carried off with the water. Some form of *agitation* is needed to get the dirt moving. A little rubbing will hasten the cleaning of dirty socks. Squeezing your sweaters gently is another way to loosen dirt. Washing machines spin or agitate back and forth to provide the necessary action. These three basics for clean clothes are necessary if you are washing clothes in a sink or in a washing machine.

Ways to hang up your nightly wash of underwear, socks, and the like.

Sorting clothes as to color, fiber content, and special finishes is critical. Emptying pockets, closing zippers, keeping clothes right side out for easy folding are other important steps. Having a particular place such as a laundry bag or a hamper or other container for soiled clothes will encourage your family to put their dirty clothes there instead of at the bottom of their closets or under the bed.

Hand Washing

One of the first problems in hand washing is to find a way and a place to hang your clothes after they are washed. One possibility is to cover a wooden hanger with washable and colorfast fabric and to hang plastic clothespins from strings to hang articles. An inflatable hanger that blows up so that clothes dry more easily is valuable. If your bathtub is between two walls, put up an extension curtain rod for hanging drip-dry clothes. Maybe you have considered other ways.

For washing your underwear and socks at night, use a mild detergent, rub gently for most items, and rinse thoroughly. Easy-care shirts can be washed and placed on the inflatable hanger and be dry to wear the next day, if desired. Both boys and girls may enjoy doing this easy-way washing. Scrub collars and cuffs well and hang the garment while it is dripping.

Some of your clothes will require special attention. Sweaters made of wool must be washed in cold water with an appropriate detergent, gently squeezed after rinsing, and then rolled in a dry towel to get out most of the moisture. Place a plastic trash bag or plastic bags from the cleaner on a spot on the floor that is out of the way of family traffic. Place a dry towel that is large enough for spreading the sweater on it. Sweaters dry slowly. Acrylic sweaters can be washed in warm water but are dried in the same manner as sweaters made of wool.

Washable raincoats when washed should be rinsed especially well, because soap residue attracts water and may also weaken the fibers. Scarfs, ribbons, and other small articles may be pressed against a clean mirror or the bathroom wall tile and dried without wrinkles. This trick is good if you have to wash while traveling.

Most clothes no longer require ironing, but a little touch-up with an iron may improve their appearance. If you have clothes that are 100 percent cotton and without durable-press finishes, ironing will be necessary. One method is to iron the part of the garment that you want to look es-

"A stitch in time" will save worry, uneasiness, and also your clothes.

pecially nice, such as the collar of a shirt, last. Compare notes with others about how they take care of their clothes.

Check-up Points

The pleasure of wearing clean clothes can be diluted if a seam has split, a zipper is broken, or a collar ripped. Keep a repair kit with neutral colors of thread and a needle handy. If you sew the rips and other items that need attention before you wash the clothes, they will be ready to wear after washing. You are thus spared major repair jobs.

Daily Care

After school, if you are planning on out-of-doors activity, change from school clothes to play clothes. Brush your school clothes to remove dust and lint. Hang them straight on the proper hanger and let them remain in your room to air before putting them away. This allows the perspiration odors to escape and will give your clothing a fresh odor.

At bedtime look over the clothes worn that day to decide what needs to be done to keep them in good condition. Eliminate all stains and spots—even a small one that you think might escape detection—and determine whether sweaters

A few minutes' care each day will keep all clothes ready to wear.

A few minutes spent each night collecting and checking the next day's wardrobe can eliminate morning rush and confusion.

can be worn again. Wipe off your shoes and place shoe trees in them for the night.

All stains should be removed as soon as possible. This should be done at this nightly check-up. If a stain becomes old, a strong remover will be required. This will probably injure the fabric. You need to remove the spots from some fabrics by dry cleaning methods. Either these should be done professionally or your mother can help you. There are some commercial spot removers that are packaged for home use. Again, your mother's experience is the best guide as to whether or not you should use them. Usually the label clearly indicates limitations and suggestions for use.

Plan Tomorrow's Clothes Tonight

The last little chore at bedtime is to lay out your clothing for the next morning. A few minutes spent at this task the night before (no matter how sleepy you feel) will save confusion when you have just awakened in the morning.

Decide what outfit you are going to wear and then check the following:

1—Check whether the clothes are fresh and well-pressed, with a crease in the trousers or pleats in the skirt.
2—Check whether your sweater is clean, free from snags, and not stretched at the neck.
3—Lay out fresh undergarments.
4—Check all buttons, fasteners, and the like to be sure that they are secure and functioning properly.
5—Gather the accessories that you plan to wear so that you can find them easily. This would include belts, pins, scarfs, tie, and tie clasp.

This daily care of your clothes will bring dividends far in excess of the time you spend. Habits such as these make for smoother living. You will have more time to enjoy yourself as these details become a matter of routine.

Weekly Care of Clothes

If you have been efficient in your nightly check-ups, by the end of the week you probably will have accumulated several garments that need reconditioning.

You Need a Schedule for Clothes Upkeep

If one doesn't set up a weekly routine for polishing shoes, pressing trousers or skirt, or washing and ironing blouses, most of one's clothes will soon be unwearable. To avoid time-consuming extra work, set aside a certain time each week for Operation Perk-up. You are probably so busy during the week that the best time will be Saturday morning. Whatever time you choose, stick to it. Don't put it off for another week, or your upkeep job will become gigantic.

Does taking care of yourself and your clothes seem like a big job? Do it gradually. Start your routine today. Experiment with grooming methods to find the best for you. You may become so expert that you will seek a career in this area. Can you name possibilities?

THINKING IT OVER

1. Think about the grooming of yourself and your clothes. Do you enjoy some areas more than others? Why?

2. Think about the grooming process in the context of your family living situation. What facilitates or deters the accomplishment of your goals, such as bathroom scheduling, attitude of family members, and facilities in general?

THINGS TO DO

1. React to the following statements made by boys and girls of your age:
   a. "I like a girl to look natural, not with a lot of makeup on her face."
   b. "I like girls to wear perfume."
   c. "Sometimes when I leave the house, someone in my family will yell, 'You're not going out like that!'"

2. Time yourself in grooming activities, such as bathing. Can you improve the time in some areas and thus cut down on the total without sacrificing quality? Look at the way you are doing it. Are you using unnecessary motions? What about supplies and equipment? Make yourself an expert and share results with others.

3. Compare costs of grooming supplies in the same store and among a number of stores. Read the labels and read advertisements, as well as listening to radio and television commercials. What kind of claims are made? Experiment with different brands. Compare notes with friends. Put it all together when you feel you have the best products for you. Be prepared to make a report in class of your findings. You might write to some of the companies and report your positive or negative results. Your comments will be appreciated.

24 Buying clothes

Buying clothes can be a pleasant experience. You imagine how you will look in your new clothes and how others will react. When you make each purchase, buy wisely, so that every time you wear the clothes you will feel good and have a happy feeling.

GETTING READY

Before you go to the store to make an actual selection, you will have to become a detective and secure certain information. Discover what you want, what you need, and why. Since the clothes are for you, the first step is to take a look at yourself. Stand before a full-length mirror. Are you pleased with what you see? If not, how do you want to look? Clothes can emphasize good points, de-emphasize less attractive points, cheer you up, and give you confidence.

Do not waste time worrying about being too short, too tall, too thin, or too heavy, or having unattractive features. There are a few ideas that may be helpful, but do not live by rules; develop a sense about what looks well on you and is comfortable.

PLAN YOUR WARDROBE

Your first step is to look at the clothes you have. Few people can afford to buy a complete new wardrobe. Make an inventory. First list the clothes that are in good condition and that you enjoy wearing. Secondly, list those that need to have something done to them to make them wearable, such as fixing a collar, shortening the legs of your jeans, or removing some stains. Also, consider whether they fit into your plans for a wardrobe. Lastly, list the clothes that you do not wear or consider unwearable. Can they be recycled in some way? If not, give them away or dispose of them in some manner after a discussion with your mother.

Make an honest appraisal of the clothes you need in relation to your activities, such as school, church, parties, work, and sports. Review this past week: What did you do and what kind of clothes did you wear? Was this a typical week? Did the season affect your activities? It might be easier if you use a form like the one below or adapt your own.

Other school outfits you have may be listed, as well as clothes for other activities. This form becomes an inventory and a wearing guide.

An analysis of each garment you have and the many uses for it is helpful. Do your colors coordinate well? Can your jeans, shirts, and sweaters be mixed and matched into different outfits? How many? In how many ways may your coat be worn? Do you have adequate clothes for each season? Do you have special clothes for the sport or sports in which you engage? In what condition are they? Have you become less interested in a sport you formerly liked and stopped wearing these clothes? What

should be done with them? Do you have a new interest and what about the clothes you will need? Do you have any clothes from an outmoded fad? Can they be remodeled? Are there some clothes that you have outgrown? Do you have any buying mistakes among your clothes? Diagnose why you made the purchase and why you consider it unsatisfactory now.

Your Buying Plan

Take plenty of time to think about all the information you have collected. What new clothes do you feel you need? What are your family's reactions? Try to plan ahead. Is your coat good for another year?

Make a wardrobe card

1. Take a 3 x 5 index card and sketch the main items of your wardrobe in pencil. Put your jeans and slacks and each category together.

2. Below each sketch make two small slits. Cut a *very small swatch* from a generous seam in your garment and place it through the slits.

3. At a glance you can tell what you have and the colors, textures, fabrics, and designs in your clothes. Put the card into a small clear plastic envelope. This card will be very helpful when you go shopping.

ANALYSIS OF CLOTHING NEEDS			
ACTIVITY	Separates Slacks - Jeans Shirts - Skirts Jackets	Dresses or Suits	Party Clothes
School	Jeans w blue checked shirt	—	—
Social			

Take an inventory of the clothes you have.

When you have decided on the colors that you like and that seem to be best for you; the features that you wish to highlight, such as your eyes; and what you want to de-emphasize, such as hippiness, you can combine all this information into the kind of image you wish to project. Discuss this with your friends and family. Is your plan realistic? Remember that your uniqueness is being yourself, not like someone else, but you can improve your appearance.

Single-breasted coats and jackets are good, and clothing should be well fitted, not tight. Smooth fabrics are better than textured ones.

To appear taller and slimmer, choose up-and-down lines and stripes, such as corduroy slacks.

To Look Taller & Slimmer, choose:

One of your problems in planning your wardrobe is that you may be growing rapidly and even different parts of your body change. Your arms may be longer, your hips have become larger, girls may be developing in the chest, your feet are larger, and it seems you need new shoes often. When you buy something, you should plan to wear it often, because you may not be able to wear it for a very long period. Think about ways you can adjust to these problems of outgrowing rather than wearing out your clothes. One consideration is the cost per wearing. Try to estimate how many times you will wear an item of clothing and divide that number into the total cost.

But, To Look Heavier & Shorter, try:

Darker, solid colors or a very small print will keep eyes from stopping at your middle where another color begins.

In contrast, to look heavier and shorter, bulky fabrics, color contrasts, crosswise or horizontal lines and stripes, light colors, and double-breasted coats and jackets are helpful. Review suggestions for color in Chapter 22.

If you decide that you need a new shirt, sweater, pants, or coat, decide which of your present clothes will be worn with it. Will the colors harmonize? For which seasons will this garment be suitable? Would it be better to purchase a middleweight pair of pants rather than a heavyweight or a lightweight? Your climate will determine the answer to this question. If you have not crystallized what you want exactly, shop around so that when you do make your purchase you know exactly what you want. With planning, the clothes you buy usually give you more satisfaction, and they may have multiple uses rather than only one, such as a shirt that can only be worn with one pair of pants.

What you buy will depend also upon the amount of money you have to spend. You may have some of your own money and your family may provide some. When you estimate the cost of your new clothes, be certain to check actual prices and make allowances for changes in prices before you really make your purchases. You may discover that you do not have sufficient money to buy everything you desire. What are alternatives? Can you or a family member sew any of the items you need for less cost? Can you decide which item is the most important and plan from there? Can you wait for end-of-the-season sales or other types of sales, such

as those on Washington's birthday? Can you reduce your spending in other areas, such as your fun money, to make up the difference? Is there any way you can make some extra money? How about taking another look at your present wardrobe and seeing what you can alter or recycle or make do?

Learn to Be A Shopper—Read Labels

Before you step into a store to buy your clothes, you can do some practicing as a shopper. *Learn to read labels*. What kind of information do they give you? Information about the fiber is important. The Textile Fiber Products Identification Act requires that all fabrics be labeled with the family or generic name of the fiber in the order of predominance. For example, you may think you are buying a jacket that is predominately wool but has other fibers included. The first fiber mentioned will be in the largest quantity and less of other fibers in the order mentioned. If the last item is wool, you have misjudged. Will this affect the comfort, usefulness, or wear of the garment? The percentage of weight of each fiber is another guide to the content of the fabric. The manufacturer's name and address are given so that you can make complaints, if necessary. In the case of wool, not only percentage is required but the type, such as virgin or new wool, reprocessed wool, or reused wool. If the latter two are mentioned, the garment will not wear as well.

Does the label give information as to whether the fabric is knitted, woven, or nonwoven? Knitted fabrics are comfortable, easy-care, and resist wrinkling. Woven fabrics are durable and retain shape. Nonwoven or felted fabrics are not as durable as knitted or woven. There is a difference in the closeness of knitting or weaving that will make a difference in wearability. Is any information given about colorfastness? Sometimes a label will tell you about dye resistance to sunlight, washing, dry cleaning, perspiration, fumes, or crocking (rubbing off). Is the garment wrinkle-resistant or wash-and-wear? Does it have a durable finish? What about resistance to shrinking? Considerable interest has been created in flame-retardant finishes—not fireproof.

What does the label tell you about the care of the garment? If a shirt, for example, has to be dry-cleaned and cannot be washed, the cost of the garment is increased considerably. Of

Think of your clothes in terms of your activities. How well do they match?

ACTIVITIES

tenis
ice skating
school
church
parties

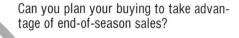

Can you plan your buying to take advantage of end-of-season sales?

What does the label tell you about the care of a garment?

What will be the cost per wearing of a new jacket?

course, if you have a wool coat, it will have to be dry-cleaned. Can the garment be machine-washed or must it be handwashed? The latter will take more of your time. Check on care required for linings and trimmings.

Learn to Be A Shopper—Read and Listen to Advertisements

You can do a great deal of comparison shopping by careful reading of newspaper and magazine advertisements. What does the description tell you about sizes, color, wearability, or other points? Compare costs and fabrics. Reading a mail-order catalogue can be informa-

tive. Radio and television commercials may give you some different slants to consider. If the price range is wide, try to determine what makes the difference.

Learn to Be A Shopper—Judge Quality and Workmanship

The quality refers to workmanship, fabric, and design. Quality affects price and may need to be considered especially for those garments that you wear frequently and that need to be durable. Lower quality may be adequate for clothes that you wear only now and then or that you will outgrow quickly. Your values will be a factor here and you may wish, for example, to have fewer clothes of higher quality for your money. Other points to consider in quality are the closeness of weave of a fabric, the design of the garment and the fiber used.

Check for workmanship and quality

⭐ Is sufficient fabric allowed for seams, hems, pleats, and for a good fit?

⭐ Do designs in the fabric, such as checks, plaids, and stripes, match at seams, especially the center seam?

⭐ Is the stitching appropriate for the fabric, straight, even, securely fastened, free from loose stitches, and sewed with thread that matches?

⭐ Is the hem wide enough to allow for alteration if you grow taller?

⭐ Are all fasteners, such as buttons, securely attached? Are trims color-coordinated and do they require the same care as the garment? Remember that decoration increases the price.

⭐ Are garment pieces cut with the grain—that is, lengthwise and crosswise threads should be at right angles—so that it hangs well?

⭐ Are sleeves, collars, and cuffs free from puckers?

⭐ Are buttonholes well made? Are facings inconspicuous?

Get Your Money's Worth!

Where and When to Shop

If you live in a very small community, you may not have much choice as to places for shopping. But most people will have considerable choice.

Discount Store · MAIL ORDER · JEANS

Discount stores usually have lower prices than other stores. There is a wide choice of sizes and styles and even high-fashion merchandise may be found. Few services are offered and some customers have found it difficult to return merchandise, particularly if labels of the manufacturer have been removed.

Mail-order buying may be done directly from a catalogue mailed to your home or from a catalogue in a mail-order house. Since you have to wait for delivery the wearing of the clothes is delayed. If they do not fit they can be returned.

The *specialty store,* as the name indicates, concentrates on a few items but you can learn a great deal by talking to salespersons in specialty shops, because they are authorities on these items. You can also gain some ideas for actual shopping.

The *thrift shop* sells used clothes and you might find a bargain there. Sometimes these stores are operated by churches or other charitable organizations. Many well-known people shop in thrift shops to get unusual items.

A *factory outlet,* as the name indicates, sells from factory to customer. Limited services are offered and you must know your merchandise to determine whether you are getting a bargain or not.

A *variety store* sells many items, including clothing. Sometimes the choice is limited, but prices are usually lower, and you might find a buy.

A *department store* may have clothes in different areas of the store that vary in price and quality. It is easy to coordinate your purchases. You can check whether a jacket coordinates with the slacks you are buying. Prices may be higher because you pay for many services. Sometimes volume of sales is large, so prices may be lower. Check on these points.

When to Buy

When you buy may depend on store sales. Slack seasons are good times for sales, such as after Christmas and after Easter, or at the end of a season, such as summer. Preseason sales offer an opportunity to select clothes at lower prices, such as buying a winter coat in August. There may be sales for goods marked in certain ways. A fire sale consists of clothes that were in a building damaged by fire, but the clothes may be unharmed and a bargain. Seconds and irregulars have have some slight defects or flaws. Check carefully to see whether appearance or wearability are affected. Samples may be offered for sale. As a good shopper, keep your eye on your objective and do not settle for something else that may be cheap but does not fit your needs. You need to plan ahead to take advantage of sales. If you need an article of clothing in a hurry, you usually have to pay more.

Arrival of Shopping Day

Now that you know what you need and what to look for in a garment, you should enjoy doing the buying that you planned. If you are buying a big-ticket item like a coat, someone older from your family will probably go with you. You have probably gone to several stores and have narrowed your choices. After checking workmanship, fabric, style, suitability for you and other points, you will want to try the coat, pants, shirt, or other item on. If the fit passes approval and the price is right, you may be ready to make your purchase.

BUYING SPECIFIC GARMENTS
Jeans

This item of clothes may be among your most common purchases. Look for closeness of weave. A heavy twill will wear the longest. An iron-on patch on the inside will lengthen the wearing period. The zipper should be heavy-duty and long enough to let you slip easily in and out of the jeans. Pockets should be reinforced with a rivet or bar-tack reinforcements. Look for rows of stitching for strength. Seams should be flat-felled for added stength. The snaps at the top of a zipper should be heavy-duty and securely sewn.

Sizes usually come in slim, regular, and husky cuts. Regulars and slims usually come in age-sizes from 8 to 20, for example. Some are sold by waist measurement plus inseam length to heel. Many jeans rest on the hip, so that measurement must be taken rather than the waist. What experiences have you had with sizing? Do you have some suggestions to share with others?

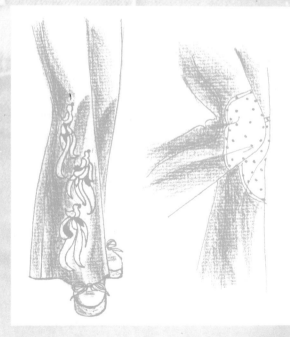

Most boys and girls prefer the all-cotton type of jeans to blends of fabrics or durable-press finishes. Cotton absorbs perspiration better, bleaches better (although this process weakens the fiber), and seems more comfortable. Cotton is a trifle warmer in the wintertime than jeans made of blended fabrics. What are other points to consider while buying? Why, for example, is there a wide range in prices? Why are some jeans more comfortable than others?

When you shop for jeans, be sure to read the label carefully to make sure that they will not shrink too much after washing.

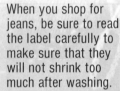

INTIMATE APPAREL
General Information

There are many types of underwear. Included are undershirts, bras, slips, half-slips, pantyhose, underpants, tights, body suits, socks, and stockings. Sleepwear and loungewear are a part of this category. Some are worn for personal comfort or for the outward appearance they give you. All underwear should be washable.

Soft fabrics are generally used. Sturdy construction is essential if intimate apparel is to hold up after many washings. Garments must fit well to assure long wear. Check with sales personnel, if you are uncertain about sizes or types. Consider the quality best suited for your purpose. Look for fiber content and other information on the label. A few points about selected types of underwear are discussed here.

Underpants and Panties

There are three general types of underpants: bikini, which is the favorite worn with low-slung jeans or pants; regular; and hip hugger, which is cut so that it rests just below the navel. Fabric is an important consideration. The elastic should have plenty of give and be securely attached. Seams should be neatly finished and invisible under clothing. There should be two thicknesses of fabric in the crotch. Sizes are by number, waist or hip measure, dress size, or small, medium, or large.

Slips and Bras

Slips are full or half. Full slip sizes are based on bust measurements or dress sizes. Half slips are usually sized small, medium, or large, or by waist measurement. Many slips are proportioned to height. Look for adjustable shoulder straps and other features that you consider important.

Sleepwear and Loungewear

Sleepwear includes shorty nightgowns, T-shirts, or grannies for girls. Both boys and girls wear pajamas. Some boys and girls like night-shirts. Robes may match the sleepwear or be of heavier fabric for warmth.

Loungewear may be dressy pajamas, long flowing garments, or other types of comfortable clothing. What points would you add for consideration in the buying of intimate wear?

SHOES

Many boys and girls wear sneakers. The hiking shoe or boot comes in a number of styles and is popular. Boots are desirable in some parts of the country. Other styles are favored by certain groups for specific purposes.

Make your choice on the usual basis of the occasion or activity for which shoes will be worn. Appearance is important—how they look on your feet. Check in a full-length mirror. Which clothes do you wear with your shoes? How will they fit into your wardrobe? Shoes may have to be changed every two to three months because your feet grow rapidly. Fit is of prime importance because shoes that do not fit can damage your feet for life. Do not buy shoes on the assumption that they will feel better after you have worn them. Have them feel comfort-

Check fit and comfort of shoes you buy.

able when you buy them. Put on both shoes and stand and walk in them to test the fit.

Check for a smooth lining that is free from wrinkles, seams that have smooth edges, and even, firm stitching without loose threads. Check to see whether the shoes have a water-resistant finish. The innersole should be comfortable and may be cushioned at the ball of the foot and reinforced over the arch of the shoe. Sometimes the innersole is treated to resist moisture and the growth of fungus. The uppers may be made of many materials, such as leather, plastic, fabric, straw, or man-made shoe material. Consider care, color, texture, flexibility, and durability.

Be certain that the shoes in which you walk the most are supportive. Do not wear old discarded shoes for working. Change shoes often for comfort and greater wearability. Brush and polish or clean your shoes regularly. Check the shape of the shoe when buying and also after wearing from time to time. The shape of the shoe should resemble the shape of your foot.

Shirts

A few well-chosen shirts can be a big addition to anyone's wardrobe. They are usually sized by neck circumference and sleeve length for boys and bust size for girls. The fabric you choose should complement other separates in your wardrobe. It should also meet your requirements for good fit, comfort, and easy care. Look for small, neat stitches, finished seams, buttonholes with tiny, close stitches, and durable fabric, if you are looking for long wear.

The shape of your face will affect the type of collar or neckline you choose. The neckline influences the casualness or dressiness of the shirt. Some styles are more attractive than others. Experiment and find a type that looks best on you. Sometimes a scarf can make an otherwise unattractive neckline wearable. Boys consider the width and length of the collar and the illusion created.

Pants

Basic measurements are waist, hip, and inseam to heel. In contrast to jeans, pants and slacks may be part wool, cotton, synthetics, and blends, and usually durable-press. Consider the care that pants require in cleaning. Can they be washed or must they be dry-cleaned? If you have trouble finding a good fit, try different brands and sizes. Coordination with your entire wardrobe is important.

Skirts

Skirts are also wardrobe builders and stretchers. They can be worn appropriately with blouses, shirts, or sweaters. A jacket or blazer may give the look of a complete outfit. A decision will have to be made about the fabric of the skirt. If wool, the problem of care is more costly because of dry cleaning, unless the skirt fabric is a washable wool. Using a coin-operated dry-cleaning machine will reduce costs, but the skirt will still probably be more expensive than skirts made from easy-care fabrics.

Before buying a skirt, a girl will wish to check the jackets, blouses, shirts, or sweaters in her wardrobe that can be worn with it. A skirt will show off hips, so if there is a problem in that area, stick to darker colors and long lines. Be certain that the fit at the waist and hip is comfortable and has sufficient ease. Is the skirt smooth both while standing and sitting? Does it ride up when one sits? Is the hem even and is there an allowance for lengthening after that next growth spurt?

234

235

DRESSES

A dress can fill many wardrobe needs. It may be worn to school, to church, and to parties. One advantage of a dress is that it is complete. A girl does not have to be concerned about the skirt or the jeans she will wear with it. Check accessories, shoes, handbag, or tote bag, and coordinate the dress with them. Consider the purpose of the dress and buy accordingly. Are easy care, durability, or dressiness important? How much money can be spent?

A dress can fill many wardrobe needs.

The type of yarn, knit, and closeness of knit will influence the texture, weight, and durability of a sweater. Loose knits do not hold their shape as well as tight knits. Sometimes loose knits are lined or specially treated so as to hold their shape better. Avoid elongated loops, if possible, because garments made with these loops have a tendency to shrink, stretch, and lose shape in cleaning.

Select your sweater according to the purpose for which it is intended. A cardigan sweater may double as a jacket and give extra warmth, especially if made of wool. A pullover sweater

Round loops are preferred to elongated loops in a sweater because the garment holds its shape better.

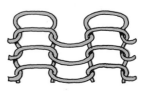

may or may not be worn over or under a thin shirt or a heavier one in extremely cold weather. Sweaters may be tailored or classic in appearance or more fashionable and unusual. When buying a sweater, consider that you might enjoy wearing it for years or for just one or more seasons. Also, consider the warmth you need or the care a sweater requires before buying. Nylon or polyester yarns demand the easiest care. Acrylic yarn sweaters can be washed, as can washable wool yarns. See Chapter 23 for hints on the care of your sweaters.

Check seams for close stitching, loose threads, bulkiness, evenness, and straightness. The ribbing at neck, waist, and wrists should be a smaller gauge knit for added stretch. Try on a sweater for fit. The armholes should be comfortable, there should be no strain at any point, and the garment should be snug but not too tight at neck and cuffs.

OTHER WAYS TO CUT COSTS

If your money did not stretch to cover all your needs, do not become discouraged but consider other alternatives. Recycle your old clothes by

1–Cutting off worn long sleeves to a new short length. If sleeves have become too short because of your growth, do the same.

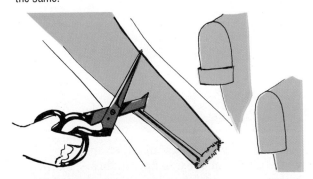

2–Patching elbows of shirts and sweaters with colorful patches that will wash.

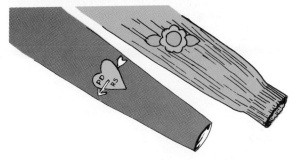

3–Applying a new contrasting collar if a shirt collar is worn. Decorate it with stick-on patches that can be ironed on.

4–Cutting armholes from undershirts and making them into sleeveless summer shirts that can be decorated with scraps of material from the variety store.

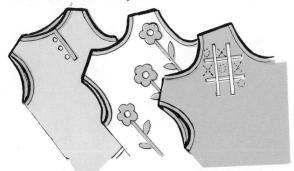

5–Fixing torn buttonholes with creative stitchery.

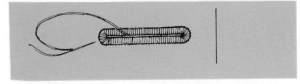

6–Making a blouse or skirt by cutting off the bodice or the skirt of an old dress.

7–Making a nightgown out of an old lightweight dress. Make the sleeves short or cut them out for sleeveless style. Cut out the neck so it will be cooler.

If you are buying an expensive item like a coat, someone from your family will probably accompany you.

Maybe you can find something on your list at a flea market.

Brainstorm for additional ideas with your friends. Look at magazines and newspapers for other suggestions.

You may be lucky and find just what you want at a garage sale, rummage sales, treasure-and-trash sales, bazaars, a flea market, a thrift shop, or other types of community events or projects. Why not set up a "swap shop" with your friends and exchange clothes. This might become a neighborhood project and would be a worthy recycling program. If you belong to a large family, maybe you have some older cousins who are willing to pass on their clothes for a small sum or some favors. Keep thinking!

THINKING IT OVER

1. Think about all the influences that affect the decisions you make about what you will wear, such as family and community approval, fashion, culture, and others. How strong are these influences? Do you feel that some of them are merely traditional and no longer important? If so, which ones? Why?

2. Think about the factors that inhibit you from having the clothes that you would like to have, such as limited choice in stores in your community, money, and other reasons. Can any of these be overcome? If so, how? Are some of your problems as large or as important as you thought they were?

THINGS TO DO

1. Evaluate the information a salesperson gave you while buying clothes. Was it useful? Accurate? Complete? Was it new to you? Summarize your conclusions.

2. Make an inventory of the places where you can shop in your community, with a list of strong and weak points. Share your ideas with others. Update when necessary.

3. Consider ways of securing information that will be helpful to you as a shopper. What are the sources and their value to you?

25 Before you sew

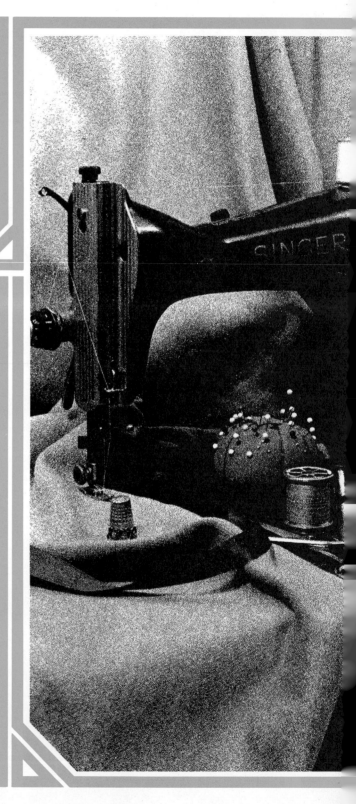

Millions of boys and girls everywhere are enthusiastic about sewing. While sewing, you can imagine you are an artist. The medium with which artists work may be clay, stone, metals, wood, ivory, plastics, wood, paints, or other materials. In sewing, you use fabric to express yourself. There is a fabric for almost every idea or mood. Isn't it fun to think of yourself as a fabric artist or sculptor?

WHY SEW?

In addition to artistic satisfaction, there are many other good reasons for you to sew. Your wardrobe can be made more personal through selection of the fabric and colors you desire and by special touches, such as use of initials, favorite appliques, interesting pockets, jackets to match, embroidery, and other ways to make the garment your own very special creation. Sewing can be profitable, satisfying, and fun. You can usually have better quality fabric than you might buy in a ready-made item. Saving money is a big plus, not only for your clothes but in making gifts. Your clothes will fit better and have better workmanship. You can make money by selling some of the things you sew and sewing can be the basis for a rewarding career. Among such careers are being a designer of men's or women's, boys' or girls', or children's clothing, being a seamstress or tailor, or having a job in the textile field. And lastly, you can apply your sewing skills to improving your ready-to-wear garments, such as changing the length of hems, correcting poor fit, or creating a new look with trim or in other ways. Do not forget that you can sew things for your home, too.

BASIC TOOLS AND SUPPLIES

There are certain tools and supplies that are necessary for sewing. Familiarize youself with them and learn how to use them efficiently. Your sewing will be easier. Following is a discussion of the major ones needed.

1–*Measuring* means a knowledge of present measures plus the metric. You will need a tape measure for taking body and other measurements. A metal-tipped tape measure 60 inches long (slightly less than a meter), plainly marked on both sides (with standard measures on one side and metric measures on the other), and made of a material that will not stretch, is the best choice. A plastic-coated one is more durable.

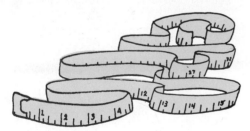

A see-through ruler or yardstick is useful when altering the pattern or laying it on the fabric.

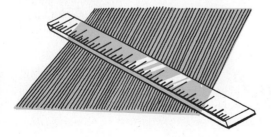

A 6-inch or 15-centimeter sewing gauge with a movable slide marker is good for measuring buttonholes, hems, and seam widths.

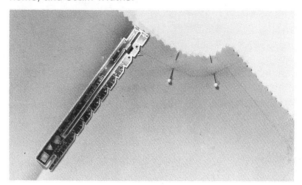

A smoothly finished yardstick that will not catch on fabric is good to measure fabric and to check on grain lines.

The yardstick can be used for marking an even hem, but a skirt marker is easier to use and more efficient. If you had to choose only one piece of measuring equipment, which one would you choose?

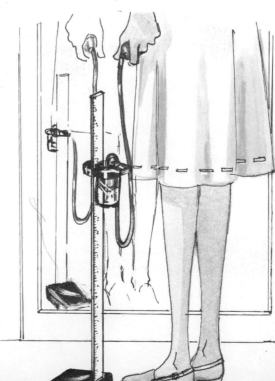

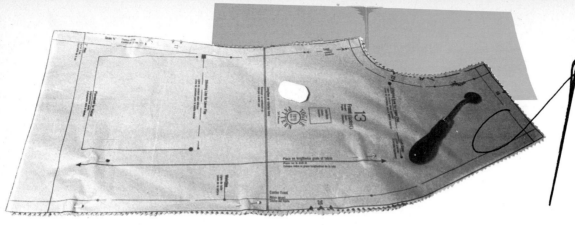

Needles should be *sharps* sizes 7, 8, or 9. The larger numbers indicate fine needles, smaller numbers thicker needles. Sharps have round eyes and are of medium length for sewing.

2–*Marking* must be accurate so that your garment will go together accurately. Use dressmaker's tracing in a color that is close to or lighter than that of your fabric. Make the marks with a tracing wheel on the wrong side of the cloth. There are many types of tracing wheels. For any marks on the right side, you may use tailor's chalk, tailor's tacks, wax, pins, or a marking pencil for lines for hems, buttonholes, pockets, and other purposes. Make sure that the chalk will rub off or the wax will melt when ironed, and that the use of other devices will not leave marks on your fabric.

3–*Pins and needles* are mandatory. Pins should be fine, sharp, and nonrusting. Pins with glass heads are easy to handle and also to see on your fabric. For synthetic knit fabrics you may wish to use very fine ball points to avoid snags and pulls. Keep pins within easy reach by wearing a wrist pincushion.

You may have to use a ball-point needle on your sewing machine for synthetic knits, otherwise your machine will skip stitches or not sew at all.

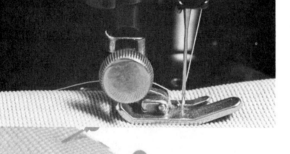

4–*Cutting* your fabric requires good, sharp shears. Shears are 6 inches or 15 centimeters in length, with a small opening in one handle for the thumb and a larger opening in the other handle for two or more fingers for leverage and control. The lower blade rests on the cutting surface.

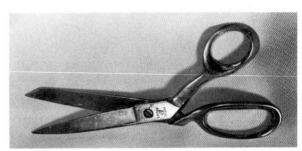

Pinking shears cut a zizzag edge and are good for finishing seams, hems, and facings. They are not to be used for cutting the fabric from the pattern before the seams are sewn.

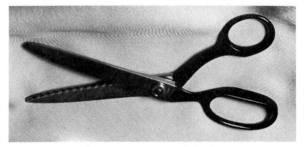

A 4- to 5-inch (approximately 10 to 10½ centimeters) pair of scissors with sharp tips is excellent for snipping thread and clipping and trimming seams. Both handles are of the same size.

Left-handed sewers should investigate equipment and supplies to make their sewing easier, such as left-handed shears.

A seam ripper helps you remove the stitches that are beginner's mistakes.

5—*Pressing* is the mark of a professional sewer, so begin early. Press slowly and carefully to assure that each seam is straight and opened out to the sewn size. A pressing cloth will prevent iron shine. A dampened press cloth helps remove wrinkles and some feel it is a must for expert pressing.

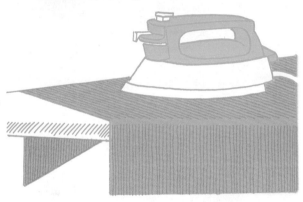

Other pressing aids are a mini sleeve board or a pressing ham for pressing seams and darts. Experiment and decide on the equipment and the ways to press that are desirable for you.

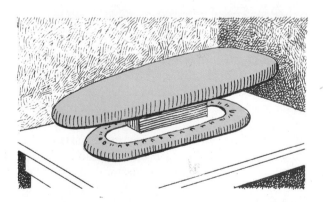

6—*Thread* should be selected a shade darker than the fabric. When unwound it looks lighter. For best results, a thread should be compatible with the fabric being sewn. Before sewing, ask yourself whether your fabric

is animal, vegetable, or chemical and choose your thread accordingly. The types of thread are silk, synthetic thread, mercerized cotton, heavy-duty thread, buttonhole twist, and all-nylon thread.

Silk is to be used with all types of silk, crepes and sheers, wool, and/or blends of these fibers, because they are all classified as protein or animal fibers.

Synthetics are to be sewn with *synthetic thread.* It has added strength and elasticity, and is ironed at lower temperatures.

Mercerized cotton is used for cotton, linen, and rayon fabrics, because their fibers come from cellulose or vegetable fibers and originate from some form of plant life. This thread is often used for other types of sewing. The most common is Number 50. Mercerized thread is especially suitable for cottons, because it is smoother and stronger than cotton thread and can take higher ironing temperatures.

Heavy-duty thread is used for sewing on coat buttons.

Buttonhole twist is used for decorative top stitching and hand-worked buttonholes.

All-nylon thread is recommended for use on special fabrics that require extreme strength and particularly strength in the seam, such as tricot, synthetic jersey, and power net.

7—*Zippers* (although belonging to notions, zippers are included in this section) are made with synthetic coils or metal teeth attached to tapes and closed with a slider. These standard zippers may be inserted by using the general zipper foot attachment that is standard machine equipment.

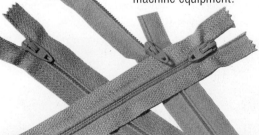

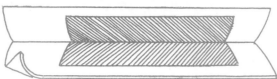

Velcro is plastic tabs or strips that can be sewn in place of traditional zippers or buttons and buttonholes. The tab or strip (sometimes called the hook) on a side grips the tab or strip on the other side (sometimes called the loop) and makes a closing. Velcro is sold in the form of 1-inch-wide tape by the yard and also in prepackaged forms of circles, squares, and special shapes for neckline and waist closings. This fastener can be used in general, creative, and lazy sewing. Velcro is sometimes used on children's clothing because they can open and close their garments easily, thus becoming more independent in dressing. For that same reason, Velcro is good for handicapped persons who may have some difficulty in dressing.

8–*Thimbles* should fit the middle finger of your right or left hand, depending on which one you use for sewing. A thimble may seem old-fashioned, but it does keep your finger from getting pricked while hand-sewing, helps you sew faster, and helps you get more even stitches. It is a sign of a professional hand sewer.

9–*Storage* for supplies, fabric, and other items, such as small equipment, is important. A basket with a handle is good, because it can be transported wherever it is needed. An old overnight bag may be covered with bright fabric or other material. A strong cardboard box may be covered with decorative paper or felt and decorated with paste-ons or iron-ons. Your choice will depend somewhat on where this holder of your sewing will be stored—a closet shelf or dresser drawer, or somewhere else.

An egg carton sprayed with paint is good for keeping buttons, snaps, hooks and eyes, and other small items. But most important, learn to use the basic equipment, supplies, and notions well.

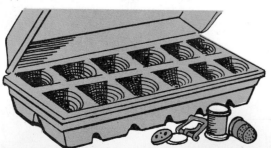

Do comparison shopping if you plan to buy a sewing machine.

Remember that your sewing equipment needs to be organized and updated periodically to serve you well with changes in fabrics, sewing machines, and sewing techniques. Visit sewing notion departments to see what is new.

THE SEWING MACHINE

The most important sewing tool you will learn to use is the sewing machine. Each manufacturer of sewing machines has specific directions for threading the machine, threading the bobbin, and operating the machine. However, the same basic parts are found on most machines, although they may be in different places on each model or type. At any rate, the main parts of the machine and the location and function of each should be studied and understood. Table 25–1 lists of the parts of a sewing machine and what each is or does.

This is only a general chart, and parts may differ on your sewing machine. Changes are made on new models, so adapt the chart to suit your purpose.

244

Table 25-1

PARTS OF A SEWING MACHINE AND THEIR USES

MACHINE PART	WHAT IT IS OR DOES
1. Head	The complete sewing machine without cabinet or stand
2. Spool pin	Spindle that holds the upper thread
3. Hand wheel	Controls the movement of the needle and the take-up lever
4. Bobbin winder switch, spindle, and tension disc	Mechanism for winding the bobbins
5. Stitch length selector	Regulates stitch size; switches the sewing to forward, reverse, or zig-zag
6. Upper tension	Regulates the amount of upper thread used
7. Feed dog	Carries the fabric as it is being stitched
8. Presser foot	Holds the fabric on the feed dog
9. Thread cutter	Cuts the thread
10. Thread guide	Holds the thread
11. Presser foot lifter	Raises and lowers the presser foot
12. Take-up lever	Takes up the excess thread and locks the stitch
13. Needle	Pushes and pulls the thread through the fabric for stitching
14. Slide plate	Covers the bobbin

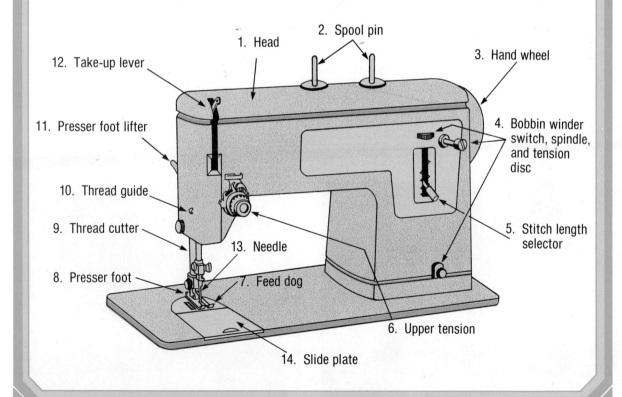

Table 25-2

SEWING MACHINE OPERATOR'S LICENSE

New to me; need help	Sometimes forget; need practice	Like an expert; do it every time	
			1. Wind the bobbin and insert it properly.
			2. Correctly thread the machine.
			3. Draw the lower thread up before starting to stitch.
			4. Start, stop, and operate the machine at an even speed.
			5. Test the stitching on a scrap of double fabric before beginning to sew; learn to judge good stitching.
			6. Stitch accurately on the required seam allowance.
			7. Keep the bulk of the fabric to the left of the machine.
			8. Draw both threads back between the toes of the presser foot before cutting the thread.
			9. Practice good posture at the machine.
			10. Know how to oil and clean the machine and replace the needle, when necessary.

Use and Care of the Sewing Machine

An understanding of the basic techniques for handling the sewing machine is essential before you sew. It takes practice to learn how to use and care for the sewing machine. During practice sessions you should become proficient.

Table 25-2, the "Sewing Machine Operator's License," presents a checklist for you to use on the care and use of the sewing machine. You might like to devise your own Operator's License, using a similar checklist to rate yourself.

General Sewing Suggestions

With practice you should feel quite confident about the use of the sewing machine. Here are some ideas to make actual sewing easier.

1–Let the machine do the work; do not push or pull the fabric while sewing.

2–Place necessary sewing equipment on the right side of the machine, away from the sewing area. This equipment would include scissors and pincushion.

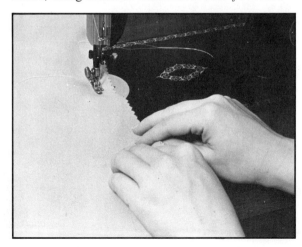

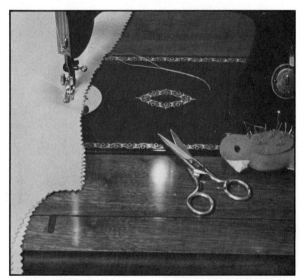

3–As a general rule, do not stitch over pins, because needles might be broken or bent. Needles or seams may become crooked.

4–Test the stitch on a self-fabric scrap for correct tension, stitch size, and proper threading before sewing on your fabric.

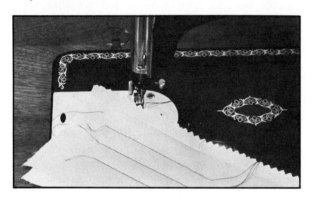

5–Use a self-adhesive tape measure or other measuring device as a permanent pinning guide and attach it to the machine case.

6–Certain attachments of the sewing machine, such as a hemmer or ruffler, make a particular job easier to accomplish, so learn to use them.

You may have other ideas to add to this list. You may wish to make a poster of these ideas so they are reminders for the entire class.

Safety Precautions

Exercise care so that accidents do not occur while you are sewing. Being aware of possible accidents will help you prevent them.

1–Check the electrical cords on the sewing machine and iron. Faulty wiring can be dangerous.

2–Operate the sewing machine at a safe speed, within your control.

3–Be certain that the needle is properly inserted in the sewing machine.

4–When threading the bobbin, disengage the hand wheel by throwing the knob counterclockwise. This prevents a needle or pressure foot from loosening and possibly causing the needle to hit against the machine, break, and hit you.

5–Use the shears correctly and carefully. They are sharp and you may be cut.

6–Use a seam ripper, not razor blades, for ripping and removing stitches.

7–Use the equipment for the purpose intended.

8–Be cautious of the effect of the heat of the iron when pressing fabrics. Melting and scorching temperatures vary among fabrics.

Once you become an expert, all of this information will become a part of you.

Buying a Sewing Machine

About two-thirds of the homes in America have a sewing machine. You may be living in such a home but your family may be interested in purchasing a new machine. You may be pleased with your present brand, but wish to have a more up-to-date machine that can handle present-day fabrics. A machine today, in addition to making a regular, even, firmly locked series of stitches, must have a zigzag of several widths, an attachment or mechanism for making buttonholes, and at least one simple stretch stitch for sewing stretch fabrics. These are the basic features to consider.

You may not have a sewing machine at home but now that you are excited about sewing, your family may be interested in buying a machine. It might be a good idea to rent a ma-

If you plan to buy a second-hand sewing machine, carefully check that new fabrics can be sewn with it.

chine at first to see how much you use the machine and if the family's enthusiasm continues. Renting a machine can spare you the experience of buying an expensive piece of equipment that may not be used. Try to determine how much you and your family would actually use a machine.

You will want to shop around and try to find the best buy. The whole family can participate because they are concerned. Your brother may be interested in the operation of the machine. Your mother may be concerned about the kind of stitches that can be sewn. Here are a number of important pointers to consider in buying:

1- Does the new machine sew straight and with even pressure?
2- Do not buy a machine that cannot stitch new stretch fabrics. That is not a bargain.
3- Check to see if zigzag and stretch stitching, as well as reverse stitching, is available.
4- Check various distributors. You can buy a machine in sewing-machine centers, department stores, mail-order houses, and yard goods stores, and from sewing-machine dealers.
5- Check various brands and features. Reports from a consumer organization on their tests of machines or your state extension service may give you information about all the brands.
6- Consider your space limitations before buying. If space is limited you may have to concen-

trate on portable models and not cabinet types.
7- Do not be lured by small hand machines that make extravagant claims. Most are very inefficient and a waste of money.

SELECTING A PATTERN

For beginners the "How to Sew" or "Easy" Patterns are helpful because they have extra tissue charts with detailed directions for certain techniques, such as applying zippers or hemming. If you plan to select a style that you have not worn previously, try on a ready-made garment of that style to see whether you like it. Also notice the fabric, the construction methods, and the price. Is sewing an advantage? If you like to sew, you will make it yourself and it will be especially enjoyable because you have tested whether you like it or not.

One of your first steps is to determine your pattern size. This is important to ensure that what you make will fit well. Do not confuse pattern size with ready-to-wear sizes which may vary according to their manufacturer. Pattern sizes are standard and are based on the measurements that are indicated here. Take these measurements with great care and accuracy. It is best to have someone help you.

Pattern books give you a wide selection of styles from which to choose.

Pattern Figure Type

Girls mature at various rates of growth, so patterns are grouped under different *figure types* with different proportions. Figure type measurements are based on your height, your back waist length, and your body proportions and shape.

Analyze your own body proportions and shape and compare them with the figures below. In addition, look at your body silhouette in a mirror to help you decide which figure most closely resembles yours. Choose your figure type before selecting your pattern size.

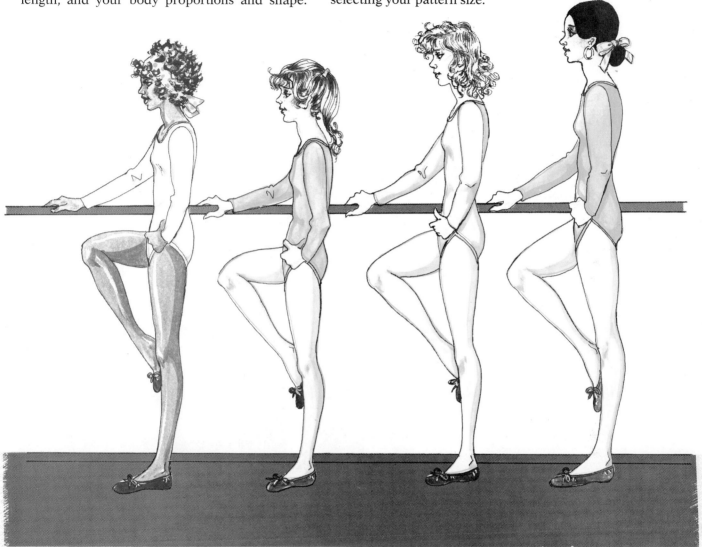

Pattern Figure Types for Girls

A Young Junior/Teen. This figure type is the slim, developing teen figure. The bust is small and high with a proportionally large waist.

The Junior Petite. The Junior Petite figure type is short—about 5 feet (1.52 meters, 15.2 decimeters, or 152 centimeters) to 5 feet 1 inch (1.55 meters, 15.5 decimeters, or 155 centimeters) with a well-developed figure and the shortest waist length.

The Junior. The Junior type is about 5 feet 4 inches (1.65 meters, 16.5 decimeters, or 165 centimeters) to 5 feet 5 inches (1.65 meters, 16.5 decimeters, or 165 centimeters) in height and has a well-developed figure but is shorter in waist length and height than the Miss.

The Miss. This figure type is about 5 feet 5 inches (1.65 meters, 16.5 decimeters, or 165 centimeters) to 5 feet 8 inches (1.73 meters, 17.3 decimeters, or 173 centimeters) tall. It is the tallest type. It is for the average, well-proportioned, well-developed adult figure.

Measurements for Girls

Measurements for girls should be taken over the slip or undergarments that are worn with the clothes.

> Tie a tape measure, a ribbon, or a string around your waist to mark your natural waistline at the narrowest point. Measure your body at the points indicated. Hold the tape measure so it is comfortably snug but not tight. Stand straight, feet together, and arms at your sides.

Write down each measurement as you take it. Copy the form in Table 25–3. Write in pencil so that you can change measurements as you grow, and you can erase the old date and write in the new one. If you are in a rapid growing stage, take measurements frequently, because you may require the next size or may have become a different type.

Your Pattern Size

Now check the bust measurements with your figure type. If you are making something that fits from your shoulders, take the pattern that measures the same as your bust measurement. If you measure between two sizes, take the smaller size, unless you are large-boned; in that case, take the larger size. When making a garment that fits from the waist, select a pattern by your waist measurement, unless it is extremely small in proportion to your hips.

How To Take Measurements

Table 25-3

TALLY SHEET FOR GIRLS' MEASUREMENTS

HEIGHT—When standing tall and straight ———— ft. ———— in.

HIGH BUST—Just under the arms above the fullest part of the bust ———— in.

BUST—Across the fullest part of the bust, straight across the back ———— in.

WAIST—At the narrowest part ———— in.

HIPS—At the fullest part. It is usually 9″ below the waist for Misses and Juniors, and 7″ below for Junior Petite and Young Junior/Teen ———— in.

BACK WAIST LENGTH—From the prominent bone at the base of the neck to the waist ———— in.

FIGURE TYPE ———————————— SIZE ———————————— DATE ————————————

Pattern Figure Types for Boys

Measurements for Boys

Pattern sizes for boys and men are based on body build, not age. There are three types: boys' patterns, teen boys' patterns, and men's patterns.

Boys' Patterns. Boys' patterns are designed for a growing boy, starting to mature, who has a young build. The height is from 4 feet (1.22 meters, 12.2 decimeters, or 122 centimeters) to 4 feet 10 inches (1.47 meters, 14.7 decimeters, or 147 centimeters).

Teen Boys' Patterns. Teen boys' patterns apply to an adolescent shape that is smaller in the shoulders and narrower in the hips than a man's. It is a growing size that ranges from 5 feet 1 inch (1.55 meters, 15.5 decimeters, or 155 centimeters) to 5 feet 8 inches (1.73 meters, 17.3 decimeters, or 173 centimeters).

Men's Patterns. Men's patterns are for the adult male with an average, fully mature build. The neck and shoulders are fully developed. The height is around 5 feet 10 inches (1.78 meters, 17.8 decimeters, or 178 centimeters).

Many in this group will be in the boys' pattern stage, because boys grow less rapidly than girls at this age. Some of this age group may be maturing early and will need the teen boys' patterns. The men's pattern size is included because you may wish to sew for your father or an older brother or a boyfriend who is older.

Body measurements must be taken to determine your pattern size and type. Take your measurements over a thin shirt and pants with no belt. Use a flexible tape measure pulled snugly but not tightly. Again, it is best if a friend or family member helps you. Write down each measurement on a copy of the "Tally Sheet for Boys' Measurements" (Table 25–4).

Additional measurements are needed, if adjustments have to be made in the pattern. Add these to your tally sheet.

Table 25–5 gives the measurements that are used in sizing patterns, expressed in both standard and metric measures. Check your measurements against this table. Table 25–6 indicates how the various measurements should be taken.

Table 25-4

TALLY SHEET FOR BOYS' MEASUREMENTS

HEIGHT—When standing tall and straight   ____ ft. ____ in.

NECK—Around the neck + ½″ for the neckband size   ____ in.

CHEST—Around the fullest part of the chest   ____ in.

WAIST—Around the natural waist   ____ in.

HIP (SEAT)—Around the fullest part of the seat area   ____ in.

SLEEVE LENGTH—From the center back neck base, along the shoulder to the bent elbow and down to the wrist   ____ in.

The type of garment you plan to make tells you which of these measurements should match up best with those on the chart.
FOR A COAT OR JACKET—Chest measurement
FOR SHIRTS—Neck and sleeve measurement
FOR PANTS—Waist measurement

Write the sizes you need for these garments here.
SIZE _____
BODY TYPE _____
COAT OR JACKET_____
SHIRT_____
PANTS _____

SOURCE: Simplicity Pattern Co.

Table 25-5

MEASUREMENTS USED IN SIZING PATTERNS FOR BOYS AND MEN

Measurements in Inches

	BOYS'				TEEN-BOYS'				MEN'S							
Size	**7**	**8**	**10**	**12**	**14**	**16**	**18**	**20**	**34**	**36**	**38**	**40**	**42**	**44**	**46**	**48**
Chest	26	27	28	30	32	33½	35	36½	34	36	38	40	42	44	46	48
Waist	23	24	25	26	27	28	29	30	28	30	32	34	36	39	42	44
Hip (Seat)	27	28	29½	31	32½	34	35½	37	35	37	39	41	43	45	47	49
Back Waist Length	11⅜	11¾	12½	13¼	14	14¾	15½	16¼	17½	17¾	18	18¼	18½	18¾	19	19¼
Front Waist Length	12⅜	12¾	13½	14¼	14⅝	15⅜	16⅛	16⅞	17¾	18	18¼	18½	18¾	19	19¼	19½
Shoulder Length	4	4⅛	4¼	4½	4¾	5	5¼	5½	6⅛	6¼	6⅜	6½	6⅝	6¾	6⅞	7
Back Width	11½	11¾	12⅛	12¾	13⅞	14½	15⅛	15¾	16	16½	17	17½	18	18½	19	19½
Arm Length	16¼	17	18½	20	21⅞	22½	23⅛	23¾	23⅝	23⅞	24⅛	24⅜	24⅝	24⅞	25⅛	25⅜
Shirt Sleeve Size	22⅜	23¼	25	26¾	29	30	31	32	32	32	33	33	34	34	35	35
Shirt Neck Size	11¾	12	12½	13	13½	14	14½	15	14	14½	15	15½	16	16½	17	17½
Height	48	50	54	58	61	64	66	68								

Measurements in Centimeters

	BOYS'				TEEN-BOYS'				MEN'S							
Size	**7**	**8**	**10**	**12**	**14**	**16**	**18**	**20**	**34**	**36**	**38**	**40**	**42**	**44**	**46**	**48**
Chest	66	69	71	76	81	85	89	93	87	92	97	102	107	112	117	122
Waist	58	61	64	66	69	71	74	76	71	76	81	87	92	99	107	112
Hip (Seat)	69	71	75	79	83	87	90	94	89	94	99	104	109	114	119	124
Back Waist Length	29	30	32	34	35,5	37,5	39,5	41	44,5	45	46	46,5	47	47,5	48	49
Front Waist Length	31,5	32,5	34	36	37	39	41	43	45	46	46,5	47	47,5	48	49	49,5
Shoulder Length	10	10,5	11	11,5	12	12,5	13	14	15,5	16	16	16,5	17	17	17,5	18
Back Width	29,2	29,8	30,8	32,4	35,2	36,8	38,4	40	40,6	41,9	43,2	44,5	45,7	47	48,3	49,5
Arm Length	41	43	47	51	55,5	57	59	60	60	60,5	61,5	62	62	63	64	64,5
Shirt Sleeve Size	57	59	63,5	68	74	76	79	81,5	81	81	84	84	87	87	89	89
Shirt Neck Size	30	31	32	33	34,5	35,5	37	38	35	37	38	39,5	40,5	42	43	44,5
Height	122	127	137	147	155	163	168	173								

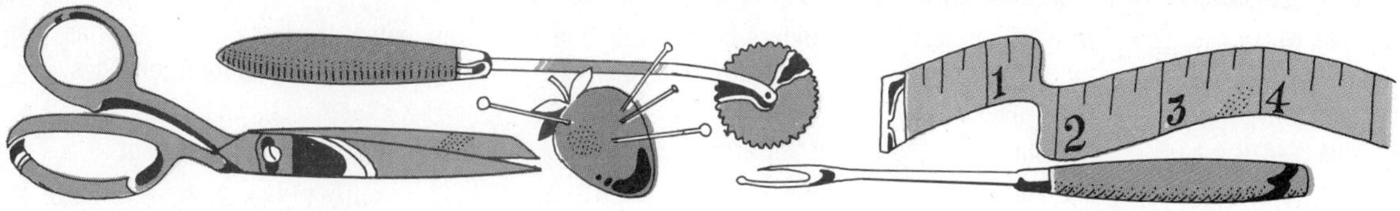

Certain information is essential for choosing a pattern size that is suitable for you. If you plan to sew a coat or jacket, select a pattern according to chest measurement. For shirts, use the neck measurement, plus ½ inch (1.2 centimeters) and the chest measurement. If there is considerable difference between your body and the pattern chest measurement, buy the pattern according to the chest size and alter the neck for your size. For trousers or slacks, use the waist measurement for your guide even for hip hugger or low-rise slacks. If the hips are much larger and the waist smaller than the pattern size, use one matching the hip size and alter the waist.

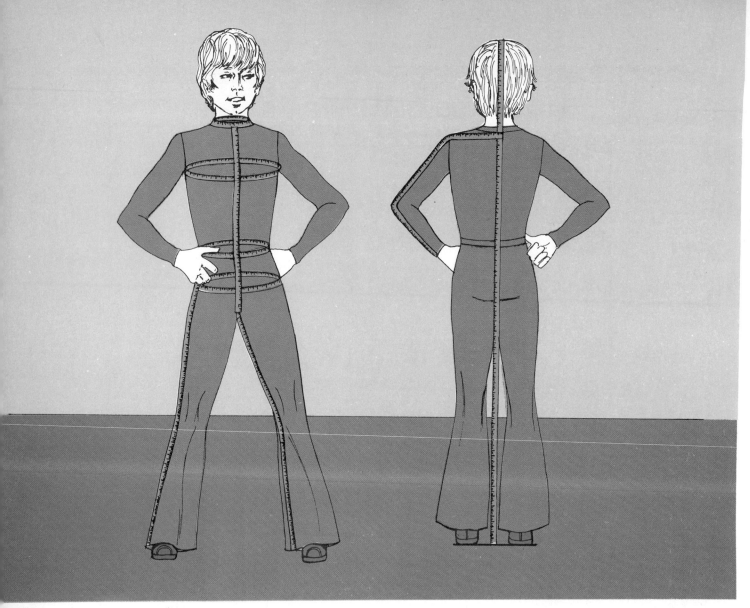

TABLE 25-6

HOW MEASUREMENTS SHOULD BE TAKEN	
BACK WAIST LENGTH	Measure from the base of the neck to the waistline in back.
FRONT WAIST LENGTH	Measure from the base of the neck at the shoulder to the waistline in front. Shrug the shoulders to locate the base of the neck.
SHOULDER LENGTH	Measure from the neck base to the top of the arm.
BACK WIDTH	Measure across the shoulders between the sleeve seams, below the base of the neck as follows: 6 inches (15.2 centimeters) for Men, 4½ inches (11.4 centimeters) for Teen Boys, and 4 inches (10.2 centimeters) for Boys.
ARM LENGTH	Measure from the top of the arm (sleeve seam) to the wristbone with the arm bent at a right angle.
SLEEVE LENGTH	Measure from the prominent bone at the back of the neck along the shoulder over a bent elbow and down to the wrist-bone. The shirt sleeve size is a ready-to-wear measurement used for reference.
TROUSER INSEAM	Measure the inside of the leg from the crotch point (where the seams meet between the legs) to the hem.
TROUSER OUTSEAM	Measure the outside of the leg at the side seam from the bottom of the waistband to the hem.

SOURCE: *Sewing for Men and Boys,* New York: Simplicity Pattern Company, 1973, pp. 14–16.

THE PATTERN ENVELOPE

There is considerable information about the materials in a pattern package that you need to know before you select your own pattern. Here is a list:

1–The *front of the envelope* has illustrations of possible styles that might be constructed from this pattern. You select the view that pleases you the most. Other information given is the name of the company, size, style number, and price.

2– The *back of the envelope* has back views and illustrations of the pattern pieces inside the envelope and descriptions of the garment. Suggestions are given for suitable fabrics. There is a section that helps you figure how much material you have to buy of a certain fabric width.

If a suggested fabric has a nap or there is a one-way print, there will be assistance on how to determine the yardage you will need. Another section lists sewing notions, such as bias tape, buttons, or zipper. The number of pattern pieces and sometimes sketches of the pieces, body measurements, length of material needed for different views, and finished length and waist of the garment are included.

3–The *construction guide* found inside the envelope is a kind of blueprint for cutting and sewing your garment. Begin by reading the entire guide sheet.

Your layout guide is determined by the view, width of fabric, and size pattern you are using. Circle your layout.

Make sure that the fabric is preshrunk, pressed, and folded, with selvages even. Some fabrics may have to be straightened.

Separate the pattern pieces, if there are more than one on a sheet.

Leave the margins. If you do, you will be more accurate when you cut your fabric. Press your pattern pieces.

Next, you are ready to follow layout directions, pin the pattern to the fabric, and check on your grain lines.

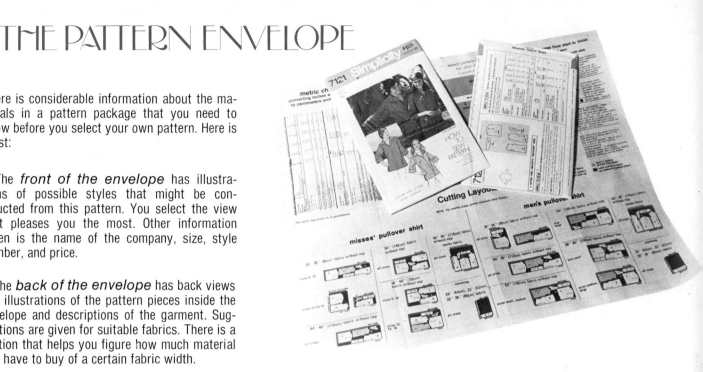

Certain markings on the pattern pieces must be understood.

A **straight arrow** is a help in placing the pattern straight on the fabric grain.

A **bracketed arrow** is a sign to place the pattern piece on the fold of fabric. You must place the pattern piece with the bracketed arrow on the fold to have a piece of the right size after cutting.

Cutting lines are solid. Solid lines also indicate placement of buttonholes, pockets, and trims.

The **seam line** (usually 5/8 inch, approximately 2.5 centimeters) is a broken line.

Notches are numbered for joining seams together.

Dots on the seam line help to match seams on collars, sleeves, and other places.

The **double line** is for lengthening or shortening the pattern.

CHOOSING THE FABRIC

Although suitable fabrics are indicated on the pattern envelope, there are many considerations to bear in mind. The fabric must be suitable for the climate or season when the garment will be worn; special finishes such as durable press should be considered, as well as the hand, or how the fabric feels when you touch it—soft, crisp, sheer, or bulky—and eye appeal and surface interest. Other questions to answer are care of the fabric, cost, attractiveness, and suitability for your purpose. A woven cotton or cotton blend fabric is often chosen for a beginning sewing project. These fabrics have been favorites among sewers for years.

It might be helpful if you try to analyze your choice of fabric for a pants suit for school wear. The pattern may suggest soft or crisp fabrics, such as knits, gabardine, jersey, velveteen, light-to-medium wools, challis, denim, pique, and broadcloth. If you want the suit to be economical and sturdy, you might prefer cotton. Cotton knits or jersey might be too limp. Gabardine, velveteen, or jersey are expensive. Pique is lightweight and dressy. Your choices may eventually be narrowed to denim or broadcloth. Now re-read this analysis.

Woven Fabric Terms

There is a language in relation to woven fabrics that must be understood. There are three *grains*. The *lengthwise grain* is parallel to the *selvage* and consists of the *warp* threads of weaving. The *crosswise grain* runs from selvage to selvage and consists of the *filling* threads. The *diagonal grain* or *true bias* is the diagonal direction across the two grain lines. This grain has the most stretch and give. The *selvage* is the outside edge on both sides of the fabric and runs the length of the fabric as it is wound on the *bolt*. It does not ravel as do the crosswise edges of the fabric.

Types of Fabric Weaves

Fabric may be woven in several ways. Weaving is the interlacing of two sets of yarns at right angles.

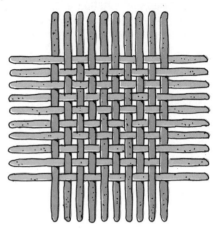

Plain weave is the regular interlacing of warp and woof (lengthwise and crosswise threads, respectively), one row after another, in an alternating pattern. Some examples of common fabrics in plain weave are gingham, organdy, voile, and taffeta.

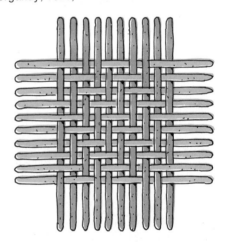

In *twill weave* the filling threads are passed over one or more warp yarns, each successive line starting one warp yarn back. This creates a diagonal line. Some examples of the twill weave in fabrics are denim, ticking, surah, and gabardine.

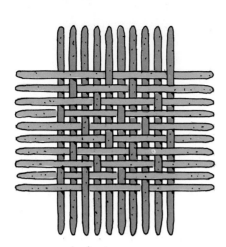

The *satin weave* is interwoven in such a way that more warp than filling threads show on the right side of the fabric. This weaving gives a great sheen to the fabric and reflects light. This weave is used for silks, rayons, and synthetics.

Knitted fabrics are usually classified into weft and warp knits. Each uses a particular kind of machine and produces a different type of fabric. The *weft type* is used in sweaters and hosiery. The threads run horizontally from side to side across the width of the fabric. Other types are the *plain knit,* also known as the *jersey knit.* This is used in T-shirts and full-fashioned sweaters. The *rib knit* has a very distinct lengthwise rib effect, providing greater elasticity. It is used in the neck and cuffs of a turtleneck sweater. *Double-knits* are made from a special type of rib-stitch fabric. These fabrics are closely knitted, made from fine yarns, and may have a patterned or designed effect. They are thicker and heavier than regular jersey knit fabric. True double knits do not have a "right and wrong" side. They are the easiest fabric to use because of their stability.

Knitted fabrics are easy to wash and dry quickly because of the openings in the knitted construction. Other advantages are that they do not wrinkle easily, are packable, take up little space, and are comfortable to wear because of their elasticity. They are not likely to stick to the skin if the fabric becomes wet. Another plus is that these fabrics can be adapted to style changes.

Other questions to ask about the fabric you choose are wearability, care—washability or dry cleaning, appropriate colors and design, cost, suitability to your needs, and a fabric that sews and handles easily because it may be your first project. A cotton fabric or a cotton blend are often chosen as the fabric for beginning sewing. This is true if this type of fabric is appropriate for the garment you plan to sew.

KNITTED CLOTHES

WORK HABITS IN CLOTHING CLASS

As an individual and as a member of a group in the homemaking room, there are some habits and attitudes toward work that you should develop in order to achieve what you set out to do. The test in Table 25–7 allows you to rate yourself occasionally to see whether you are achieving better standards for yourself when you sew. Give yourself a score of 3 for each item you always do, 2 if you do it when someone reminds you, and 1 if you forget quite often. One way to achieve satisfaction from your accomplishments is to take pride in your work.

Table 25–7

TESTING YOUR WORK HABITS

Sometimes forget: score 1	When I'm reminded: score 2	Do it every time: score 3	
			1. Before I begin sewing I wash my hands and see that my nails are clean.
			2. My sewing box, tote drawer, or envelope is orderly.
			3. All my materials are on hand when required: pattern, fabric, shears, thread, bobbins, needles, and so on.
			4. I am unselfish in using and sharing equipment and supplies.
			5. I use a thimble.
			6. I use good posture at work.
			7. I ask the teacher to check my layout before beginning to cut.
			8. I check to make sure each step is correct before the final stitching.
			9. I plan each step carefully to avoid mistakes.
			10. I check the machine for proper tension and stitch length by stitching on a double scrap of my fabric before sewing on my garment or project.
			11. I press all seams open as each one is finished.
			12. I work quietly without unnecessary talking or noise.
			13. I put my sewing supplies away neatly and promptly.
			14. I do my share to keep the classroom clean and orderly.

THINKING IT OVER

1. Using the analysis in the section "Choosing the Fabric" as a "think-starter," establish a model for selecting the fabric for a sewing project. Test it on one or more of these possible projects: a pillow, an apron, a bathing suit, or a jacket.

2. If you were an inventor, what would you design in the way of new sewing equipment?

THINGS TO DO

1. Have an identification contest. Number a series of fabric samples and see how many you can identify as to name and suitable purposes, and make a judgment on whether they are inexpensive, somewhat expensive, or expensive.

2. Teach a younger brother or sister or someone else you know how to sew.

3. Compare the cost of articles you can make with those that are purchased. Establish criteria for making your judgments.

26 Sewing basics

ST (SEWING TIME) is here! You are eager to add something new to your wardrobe, to make a gift, or to sew something that will brighten your home. You have your sewing tools by now and have become familiar with the sewing machine to the extent that you are confident about handling it.

SUGGESTIONS FOR PROJECTS

If you are a true beginner, you may wish to select a sewing project that will improve your basic skills, such as stitching, becoming more confident about using the sewing machine, or cutting and putting fabric together. If you feel that you have a little know-how, you might choose projects that will give you some new experiences or will improve your present skills. If you consider yourself an old hand, you might like to select one of the projects that appeals to you to help you "tune up" for more advanced work. In addition, you might be encouraged to take a project and change it to fit some of your own ideas, or to redesign it completely. No matter how you feel about your ability as a sewer, you should select something that you will enjoy doing and that you feel will add something useful to your life.

Rectangles of different widths and lengths and colors may be put together in a design for a pillow. Patchwork effects can be very attractive from putting together a few squares or rectangles to more complicated designs that you may develop.

If you are a beginner you may wish to work with cotton or polyester and cotton-blended fabrics. If you are an advanced sewer, you may try more expensive and elegant materials for a pillow for the living room sofa or a chair.

Pillows, Pillows, Pillows

Collect scraps or buy remnants. Try to assemble fabrics that are similar, such as cottons, silks and velvets, or textured materials. Use them for making rectangles of different lengths and widths that can be combined in numerous ways. You may even start a fad!

To make a rectangle, cut a strip of cloth at any length you wish. Next decide on the width. Suppose you want a rectangle that is 6 inches (15.2 centimeters) wide when sewn. To the 6 inches you will have to make a seam allowance of ⅝-inch (1.6 centimeters) on each side of the cloth or 1¼ inches (3.2 centimeters) for both together, making a total of 7¼ inches (18.4 centimeters). Place the two right sides of the fabric together and stitch along the long side.

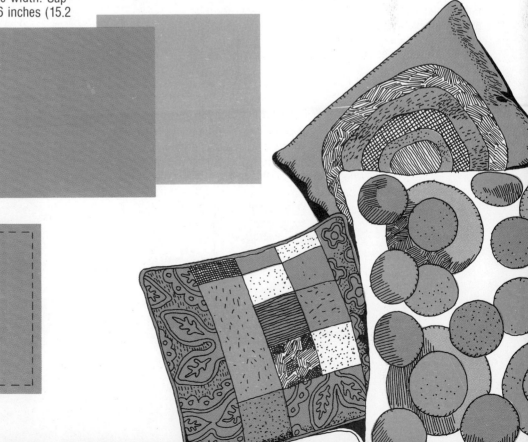

Ideas!

A throw for the bottom of the bed or an entire quilt, if you are ambitious, may be made.

Snake shapes may be made from a single or double rectangle that is very long. Loop it, knot it, put a face in the middle, or dream up other ways to make an interesting pillow or bed decoration.

Other Types of Pillows. Be observant when you visit in the homes of others and when you are in home decorating and furniture departments in stores or in needlecraft shops, for ideas on making pillows. Some communities have pillow stores, especially for the very large pillows. Newspapers and magazines may have ideas for pillows that you can adapt. Here are some suggestions that you may change to please yourself or to suit the materials that you have on hand.

a "pull - bag" pillow

This technique can be used to cover an old sofa cushion or a bolster pillow. You may wish to make one of the popular large pillows that may be placed on the floor for your friends to sit on when they visit you. Knit fabric is good because it stretches for a good fit, but other fabrics you have can be used.

1–Measure the length of the pillow to be covered or the inner pillow, if you do not have an old one to cover. Measure the thickness of the pillow and add half of this measurement to the width of material, plus seam allowances for each side.

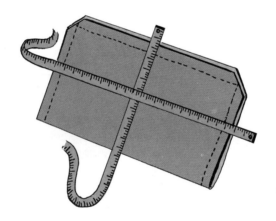

3–You may wish to have different colors or fabrics on each side. In that event, measure and place the two right sides together and sew lengthwise, leaving the two smaller ends open.

4–Pull the bag over the pillow and pull the drawstrings at each end tightly. Tie the drawstrings securely and place them inside the pillow. Leave the pillow as it is, place a decorative button at each end, or create your own idea for a finish. This method is not appropriate for round pillows.

2–Allow ⅝ of an inch (1.6 centimeters) on each side for the seams. Make a small hem at each end, large enough to pull a drawstring through. When the hem is finished pull the drawstring through.

Ribbons for a Pillow

An attractive pillow may be made by weaving strips of ribbon or trimming. You may vary the widths of ribbon for the lengthwise threads for variation.

Select a backing fabric for the weaving and cut it the same size as the finished weaving, adding ½ inch (1.2 centimeters) on each edge for seam allowances and finishing.

Place all the lengthwise ribbons or trimming side by side so that none of the backing fabric shows through the ribbons.

To keep the ribbons in place, anchor each ribbon with a T-pin or straight pin on an ironing board or a piece of corrugated cardboard. The latter can be held on your lap. If you have a complicated design, make a copy of the design and keep it near you so that you know which ribbon or trimming to weave next.

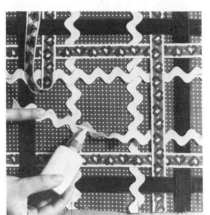

2—One is basting the ribbons securely to the backing fabric and then stitching by machine on all four sides ½ inch (1.2 cm) from the edge on each side. Be certain that the ribbons have not moved but are secure.

3—If you feel that you have had sufficient practice in stitching you may wish to use fusible web to secure the ribbons. Place a piece of fusible web, the same size as your fabric backing, under the ribbons but on top of the backing. When your weaving is completed, iron so the web will fuse the backing with the ribbons.

Another method is to use white glue for anchoring the ribbons to the backing.

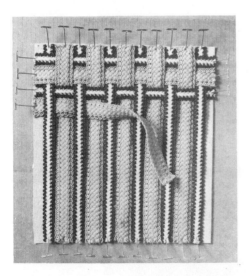

1—Anchor the first horizontal ribbon with a pin ½ inch (1.2 centimeters) from the first vertical ribbon and begin your weaving according to plan, weaving over and under the vertical ribbons. Repeat with the remainder of the horizontal ribbons, anchoring each at both ends.

There are several ways in which the ribbons can be secured to the fabric backing.

If your pattern is rather open and shows a great deal of the backing fabric, the ribbons or rickrack may be anchored with white glue. It is especially important that the intersections be well glued.

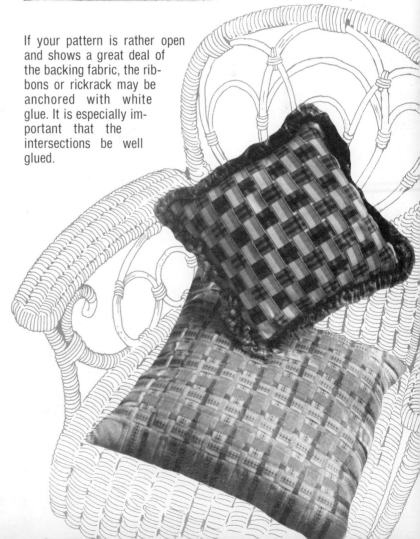

Make your own design for other pillows by collecting the scraps of fabric you have. Take a sheet of paper and work out ways to put them together. You might sew strips of the same or different widths together. The fabric may be plain or printed. If you have a number of small pieces consider making them into various shapes, such as circles, squares, diamonds or abstract designs.

Look at your fabrics and decide what the background should be, plain or printed, and which type of fabric is best.

On a piece of paper, try out your design or designs and select the one that pleases you. This is a form of appliqué. To hold the pieces to the base fabric, several methods may be used.

Decorative stitches such as overcast hemming, featherstitching, or blind hemming can be done by hand. Zigzag, satin, or other decorative stitching may be done by sewing machine.

Use fusible web for attaching the pieces.

You may embroider the pillow you make by using any embroidery stitch or a combination of the many kinds of stitches. The fabric should be durable. Cotton is the easiest material to work on. Silks and woolens are luxurious but more difficult to work on. You can make your own design or buy a pattern of one you like. What other kinds of pillows can you make? Share ideas.

Patchwork

Colonial homemakers used patchwork as a way of using all the materials they had on hand,

Patchwork of squares may be put together to make a quilt.

even small scraps. Quilts are most commonly considered for patchwork projects, but in recent years there have been many other uses. Look at books that have some of the old designs with charming titles, such as rail fence, starry path, morning star, flying geese, king's X, and peace and plenty. Talk to older persons in your community and find new names and stories about quilting bees and ways that patchwork was used.

Patchwork projects for you might include a pillow or a wall hanging with an interesting design, and like the pioneers you might give the pattern a name. A tote bag, curtains, place mats, a scarf, or a shawl are other possibilities.

Needlepoint, which is a popular hobby today, can be used to make a variety of useful and colorful items.

20" x 10" for smaller pocket
20" x 14" for larger pocket

To Measure Caddy:
Take a piece of chalk and mark, as illustrated, on the outside of *one* piece of your "caddy" fabric. These marks will help you place the pockets accurately.

16"

8"

21"

12"

←12"   12"→

←19"   8"   19"→

CAN YOU USE A CADDIE?

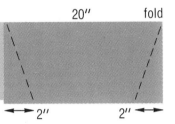

20"   fold

2"   2"

Keep the cut edges together, right sides outside, and machine-baste raw edges together.

To Make Pockets:
Smaller pocket:
Fold the 20" x 10" fabric strip in half lengthwise, right sides outside and measure in 2" from either end at bottom. Draw a line from the corner of the folded edge to the 2" mark on each side, cut off this excess amount.

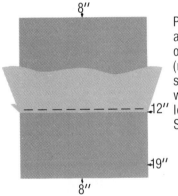

8"

12"

19"

8"

Press a 5/8 seam allowance on the bottom edge of the pocket. Pin pocket (right side out) to right side of caddy at 12" line, with unfinished seam allowance folded upward. Stitch in place.

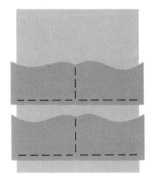

Machine stitch down center of pocket, back-stitching at upper and lower edges to secure. Fold pocket sections toward center to keep clear of side edges, pin. Stitch side edges of pocket to caddy, keeping edges even.

Repeat for second pocket, placing pocket on 19" line.

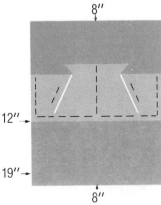

8"

12"→

19"→

8"

Joining Front and Back of Caddy
Pin back to front, right sides together, matching centers and edges. Stitch 5/8" seams, leaving approximately 5" open at bottom for turning.

Turn, finish bottom opening with machine stitching.

A caddy can be a shoe bag with pockets sewn on a backing fabric, that may be hung on your closet door. Another caddy is similar, but the pockets are of different sizes, depending on the purpose. For example, you may tuck a caddy securely under your mattress, leaving access to the pockets. Here you may store your transistor radio, the latest paperback that you are reading, a flashlight, tissues, pencils and a pad for notes, and other items that you might like near you. Some articles may be too heavy. Experiment. Use a stout material such as muslin, denim, or chintz. For each pocket, measure the article, allowing sufficient room for it to slip out easily. Make a sample pocket for testing.

FABRIC REQUIRED
35″   2⅛ yards
45″   1¾ yards

STEP 1 Prepare the bag
Prepare two pockets as follows:

a–Press under 1/4″ (6mm) on upper edge. Press upper edge to INSIDE along fold line, forming facing. Stitch, as shown.

b–Pin WRONG side of pocket over RIGHT side of one bag section, matching small and medium dots.

Baste raw edges to bag.

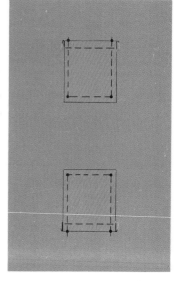

STEP 2 Sew the handles and bottom section
Prepare two handles as follows:

a–Fold handle in half lengthwise with RIGHT sides together. Stitch long edges.

b–Turn handle RIGHT side out bringing seam to center on underside; press.

MAKE A TOTE

c–Pin underside of handles to bag (over pockets) matching small dots.

Stitch close to long edges of handle as far as small dots, as shown.

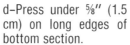

d–Press under ⅝″ (1.5 cm) on long edges of bottom section.
Pin WRONG side of bottom section over RIGHT side of bag, covering raw edges of pockets and handles, matching small dots.
Stitch close to long edges, catching in pockets and handles.
Baste side edges.

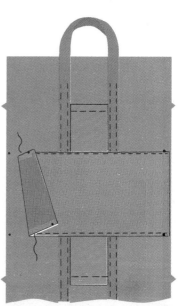

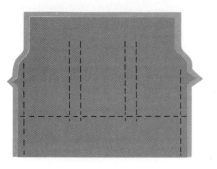

e-Fold bag with RIGHT sides together, matching notches. Stitch notched edges.

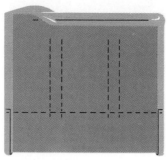

f-Press under ⅝″ (1.5 cm) on upper edge of bag.

If you prefer, fold points of bag up to medium dot at seams, as shown. Stitch thru all thicknesses, as shown.

Need a clutch bag?

FABRIC REQUIRED 35″ 3/4 yard
Foldover band
1-1/4 yards of 1/2″ or 5/8″

STEP 1 Prepare the bag
a–With RIGHT sides together, pin bag sections together, matching notches. Stitch notched edges together.

b–Trim seam; press open.

c–Fold bag in half with WRONG sides together, having raw edges even. Pin. Baste raw edges together.

e–Encase all raw edges in fold-over braid, folding out fulness at corners and turning under ends at lower edge.

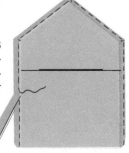

d–Fold lower edge (straight edge) of bag up along fold line. Baste raw edges together.

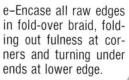

STEP 2 Finish the bag
Turn upper edge of bag down and fasten with large snap. If you prefer, a purchased applique can be sewn to bag.

SUPER SIMPLE ADJUSTABLE APRON

With this pattern you can make this useful apron. The steps here outline how simple it is.

UNIT 1-preparing apron

Press under 1/4" (6 mm) on all edges of apron.
Press all edges to INSIDE along seam line; stitch.

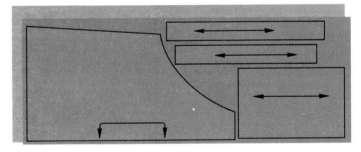

UNIT 2-neck strap and tie ends

a-Fold neck strap in half, lengthwise, RIGHT sides together.
Stitch long edge in 3/8" (1 cm) seam.
Trim seam.

b-Turn strap; press.

268

a–Stitch along seam line on side and lower edges of lower pocket; trim to 1/4″ (6 mm).

Press edges to INSIDE along stitching.

e–On INSIDE, pin neck strap to upper edge of apron, matching small and medium dots. Adjust to fit. Stitch, as shown.
On INSIDE, pin tie ends to side edges of apron, matching small and medium dots. Stitch, as shown.

c–On OUTSIDE, pin pocket to apron along lower pocket line, matching centers, small and medium dots.
Stitch close to side and lower edges.
Stitch along stitching lines, as shown.
If you prefer, also stitch along center front line.

b–Press under 1/4″ (6 mm) on upper edge.
Press upper edge to INSIDE along seam line; stitch.

Feather Stitch

Running Stitch

Blanket Stitch

Outline Stitch

Cross Stitch

Chain Stitch

APRON VARIATIONS

USE OF PATTERNS

By this time you may feel that you are sufficiently skillful to graduate into something more advanced. You might like to get a pattern for a dashiki, an African-type blouse, that is equally appropriate for boys and girls. From the same pattern, you can make a long length and it becomes a caftan. This may be worn around home for lounging or on the beach. This garment will give you considerable practice in top stitching. You may have your eye on another type of pattern for something you wish to sew. Review the information in Chapter 25 on selecting a pattern, the information on a pattern envelope, and choosing the fabric.

Construction Processes

In the construction of a simple garment or accessory, there is an orderly sequence of processes that must be completed if the project is to be successful. A quick run-through of the processes involved in making a blouse, for example, will illustrate this order and sequence. Most garments follow a similar pattern of construction steps with slight variations. These steps are

1-Selection.
   a. Select the pattern.
   b. Select the fabric.
2-Preparation.
   a. Lay the pattern.
   b. Cut out the garment.
   c. Transfer the markings.
3-Construction.
   a. Pin-baste and sew the darts.
   b. Choose appropriate seams.
   c. Pin-baste and stitch the seams.
   d. Press the seams.
   e. Finish the neckline.
   f. Finish the sleeves.
   g. Finish the hem.
   h. Make trimming suitable to the blouse.

Using a Commercial Pattern

When you are making a garment or accessory and are using a commercial pattern, the most important step in the process is to understand and learn how to use the guide sheet that comes with your pattern. This sheet contains all the information needed to make the garment. Generally, one side is devoted to cutting instructions and the other to detailed construction steps

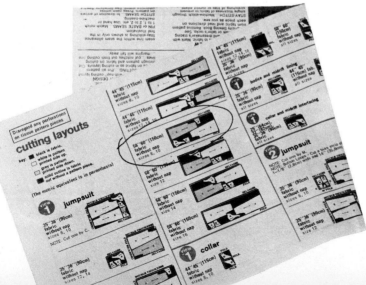

and techniques. Sometimes a pattern company will have the cutting instructions on one sheet and the sewing instructions on another.

CUTTING INSTRUCTIONS ON THE GUIDE SHEET

A general study of the cutting instructions will show that *before you can place the pattern on your material* properly you must do seven things:

1-Choose the style or view you want. Circle it.

2-Select the layout to be used. Note that the layouts are arranged according to (a) the *view* or style, (b) the *width* of the fabric, and (c) the *size* of the pattern. Find and circle the specific layout for your garment and underline the three key items you used as a guide.

3-Identify the pattern parts you will need by writing your name on each piece in pencil. Use the diagram that shows all the pattern pieces and the layout you will use. Take out the pattern pieces you need. Fold the remaining pieces and return them to the pattern envelope.

4-Learn the pattern symbols. All notches, perforations, or dots have a purpose. Study the instruction sheet and learn what *each* marking means and how it is used. The two most important markings on the pattern are the symbols for the *grain line* and for *cutting on the fold.* The *grain line* indicates that you must place your pattern piece parallel to the selvage edge of your fabric. Knits do not have a grain, but a "rib" must be followed in place of a grain. *On the fold* means that the pattern piece given is *half* of what will be required when cut from the material, like half a skirt or blouse back. Use care in placing the side of the pattern *on the fold* of the material before cutting.

5-A gauge is used as a standard guide to help you sew the same distance from the edge. An easy way to make a gauge is as follows:

   a. Take a piece of heavy cardboard about 3 inches by 1 inch. Mark off ⅝ inch (2.5 centimeters).

   b. With a scissors cut straight in on the mark about ½ inch (1.27 centimeters).

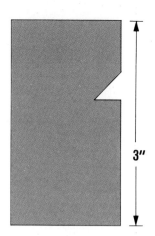

Make a seam gauge and a hem gauge.

3"

c. Cut a notch out leaving a ⅝ inch marker. A hem gauge is made the same way, but instead of a notch at the ⅝ inch mark, it may be at the recommended hem width.

6-Press your pattern before measuring it or cutting the fabric. Compare your body measurements with those of the pattern. Make alterations where necessary. Basic measurements to check are waist and hip width, skirt or pants length, and back waist length. If necessary, refer to a sewing book for assistance.

7-Test your fabric for shrinkage. Take a 1½ inch by 2 inch (3.8 centimeters by 5 centimeters) swatch and trace this carefully on a piece of paper. Press the fabric with steam or wet it with water, depending on how you will eventually clean your fabric. Compare the size with that of the original tracing. If any shrinkage has occurred, preshrink the entire fabric. Also straighten the ends and grain of the fabric, if necessary. You are now ready to lay out the directions of your pattern cutting guide.

Placing the Pattern on the Fabric

You are now ready to pin the pattern on the fabric, cut it out, and transfer the important markings. The layout you selected will indicate whether your pattern pieces are placed on the fold of the fabric or on a double thickness of fabric. Follow your Pattern Cutting Guide for placing the pattern on the fabric. There are three basic points to remember in placing the pattern on your fabric:

1-**Use sufficient pins to hold your pattern securely to the fabric.**

2-**The proper order of pinning is (a) on the fold line or grain line *first*, (b) flatten out and place pins at each corner, (c) place a few pins along the sides to hold firmly.**

3-**Keep the fabric flat on the table and free from wrinkles while pinning.**

SEWING TIPS

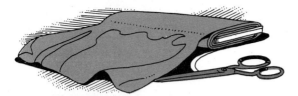

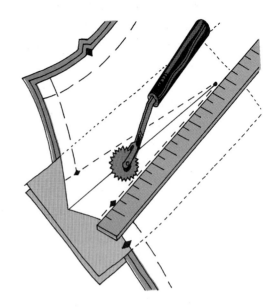

If the fabric is to be folded, make sure that the selvage edges are even.

Pins may be placed parallel to the edge of the pattern piece or at right angles to the edge. Whichever method is used, be sure the pins are in far enough from the cutting line so that they will not be caught in the shears.

Before beginning to cut, make a final check of the layout to be sure every pattern piece you will need has been placed on the fabric.

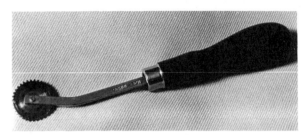

To cut the garment, hold the shears properly and use long, full strokes. Cut exactly on the cutting line, being especially careful not to cut out of line around curves and at the corners, and in cutting the notches outward. Allow all pattern pieces to remain pinned to the fabric and fold neatly.

The last step in cutting is to transfer the necessary markings from your pattern to your fabric. Darts, pleats, gathers, and placement of pockets are some of the things that may need to be indicated on your fabric. Tailor's chalk, wax, or a tracing wheel and special carbon may be used. Your teacher will help you use the one best suited to your garment.

Dressmaker's tracing paper is a special coated paper used to transfer pattern markings. It is available in a variety of sizes and colors. Whenever possible, white or light colors should be used, since dark colors do not clean easily from the fabric. To mark a single layer of fabric, place the sheet of tracing paper with its face against the wrong side of the fabric. For double fabric, use two pieces of tracing paper, each facing the wrong side of the fabric under the pattern. With the tracing wheel and a ruler as a guide on straight lines, mark over the construction symbols using only enough pressure to make a light mark.

After you remove the pattern and put it away neatly for future reference, you are ready to begin the construction of your garment. You have completed the work covered on the first side of your instruction sheet.

PUTTING THE GARMENT TOGETHER

The next step is to put your garment together. The other side of your guide sheet will have each step listed in the order to be used in putting the garment together. The order for assembling the parts of your garment is determined by the de-

UNIT METHOD OF CONSTRUCTION

Units in Your Basic Blouse

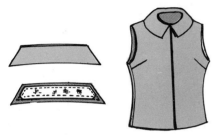

Unit 1–Front-interfaced. **Unit 2**–Back-stitched to front.

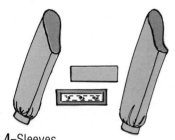

Unit 3–Collar–interfaced–attached to blouse.

Unit 4–Sleeves.

Unit 5–Cuffs–interfaced–stitched to sleeves.
Sleeves stitched to blouse.
Hem and finishing details added.

Units in Your Basic Skirt

Unit 1–Front.

Unit 2–Back–zipper attached–stitched to front.

Unit 3–Waistband.
Hem and finishing details added.

Units in Your Basic Dress

Unit 1–Front.   **Unit 2**–Back–zipper attached–shoulder seams stitched.

Unit 3–Neck Facings–stitched to dress–side seams stitched.

Unit 4–Armhole Facings–stitched to dress.
Hem and finishing details added.

SOURCE: © Copyright 1976 by Simplicity Pattern Co. Inc.

sign. However, the usual procedure is to baste darts, tucks, or gathers on the blouse or skirt. Then stitch them on the machine and press the fabric.

In constructing a simple dress, the bodice is usually completed first, then the skirt. Finally they are put together and finishes such as the hem or trimmings are done last. This is often referred to as a *unit method* of construction, since the main sections of the garment are put together as units, each being assembled before the next part is done.

Darts. A regular *dart* is a fold of fabric stitched wide at one end and tapering to a point.

Darts are used for fitting by controlling fullness or removing excess fullness where it is not needed. They are frequently used at the underarm seam to control fullness over the bust and at either side of the skirt back to allow for ease and fullness over the hips and for a smooth fit, or in a dress or sheath to control waistline fullness.

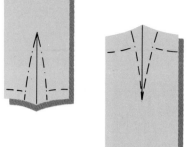

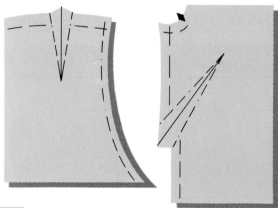

curved

Outward—waistline of dress bodice front.

Inward—skirt front, slacks front.

straight

Front underarm

Shoulder

Skirt back

Bodice back

Elbow

Tucks. A *tuck* is a fold of material usually the same width throughout and often made on the right side of a dress or blouse for decoration. Tucks may be stitched either by hand or machine.

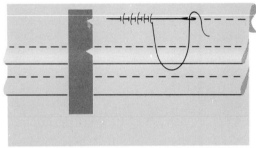

Pin-Basting and Stitching. Pinbasting and stitching the seams will be the next steps in the construction of your garment. You will notice if you examine seams on ready-made garments that in most cases a plain seam is used. On the yoke of a boy's shirt a top-stitched seam may be used.

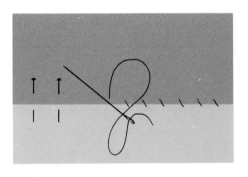

A *plain seam* is made by stitching two pieces of fabric together on the wrong side (right sides of the fabric together) after they have been pin-basted.

A *top-stitched seam* is used for decoration or to hold a seam edge in place. The finished edges of collars and cuffs may be top-stitched as a decorative touch. Yoke seams in blouses and shirts are top-stitched.

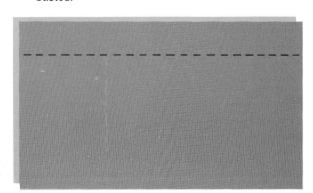

Finishing Steps

If you examine the inside of a garment made by a skilled seamstress or tailor you will notice a clean, finished look. This is achieved by careful pressing during construction and neat finishes on hems, necklines, collars, facings, and the like. When you complete your garment, give it a detailed check on the *inside*. Are the threads at the ends of darts knotted and clipped? Are facings applied neatly and well finished around the edges? Are seams pressed open or flat? Are all loose threads, pins, and materials used during construction removed? Does your garment have a neat look when turned inside out?

> ### Making a Hem.
> These are the steps in putting a hem in a skirt or dress:
>
> 1—Put on the dress or skirt. Wear shoes regularly worn with the garment.
>
> 2—Ask your partner to mark the bottom of your skirt with a row of chalk marks or straight pins placed parallel to the bottom of the skirt and each one the same distance from the floor. To find the best length for you, have someone measure the distance from the floor to the hemline of a dress or skirt you think looks well. Use a yardstick or skirt marker. There are also skirt markers available which allow you to measure your skirt length by yourself.
>
> 3—The row of pins or chalk marks indicates where the bottom of your finished hem will be. Baste on the marking row of pins, remove the pins, and cut an even hem width. A hem gauge is important. Now turn up the hem, finish the edge, and sew the hem. See the Pattern Directions for special techniques.

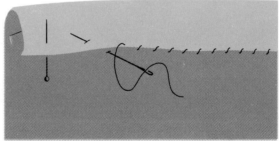

Blind-hemming

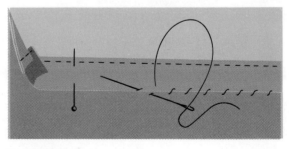

Seam-taped hem, top stitched.

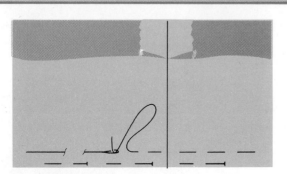

Turn on pin line. Pin or baste.

Final Pressing. The final complete pressing is most important and is the last step in the construction of a garment. It is hoped you will wear or use your project proudly and that the satisfaction you have derived from this initial project may spur you on to try other projects soon—perhaps more difficult ones.

Fashion Silhouettes and Vocabulary

One of the basic requirements for becoming an expert in clothing construction is to be able to recognize and identify popular and classic fashion silhouettes. For example, do you know the difference between a Peter Pan collar and a convertible collar? Between a V neckline and a scoop neckline? Not only do they change the style of a dress or blouse, but they require differ-

ent construction techniques. Necklines, collars, sleeves, skirts, dresses, and trousers or slacks have many distinctive outlines.

Try this experiment: Use the outline of the shift or the basic sheath shown below and add each of the sleeve silhouettes to it one at a time. Note the difference in the result. Try combining neckline and collar outlines to harmonize.

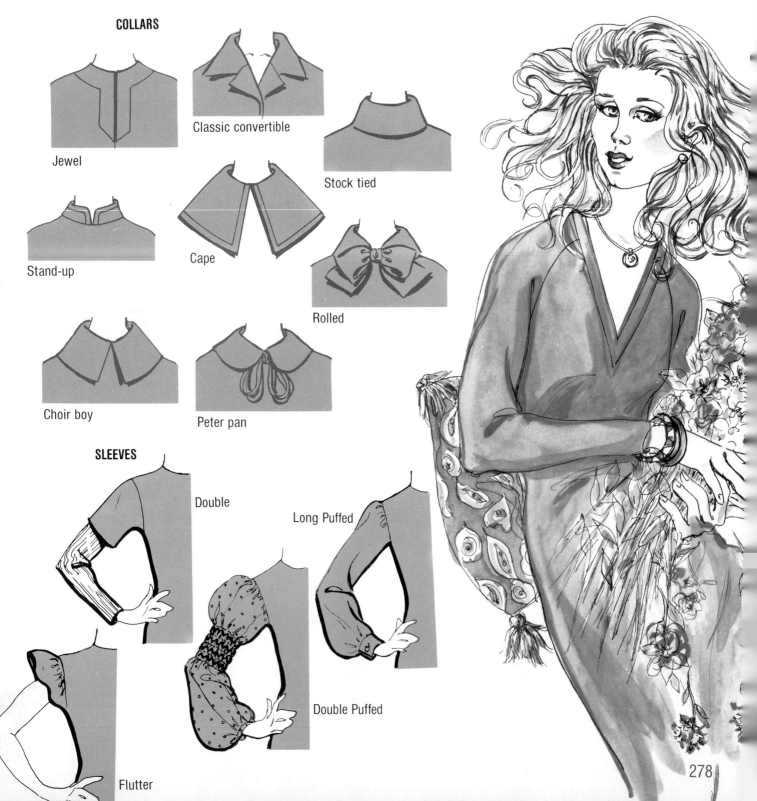

COLLARS

Jewel

Classic convertible

Stock tied

Stand-up

Cape

Rolled

Choir boy

Peter pan

SLEEVES

Double

Long Puffed

Double Puffed

Flutter

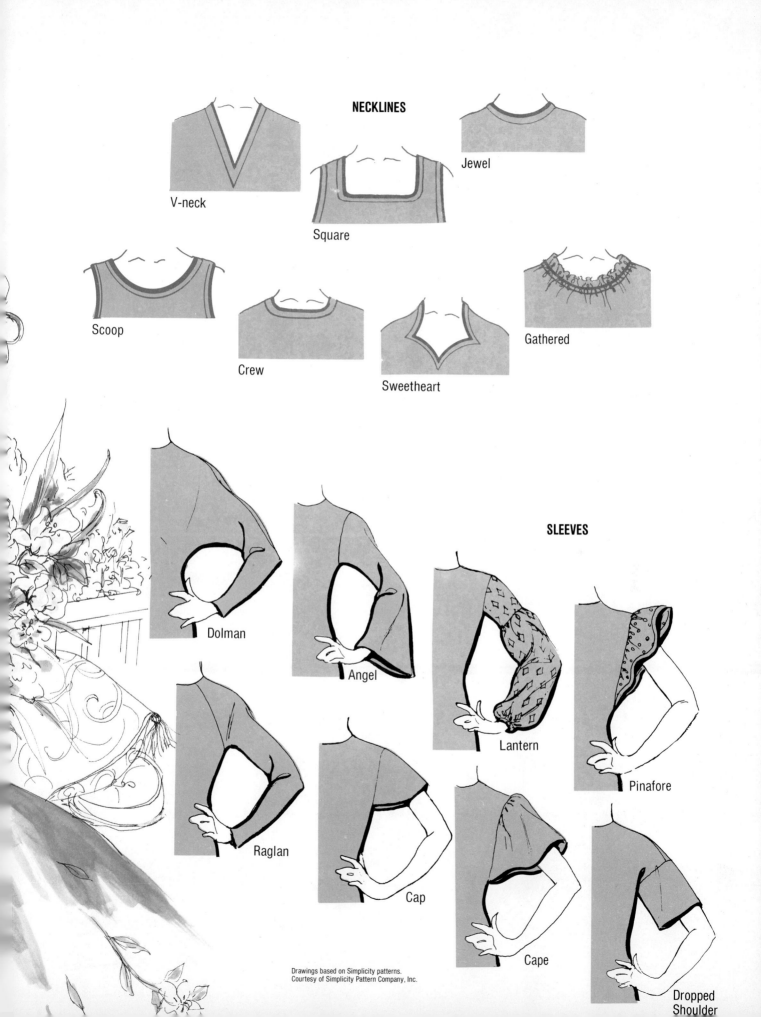

NECKLINES

V-neck

Square

Jewel

Scoop

Crew

Sweetheart

Gathered

SLEEVES

Dolman

Angel

Lantern

Pinafore

Raglan

Cap

Cape

Dropped Shoulder

Drawings based on Simplicity patterns.
Courtesy of Simplicity Pattern Company, Inc.

To make over old clothes so they will have a new look or to sew something from old towels, sheets, scraps and remnants, or other household materials, can be a creative challenge. It can be a necessity if your family has money problems as do so many families in these days of economic trouble.

What, for instance, can be done with old *towels?* Washcloths, patchwork or striped aprons from less worn parts, or bathroom curtains, are possibilities. Bathing trunks and halters, place mats, or a baby's bib are other ideas. Stuffed toys are good because they can be easily washed. In fact, all these ideas require little effort in washing and do not have to be ironed, so energy is saved. Ask yourself what you can do with old neck and head scarfs, napkins, or fancy handkerchiefs.

Apron

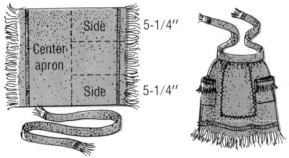

Side   5-1/4"

Center apron

Side   5-1/4"

1–Cut towel in half and cut sides from other half. Join cut edge to center, matching fringe.
2–Add pockets and rickrack trim.
3–Seam ties together. Put seam at side, leave fringe at ends.
4–Make 2 rows of gathering stitch and add to right side of waist band.
5–Fold band over and top stitch. Hem ties.

Place mat

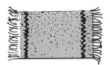

1 Hand Towel—1 yd. rickrack for each. Fold a 1/2" tuck along each fringed end of towel. Sew rickrack over this tuck.

Curtains

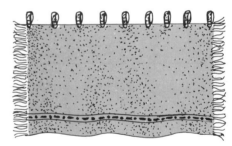

(2 Bath Towels)
Sew fringe 1" from selvage edge. Use clips across hemmed edge, or sew on rings.

SOURCE: Courtesy of Procter & Gamble from *Free sewing and Decorating Booklet from Bonus*

Make minishirts or collar and cuff sets to wear with your sweaters.

Tie and dye old sheets or parts that are still usable. Make a skirt, halter top, or a pinafore. Some of the colored or print sheets may be used as they are without dyeing. Make a ruffle for under your bedspread. A sheet might make an attractive light summer coat. Curtains and dresser scarves are other possibilities.

Drawings based on Simplicity patterns.
Courtesy of Simplicity Pattern Company, Inc.

Drawings based on Simplicity patterns.
Courtesy of Simplicity Pattern Company, Inc.

Create a new neckline, decorate with ribbon, lace, or tape. If it is faded, dye it another color, or use a wax-and-dye or batik technique and create an interesting design. Make a cardigan by putting a zipper down the front of a *pullover.* Take an *undershirt* and insert a crocheted doily in the front. Put fun patches over worn spots.

You can use some of these ideas with old *sweaters,* such as cutting off old sleeves or making a scoop or other type of neckline. Stitch just above where you intend to cut, to prevent raveling. Crochet around the edges or use decorative embroidery stitches. Add other types of trim, such as lace or rickrack.

RECYCLING RECYCLING

Make a *minishirt* to wear under sweaters from an old shirt or collar and cuff sets. Cut off the worn collar and sleeves of an old shirt and replace them with a contrasting fabric for sleeves and trim. The bottom part of *T-shirts* may be cut off for a short shirt for hot weather.

Blue jeans can be recycled by cutting off the lower part of the legs and wearing them as shorts. Seams of the legs may be opened and some of the material from the legs that has been cut off can be inserted to make a skirt. The top of the pants may have handles or drawstrings added and become a bag. Cover worn spots with attractive patches (the side of a wornout boot makes an unusual patch), iron-ons, or appliqués. What ideas have you discovered?

283

Make a jean top from an old dress or blouse and trim with rickrack. Make a yoke to renew an old dress. Make a top to wear over sweater and jeans.

Fix up your bangle bracelets.

Discuss recycling with your friends and see how many ideas you can develop together. Have an idea bulletin board that gives ideas and solicits suggestions from others. Take some of the best ideas and use them in a column for your local newspaper. You can have fun and save money as well.

THINKING IT OVER

1. Have you or a friend of yours had the experience of recycling clothes and the idea attracted attention and others borrowed it? Try to reconstruct how the process of thinking it through took place. Was it accidental? Did it take a lot of thinking? What happened? Could you or your friend do the same thing now in terms of recycling something else?

2. As you read this area on clothing, you may have noted that in many places, it was assumed that the content pertained to either boys or girls. What is the situation in your school or community? Do you wear and sew similar clothes? If so, for which occasions? What does this mean to you?

THINGS TO DO

1. Plan now to compare wearing qualities of the clothes you make and the clothes you buy. What kind of record would you keep? What would you look for? Compare the costs.

2. Analyze your experiences of sewing. What was pleasant? What was unpleasant? What would you change?

3. Each student might like to keep a record such as the following:

PATTERN STUDY

Name of pupil _____ Name of pattern _____
Pattern number _____

1. How much material did the style require? _____ How much did you buy? _____
2. What is the name of your fabric? _____ How wide is it? _____
3. What view of the garment are you using? _____
4. How do your measurements correspond to those on the pattern?

	Pattern measurements	My measurements
Bust	_____	_____
Waistline	_____	_____
Hip	_____	_____
Skirt length	_____	_____
Waist length	_____	_____

5. What is the seam allowance? _____
6. Name pieces of pattern you use more than once. _____
_____

7. What markings on your pattern indicate the following?

   a. Cutting line _____

   b. Seamline _____

   c. Seam allowance _____

   d. Center front _____

   e. Center back _____

   f. Darts _____

   g. Place for pockets, buttons, etc. _____

   h. Matching collar seams _____

   i. Joining seams _____

   j. Fold line _____

   k. Lengthening or shortening the pattern _____

   l. Placing the fabric on the grain _____

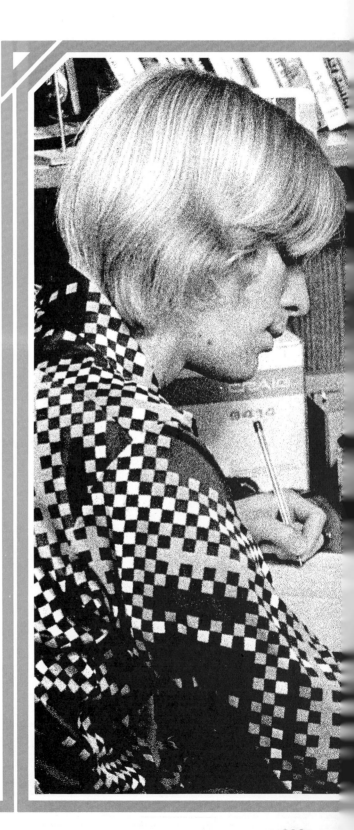

area seven

Being a Good Manager

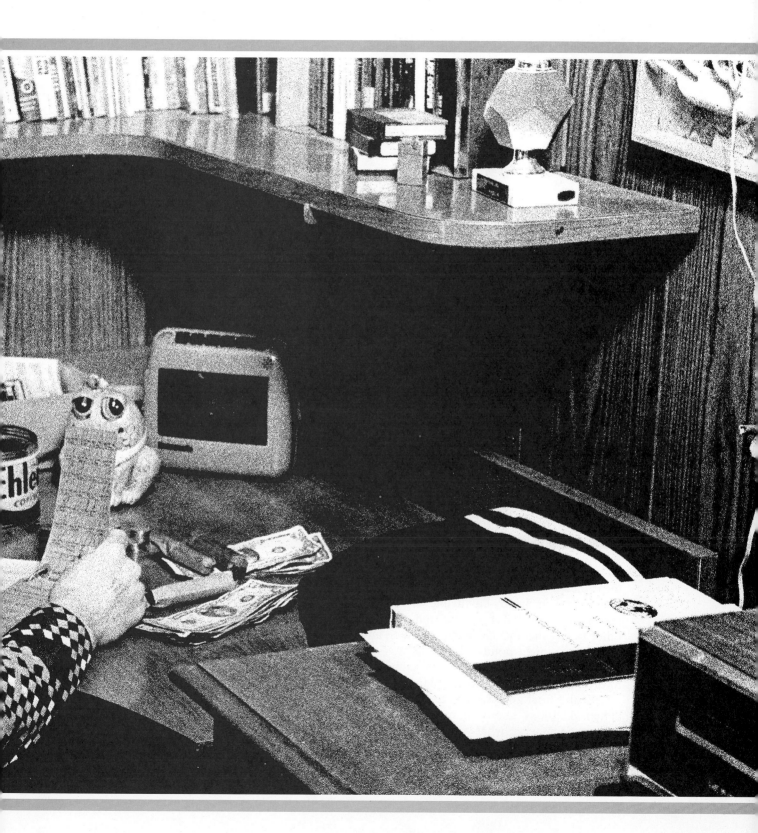

27 Managing what you have

The title of this chapter may seem like a joke. You may feel that only wealthy men and women are concerned about managing what they have. But you do have assets and when you think about them you may become quite excited about their possibilities.

Suppose you begin a list. Experts generally include time, money, health, and energy to be active; knowledge and experience in certain areas, abilities and values; possibly equipment and space to carry out some of your interests; some expertise in planning; and attitude. These are the assets in varying degrees that are used to help you to manage your daily living. Are there other resources that you feel are important?

The next consideration for becoming a good manager is to think about the best way to use these means in solving problems and making decisions in your day-by-day living. Of course, you receive a great deal of advice from parents and other family members, friends, advisers, and experts. They might point out various ways to act and the possible consequences of each act, and information or other forms of guidance.

In the final analysis you have to make the actual decisions about many things, such as what you will wear, what you will select for your lunch in the school cafeteria, or how you will make up with one of your best friends. Psychologists tell us that your decision usually reflects your knowledge, experience, and maturity. Maturity does not mean you have to be old to make wise decisions. Maturing refers to the process of developing the ability to make decisions. If you have opportunities to make decisions on your own and to learn about how to make them, you will probably be more mature than someone who has not had this experience.

In making any decision, it is wise to think about the effect of your decision on other people. If, for example, you insist on having money to buy something, will your mother or father have to give up something that they desire? Sometimes a decision has a bearing on something else. You may want to have a bicycle but may live in a city apartment and have the problem of finding a place to garage it. No doubt you can add other points to consider.

We might learn something from looking at the steps that experts in business and management use in making efficient decisions. Most of them recommend making a decision in steps. Here is one formula you might like to try and you might improve on it for your own use.

1– Make a statement of what you want to have happen and why, such as finding a job after school so you will have money to buy a record player.

2– Analyze the difference between your present situation and what it would be like if the change you desire took place. This helps you decide whether what you want is really desirable. Think about the effect on other people; for example, would some members of your family be concerned about the loud music?

3– Think about all the ways you can reach your goal of a job after school and test each idea in your mind. Some possibilities are these: Where do your friends work and could they tell you about possible openings? Do you have a special skill or service that you could sell? Are you a good "fixer," pet tender, errand runner, cake baker, or baby sitter? Brainstorm about other ideas.

4– Select what you consider your best idea and develop a plan of action. This is sometimes referred to as your operations. Here is an opportunity to survey your assets and use them to your advantage.

5– Think carefully about any possible roadblocks that might keep you from doing what you plan. Does any member of your family object to your working? Are all the good jobs too far away? Are jobs scarce? What other obstacles are there?

6– Re-examine your plan and see if you can improve it by making changes that might take care of the possible blocks to reaching your goal.

7– Act.

8– Analyze what you did and how you might have done it differently or better.

You may feel that all these steps are too much work. If the decision or problem you face is important, the use of this formula may prevent failures or other forms of disappointments. The

Take an inventory of your assets.

289

Will a decision you make inconvenience your mother?

Would a part-time job help you with your money problems?

more you use this formula, the easier it is for you to think in this way. And you may develop your own steps for action that are equally good.

Important decisions may relate to the kind of person you want to be, how you get along with your family, money problems, health, physical or mental handicaps, use of time, community responsibilities, or planning for the future. These are some of the major areas that may concern you but there are others that may be equally important to you.

Two of these decision-making categories, the use of money and the use of time, will be discussed. Some of the other areas are discussed elsewhere in this text.

MONEY

Before we begin to think about money, suppose you consider how you feel about money. Is it very important; important; important in relation to some things, such as buying sports equipment; a matter of indifference—that is, it is neither important nor unimportant; of little importance; or of no importance? Are your feelings pleasant or unpleasant? Analyzing these feelings

Does money seem to fly out of your purse?

may help you understand your reactions towards money.

Does money seem to slip through your fingers? Are you the type that can't stand being prosperous? Whenever you have a little extra money, do you immediately plan ways to spend it? Or maybe you are the kind of person who hoards money—you'd rather put money in your bank than spend it. Though ways of spending differ, most people would like to have more money than they already have.

SOURCES OF INCOME

Assuming that this is true, let's answer the question, "Where do we get our money?" Most of us can count on three sources: allowances, work for pay, and gifts of money.

Your Allowance

One of your main sources of income may be your allowance. This is the amount of money that your father, both your parents, or the whole family have decided you should have each week. It is your share of the family's money to spend. You may be allowed to spend it as you please or you may be required to cover certain items with it. In some families, an allowance must be used for carfare, school lunches, movies, comic books, and the like. To avoid problems, it is well to have a clear understanding with your family about any expenses that must be met from your allowance.

Size of Allowance. You may feel that your allowance is too small. But there are many points to consider in determining the size of an allowance. Certainly your allowance must be in line with your family's income. Your family will consider, no doubt, the ability you have shown to spend money wisely. Can you think of other points that should be mentioned? How could you discuss this matter with your family? Put yourself in their place and try to see their point of view.

Work for Pay

Many young people supplement their allowance by taking some kind of job. Why not make a list of the ways in which you might earn money. Here is a sample list. Check the ones you have done. What are other possibilities?

☐ 1-Baby-sitting
☐ 2-Running errands for the neighbors
☐ 3-Working a newspaper route
☐ 4-Selling things you make, like wood carvings
☐ 5-Making deliveries for a neighborhood store
☐ 6-Washing and waxing cars
☐ 7-Mowing lawns
☐ 8-Gardening
☐ 9-Taking care of someone's pets
☐ 10-Tending a neighbor's garden
☐ 11-Raking leaves
☐ 12-Others

There are many ways to earn money.

291

In some families, no one is paid for any jobs done around the home. In other families, special jobs are paid for, especially if the work benefits only one family member.

Gifts of Money

Another source of income is gifts of money from family friends or relatives. Sometimes they suggest how you should spend the money by saying, "Buy something you like," or "Use it for the movies or a ballgame." And often the money is just given to you.

Have you ever thought about why this money is given to you? Is it because of family friendship, a return for a kindness you did the giver, or for a special occasion, like your birthday? What are possible ways for you to express your appreciation besides a simple "thank you"? Do you make special plans for money received in this manner? It might be a good idea to use the money for something you have wanted very much but could not afford.

YOUR FAMILY AND MONEY

Since money seems so desirable, we may harbor some queer notions about the best way to get more of it. What is your honest opinion about such practices as asking your father for money

Every family member can contribute something to family money planning.

when your mother has refused you? Or the reverse process? Do you ever nag for money—keep asking and asking with the hope that you will eventually get it? Is bartering one of your schemes—promising to study hard or behave well if your parents will increase your allowance this week?

Analyze the kind of thinking that underlies these actions. In the first place, you are not a very pleasant person to have around when you indulge in begging, bargaining, and similar activities. It's hard for us to remember that money does not grow on trees. The money in most families comes from earnings. The sum you ask for may represent several hours or days of work by your father or mother. Your parents have to decide what is the best use for the money they earn. Your request may not be as important as other family needs. When you are given money you are actually sharing the rewards for work done by others. A good question to ask yourself is "Do I deserve this?" Another point to consider is that money given to you represents a choice on the part of the giver. He or she could have bought something for himself or herself instead of giving the money to you.

How Much Are You Worth to Your Family?

On the bright side of the problem of family finances is the opportunity you have to reduce family expenses. There are certain responsibilities you can assume that will actually save money. You might shine your father's shoes, wash the family car, bring the groceries home for your mother, or keep a vegetable garden to supply the family table. For the fun of it, you might figure out how much these services would cost if someone outside the home had to be paid to do them. But remember that such services are actually your contribution to your family's welfare.

Family Feeling About Money

It is also well for you to learn how your family feels about money. What do they consider good things to spend money on? A car, a home, good books, records, music lessons? Are they saving for your future education? If you think about this situation seriously, it will help you understand why some of your requests for money are refused.

Have you thought about what some of your family's important expenses are? Your parents may have financial responsibilities they have not

You cost your family a great deal of money.

discussed with you. And since they are eager to keep their children happy, you are being very selfish if you burden them with constant requests for money. Bear in mind that there are reasons that they cannot grant all your requests.

How Much You Cost the Family

The services your parents render you are really quite costly. Suppose you were to eat the majority of your meals in a restaurant rather than at home. How much would it cost? How much rent would you have to pay for a room like yours? Your parents don't want you to consider these items. That is the wonderful part of family life. Everyone shares and gives.

HOW YOU SPEND YOUR MONEY

With these points still in mind, look at the way you spend your money. Think of all the ways you spent money this past week. This list might include:

- at school, for milk or soup in addition to lunch from home
- Snacks—ice cream, candy bar, popcorn
- Movies
- Records
- School carnival or dance
- Sports equipment
- Hobby material, like stamps for collection
- Present for someone
- Some trinket, such as a special pin that everyone was wearing

What are other items that might be included? Do you have any serious leaks in your pocketbook?

Have you ever tried keeping a simple account book? It isn't difficult. Just cover a notebook with fancy paper or material. Paste letters on the cover which spell "My Accounts," "Where My Money Goes," or the like. You can think of

An analysis of your spending may be helpful.

Table 27-1

MY ACCOUNTS		
Week of:		**Total Income:**
SPENT ON	**AMOUNT**	**COMMENTS**
Books and magazines		
Hobby		
Presents		
Recreation		
School lunch		
School supplies		
Snacks		
Things to wear		
Others		
Summary		
Total Income	_____	
Total Spending	_____	
Total Savings	_____	
Or Deficit	_____	

your own title. Headings in the book might be like those in the table above. You may add other headings if necessary. Some of these headings may not be needed. You may eat your lunch at home or bring all your food from home, so that there will be no spending in that area. In other words, your account book should be personalized. It should tell *you* what *you* want to know. You might have a few headings or you may wish to have a more detailed account.

An example of a very simple accounting plan follows.

You might have a page for a week, a month, or whatever period of time seems best to you.

After you have kept track of your money for several weeks, analyze your spending. Where is your money going? Could you distribute your spending more wisely? Have you spent any money foolishly? If you could re-spend your money, would you do it in the same way?

Keeping accounts will help you to see where your money is going.

	MY SPENDING		
DATE	AMOUNT SPENT	ITEM	COMMENTS
Jan 9	$.50	Stationery	Mom's Birthday

SAVING YOUR MONEY

Your family may encourage you to be a good shopper and be thrifty as well. Most boys and girls have banks for saving pennies, nickels, dimes, and quarters. Do you have a bank? What do you do with the money you save? It can be fun to save for something you want, like a baseball bat or a record. To do so you will have to make a plan for keeping account of your money. You may already have a system for putting aside some money for such purposes. Some students get into the excellent habit of saving 10 percent of all of their income. One boy did it this way. If someone gave him a dime, he would put a penny in his bank. If he was fortunate enough to receive or earn a dollar, he would save a dime. Thus he not only saved for specific purposes but he always had some money on hand for emergencies.

Money for the Future

It is frequently difficult to look ahead and anticipate something you will need next month or at an even later date. Some kind of savings plan comes in handy on these occasions. You also have to check yourself from spending your money before reaching your goal. Sometimes, of course, your ideas change. You may have had your heart set on a volleyball. Later, a decision to buy baseball equipment may seem more sensible. Often it is wise to save a little during the year so that extra money will be available when you are going to camp or visiting friends or relatives away from home.

BORROWING MONEY

What do you think about borrowing money? Certainly a person who is always asking for money can become quite a pest. Here are some rules to guide you in deciding when and if it is wise to borrow:

1-Borrow only in emergencies, such as when you have lost your lunch money at school or your bus fare home.
2-Don't borrow from your family or friends unless you can repay the money promptly. Few persons have money to spare and you may be making it inconvenient or even a hardship for them by using their money.
3-Promise to repay within a specific time—as soon as possible—and be sure to keep your promise.

Borrowing money is a bad habit.

4-Don't get the habit of borrowing. Borrowing may lead to carelessness about staying within an allowance.
5-Realize that borrowing money is a serious obligation and a reflection on your character.

Intelligent people do not let themselves get into a situation where they need to borrow. If you plan carefully, there will be no normal need to ask someone else for money. When you borrow you are spending beyond your needs and are really spending next week's or next month's income. When an emergency arises and you must borrow, plan to repay your family or your friends with some additional kindness for the favor they have extended to you. But the best action of all is to avoid borrowing completely. You will spare yourself many troubles and you will have more friends.

PROBLEMS WITH MONEY

All of us have problems concerning money from time to time. Maybe you do not have an allowance and have to ask your parents for money for all your needs. Maybe you can talk to them about letting you have a definite amount every week. This will teach you how to handle money. You will learn to make decisions involving spending money. If you are a member of a large family, you may not have as much to spend as a friend who is an only child. You will have to make the most of the situation and be glad you have brothers and sisters for companionship rather than extra money.

Sometimes it may appear to you that all your friends have more money to spend than you have. If they actually have more and if it makes you unhappy, perhaps you need to find some friends with incomes near your own. Otherwise, make the best of the situation.

There may be times when you want something very much but can't afford it. How do you meet this problem? There may be a number of solutions. Is there a substitute—something that is less expensive but will serve the same purpose? Or could you earn some extra money to cover the extra cost? Spend a little time thinking about what you want. Is it as important as you seem to think it is? Would it give you as much happiness next week or next month? If all possible solutions fail, you will have to face your disappointment as best you can. What are some ways in which this might be done?

Occasionally you may feel that everyone in your group of friends has something you cannot afford. This might be something to wear, some form of recreation, or even something in the home. Reread the suggestions given in the last paragraph and apply them to this problem.

Losing Money

One of the most serious problems that might arise is losing money. It may not be pleasant to face, but losing money is usually the result of carelessness. It may be true that your pocket had a hole in it or your purse didn't catch properly when you closed it and money fell out. But even these possibilities could have been checked. Here are some pointers that may be helpful:

1-Have a purse or wallet that is large enough to hold your money.
2-Arrange your money so that you can find it quickly and will not confuse a quarter with a nickel. A coin purse and billfold combination is a good idea. Then you will not mix your silver and your bills.
3-Carry only the amount of money that will meet your needs for the day. It is unnecessary to carry all your money around with you.
4-Decide on a safe place to keep your money at home. Don't scatter your money. Keep it in one place. Count it at regular intervals so you know how much you have.

Check your wallet for holes and count your money to safeguard it.

5-Work out a plan for checking on the money you carry with you. Count your money when you leave in the morning and when you come home at night.
6-Don't be careless about leaving your purse. Keep it with you.
7-Don't count your money in the presence of others. It is very impolite.

Losing your money is very upsetting, but it is even more serious to lose money that belongs to someone else. You need to be especially careful when you are sent on an errand for someone in the family or for a neighbor and are given money to pay for the purchase. If you are treasurer of a club or other group, you will feel especially responsible for the members' money. It is a good idea to count the money carefully when you receive it and keep accurate records so that you are certain of the amount for which you are responsible.

If you do lose money that belongs to someone else, you may have to work out some plan for repaying it—perhaps over a period of time. Whatever plan you decide on, be sure to stick to it, and be certain that the idea is agreeable to the person whose money has been lost.

Another problem is the importance of meeting family crises, such as loss of a job, illness, an accident, adding the responsibility of taking care of one of your grandparents, or similar strains on the family budget. How have you met such a situation or how would you meet it? Higher prices is a money problem that faces all of us. What can be done?

Although a discussion of saving, spending, keeping money safe, and making plans for your money is important, some thought should be devoted to the purpose of money. We have money as a simple means of getting what we want. In pioneer days, people had to use barter. If they needed someone to fix their fence, they might pay their neighbor with grain or some other service. Today such a system would be terribly complicated. Can you imagine giving the bus driver three eggs for a ride to school? Yet you can see that it is not money itself but the goods or services bought with the money that are really important.

When pocketbooks are lean, barter can be used effectively among friends. For example, what could you offer in exchange, to a friend that could style your hair, tutor you in a difficult subject, teach you to knit, fix your bicycle, or give you some fresh ideas on playing your guitar or banjo? Not only may services be offered but you may also have things, such as paperbacks you have read, records, clothes, or other items.

How will a family crisis, such as a flood, affect your pocketbook?

Have you had experience in this type of enterprise? What suggestions do you have to offer?

To go one step farther, we must realize that money cannot buy everything. A rich person is not necessarily a happy person. Think of all the things in your life that money cannot buy but that are very precious to you. For example, you can't buy the love of your parents or your sisters and brothers. You can't buy friends. There is no price on certain types of fun you can have with your family. Think of the times when something has happened to make everyone laugh. What makes you really happy? Can these things be bought? In other words, everything does not have a dollars-and-cents value.

TIME

Are you an expert on saving time or do you have clock troubles? Has anything like this ever happened to you? You looked at television or talked on the telephone and failed to get your homework done. The next morning you tried to snatch a few minutes of the studying you had planned to do the night before. This made you late for breakfast. Then you didn't have very much time to pack your lunch and you forgot the banana you were going to have for dessert. Does it seem to you on days like this that you never catch up?

Advantages of Planning Time

But what is the advantage of being an expert on saving time? Do you have to be a slave to the clock? Is life any fun that way? Let's look at the other side of the picture and see some of the advantages of a schedule. Suppose everybody decided to eat dinner at a different time? Sometimes variations are necessary, but isn't it much more agreeable when you can look forward to having your evening meal at approximately the same time each night? Suppose trains, planes, and buses didn't run on a schedule? If a storekeeper opened up any time between 8 A.M. and noon, you would be quite disturbed if you wanted to buy something at 8:45 and the store wasn't open, wouldn't you?

What Do You Do with Your Time?

Everybody has 24 hours each day—no more, no less. Have you ever thought about what happens to *your* time? Take a look at your day. Where do your activities take place? What do you do at home? What do you do at school?

Do You Have Clock Troubles?

What do you do in your neighborhood or community? Do part-time jobs, such as baby-sitting, running errands, or delivering papers, demand some of your time? What are other ways in which you spend your time? Does the season of the year make a difference?

Time for "Doing Good"

Sometimes you have "do-good" jobs as part of your club or religious work. These may include visiting shut-ins, telling stories or reading to children in a local orphanage or hospital, or helping in a community litter or recycling campaign.

Time for Improving Ourselves

Developing yourself personally takes time. You may have an interest in music. If you play an instrument, you will devote considerable time to practicing. Listening to good music develops your appreciation of it. Reading is important in broadening your knowledge of people and the world, and is a pleasant way to relax as well. Time may also be set aside for browsing through the library and borrowing books. Some of us may spend extra time for art or dancing classes. Knowing about sports and being able to take part in games will help you be a more interesting person. Learning to speak or write another language might be another good use of your time. You might be able to start a warm friendship with a pen pal in another country. How much time do you set aside for personal improvement?

Activity Time

Here is a list of activities you may engage in every day. Think of the time you spend on each one. On which activities are you spending most of your time? Which ones demand the least of your time?

- Dressing and undressing
- Eating
- Sleeping
- Helping at home
- School homework
- Care of clothes
- Telephoning
- Sports
- Parties
- Movies
- Religious services
- Clubs
- Music
- Radio listening
- Television viewing
- Reading
- Friends
- Hobby
- Pets
- Work for pay
- Others

What are your conclusions after examining your list of daily activities?

Analyze How Time Is Spent

Do you feel that your time is well-balanced? Are you spending too much time in any one area—more than is necessary, perhaps? Is there sufficient time for health activities, like eating, sleeping, and exercise? How much time do you spend with your family? Do you allow enough time for your school work at home? Are you devoting some time every day to improving yourself? Would you make any changes in the use of your time? If so, what?

Planning a Schedule

If you are interested in using your time to better advantage, you might like to plan daily or weekly schedules. First, look at the list of your daily activities that you made. Are there weekly jobs or other items that should be added? In the beginning it is wise to make a rather detailed schedule for each day.

How Well Can You Estimate Your Time?

As you go along during the day, check yourself often to see how well you have estimated your time. Did some activities take more time than you had allowed? Did you do some things faster than you had expected? Did you have to make some unexpected changes?

Timesavers

Another suggestion is to think of all of the tricks to save time. Is there something that you could learn to do more quickly? Are you washing your clothes, for example, in the fastest way? How long does it take you to dress? Could you run a race with yourself and see if you could improve on that time a little each day?

Start the Day Right. The way you start the day is important. Do you have trouble getting up? Are you the type that likes to stay under the covers for another ten minutes? If you think about something very pleasant, it will encourage you to get up. After all, you have to get up, and postponement only brings problems, making it necessary for you to rush.

Do you plan the night before what you will wear the following day? Having your clothes ready will save many minutes in the morning. You will be able to dress much more quickly.

A Place for Everything. Sometimes we lose time because we can't find things. Do you have your closets, desk, and chest drawer arranged so that you can locate everything quickly? Have you ever found yourself looking for a pen or pencil to do your homework? Or maybe you couldn't find those blue socks you wanted to wear? Arranging your tools so that you can find them may save many minutes.

Find the Best Way. Maybe the way you are doing something is not the most efficient way. If you are peeling potatoes, for example, maybe your knife is too large or dull. Think of the things you do every day. Pretend you are a management expert. Are there some steps in a job you could skip or do more easily? For example, you probably can save yourself several trips by using a tray to carry dishes and silver for setting the table.

Best Time to Do Things. Another important point to consider is the best time for each activity. When is the best time in the evening for you to do your homework? Or maybe you prefer to get up early in the morning to study. When do you wash your clothes? Is it at a time when you will not interfere with some of your mother's work? Is it better to do it once or several times a week?

Plan Ahead. Are there ways of doing things to save you work later on? For instance, if you keep your room neat, you won't have all that clutter to pick up at once. On some jobs, if you do a little work each day rather than all at once, it won't seem like such a mountain. Writing a term paper is an example of this. You might do your reading and other research, outline it, make a rough draft, and then rewrite it. Each step could be done on a different day—provided you have sufficient time to do an assignment that way. Start as soon as you can. Don't put it off.

Influence of Attitudes

Your attitude toward a job makes a difference in the amount of time it takes. Time flies quickly when we enjoy what we are doing and drags when we dislike it. Doesn't it seem like a good idea to do the jobs that are not so enjoyable as quickly as possible in order to have more time for the things we like to do? No doubt there will always be some kinds of work we like to do better than others.

It might help if you looked at the reasons for liking or disliking a job. Is it because the job has to be done so often that it is monotonous? Is it satisfying? Maybe you don't feel your work is appreciated. Sometimes thinking about the benefits that you or other people will receive as a result of your work is helpful. It may be possible to change your attitude about some of your jobs so that you will learn to like them. Being happy at work makes life much more interesting.

Viewpoints About Time Differ. You must also realize that people have their own ideas about the good use of their time. Sometimes we think people lazy because they are not active. Such people may actually be very busy planning something important . . . or they may not be feeling well.

How Important Is Time to You? You will use time more wisely if you first realize how important time is to you. You can find time for the things you really want to do if you try. Moreover, remember that when you waste time you frequently increase the responsibilities of other family members or of your friends. Time must be considered in relation to the plans of others, as well as to your own.

THINKING IT OVER

1. Bill earned money by running errands for the neighbors. Because he was so busy, his mother had to do the errands for the family. What do you think about this situation?

2. Some of the richest men and women in the world believe they learned how to handle money when they worked in after-school jobs. What could you learn or have you learned from such jobs about handling money?

3. Think about the ways various members of your family use their time. How may your use of time help or hinder them from doing their work well?

4. Have you considered the possibilities of planning while you are doing something else? While you are combing your hair, for instance, you might be thinking about what you will do on Saturday or the best way to write that term paper. Could you give other examples?

THINGS TO DO

1. Make a list of the kinds of jobs you can do in your community. What are the various rates of pay? How can you find out about jobs? You might like to consider them according to seasons of the year.

2. Talk to your grandfather about ways in which he earned money at your age.

3. Experiment with jobs at home that might be done to music, such as washing dishes. Be prepared to report your results to the entire class.

28 Managing your fun money

Fun has many meanings depending upon who you are, where you are, and how much money you have, although the last item may be debatable. Sometimes fun may mean freedom from work, relaxation, rest, a happy time, pleasant companionship, or doing something you enjoy. What does it mean to you?

In addition to these generally accepted ideas about fun, there are other benefits that may come to you from leisure-time activities. A hobby, for example, may turn out to be preparation for the work you will do in the future. Some of your best friendships may be developed on a camping trip. Members of your family may be appreciated more after a vacation together. You may earn additional education by the skills you have learned, for instance in photography or dramatics, or even playing the drums! Some of your fun activities may give you pleasure for the rest of your life.

GENERAL POINTS TO CONSIDER IN YOUR BUYING

In these days of energy shortages, money pinch, and high prices, you may wish to give careful consideration to the way you spend your money. For some types of fun, you may have to save for quite some time. You will have to make decisions about the fun activities that give you the most pleasure. Why go to a movie that you won't enjoy and waste your money?

First, review the steps in making a decision that were discussed in Chapter 27. You may wish to buy a book on a certain sport in which you are very much interested. You may reach the conclusion that you cannot afford to buy it. What are the alternatives? If you have a community library, you may find it there. If it is a sport in which a number of your friends are interested, you might pool your money and buy it together and pass it around. Watch for book sales. Sometimes there are drastic reductions and you might be able to buy it at a greatly lowered price. Perhaps a neighbor has a copy and will be willing to lend it to you. You should take good care of it and perhaps do a favor for your neighbor in return. What are other possibilities to meet this or a similar desire?

If you are going to buy an item that is rather costly or that represents past savings and will not leave much money for anything else, you will want to do plenty of homework before you actually shop. This may include looking at catalogues, talking to friends who have previously made purchases, reading magazine articles and books on the subject, looking at the item in different kinds of stores and talking to the sales clerk to secure information, and testing your information on your family and friends so that they can raise questions that you may not have considered. Finally, you may narrow down your facts about several different brands or types of merchandise, listing the strengths and weaknesses of each. All of this has to be matched to the criteria you have set up for the article.

There are many other questions to answer. Can you begin with a less expensive type, such as in a camera, and then develop skills required for a more complicated and expensive model, later? This is also good insurance, because your enthusiasm for photography, for example, may decrease considerably after several months. Will a secondhand model of the article you plan to buy be satisfactory? Can you rent or lease the article more cheaply? If it requires repairs, where can you take it? In the case of a bicycle, will a de-

Many benefits may come from leisure-time activities.

partment store offer repair services or is it better to buy a bicycle in a bicycle store that also does repairs? What are the guarantees? Have you compared paying cash with buying on the installment plan? What do mail-order houses have to offer and what assurance do you have about the quality of the product? Can you return your merchandise if it is unsatisfactory? Are the instructions supplied adequate? What kinds of stores seem to be the best places in which to buy? When you have made a tentative selection you may want a family member, a good friend, or someone else whose judgment you respect to give an opinion on your choice. Answering all these questions will assist you in making a better decision. Do you have other points that you believe should be explored before making a purchase?

Bicycles & Bicycling

Your first concern may be the purchase of a bicycle that will provide you with fun and may also be considered a necessity, in some instances.

There are three basic models of bicycles. The *middleweight* model has a sturdy frame, heavy wheels, balloon tires, and coaster brakes. It is slower and requires heavier pedaling than other styles, but is comfortable for boys and girls because of its low riding position. This model is recommended for beginning riders.

The *lightweight* model has narrow, high-pressure tires and usually comes with hand brakes and from 3 to 15 gears. These different gear speeds allow for adjustment to riding and road conditions. American and European models are available. A popular model is the low-cost 10-speed bicycle that is quite satisfactory for all riding conditions. This bicycle is designed for speed rather than a soft ride.

The *high-rise* model has high handle bars, an elongated saddle, and rear saddle support behind the seat. For purposes of safety, these bars should not be less than five inches above the seat. The bicycle may have hand brakes and multispeed gears or coaster brakes and no gears. This bicycle handles very easily, but is less stable. This type is recommended only for the experienced rider, because it requires more skill in handling.

A bicycle should be maneuverable and stable. Unfortunately these factors operate against each other. A large wheel base, for example, will increase the stability of your bicycle and is recommended for straight riding and beginners, but is more difficult to handle when turning corners and avoiding traffic.

Select the correct size for you. Here is the way you decide. Sit on the bike and grasp the handlebars as though you were actually riding. Adjust the pedal down to its lowest point with the ball of the foot touching the pedal, and lean forward slightly. The bicycle is the right size if there is a slight bend in your knee.

In addition, check for safety attachments required by traffic regulation agencies. Read the laws of your community and state. Usually, adequate well-functioning brakes, a bell or horn that can be heard at least 100 feet away, a front lamp with a white light visible 500 feet away for a designated sunset-to-sunrise period, and a red reflector, 3 inches in diameter, in the rear for use during the same period, are required. The wearing of light or white clothes at night is suggested. Generally bicyclists are required to obey all traffic regulations that pertain to automobile drivers.

There is a wealth of knowledge available and much is required to select and operate a bicycle sensibly, so try to be well-informed. If your funds are limited, you may wish to consider buying a second-hand bicycle. Giving your bike good care will make it handle easier and last longer. There are many possibilities for fun with a bicycle. Why not share ideas with your friends and classmates?

Some of the many ways in which you can spend your fun money are discussed with suggestions to help you to secure the best buy.

ENTERTAINMENT

Plays, puppet shows, pantomimes, musicals, operettas, movies, special concerts of a rock band or a country, rock, or pop singer or singers, opera, ballet, documentaries, television programs, lectures, exhibitions, fairs, square dancing, and many other activities and events might be considered in this category. Attendance at any one will depend on your interest and your pocketbook. For some of these occasions you might be attending with your family. At others, you would probably go with friends. Your companions might be as important as seeing the show.

Ice skating is fun and cheap.

You can find out about the quality of the entertainment by reading about it in the newspaper, reading reviews, looking at handbills or posters that may be distributed, but most important, talking to persons whose judgment you trust and who have somewhat the same tastes as you do. If your budget permits it, attend a show of a type that you have never heard or seen, such as a symphony concert, if you like that kind of music. Not only can these functions give you enjoyment and sometimes new ideas, but they also provide you with topics of conversation.

VACATIONS

With fuel shortages curtailing the use of the family car and with rising costs of travel, your family and you may decide to change your vacation patterns to something less expensive. You might try a train or a bus trip to a pleasant spot not too far from home.

Plan carefully ahead of time. Secure as much information as you can about vacation possibilities and discuss them with your family. Write for information and talk to friends and relatives who may have visited some of the spots that interest you. Make reservations for travel and places to stay well in advance. Choose among hotels, campsites, or motels. Some motels are quite inexpensive because they offer only essential services. Help your family find money-saving and fuel-saving ideas.

Here are a few suggestions. Visiting a national park can be interesting and pleasant. Some states, such as West Virginia, Ohio, Kentucky, Tennessee, Georgia, and South Carolina, have family resorts in state parks. New Hampshire, Vermont, and California have state park camp grounds. You may live near or in one of these states and can take advantage of these opportunities. Public parks can often be found off dirt or gravel roads. Cruises on river boats on the Mississippi and Ohio rivers or on steamers on the Great Lakes are often inexpensive. Some colleges offer summer programs for families and make available their dormitories and dining halls for reasonable cost vacations. Classes in crafts, lectures, a swimming pool, hiking trails, tennis courts, and other attractions give this kind of vacation considerable appeal.

Visiting a strange city may provide a good family vacation.

Avoid covering too much territory on a vacation.

If you live in the city, a vacation on a farm may attract you. Sometimes there are separate facilities for guests, but often they eat and live in the farm home with the family. Some families swap homes for vacations—for example, a family in Oklahoma might exchange homes with a family in Connecticut. Details have to be worked out

Craft classes are inexpensive, fun, and available in most cities.

carefully, but families who have experienced it have felt that the vacation was delightful and less costly. Household chores continue, but most families do not seem to mind. If funds are very limited, a vacation might be planned at home with each day bringing a different experience such as a picnic, a bicycling trip, a visit to a museum, a nature walk, or a baseball game.

You may decide to visit a city. Most metropolitan areas have information centers about the chief attractions as well as where to stay and to eat. Study the map of the city so that everyone in the family knows it well. Familiarize yourself with the modes of transportation. Using city buses is a good way to go sightseeing. Taxis can be very expensive. Before entering a restaurant, read the menu posted on the door or in a window for prices. Be wary of anyone who solicits you on the street to buy jewelry, Oriental rugs, or other items. Be sensible about what you buy and what you spend for presents to take to friends and relatives at home. Plan ahead how much you will spend and for whom you will buy gifts. Know where you can locate a doctor or anyone or anything else for which there may be an emergency.

Here is some general advice. Avoid covering too much territory on a vacation. Less money is spent and the trip is more enjoyable on the whole if less ground is covered. Travel off-season and to less well known spots to save money. Do not plan to take your vacation at times when holidays occur. If you have a packaged tour, be very certain about what is included, such as number of meals, transportation, tips, supplement for top of the season, taxes, services, and other items. Do some thinking about all the benefits that a vacation can bring to each member of your family. Make it special, not routine.

OUTDOOR ACTIVITIES

Taking part in outdoor fun can be like having a mini-vacation. Skiing, camping, hiking, kite flying, boating, sledding, roller or ice skating outdoors, sunning, or jogging are some examples of outdoor activities you can participate in. The cost can vary from using a castoff garbage can lid for slipping and sliding on ice and snow to an expensive family camper. Because of the safety element in many of these pursuits, it is well to check on workmanship, durability, steering mechanism where indicated, and on other aspects of necessary equipment. Other questions

A camping trip might be a good vacation plan for your family.

to consider are the opportunities in your community for participation in these activities, knowledge about the use and care of the equipment, and important safety factors.

Sports

Sports not only provide fun but also promote health and offer companionship. If you can play tennis or volley ball, for example, it may

Swimming is not only fun but it promotes health.

help you become part of a group you admire. Many sports are played around the world so you can play with someone in almost any country and communicate with that person. Some of the sports you may select are softball, baseball, tennis, Ping-Pong, volleyball, football, hockey, fishing, swimming, track, and others. All of these require space and equipment. Survey your community to see what is provided. Often public facilities can make participation in these sports rather inexpensive. Some of them offer lessons free or at a nominal cost. Many of these sports are provided for you in school. You may wish to experiment with the sport or sports to determine those that you enjoy and in which you find you can do well. How much they cost is another determining factor. Often what you learn to do at this age will give pleasure in later years.

MUSIC

Having your own guitar may be your most important musical interest at the moment. But have you considered the cost of the instrument and the lessons required to learn to play it? Because so many young people are interested in a guitar or an instrument of this type, the advertisements are very tempting and must be examined carefully. Door-to-door salesmen have attractive offers on the installment plan, but are often unreliable. Get all the information you can from reliable sources and do comparative shopping with someone who is an expert.

Your interest may be in equipment that will bring you the music of others, such as tapes, cassettes, cartridges, radio, television, or a hi-fi system. There are a number of possibilities. If you want music while reading or for dancing, a portable phonograph may be suitable. Realize that the lighter or more portable the machine is, the poorer the quality of music. Shop around for your best buy and be certain you know what you want.

A tape recorder has a number of uses. You can play cassettes of the kind of music you like. The quality is not as good as that of records. You may record the music of a television special of your favorite rock, pop, jazz, blue grass, or blues singer or programs of classical music. Be certain that you recorder is a battery/AC type. Batteries are good when you are not near an outlet, but they are heavy and expensive and have a comparatively short life. A tape recorder is good for sending messages to friends far away or letting

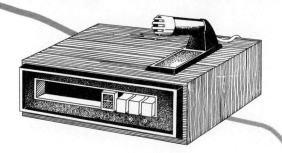

Is buying a guitar worth the money?

the music is reproduced better. If you wish stereo fidelity you may have to save and buy a component at a time because each one (FM tuner, amplifier, record changer, turntable and speakers) is very expensive, but this may be where you wish to place your money.

There are many "lures" for the buying of records, such as record clubs in which you are required to buy a specific number, and other combination mail-order offers. You may be saddled with a number of records that do not appeal to you in these package deals. You should find out to what extent your choices are limited. Look at the form you have to fill out to see what you are actually getting. Do you have to pay for handling, packaging, or mailing in addition to the price? If so, your bargain may not be a bargain any longer.

You may yearn for a colored portable television set so that you can look at the programs you enjoy and not have to share a set with other family members with different tastes, particularly in music. The size of portables is measured by the length of the diagonal across the picture tube. The most popular seems to be the 12-

them hear your latest original song or poetry. Before buying one listen to a cassette on it for quality.

Tape recorders with cassettes are cheaper than reel tape recorders but the latter are more satisfactory because the tone quality is better and reels are cheaper than cassettes.

A radio with a phono input in which a phonograph or a tape recorder may be plugged is another possibility. FM radio is best because

What thought do you give to the buying of records?

inch model. Color sets are becoming less expensive but continue to cost much more than black-and-white sets. The automatic sight and sound controls in the latest sets eliminate the warm-up stage. Test the various sets on these controls.

Smaller sets that measure between 7 and 11 inches are very portable and can be operated on batteries as well as electric current. Battery current lasts only about 4 hours but can be recharged. Many of these small sets have a screen for outdoor viewing. Check to see if this screen is a snap-on variety so the set may be used both indoors and outdoors. Solid state components instead of tubes produce a set that does not heat up easily and takes much less electricity. Secure information about the type of antenna needed for good reception. Determine what your set's warranty or guarantee covers. For how long? Are parts replaceable and is the labor cost included? Before closing the sale, practice operating the set, check the picture quality and the sound for clearness and tone, and check delivery service.

HOBBIES

The possibilities for fun in this area are almost limitless. Some choices are collections of stamps, coins, antiques, comic books, and other items; photography; basketry; candle making; ceramics and enameling; furniture making and other woodwork; jewelry and metalwork; needlework; rug making; gourmet cooking; toy making and folkcraft; weaving and macrame; and model airplanes.

For a beginner, it is well to start slowly, because your interest may dim after you have spent your savings on an expensive kit or equipment. You have an opportunity to experience many of these hobbies through school activities. Let this help you to decide your direction. Some hobbies may be too expensive, so select a hobby that suits your pocketbook and consider other alternatives, such as sharing equipment with a friend. Make an analysis of your skills. If you are all thumbs, start with a hobby that does not require precision and work till you develop skills that will enable you to tackle more difficult projects. Do you have adequate space to carry on your activities? What is the reaction of your family? Is adequate assistance available to supply the information you will need? There are many benefits involved in pursuing hobbies. You will

What Are You Interested In?

become acquainted with others who are interested in the same hobby and share ideas. Sometimes there are clubs for persons interested in a particular hobby.

FUN WITH CULTURE

Do you include culture in your fun money budget? Classical literature, music, and art may head the list. Some of this you may enjoy at home with other family members through books of fiction, biography, and poetry written by renowned writers or art books that have reproductions of the works of famous artists. You may listen to recordings of classical music or get it on FM radio or on your public television station. Occasionally you may manage to go to an actual opera, an historical play, or a famous ballet.

Survey the possibilities for museums in your area. Their collections and exhibits can be most enlightening and enjoyable. Museums offer other possibilities such as an opportunity to buy excellent reproductions of famous paintings for framing and hanging in your home. Some museums sell authorized copies of ancient and modern sculpture in durable materials, that duplicate the dimensions and textures of the originals. Reproductions of ancient jewelry and wood carvings are other examples of interesting and comparatively inexpensive items that may be bought in museums. A family membership in a museum may offer you a magazine and other literature, as well as special privileges.

Paperback books are an inexpensive way to build a good library.

Secondhand stores are good places to find used books on art and literature. Paperback books have reproduced many of the great books of the world and are usually very inexpensive. You may wish to make an interesting cover for the book to make it more durable and so it will look attractive on your book shelves.

Why not make an inventory of how you are actually spending your fun money? Is it lopsided—that is, is most of your spending for sports? Could you make it more balanced and reach out for something you have never considered previously?

THINKING IT OVER

1. Look at the main categories in this chapter. With each category, ask yourself what if anything you are doing in this area, what you would like to do, and what you can do.

2. Think about ways that you could bring fun to others—for example, to orphan children, the elderly in a nursing home, veterans in a hospital, or someone who is lonely.

THINGS TO DO

1. Do some brainstorming alone or with others about unusual ways to have fun. Why not try a few?

2. Survey your community for fun possibilities. Make a leaflet or a poster sharing your information with others, do a radio show, or write a short article for your local newspaper.

3. Analyze fun opportunities that are free or cost little. Think of ways to share this information.

29 Managing at home

Imagine that you are a home executive assigned to help your family efficiently tackle the many jobs that must be done again and again, many every day. Sit down at a desk and do some brainstorming about efficiency.

Most families are very busy. This means that everyone on the family team has to do his or her share around the house. What you do might depend on several things. You may be assigned a job because you can do it better than anyone else in the family. Members of the family differ in what they can do and what they like to do. Your sister might like to do the dishes, your brother to run the vacuum cleaner, and you might prefer making beds.

It is a good idea to learn how to do many jobs. Maybe you will change your mind about some of the things you thought you didn't like to do. Some jobs may be given to you because you are the only one home when they need to be done—for example, starting supper because the rest of your family gets home later.

JOBS TO BE DONE AT HOME

Let's take a look at the homemaking responsibilities that have to be undertaken. Cooking and serving the family meals is a big order. Although your mother may be the foreman, she needs helpers. Cleaning the house—dusting, vacuuming, washing windows—is another important job. Laundering requires attention, even if some clothes are sent to a laundry. Care of porches and yard must be considered, unless you live in a city apartment. Shopping for groceries and household supplies will have to be done by your mother and other members of the family. Can you think of other home responsibilities?

Cooperation on Home Jobs

Sometimes a job can be made a team operation. A younger or older sister or brother may work with you. You might divide the cleaning chores on a room basis, each of you taking charge of certain rooms. One family tried streamlining the work. One person made all the beds. Another did the vacuuming in all the rooms. The waxing was assigned to someone else. Cleaning the kitchen and the bathroom was considered one job. This kind of operation requires the closest cooperation. Some families might not like it. It is wise for the family to discuss who does what.

In keeping house, some jobs have to be done every day, like preparing meals, some several times a week, like shopping, some once a week, like mending, and others less often. A family schedule for the time of each job will make for a more efficient household.

When the family is planning its work, you might offer to take certain responsibilities. What kind of work do you know how to do now? Which jobs could you learn to do? What would you like to do?

One suggestion for your planning is a consideration of the following:

★ Know your goals.
★ Make decisions.
★ Face your attitudes toward work and home responsibilities.
★ Analyze the necessary steps.
★ Collect needed resources, such as the proper tools and ways to save time and energy.

Know Your Goals. When you look at everything that has to be done and think about who can do the work, some order of importance must be attached to the jobs. Then you will know which job needs attention first, which jobs require the most attention and which the least attention, you can then rate the skill required of each job. You may present your ideas to your family and an overall plan may emerge, including what your work will be.

Make Decisions. When you have your assignment, you will have some decisions to make. When will you do your work and how will you do it are important. This experience will help you in other planning because making decisions has to be learned. You cannot be very efficient if you have trouble making up your mind. Take the time you feel is necessary but when you have enough information, make the decision and do not put it off until a later time.

Be a home executive with your own think-tank.

Face Your Attitudes Toward Work. Doing a job as willingly and as cheerfully as possible will be more satisfying and pleasant. If you keep thinking about the monotony and uninteresting aspects of a job, you are more likely to find irritations and frustrations, so why punish yourself? There will always be work in life that you like to do and some that you dislike. So doesn't it seem sensible to do your work in the best spirit possible?

Give jobs a priority rating.

Family members can work together and make these jobs more pleasant.

Analyze the Necessary Steps. Make a study of the steps and motions necessary for your jobs, like a real expert. If you learn to do jobs easily and quickly, you will establish habits that will be helpful to you all your life. You do not inherit efficiency, you learn it.

Time and motion studies have been done in research in industry and in some homes. Each step in a job is actually timed. Photographs or motion pictures are taken of the worker while on the job. Experts can then decide if a change of position, a different use of a hand, or another body position will make the job easier and safer to complete. This may sound technical, but think of the motions and minutes that might be saved over a period of time. Fatigue is generally lessened and backaches and other discomforts may be reduced. The minutes you save can be spent in doing something you like.

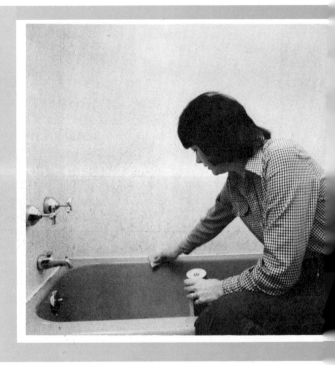

Can you save time and energy cleaning a bathtub?

Ask yourself a number of questions in regard to a specific job. What preventive measures can be taken to cut down the work? For example, if everyone takes off coats, boots, and outer wearing apparel as soon as he or she enters the house, less dust and dirt will be tracked around. Do you do only the work that is necessary or are you like a whirligig when only a few motions—for example, in making a fruit salad—are important? Are the steps you take in doing a job the best way or would a different order be more efficient? In making a bed, for example, fixing all the covers on one side of the bed and

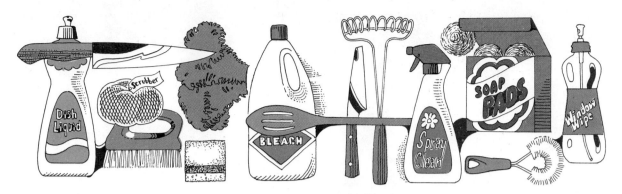

then moving to the other side and fixing covers there has proved more effective for some persons. Do you use only the muscles that are necessary? Using and tiring extra muscles is questionnable.

Collect Needed Resources. Are you familiar with the best tool for the job? For chopping, mincing, or cutting vegetables into strips, for instance, a large knife, specifically a chef's knife, is best. All knives should be sharp and have handles that are easy to hold. Take a look at each job and decide on the equipment before you begin to work. What do you need for cleaning a bathroom? For dusting? For cooking? Can you think of multiple uses for the same tool, such as a paring knife? Some homes are cluttered with equipment that is seldom used.

Which methods are most suitable? For cleaning a kitchen sink, which cleansing agents are best and do you use a cloth, a sponge, a plastic scrubber or something else for the process? These are the kinds of questions you will have to answer. It may be necessary for you to experiment to determine what is best in your situation.

Sometimes you are at a complete loss as to how to do a job and your mother is not at home to ask. You might keep a file of government pamphlets handy for this purpose. Your local extension office may have copies. Soap and detergent companies often offer free booklets on cleaning in their advertisements in a magazine or newspaper and sometimes on television. You may make your own booklet by combining the methods that seem best to you. Talk with neighbors and friends about how they do certain jobs.

In addition to using the best method and equipment, other devices may make work more pleasant. Listening to the radio is one idea. Music that has a strong beat may help you develop a good rhythm while working, so you will be less

Sing, whistle, listen to the radio, play a record, or anything that will get you into a good rhythm for your job.

fatigued. Plan for periodic rest periods. Set an alarm clock or a timer and take a five-minute rest every hour or set your own schedule that suits you.

You can further improve your planning and decision-making in buying food, cooking and preparing meals, and other areas of home responsibility that are discussed elsewhere in this book. Cleaning at home will be discussed here.

CLEANING AT HOME

All families have as one of their goals a clean home. This is important not only for the enjoyment of the family but for health reasons as well. You know how good it makes you feel after you have helped clean your home and everything is shiny. Psychologists tell us that our surroundings make a big difference in how we feel about our home, our family, and ourselves.

It is a pleasure to walk into a clean living room.

Silverware must be polished periodically.

As a home executive you will need to analyze the best ways for reaching the goal of a clean home. Here are some suggestions. What are the types and sources of soil and dirt? What are the best ways of removing soil? What preventive measures can be taken? How can your home be kept clean and orderly with the least effort every day?

Types of Soil

Why not start with a list of all the kinds of dirt you might find in your home? What about soot from your heating plant or from factories in your area? What about the exhaust from cars and trucks? The sidewalks near your home collect various kinds of litter which may be brought into the house. In dry weather you may have sand and dust. In wet weather you have mud. When you have open windows, dirt may blow in.

Indoors there are deposits of grease and smoke from cooking and eating. With casual eating in many places in your home this multiplies the possibilities of grease deposits and crumbs from food.

Lint from rugs, from the clothes you wear, and from household linens, such as sheets, towels, upholstery, and the like is another source of soil. Your skin is oily and that accounts for the finger marks on mirrors, door jambs, furniture, and other places. Bathroom and sink fixtures may become dull and require polishing. Table silverware will require polishing periodically.

Removal of Soil

What are the best ways to remove these types of soil? Loose, dry soil is best removed with a vacuum cleaner attachment, a moist cloth, or a cloth with furniture polish. If a dry cloth or duster is used, the dust is only moved and not picked up. If the soil is greasy, some kind of solvent is required. Soap and water, detergent and water, or special household cleaners will dissolve grease. What you use will depend on what you are cleaning, such as woodwork, or the upholstery of a sofa.

Some kinds of dirt, such as paper, grass, or dried leaves, may have to be swept up if they are too large to be picked up with the vacuum cleaner or picked up by hand. If something is spilled, it should be wiped up immediately and removed with the cleaning agent best suited for this purpose. Appropriate polishes and cleaners

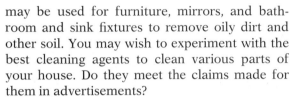

may be used for furniture, mirrors, and bathroom and sink fixtures to remove oily dirt and other soil. You may wish to experiment with the best cleaning agents to clean various parts of your house. Do they meet the claims made for them in advertisements?

Equipment and Materials. We live in a modern age and so must have equipment that will assist us in meeting modern needs. Basic equipment might include a vacuum cleaner with attachments; a carpet sweeper or something similar to use between vacuumings; a dry mop with an oily or dust-lifting substance on it for dusting plain floors and for other purposes; a broom; a dustpan; a wax applicator, if your home has waxed floors; a wax polisher, unless you use a self-polishing wax; a self-wringing mop made of cellulose, sponge, sponge rubber, cellulose yarn, or cotton string; and a bucket for mopping and cleaning walls and woodwork.

Brushes of various types are handy such as toilet bowl brush or mop. A kitchen stepladder and stool combination is good for sitting to do some food preparation jobs in the kitchen and for reaching into tall cupboards and closet shelves.

Not only must you have adequate tools but they must be kept in good condition. Read the instructions that come with each piece of equipment carefully. Do not assume that all models or brands operate in the same way. Manufacturers test their equipment and work out the best instructions possible. File this booklet because the information is invaluable. Soon your younger brother or sister may be in line for vacuuming responsibilities and the instruction booklet will be helpful to them. A machine must be operated correctly so that it will last longer and clean better. Also, file the name and address of the shop or store where repairs can be made and where parts may be purchased for replacement. Keep your equipment clean for better operation.

Read the instruction booklet that comes with equipment for efficient operation.

Storage of Cleaning Equipment.

If possible, there should be a separate closet for equipment and cleaning materials or at least a specific part of a closet. Digging into a closet and pulling out a vacuum cleaner that is behind coats and other clothes can be discouraging. With cleaning materials, it is easier to place them where you can see them and thus check on supplies that are needed. It is also convenient to have everything handy. Hooks and brackets for hanging the broom, mop bucket, and the like are helpful. A pegboard is good for vacuum cleaner attachments, brushes, and mops. Shelves that are not too deep are efficient. You will not have to shove everything around to find the bottle or can you need. A caddy with many different-sized pockets is good for holding brushes, cloths, and some containers that are frequently used. This may be hung on the back of a door.

A basket has been found useful in some homes for keeping the most common cleaning agents, together with cloths, sponges, and brushes. One woman uses her son's small wagon

Certain cleaning materials should be kept on hand so that your job will be easier and so you will not be frantically searching for substitutes for furniture polish

Appropriate soaps and detergents
Bleach
Window and glass cleaner
Silver and other metal polishes
Scouring pads, made of steel wool,
plastic, or fiberglass
Oven Cleaner
Rust remover
Floor wax
Furniture polish or wax
Scratch-concealing polish for furniture
Spot remover

Store equipment and supplies
in one place if possible.

because you have run out. Here is a suggested list. You may have some bright ideas about substituting some of these items or preparing your own cleaning agents.

Carpet and rug cleaner and perhaps
a machine to do your own cleaning
Ammonia
Baking soda to clean your refrigerator
and for other uses
Upholstery cleaner
Paint and wallpaper cleaner
Deodorizer and disinfectant
Drain opener
Insecticide
Water softener, if necessary
Cleaning cloths, sponges, brushes, and the like

to place everything on, and then pulls it wherever she needs it. Do you have some creative suggestions for placing cleaning supplies and equipment while cleaning and for storage?

Preventive Pointers. If you can prevent dirt from coming into the house and lessen the dirt in the house your workload will be lighter. Think of ways in which you can prevent family members from bringing dirt into the house. Keeping doormats before all doors leading into the house and encouraging everyone to rub shoes or boots well before coming into the house is helpful. Having a closet near these doors so that wraps and boots can be removed is good. Orientals slip into house shoes, a custom we might adopt. Smooth fabrics in furnishings collect less dust. Clean before dirt is well lodged. A very dirty rug, for example, may never be revived completely. Work promptly on picking up, wiping up spills, cleaning the refrigerator, cleaning the sink and kitchen counters after dishwashing, and disposing of old newspapers and magazines for recycling.

Establishing Standards. How clean is clean? And how often should you clean to have a clean house? Your family and you will have to establish these criteria. There are factors to consider. If your home is small and your family is large, you will have to clean more frequently, because more dirt is brought into the house and more accumulates inside. Where you live makes a difference. Cleanlinesss can become a habit as easily as messiness. Standards should be agreeable to everyone in the family. If someone in your family is careless, other members are less comfortable and relationships may suffer. Sometimes standards must be lowered in an emergency, such as illness in the family. Certain values and goals of the family are reflected in a standard necessary for health, safety, and comfort. What do you think should be included in standards?

THINKING IT OVER

1. Maybe you feel that certain things keep you from being efficient. What are they and what are possible solutions?

2. Imagine a home that has excellent standards of cleanliness. Now imagine a home the exact opposite, with very low standards. Describe these two homes. Share your ideas with others. Did you agree or differ widely with others? What are possible reasons? Giving 10 to the best standards and 0 to the worst standards, where would your standards—ones that you could be comfortable with—be on this scale?

THINGS TO DO

1. Do you feel that in your home you have made satisfactory choices in the selection of various cleaners? If not, what would you do to improve it? Why not write to the company about your idea?

2. Study a number of household magazines that have articles about the care of a home. Are the suggestions good (ones you could use), reasonable, or questionable? State the reasons for your ratings.

3. Visit a supermarket in the section that has cleaning supplies. Did you find any products with which you were not familiar? Read the labels. Are these things you would like to try? If so, why?

319

30 Managing home ecology

Ecology may be a common word in your vocabulary. Certainly pollution is. Although you realize that the problem of safety for health is serious, you may have reservations about what you can do. Perhaps your feeling is that the responsibility belongs to scientists, engineers, the government, and others. But you can participate. Maybe you took part in an Earth Day program or project that your school sponsored or you helped collect cans and newspapers for recycling. Wouldn't it be a good idea for you to become a home ecologist and plan ways to keep pollution to a minimum and to save natural resources as they relate to your home?

WHAT IS ECOLOGY?

The root of this word is "eco," which has its origins in the Greek word *oikes*, meaning *house* or *household*. "Logy" comes from the Greek *logos* meaning *word* or *wisdom* about some subject. Ecology, then is knowledge about the household. The meaning of the word has been extended to refer to the whole environment of the earth in which life exists. What pollution does to our environment, then, is a part of the study of ecology.

POLLUTION

Pollution means making something foul, unclean, or dirty. The main types of pollution about which we are concerned are air, water, and land. In breathing we take 14 to 18 breaths per minute of the air that is available to us. The quality of the air varies depending on whether we live in a crowded city, near an industrial area, in the mountains, or on a farm. A survey of the country indicates that there is an average of 40,000 particles of dust in each breath and an additional 30,000 particles of ashes, carbon monoxide, acid mists, nitrogen oxides, strontium 90, and even tiny bits of asbestos from the brake linings of cars and trucks, as well as other contaminants. In addition, air pollutants can erode stone, blacken buildings, disintegrate fabrics such as nylon hose, fade dyed fabrics, and interfere with the process of photosynthesis so plants cannot grow and animals will not have the food they need, which in turn affects the human food supply. In addition, air pollutants irritate eyes and cause respiratory diseases, headaches, fatigue, and kidney damage. People who have asthma, hay fever, or respiratory diseases have greater difficulty in breathing. Diseases of the heart and lungs may be aggravated.

The world is not running out of water, but it may run out of water that is fit to drink. When rain falls through polluted air it picks up many contaminants and poisonous gases, and as it passes through the soil it adds pesticides, fertilizer salts, sewage from septic tanks, storm sewer refuse, and industrial wastes. The litter of junked cars, bottles, old mattresses, and other garbage can add special taints. The ways in which our water can become polluted are endless.

In a similar manner, through the misuse of technology our land has become polluted. More than a 100 million tons of refuse accumulate every year on the land. Major causes are the widespread use of chemical pesticides and herbicides and the wastes of municipal, industrial, and other sources. The destruction of wildlife habitats in fields, forests, and marshes, and the extinction of species of animal and plant life is serious. The indiscriminate littering of highways, sidewalks, parks, and other places is a disgrace.

All these pollutions affect the way we live in our homes. And it is important to you to examine the possible ways that home living further complicates the pollution picture. We are also concerned about the use of limited energy resources and other ecological problems.

In your role as home ecologist you will select areas to study. Included might be home use of energy, waste disposal, transportation and its effect on ecology, noise pollution, littering, air pollution, use of water, and house plants and animals.

ENERGY

The first step is to get acquainted with the kinds of energy you use in your home. What kind of fuel is used for heating and cooling? For cooking? For kitchen appliances? For cleaning equipment? For amusement, such as radio, record

Be a home ecologist and examine ways in which your home can reduce ecological problems.

Polluted water leads to many problems.

player, or television? For bathroom equipment, for shaving or brushing teeth? For heating water? For outside of the house, such as for mowing, or for tools? Review what is used—oil, natural gas, or electricity. How is water used by your family? Can you make decisions that are *energy-sufficient* and not *energy-expensive?*

What do your bills tell you about the way you use energy?

Energy costs money. Does your family pay water, electricity, natural gas, or oil bills or are these included with your rent? Do you have meters that you can learn to read? Maybe a family member is already reading meters and can teach you. Try to identify the home activities that make the meter spin. Look over past bills, if they have been filed, to make an analysis of your use of energy fuels. Has consumption increased or decreased? In the past year have you added new appliances? Is there one appliance that you now use more frequently than before?

Make a list of your appliances and decide with your family which are necessities and which are luxuries. Another way to get some notion about the use of appliances at home is to sort them according to the room in which they are used. How many outlets are there in these respective rooms? Is there a possibility of overload?

Look at Table 30–1 and check the estimated number of watts an appliance takes. A watt is a unit of power in electricity and measures how much electricity is required for something to work. This information may help you decide which appliances are luxuries

Americans are consuming energy almost faster than it can be produced, so it is imperative that every family start saving energy. There are a number of suggestions. Encourage your family to turn out every light that is not needed. For example, if the equivalent of a 100-watt bulb burning 24 hours a day were turned off for a year, you would help save 60 gallons of oil. In addition, every time you leave an unnecessary light burning you are contributing to air and water pollution because the generating plant's burden has been increased.

Among other ideas are to fill washing machines full and to use cold water for rinsing. Do not overdry clothes. Synthetics take 10 to 15 minutes to dry, durable press 20 to 25, and towels, 30 to 40 minutes. Use tightly lidded, flat-bottom aluminum pans for best heat conduction and retention in cooking. Every time you take a peep in the oven, the temperature drops 25 degrees. Fluorescent bulbs give three to four times as much light as a regular bulb of the same wattage and will last seven to ten times as long. For example, a fluorescent bulb rated at 15 watts actually uses 4½ watts and takes 66 hours to use one kilowatt hour of electricity. Colored bulbs tend to give 10 to 25 percent less light than white ones. Dark walls and dark-colored draperies require lamps of higher wattage to have the same

Table 30-1

ENERGY CRISIS AND WATTAGE CHECKLIST

	Average Wattage	Est. KWH Consumed Annually
FOOD PREPARATION		
Blender	386	15
Broiler	1436	100
Coffee Maker	894	106
Dishwasher	1201	363
Frying Pan	1196	186
Hot Plate	1257	90
Mixer	127	13
Range, with oven	12200	1175
Toaster	1161	39
Waste Disposer	445	30
FOOD PRESERVATION		
Freezer (15 cu ft)	341	1195
Refrigerator (12 cu ft)	241	728
Refrigerator (Frostless 12 cu ft)	321	1217
Refrigerator/Freezer (14 cu ft)	326	1137
Frostless 14 cu ft	615	1829
LAUNDRY		
Clothes Dryer	4856	993
Iron (hand)	1008	144
Washing Machine (automatic)	512	103
Water Heater	2475	4219
(quick recovery)	4474	4811
HEATING AND COOLING		
Air Conditioner (room)	860	860*
Bed Covering	177	147
Heater (portable)	1322	176
Heating Pad	65	10
HEALTH AND BEAUTY		
Hair Dryer	381	14
Shaver	14	1.8
Tooth Brush	7	0.5
ENTERTAINMENT		
Radio	71	86
Radio/Record Player	109	109
Television		
black and white		
tube type	160	350
solid state	55	120
color		
tube type	300	660
solid state	200	440
HOUSEWARES		
Clock	2	17
Floor Polisher	305	15
Sewing Machine	75	11
Vacuum Cleaner	630	46

* Based on 1000 hours of operation per year. Figure will vary widely depending upon area and size of unit.

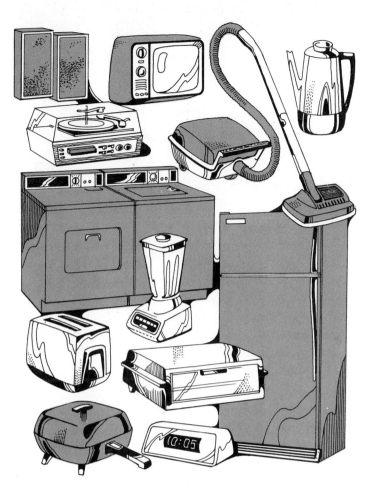

Which of these appliances are considered necessities for your family and which are considered luxuries?

light as light-colored walls and accessories. Use the fluorescent bulbs for reading and save energy.

Families may have to re-examine what a comfortable temperature is. Heating and cooling use up more wattage than appliances. Energy use may be reduced in a number of ways. For heating, the use of storm windows and doors is helpful. Check the attic for leaks. If your home has a great deal of glass, double panes may reduce heating bills. Close the vent when the fireplace is not in use. Lower the thermostat for sleeping. Lowering your thermostat by 1 degree, you save 3 to 4 percent of your fuel and by lowering it 5 degrees, you use 15 to 20 percent less fuel. Wear more clothes, such as sweaters, over your regular garments. For cooling, using less lighting, shading windows from direct sunlight, and closing light-colored draperies to the sunlight can reduce heat by 50 percent. Avoid using the air conditioner unless the weather is unbearable.

What is a comfortable temperature for your family?

WASTE DISPOSAL AND RECYCLING

Did you know that the annual "discard" of Americans amounts to 48 billion cans, 26 billion bottles and jars, 4 million tons of plastic, 7.6 million television sets, 7 million cars and trucks, and 30 million tons of paper? Much of what we throw away does not disappear. Our trash is usually poured into an open dump. If allowed to

What do you think should be done about city dumps?

burn, it pollutes the air. Liquids leaching out of the dump, especially after a rain, will pollute the water. The dump is also a breeding place for rats and insects. Open dumps are unsightly, unsanitary, ugly, and smelly. Furthermore, more cities are running out of places for dumping. There are some ingenious ideas about using the waste for fuel. Some experts believe that the energy value of American refuse every year could be equivalent to 290 million barrels of low sulphur oil or 800,000 barrels a day, which is equivalent to 5 percent of our daily domestic oil use and two-thirds of our former imports from Arab countries. The Environmental Protection Agency estimates that more than 1 billion dollars' worth of minerals could be mined annually from the nation's garbage. From an industrial standpoint, there are plans to recover glass to be recycled into a new product for paving highways, metals to make new metals and metal products, wood fibers for fiberboard house siding, and organic materials for compost, charcoal, or crude oil. Have you read about other possibilities?

Basic to all of this is the need to reduce solid wastes regardless of whether all these ideas materialize. Why not make a survey of what your home throws out every week or even for a shorter time? Take a look at your garbage can. Are you surprised or shocked at the kinds of food that are wasted? Saving food would help the food budget and leave more food for the hungry world. Some of the wastes, such as rinds, peelings, vegetable tops, and the like, make good fertilizer if you have a garden or make a compost heap.

Bottles and cans can be recycled. Find out whether centers have been established by the manufacturers with the assistance of the community. If not, perhaps it can be encouraged. The recycling of paper is of great value because fewer trees will have to be cut and water will be conserved. If all of these items can be recycled, the load of removing trash is lessened. Aluminum cans are recycled now, and an effort is being made to do the same for steel cans, called tin cans. Another way to save trash is to take a tote bag to the market and save on paper bags. In buying paper goods, choose light-colored ones, because the dark-colored take longer to disintegrate. Save gift wrappings for other occasions.

There are many items for which methods of recycling must be sought, such as worn out-pots and pans, pens, short pencils, old notebook covers, old books, and the like. A few of them provide materials for clever collages and art forms, but all of them cannot be used in that manner. Of course, some items are probably discarded before full use is made of them. "Waste not" must be our byword.

What opportunities does your community offer for recycling?

TRANSPORTATION

You may interest your entire family in examining the best ways to save energy to reach destinations. Cars are considered the most wasteful means of transportation. Per gallon of gasoline, cars are only one-sixth as efficient as city buses and one-seventh as efficient as commuter trains. Of course you may live where there are no buses or trains. But there are ways to cut down on automobile use. Workers can use car pools for transportation to work, and in some communities homemakers have a car pool to do their shopping. You might think of ways in which a number of trips can be combined into one, such as a dental appointment for one member, a beauty parlor appointment for another, and some shopping for a third member. Bicycles for short trips do not require gas, only human energy, and they do not contribute to pollution. Bicycling is good for one's health. A basket will hold groceries and other articles. You may find you could avoid many trips by car by walking, which offers many benefits other than saving fuel. What other suggestions do you have for transportation?

NOISE POLLUTION

Noise is sometimes called the invisible pollutant. Noise in the home is reaching levels that can harm the human ear. Among the worst offenders are electrical appliances, such as dishwashers. garbage disposals, vacuum cleaners, high-speed blenders, shop tools, and washing machines. If several are going at the same time, the noise can be quite an irritant. Poorly insulated walls and ceilings and the location of homes in noisy areas are other noise problems.

The noise level must be considered. Decibels are the measure of sound intensity at its source. The decible level starts at 0, the hearing threshold, and goes to 180, the level at which a rocket is launched. Brief exposure to noise levels over 140 decibels causes pain and may rupture eardrums, resulting in permanent hearing loss. Continuous exposure for eight hours to noise levels of approximately 85 decibels can cause permanent hearing loss. Loud music has its drawbacks.

The decibel level of home noises can be of interest. The quietest appliances are the refrigerator, air conditioner, and clothes dryer, with decibels lower than 60. Even at this level, there may be interference with sleep. The continuous

To what places can you walk from your home, such as church, post office, and other places?

noise can be distracting. Clothes washers, food mixers, dishwashers, vacuum cleaners, and electric knives are in the 60 to 70 decibel range. Sewing machines, food blenders, electric shavers and food grinders have decibel levels between 70 and 80. Appliances above 80 decibels include yard-care tools and shop tools.

Some suggestions to abate home noises include the use of noise-absorbing materials on floors, especially where there is considerable traffic; heavy draperies; upholstered rather than hard-surfaced furniture to deaden noise; and the use of a foam pad under blenders and mixers. Keep sleeping areas away from noisemaking equipment. Urge family members to use headsets when they are the only one interested in listening to a high fidelity program. Limit children's toys to those that do not make explosive noises. Help your family cut noise to a minimum, because health can be affected and frustrations may mount with high-decibel noise levels.

LITTERING

Littering accounts for a small amount of our solid wastes but it is the most obvious and offensive form of pollution, in the opinion of many. In addition, it costs 35 cents in taxes to pick up a pop bottle, candy wrapper, or similar item discarded along our highways or in our parks. Lit-

What makes the most noise around your home?

ter attracts rats, feeds fires, causes accidents, and degrades a neighborhood. People throw litter on the ground. Only people can eliminate it.

Take a litter walk around the block near your home or school. What kind of litter is there, and in what amounts? How much is biodegradable (able to disintegrate)? You can test this characteristic by making some "litter gardens." Line three or four shoe boxes with plastic wrap and half-fill them with soil. Plant a hair clip, a piece of plastic wrap, a piece of wood, some aluminum foil and a small piece of newspaper. Keep the soil slightly moist. Plant other items you would like to test. Identify each one by placing its name on a toothpick and placing the toothpick near the planting. After a week, dig up each item and assess what has happened. Repeat the process in another week and for several additional weeks, if you are interested. What did you learn about the durability of certain litter?

You may wish to plan a campaign to eliminate litter in your community. You might wear signs: "Don't Be A Litterbug!" or "Stash Your Trash." If a group of you will wear them, the effect can be quite dramatic. Take around trash bags during half time of a sporting event to collect trash among the spectators. What clever ideas do you have?

MISCELLANEOUS IDEAS

Take a shower instead of a tub bath and save 5 gallons of water. Make an analysis of all the aerosol cans you use in your home. What are you spraying into the air? Have you given any

Look at this littered spot and think of ways to make the place attractive and to keep it free from litter.

thought to pet pollution? How many pets should a family have and what will determine the number? Can you have too many? If you live in a city, what do you think can be done to keep sidewalks and curbs clean from pet use? Do you give leaky faucets prompt attention? One leaky faucet in extreme instances may waste 50 gallons per day! Keep a chilled container of water in the refrigerator instead of letting the water run until it gets cold. Is your lawn oversprinkled? Are you guilty of digging up plants in the woods?

In the days ahead the necessity for saving energy and not polluting our land, water, or air will be even more critical. Our environment must be protected and you can help.

THINKING IT OVER

1. Think about the role of your family in making our earth a better place to live. What are they doing that you like? What would you like to improve? How?

2. How interested and how responsible do you think people are about our ecology? Why are some people more responsible than others?

THINGS TO DO

1. How familiar are you with community action programs where you live? Where can you secure additional information? Do you see other programs or projects that might be helpful? Discuss ways to get some of them started.

2. Plan bulletin boards, posters, mobiles, or exhibits; write poetry, a play, or a scenario for a puppet show; or do something else that is creative to show your feelings about this serious problem or to arouse others to action.

31 A place of your own

Every member of a family usually has some part of the home that is strictly his or her own. You may live in a very crowded home, but even then there is usually some place that you can feel belongs to you. You may be lucky enough to have a room of your own or to share a room with a brother or sister.

In addition to the place where you sleep and do your homework, you may have a shop or playroom in the basement for your hobby or for recreation. If you have a large attic, you may have a spot there for things you are collecting. If you live in a small city apartment, you and your family may have to do some careful planning to provide you with a place of your own. In any home it might be a good idea to have a meeting of the family to decide who shall have what.

DOES YOUR ROOM EXPRESS YOU?

If someone who didn't know you walked into your room or your part of the home, what would he or she be told about you? The room's general appearance says a great deal. Is it orderly or does it look like a wreck? Are you clever about arranging things so that the space has been used to best advantage, or does the room look cluttered? If you share a room, have you worked out some kind of system with your roommate about keeping the room attractive?

Each thing that one sees in your room helps tell a story about you. Is your room streamlined or crowded? What do you have on display? Which of your interests are evident?

In other words, your room will reflect your personality and your interests. Take a look at your room with this thought in mind. What impression does it make?

THE IMPORTANCE OF YOUR SPACE

Have you ever thought about all the things you do there? Here is a list of some of the activities that may take place there:

1–Doing homework—school, club, or church
2–Doing things with hobbies
3–Entertaining friends
4–Showing souvenirs
5–Storing belongings
6–Thinking, dreaming, and planning
7–Reading
8–Sleeping

You will think of other activities, of course. All of them call for certain kinds of furniture and room arrangements. Suppose we consider each one.

Homework

Although you may do homework anywhere in the house, it is a good plan to have one place where you keep your school supplies and do your assignments. If you have no definite place, you may find it more difficult to settle down and get to work promptly, and you are almost certain to lose or to misplace important papers and books.

The equipment needed for study includes a desk and a comfortable chair on which you can sit up straight. A good lamp, a place for your books, and some place for supplies are other essentials.

Your Desk. You may be quite happy with your desk. In that case, it is not a problem. If you don't like your desk, there are several things you can do. A piece of plywood can be placed between two unpainted chests with enough room for your chair. This will give you a fine working surface. If you don't have room for two chests, use one and put metal legs at the other end of the piece of plywood. A large shelf on hinges which can go back to the wall when not in use is often used. This saves space. Look over the various magazines, at home and in your school or public library, and see if you can find suggestions of other ways to have just the kind of desk space you need.

Do You Have a Typewriter? If you have a typewriter, there must be room under the desk or at the side of the desk to keep it when not in use. In the desk drawers you will keep paper, pencils, pens, eraser, ruler, and other things you need for your homework.

Your room is a good place to display your collections and hobbies.

What does this closet tell you about the person using it?

This room is planned for homework.

Some do-it-yourself ideas for making a desk.

Books Must Have a Place. Books may be placed at the back of the desk between bookends—which you might make. If there isn't room, a hanging bookcase over your desk is attractive. But be sure that you can reach the books and that the shelves are sturdy enough to hold them. You may prefer a bookcase at the end of your desk or somewhere else in the room. At any rate, you will want some arrangement whereby you can keep your schoolbooks together and find them easily. If you have books in your room that you are reading for other purposes, you must also find a place for them.

Lighting. A good lamp is most important. Pinup lamps are good if space is limited. Then the entire top of the desk is yours for working space. Swing-arm lamps will enable you to bring the light to the spot where it is needed. If you have a shelf over your desk, a fluorescent light might be mounted under the shelf to throw light on the desk. To prevent glare, use lamps that have a bottom glass shield or a shade that diffuses light well. A lot of ruffles or other decoration on a shade reduces the amount of light. In addition to the lamp on your desk, you must also have good light in the room itself. It is a mistake to have the light shining on your work and leave the rest of the room in darkness.

330

Wastebasket. Some type of wastepaper basket will save you many steps. If you do not have one, you can easily make one from a round carton which you can cover with plastic paper or some other material. Cut-out pictures from magazines, maps, cartoons, or other devices pasted on the carton make a clever basket. Shellac or varnish it to keep it in good conditions and easy to clean.

You can make your own waste basket by covering an ice cream carton with oil cloth, plastic material, magazine pictures, fabric, or other materials.

Your room is a comfortable place for you and your friends to talk.

Entertaining Your Friends

On your way home from school, you may be accompanied by some of your friends. You may be discussing an interesting subject, and you may take everybody up to your room. You look around for some place to seat everybody. It might be a problem. To be ready for such a situation, have plenty of cushions around. Your friends won't mind sitting on the floor, if you can give them a good cushion. In addition, when your friends come to see you, you may give them something to nibble. See Chapter 19 for ideas.

Your Souvenirs. Almost everyone saves things that have a personal meaning. It is nice to be able to keep them in a place where you can see them. If they are not too personal, your friends might like to see them too. You may have school pennants, postcards from friends, party invitations, cartoons, or the snapshots you have taken. Maybe you have a silly baby picture of yourself that you like. Other items might be a program of a school play you were in or pictures of stars of stage, screen, TV, and sports.

You can't just put all these things on the wall or pin them to the curtains, so why not have

a special place to hang them? Here are a few ideas which you may adapt to suit your purpose. One is to take a burlap bag and wash and press it. You might dye it if you wish. Put a heading in the top and the bottom large enough to hold a

Why not embroider and applique a dresser scarf with your own flower or other design on cotton or easy-care material?

curtain rod from the variety store. You might hem it with sticky tape—the kind that holds rugs together is very good. Put pieces of rope, fancy string, or something similar at the ends of the rod to hang it up on the wall. Put a rod at the bottom as a weight. You can buy decorator's burlap in white and colors. It may be used in the same manner as the burlap bag. Make careful arrangements so that this burlap piece will fit on the best wall space you have.

Another idea for a display piece is to take chicken wire or coarse screen and paint it gold or silver. Cover a piece of painted plywood or plasterboard with the wire. The wire is excellent for hanging articles. A pegboard or a magnetic board are other possibilities. You will want to change this show-off board often so your friends will be interested in seeing your latest collection.

You might like some kind of bulletin-board arrangement whereby you can keep your latest baseball or football statistics and pictures of athletes. If you have an oversize pegboard, you can hang some of your sports material, as well as other equipment you use often. It might also help you solve the storage problem.

A perforated hardboard wall provides a place where you can hang sports equipment and shelves for books.

Personal Touches. You might want to have something in your room that may have belonged to your grandmother, such as a shawl that you can use as a throw at the bottom of your bed or a pincushion top in needlepoint or cross stitch that you can frame and hang on the wall. Maybe you can plan your own sampler and embroider it and think about giving it to one of your own children some day. You might make your own bookcases or shelves, wood carvings, or ship models. You might have a fishbowl or tank, or plants.

Now that you have learned to sew, you can make patchwork pillows, curtains, a bedspread, or stuffed animals. A cloth collage of different fabrics and shapes or with an appliqué design are among many ideas for wall hangings. Combine appliqué and embroidery for a handcrafted look. Pad your appliqué to produce a three-dimensional effect.

Make your own rug (small for the first one, and larger when you are more expert) of yarn, your old jeans, old curtains, felt strips, string, stockings, or rope. Get a good book on homemade rugs from your library or get ideas from an expert. You might make your own loom and weave the pieces that are to be sewn together for the rug. Friends will like to be in a place that has your own personal stamp on it.

Reading

Sometimes you may read in the living room or some other place in the house, but if you really want to concentrate, you may prefer to read in your room. It would be a fine idea to have an easy chair placed where the light is good. Keeping some books or magazines in your room to read whenever you have a few extra minutes is a good idea. You may set aside a special place to keep your magazines. Some of them can be discarded when you have finished reading them. Others you will want to save for one reason or another. At times you will be bringing books home from the library. You will want to have a place for them and perhaps some kind of reminder about their due dates. In your planning, be careful not to overlook the importance of providing for reading in your room.

Sleeping Is Important

To be keen and alert during the day, one must sleep well. Your bed should be comfortable and should be placed so you will not have the light shining in your eyes in the morning. If you like to read in bed, you should have a good bed light for that purpose. Plan to ventilate your room in such a way that a draft will not blow on you while you are asleep.

A Place for Everything and Everything in Its Place

Are you a drawer stuffer? Do you have trouble finding a place for everything? Are you always bothered with an overflow of some kind? There are several answers to this problem. First of all, examine your belongings to see whether you are saving things unnecessarily. Look at that top drawer—an old math paper that should have been thrown out long ago, the wrapper of a candy bar, some scratch paper on which you outlined that social studies committee report, a sock that has no mate, and a grocery list that your mother gave you last week. Throw out the trash. If there are things you must keep, just rearranging a drawer will usually bring you more space.

Another idea is to start fresh and carefully plan the drawer space you have. Remove the contents of each drawer and take a good look at them. How much space do you have? Have you been digging down to the bottom of the drawer for things you need? Or are you forever opening the lid to a box? Why not have partitions and open containers? They will enable you to see what is in a drawer at a glance and quickly find the things you are looking for.

There are many ideas for containers, depending on what you are storing. Pasteboard egg cartons can be separated and painted in a gay color or decorated in some manner. Here you can keep the small items you are always losing. Mark off a drawer with cardboard dividers for your hose, underwear, sweaters, and other items. Organize your things so that you needn't cause an upheaval every time you look for something. For example, keep all ties or scarves of one color together for greater efficiency.

One way to rearrange your dresser drawer is to find shoe or other types of boxes and fit them into the drawer. Designate each space for a specific item of clothing.

It is not sufficient just to put things in order. You pass the test only if you can keep them that way. If you can't, either you are not returning your things to their proper place or your system needs to be re-examined. Maybe you aren't keeping things in the most suitable place. Decide on the handiest place for everything. Where, for example, do you comb your hair? Shouldn't your comb and brush be there? Where do you dress? Which clothes are needed every day? Which are used occasionally? The things you use most of-

A candy box with its tiny compartments is good for small items and jewelry. Cover the top and box with a fabric or fancy paper, or use an art technique on it.

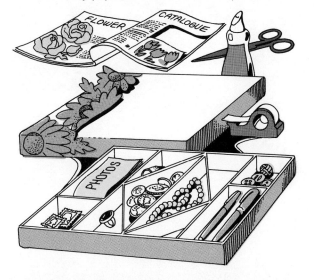

ten should be in the upper drawers and those you use less often in the lower drawers. If you have to share a dresser with your brother or sister, you will want to plan the division of space. Always putting things away will do much to keep your room orderly.

PRIVATE: KEEP OUT!

There will be times when you will want to be alone in your room. Everyone has to be alone at times. When we are quiet, we can usually do our best planning. There must be some time for just plain dreaming. This may be dreaming about what you will do next summer, what you will do when you grow up, or how you can stretch your allowance. Sometimes it is nice to have a few minutes by yourself to think about the pleasant things that have happened to you during the day. Maybe your best friend paid you a wonderful compliment. Or your father brought home something that you have wanted for a long time. You may have made an important goal for the team, or learned how to cut the figure eight on the ice. If we take time to think about it, something pleasant happens to us every day. We should never allow ourselves to forget that fact.

Then, of course, there may be days when things don't go so well. Your feelings are hurt,

It is important to have a place or places where you can read comfortably in a good light.

Everyone needs a place to think and dream.

you are disappointed, you are scolded about something you feel isn't your fault, or you are angry about something your best friend may have said. It is very helpful to retrace the steps fairly and honestly. Maybe there was some blame and misunderstanding on both sides. There usually is. Decide on a course of action. Can you apologize? Maybe the best thing to do is to get busy on something else. Read a book, work on your hobby, or go for a walk. The sooner you forget about some things, the better. Thinking negatively about anything does not help it. But you need your room as a place to think about things and to remember that difficulties do not last forever.

EVERYBODY HAS PROBLEMS

If you share a room, you may have some difficulties that demand adjustment. Your sister or brother may bring friends in at the same time that you bring yours in. You get your things mixed up. She or he may not make the beds as well as you do. What can you do? The best course is to talk it over and reach some decisions. Maybe your sister or brother should have first turn at the room after school on certain days and you on other days. If you have a feeling that you need to be alone at times when your room is occupied, you may have to go out of the house or find another isolated spot somewhere in the house.

Think about the space that belongs to you at home. Are you appreciative of it? Do you really use it to best advantage? Of course, there is a great deal of space that is shared by the whole family and you will want to be responsible for keeping it as neat and attractive as possible. Just as your room tells about you, so does your whole house tell about your family. It should always tell the best story possible.

THINKING IT OVER

1. Think about the things you have in your room. Where did they come from? Could they form a kind of biography about you? What do they tell about your past? Can you see anything about your future in your room? What is it?

THINGS TO DO

1. Make a project of planning better storage space in your room. Where will you get ideas?

2. Dramatize a problem that may arise when you share a room with someone. Would you have solved the problem in the same way? If not, how would you have solved it?

3. Think about how age affects the way one feels about what is important in a room. What does your younger brother or sister consider important? An older brother or sister? Your mother and father? Your grandparents? What problems do they have in common?

4. Look through magazines and booklets for ideas on the best ways to arrange dresser drawers, to plan a desk, and to display your souvenirs. Share your ideas with others in the class. Plan a skit for an assembly program around the best ideas.

32 Managing family health emergencies

How well do you manage in emergencies? There may be times when your family and you will have to face illness, accidents, or the possibility of physical or emotional handicap of one or more family members. Many will be minor, while others may be long-term in nature.

You can become an important person in the home during any temporary or long-time confinement of a family member. In the case of a short illness, the family routine may be changed for a while. Certain adjustments may have to be made. It may be up to you to do the work usually done by the person who is ill. Somebody will have to be a pinch hitter. And the sick family member will need care. What do you usually do in these circumstances? Are there some things you haven't done that might be done? Can you arrange to do some of them the next time?

HOW YOU CAN HELP

What you do will depend somewhat on the person who is hurt or ill. If your mother is disabled, you may have to take over many responsibilities, especially if you have no older brothers or sisters to help. If younger brothers or sisters are concerned, you may have to help your mother take care of them and give her an extra hand with the running of the house. When your father is ill, you might run errands for him or do other things to help him. If your younger brother or sister has a communicable disease, like chicken pox, and you haven't had it, the best thing you can do is stay away from the sick person and help in other parts of the house. In some homes, a member of the family may be handicapped or an invalid and need special care. Whatever the situation, you can play the part of an assistant nurse or housekeeper.

You will want to be helpful wherever you can. If other members of the family are bed-ridden, your mother may need the most help. First of all, try to be especially kind and thoughtful. Being cheerful and boosting her morale will mean a great deal to her. Offer to help. She may want you to wait on the patient, go to the drugstore for medicine, shop for groceries, or make telephone calls. It may be necessary for you to take on some added home responsibilities. You might make the beds, do some cleaning and straightening of the house, or help prepare some of the family meals.

When your mother is ill, you probably will have greater responsibilities. With your father or older sister or brother, you might plan how the jobs will be divided. It may help to make a list of all the things that must be done. This would include care of your mother and everything that needs attention in the home.

After a decision has been made about your duties, it is a good idea to make a schedule. Since you will have more to do than usual, it is important to keep to this schedule so as not to get behind with your schoolwork.

FOOD FOR THE SICK

Whoever is ill or hurt, one of your assignments might be the preparation of some of the special food for the sick person. Here you will have to follow the doctor's orders. If a liquid or soft diet is ordered, there are a number of dishes you might prepare.

Prepare a tray that is attractive and has appealing food.

Preparing Soup

Most people who are sick can take some kind of soup. You might find an interesting soup recipe in your favorite family cookbook and prepare it. Since time is precious, you will probably use canned or packaged soups to make a tasty soup. Even with this type of soup you can have fun doing something different. Following are some ideas to start you thinking. You can use these ideas and adapt them to produce something very special to please the invalid and the rest of the family as well.

1-Combine packaged or canned chicken noodle and tomato soups. Sprinkle parsley flakes over the top of the soup just before serving.

2-Cream chicken or cream mushroom soup is delicious with grated cheese added.

3-Combine green pea and tomato soups. Garnish with crushed potato chips sprinkled on top.

4-Thin canned vegetable soup with milk instead of water.

5-Combine green pea soup with noodle soup. Grated raw carrot makes a pretty garnish, if the doctor allows the patient to have raw vegetables.

6-Serve cold soups in hot weather, if the patient is feverish and would like something refreshing. Soups good for chilling are tomato, cream of chicken, cream of tomato, cream of celery, broth, or bouillon. Broth and bouillon are especially tasty poured over ice cubes in a glass with a slice of lemon. Serve cold soups in chilled cups or bowls.

You will think of and find many other good combinations. Watch advertisements and magazine articles for additional suggestions. Best of all, do a little experimenting and originate your own recipes.

Soup Accompaniments. Try to think of something different to serve with soup. Here are a few ideas:

1-Various kinds of dry cereal to take the place of crackers are a nice change.

2-For your younger brothers and sisters you might use animal or fancy cookie cutters for cutting bread into interesting shapes. The bread can be toasted and spread with butter or margarine. Peanut butter or cream cheese is also good if permitted in the diet prescribed for the sick person.

3-When making croutons for soup, toast the small cubes of bread after they have been cut. If all sides are browned they will be tastier. Sprinkling the croutons with grated cheese or paprika or both also adds to their flavor.

Cool Drinks for the Patient

Maybe you remember the last time you were ill and your mother brought you a frosty drink in a tall glass. You were kept guessing about what it was. Why not try your hand at making an interesting and refreshing beverage? Here are some ideas to start you off.

1-**Iced coffee or iced tea** is almost always pleasing. Why not make frozen tea or coffee cubes? The quickest way is to use instant coffee or

tea. Read the directions on the jar and make it twice as strong. Pour the tea or coffee into an ice cube tray and freeze it. When you are ready to use the cubes, put two or three in a glass. Then fill the glass with cold water. Sugar and cream may be desired with the iced coffee. Slices of lemon or orange make iced tea more refreshing.

2-**Fruit Egg Nog.** In a mixing bowl, place ⅔ cup of pineapple, orange, or pear juice, or a combination of the three, and one egg. Beat the mixture until foamy and creamy-looking. Pour it over cracked ice in a tall glass.

3-**Fruit Fizz.** Place a large spoonful of a fruit sherbet, such as pineapple, lemon, or raspberry, in a tall glass. Add an ice cube. Fill the glass with cold ginger ale, root beer, or some other carbonated drink.

4-**Milk Frosty.** Fill a tall glass ⅔ full of cold milk. Add a large spoonful of ice cream or sherbet.

5-**Orange Zip.** Place 3 tablespoons of frozen orange juice in the bottom of a tall glass. Fill the glass with cold ginger ale. Garnish with a spoonful of vanilla ice cream.

6-**Maple Cooler.** Place ¼ cup of instant nonfat dry milk solids in a mixing bowl. Add ⅓ cup of cold water. Beat 3 to 4 minutes. Add 2 tablespoons of lemon juice. Beat the mixture until it is stiff. Add 2 tablespoons of maple syrup. Pour the cooler over chipped ice in a tall glass. You may want to serve this with a spoon. Adding a mashed banana is a nice variation.

7-**Peppermint Shake.** Empty the contents of a small can of evaporated milk into a jar. Add 3 tablespoons of frozen orange juice, 1 tablespoon of honey, 3 drops of peppermint extract, and 1 cup of chipped ice. Mix it in an electric blender or shake it vigorously in a closed jar until frothy. Serve at once in tall glasses.

Serving Food to the Sick

The way food is served to a sick person is very important. A pretty tray makes the food more attractive. Here is a check-list to help you plan your serving.

1-Select a tray that is the right size. A glass of fruit juice looks silly on a large tray. A tray that is too small will crowd the dishes. If you have only a small tray, serve in courses. This may be a good idea anyway, because the sight of too much food at once may dull the sick persons's appetite.

A cold fruit juice drink can be refreshing to a sick person.

338

Follow the doctor's orders when choosing foods to serve someone who is sick.

2- Select a pretty tray cloth. A place mat might be the right size. If you don't have a tray cloth, think of a good substitute. A pretty kitchen towel or a large napkin might be folded to the right size. Don't have it hanging over the edge of the tray. It looks untidy and accidents may occur.

3- Select dishes that go well together. If a small child is being served, it might be wise to use dishes that do not break easily. Attractive paper dishes may be used on occasion.

4- If you want flowers on the tray, place them in a low dish. A tall vase tips easily.

5- Another suggestion is to tuck a surprise under the napkin or some place on the tray. For a small child it might be an animal cracker. For your father it might be a funny cartoon or a joke pasted on a card. A cheerful poem might be nice for your mother. Everybody likes surprises.

6- Set up your tray as you would a place at the table.

ENTERTAINING DISABLED CHILDREN

A problem in many homes is to find ways to interest small children when they are almost well but still have to be confined to their beds or at least to the house. Here is another opportunity for you to be helpful. A few suggestions of things a child might like to do are listed here. You can add ideas of your own.

1- Blow into an empty bottle to make interesting noises or play a tune.

2- Paste an interesting magazine picture on thin pasteboard (a shirt cardboard is good) and let the child make a jigsaw puzzle by cutting it into pieces.

3- Blow soap bubbles. If a bubble pipe is not available, dip an empty spool or a stick of macaroni into soapy water.

4- Place a bowl of tropical fish or turtles where the child can watch their movements.

5- If there is a tree near the child's window, he or she might like to watch birds with a pair of field glasses.

6- Spread a piece of oilcloth or plastic material on a tray or breadboard. This may be used for making things with clay.

7- Make rainbows with a prism.

8- Make a mobile of materials around the house—string, paper, foil, paper clips, and similar items.

9- See what can be done with a magnifying glass.

Think of interesting ways to entertain a sick child.

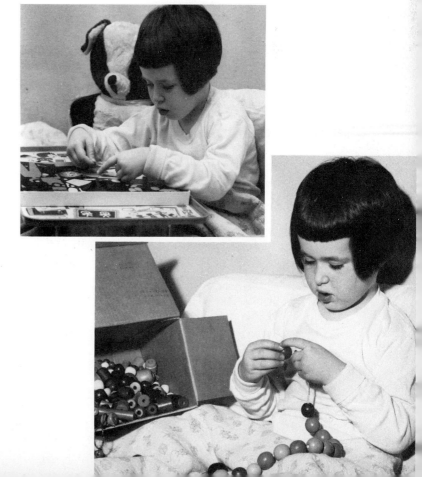

10–Make puppets from paper bags, vegetables, or light-colored cotton socks.

11–Make toy animals or other objects from pipe cleaners.

Your family will be very grateful to you if you assume the responsibility of seeing that your brother or sister is not lonesome. Some of these ideas might be used for a neighbor's child or someone else you know. In fact, some of the activities are good fun for a child whether he or she is sick or well. Some of the ideas are good for parties, too.

THE FAMILY MEDICINE CHEST

Now that you have given thought to helping at home during sickness, you may wish to check on your home medicine chest, not only for illness, but also in the event of accidents. Consult with your family and perhaps your family doctor about suggestions for supplies.

First, take a good look at the medicine chest. Is there an accumulation of empty, squeezed tubes and bottles containing old prescriptions that should be thrown out? Are there items you might need in an emergency? Your hygiene book or pamphlets from a life insurance company are good sources of information about the things that should be kept in a medicine chest. Here is one recommended list. You can make your list from these suggestions:

Absorbent cotton	Medicine dropper
Adhesive tape (various widths)	Milk of magnesia
	Ointment for burns
Aspirin	Petroleum jelly
Bicarbonate of soda	Rubbing alcohol
Eyecup	Scissors
Fever thermometer	Spirits of ammonia
Gauze bandages	Throat swabs
Gauze pads	Tongue depressors
Antiseptic	Tweezers

The medicine chest does not usually have room for the following items that should be available. They must be stored elsewhere:

Atomizer spray
Disinfectant (for cleaning the sickroom and bath)
Hot water bottle or heating pad
Ice bag
Rubber gloves
Syringe

Is your medicine chest in order?

Now check the things in your medicine chest against your list. What is missing? Does your family think there should be additions?

If you find any bottles of prescribed medicines in your medicine chest, check on the dates. It is a good plan to ask your doctor when a prescription will deteriorate, and put a label with that date on the bottle and encourage your family to look at the date before taking a dose. In addition, find out whether the medicine should be refrigerated or kept out of light, and other aspects of keeping qualities.

ACCIDENTS

Illness is not the only emergency that has to be faced. Few families escape some accidents of minor or major proportions. Your family and you will want to be prepared. That means a knowledge of first-aid procedures; simple remedies for burns, cuts, bruises, and other hurts; and knowing whom and where to go to for help in a serious emergency, such as a small child swallowing poison, a broken leg, or an injury in an automobile accident. Preventive measures, however, may be your first step.

IMPORTANCE OF SAFETY RULES

Has you family made safety rules that everyone in the family tries to remember and practice every day? If not, perhaps the family would like to elect you their rule maker and have you present some rules for their consideration. These are general rules that you might like to adapt to your own situation.

SAFETY MEASURES

1–Always use a solid ladder or step stool—never a makeshift of a rickety chair or bench with boxes.

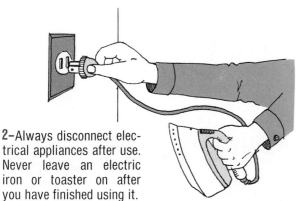

2–Always disconnect electrical appliances after use. Never leave an electric iron or toaster on after you have finished using it.

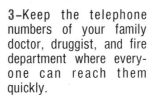 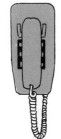 

3–Keep the telephone numbers of your family doctor, druggist, and fire department where everyone can reach them quickly.

4–Always place a lighted match under the faucet or in water before discarding it.

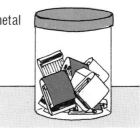

5–Keep matches in metal or glass containers.

6–Always keep things in place so that people will not stumble over them.

Don't

7–Keep everything repaired, especially furniture, steps, and electric cords.

Room Hazards

In addition to observing these general rules, it is a good idea to examine the house room by room for safety hazards.

Bathroom

1– It is very easy to slip and fall in the bathtub or while taking a shower. A rubber mat in the bottom of the tub is a "must." If none is available, a large towel placed in the bottom may be used as a temporary substitute.

2– Keep an eye on the soap. If you lose it in the tub, take time to find it, since slipping on soap can be a serious accident. Keep soap in a container when not in use.

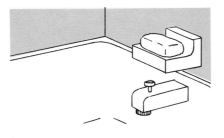

3– Don't be absent-minded and touch an electrical switch, socket, or appliance while you are wet.

4– Don't answer the telephone while you are wet.

5– If possible, there should be a grab bar near the tub for pulling yourself out of the tub or to hold on to while taking a shower.

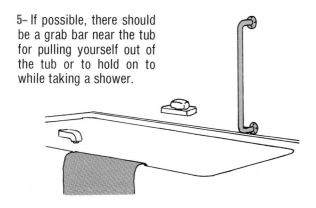

6– Keep a first-aid booklet in the medicine chest or in some spot where it can be easily found.

7– Some families paste the antidotes for common poisons on the door of the medicine chest so that they will be handy.

8– Don't help yourself to the contents of the medicine chest. A healthy person does not need pills or other remedies. A sick person should have competent advice before taking any kind of medicine. Some people try all sorts of remedies for a cold, for example, taking several at the same time. Self-dosage should be avoided. Only harm can result from this kind of practice.

Take a look at your bathroom. How safe is it? And now for the bedrooms.

Bedrooms

1– Keep some kind of light near the bed and turn it on when necessary. If for some reason it is impossible to have a light near you, a good substitute is to keep a flashlight handy. This is especially good if you share a room with someone and do not wish to waken the other person with a bright light. Make sure the batteries in the flashlight are fresh.

2– Keep the closet door and bureau drawers closed. They may block the path of someone coming into the room and cause painful injuries.

Don't

3– If you have scatter rugs, be certain that they are firmly anchored to the floor with nonskid backing to prevent skids and falls.

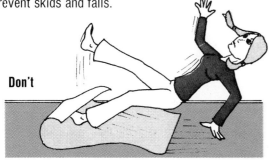

Don't

4– Keep such articles as clothes and toys off the floor.

Don't

5– If you sew in the bedroom, exercise special care to pick up any needles, pins, and scissors and return them to sewing box or drawer. It is a good idea to have a place for everything and keep everything in its place.

Do you have any suggestions for improving the safety of your bedrooms? Next is the living room.

Living Room

1– Keep everything in place. Scattered newspapers and magazines, toys, record players, and the like can be the cause of tripping and bad accidents.

Don't

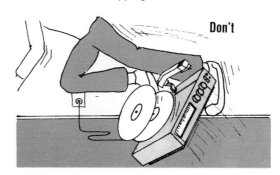

2– Chairs and other furniture should be checked periodically. It may look funny when someone's chair collapses but an accident of this nature is not amusing and can be very serious.

Don't

3– Check multiple extension cords. They may trail around the room and provide many opportunities for serious accidents and at the same time overload your circuit.

Don't

4– Look at the rugs and carpeting in your home. Small rugs should be anchored with nonskid material. The edges of large rugs should be fastened securely to the floor so that they will not turn up and trip someone.

343

5–If you have a fireplace, check it for safety. Do you place a screen across the fireplace when it is burning? Is the chimney checked periodically?

6–Is the furniture so placed that paths of traffic are clear? Walk around your living room. Is the path fairly direct from easy chairs to television, to the piano, to the fireplace, or whatever the arrangement may be, or is it a crooked path?

Don't

What changes, if any, would you make in your living room to make it a safer place?

Attic and Basement. Do you find many unused articles in the basement or attic? There may be old newspapers or magazines that someone hopes to read some day or to use in some other way. Collections of this kind are a definite fire

hazard. In addition, each member of the family collects other items he or she intends to use some day but never will. These take up space and block traffic lanes. Attention should be given to storage facilities for little-used and out-of-season materials.

Don't

Outdoors

1–Have a definite place for storing all outdoor toys, bicycles, wagons, game equipment, and garden tools. Rakes or other tools with sharp edges should not be exposed.

2–Do not leave toys or other items on the walks. This is especially dangerous for anyone who may walk there at night.

Don't

3–Discourage children from running with popsicles or lollypops in their mouths. They may fall while running and suffer serious injuries.

4–Sprinkle ashes or sand on slippery walks in the wintertime if you live in a cold climate.

5–Keep the lawns and yard clear of broken glass, nails, or similar articles.

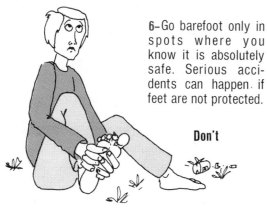

6–Go barefoot only in spots where you know it is absolutely safe. Serious accidents can happen if feet are not protected.

Don't

In spite of safety rules, daydreaming or carelessness may lead to an accident. For a minor burn, apply an ice pack or ice in a plastic bag. Bumps, bruises, and insect bites may be treated in the same way. Splinters may be carefully removed with tweezers or a sterilized needle. Apply hydrogen peroxide to a small cut. Broken bones, severe burns or cuts, animal bites, or poisoning require the immediate attention of a doctor.

THE HANDICAPPED

There are millions of handicapped persons in the United States and family members may be responsible for their care. You can be especially helpful in developing their independence. If someone in your family has to use a wheelchair or crutches, has only one hand or arm, is partially sighted or blind, or deaf, you can aid this person in working out ways to enable him or her to dress, bathe, eat, and carry on life activities alone or with little help. This is not easy, but if everyone in the family gives encouragement, it is easier. If the handicapped person is able to do as much as possible independently, time is released for the family members and they do not have to spend so much time on patient care. Do not be overeager to help. This makes for dependence, not independence.

Personnel in rehabilitation centers will suggest many ways to handle these daily activities, but you will want to read, talk to others, and experiment if you believe that a procedure different from your present one would be an improvement. Not only must everyday living be eased, but every attempt must be made to have this family member continue contacts with the outside world, such as attendance at sports events, plays, movies, concerts, and other events of interest, visiting friends, going to parties, and the like.

The disability will determine the adjustments that have to be made. You might start with the area in which the disabled person has a strong desire to help himself or herself. For example, a man with little strength in his hands wanted very much to be able to dial the telephone and talk to his friends. He found he could hold a stick in his teeth and accomplish his desire. That might not work for others, but a way can be found, whatever the need. The telephone company has suggestions. A girl in a wheelchair found she could dress herself when her clothes were closed in front instead of the back—with a zipper, Velcro closings, or large snaps. A boy wanted to prepare his lunch when the rest of the family was away at work or school. By placing a hot plate on a table which his wheelchair could go under, he could have something hot. The regular range in the kitchen was difficult to reach. These are only a few examples of ways to give self-assurance.

In the event that someone in your family has an emotional illness, it is best to secure the advice of the psychiatrist of the best ways you

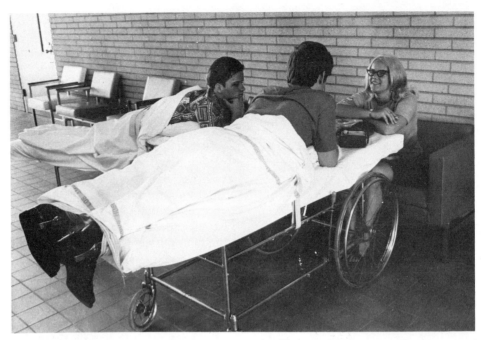

Help a handicapped person to develop a sense of achievement.

can help. Affection, encouragement, and an interest in the patient are helpful in dealing with physical or emotional illness. Your attitude to a physical or mental health handicap can make a difference in your household. Being as positive as possible in your attitude is helpful for you and it is also helpful for the handicapped member of your family.

THINKING IT OVER

1. Think of ways in which illness might be prevented in your family. How might you encourage and plan for a "Be-Well Winter" or a "Best-Health-Ever Year"?

2. Think of special safety hazards as they affect persons of various ages. Start with the infant and advance to old people.

3. Consider situations of an emotional nature that may lead to accidents because a person is upset. Some examples are having a quarrel with someone, worrying about something, or being very angry. Can you give examples of accidents that have happened to persons in such circumstances? What advice would you offer?

4. Imagine the feelings, reactions, thoughts, and actions of family members when they realize that a family member has been handicapped physically or emotionally. Maybe you can talk to someone who has experienced this situation. Share your ideas with others.

THINGS TO DO

1. Look in your newspaper. Find stories about home accidents. What types of accidents were they? How might they have been prevented?

2. Which type of accident occurs most often in your community? Is there some reason for this? Would it be possible for your class to plan an accident prevention campaign of some kind? Committees might be chosen to brainstorm about possible ways of solving this problem.

3. Make plans for ways to bring happiness to some of the invalids or shut-ins in your community. The class might be divided into groups with different responsibilities. One group might take turns visiting, writing notes, or making things. Another might present a short puppet show, prepare some interesting food, or make scrapbooks of poems, pictures, or short stories. This type of activity might be adapted to your local hospital.

4. If possible volunteer to work in a rehabilitation center, a hospital ward where the patients are physically handicapped, a nursing home for the elderly with inmates who are physically handicapped or senile; or an institution for retarded children. In what ways are these individuals independent? In what ways do they need help? Plan ways in which you might help them to be more independent.

33 Creative family living

Many families have developed imaginative and unusual ideas for doing everyday activities or for their life-style. It has become the Smith or the Jones way of giving gifts, rinsing clothes, or preparing fried chicken. Has your family created a custom that is unique? Are you carrying on an idea that your grandmother started? Does your family have a reputation for being inventive in crafts or toymaking or in other areas? What is special about your family?

FAMILY TREASURES

Most families have certain keepsakes, usually something that belonged to older relatives, such as your grandfather's watch, a plate from your grandmother, or a favorite rocking chair of a great-aunt or uncle. There may be an old family bible that has family happenings written in it or an old album of family photographs. Even migrant families who have little room to keep anything do have some family treasures, such as a framed photograph of the wedding of parents or grandparents or a brooch that belonged to Cousin Hattie. These cherished items will vary from family to family.

Where does your family keep these things from the past? Are they put in a safe place and how are they protected from deterioration? Has thought been given to the display of some of them? In one home, for example, a primitive watercolor of a landscape painted by a great-grand-father is proudly hung on the living room wall. An old watch may be mounted and placed on a shelf or an end table. If it still keeps time, it can be useful. Old afghans may be placed at the foot of a bed or at the end of a sofa to be used as a throw. Why not share ideas about family treasures and gain some ideas for yourself?

What kind of collection of keepsakes are you making for your future family? These treasures give a feeling of security and satisfaction and help you to realize that you are a part of continuing family life. With rapid changes in living and with considerable moving from home to home, it is good to have things around you from the past.

Family Records

Your family may have kept a baby book about you but may have few records after that. Families are beginning to realize that these records can have much meaning in later years. In some families tricky records have been made. Children have been encouraged to keep a scrapbook of some of their best school papers and artwork. If their names appeared in the local paper this was added, with the date. In another family, a kind of personal history was kept with information about height and weight, a recent snapshot, and other items of development. In another family, clever sayings or humorous events were described. For example, a small child of three during gardening time wanted to plant a cookie for a cookie tree. This was added to her book by her parents.

All legal items such as birth certificate, social security number (if and when you secure one), baptismal certificate (if you have one), report cards, diplomas, or a record of courses taken at school should be kept in a safe place so you know where to find them, because they will be used often all during your life.

A record of club activities, participation in sports, offices held, committee assignments, tal-

ents in music, art, or other areas, or community involvement should be carefully documented for that day when you write a résumé for a job. All of this is good management.

Think about the best place or places to store these various records. That may determine the size of the scrapbooks or notebooks in which you will keep your information.

The use of tapes and photographs for many purposes should not be overlooked. One family took colored photographs of the wall of every room and other shots that illustrated their home furnishings. This was kept in the event that an insurance claim had to be made. Bills of purchase of important furniture should be filed for insurance purposes and for a possible sale of some of these items.

Photographs and tapes of family members at holiday or other occasions are precious when viewed or heard years later. Tapes might be made of family conversations at such times. The home motion-picture camera adds action to the scene. In one family, a son who was an artist added his artistic impressions of an important family event. Sometimes unplanned photo-

Tapes and photographs of family events are appreciated later.

graphs, such as mother and father coming home from work, small children playing in the backyard, or a grandfather rocking a grandchild, have appeal. One family found that the photograph and the letter that accompanied a holiday card was actually a family history as they reread the letters and looked at the photographs for a period of years. How do you keep records? What other kind of records do you think are important?

FAMILY RITUALS

There may be certain traditional ways of doing things in your family, such as what you eat and how your Sunday dinner is served. Professor James Bossard in his book *Ritual in Family Living* says that family rituals should not be confused with those used in religious services. A ritual is not awesome or mysterious. Rather it is a pattern or procedure found in family living that is well defined and is done again and again in the same way. Generally these rituals give a feeling of satisfaction. Research findings indicate that rituals are usually found in happy families.

These rituals vary from family to family. In some homes a bedtime story may be read by the father, mother, or older sister or brother. Special stories suited to seasons and holidays are emphasized in some families. One family always

included some children's poetry among their readings. Being dramatic while reading is remembered by children. Sometimes the reading is not at bedtime but at another hour that is more suitable to family schedules. In some families, the reading of the newspaper is shared and current events are discussed. This is not only interesting but also establishes the newspaper reading habit.

Saying grace at mealtime may be a ritual that was established in your grandfather's day and has been transmitted to your family. Sometimes the grace is sung and family members hold hands.

Many families have special ways of greeting one another. Arrival at home may be announced with a loud whistle, a "Hi," or several quick rings of the doorbell.

Sunday night supper may be a time for cooking together, with each family member preparing his or her specialty. It may be eaten before the television set while watching a favorite program or in the kitchen where it is cozy. Sunday night may be a time for inviting guests for an informal meal.

Birthday celebrations often become rituals with the blowing out of candles and the giving of gifts. A certain kind of cake may be the birthday cake. In one instance, the family birthday gift to a child every year was a silver dollar. In another family, a penny was given for each year of the child's age.

Reading to a small child will help you to prepare for future parenthood.

Birthday celebrations may be a family ritual.

Certain decorations may appear on Christmas trees year after year. The time and the way the tree is decorated form another ritual. In one family taking off the decorations became a kind of family party. The way Easter eggs are decorated and distributed is another ritual.

The kind of manners family members have may be a family characteristic. This may include the way a telephone is answered, guests are greeted, or service people are treated. Giving valentines to friends or to one another in the family can be pleasant.

To maintain these ways and rituals requires family management. What are some of your family rituals? How did they originate?

EVERYDAY WAYS

There may be some activities that occur every day that have important meanings to you. In most families, for example, one person is the early riser and may start the coffee for breakfast. Another family member may bring in the mail every day. Someone in your family may take the responsibility of calling your grandmother every day to inquire about her welfare. What do you do every day for your family?

CLEVER IDEAS FOR HANDLING MONEY

Some families have found clever ways for saving money. One family, for example, in analyzing its

spending, found that a very large sum was being spent on presents for parties, as hostess gifts, and for new babies, weddings, and other occasions. Several decisions were made. One was to keep a shelf for potential gifts purchased on sale days throughout the year. Every family member kept an alert eye for word about bargains. Another idea was to make as many gifts as possible.

The stuffed animal suggested in Chapter 31 or variations of it are a possibility. Making gifts from quilt blocks as suggested in Chapter 26 will have appeal to the receiver. Homemade food such as preserves, relishes, cookies, or fruitcake are good. In one home cookies are baked and placed in small boxes placed near the front door so that when guests call during the Christmas or Hanukkah holidays, they are given a box as they leave. Food or flowers from your garden may be offered for birthdays or when you are a guest in someone's home.

Collect interesting rocks that might be used for paperweights. Make a bracelet of colored buttons strung on elastic thread. Make a picture book for a small child. Some of your family crafts, such as wood carving, needlework, or basketry, are good sources of gifts. Keep a file folder on homemade gifts as suggested in newspapers, magazines, or radio or television programs.

Gift wrappings are expensive, too, so make your own. The want ad section of the Sunday newspaper makes an interesting wrapping paper when tied with a bright ribbon or yarn. Make a simple stencil out of a potato and decorate the paper. Brown wrapping paper or brown bags can make very attractive wrappings. Cut out white snowflakes by folding and cutting paper and paste them on. Make a design from odd and different colored buttons on the paper. A pressed leaf or flower adds interest. Another idea is to sprinkle a few sequins on the paper for sparkle. Paint designs such as a train or blocks for a child's gift. Use colored felt pens and write *To* and *From* right on the package.

Recycle coffee cans, glass jars, or boxes to hold your gifts. Decorate them if you wish. Make your family gift cards by buying plain colored 3-by-5-inch cards and fold them. Put a simple design on them; it could be your own or family logo or insignia. Recycle bits of yarn, string, cord, or ribbon for tying the presents. All of this becomes a management project. Make lists ahead of time based on past experience of the number and kind of gifts you or your family will give, and plan when and by whom they will be

made. Update this list from time to time.

Other money ideas include finding clever ways to earn money. See Chapter 34 for ideas. Some families might like to adapt the money planning that was done by the family in the story *I Remember Mama*. Each week the family sat around the table and allocated the family income according to its needs. Sometimes certain less urgent items had to be postponed until the following week or later. Each need was placed in an envelope. Planning together as a family was good, because each one had an opportunity to express his or her ideas and to make suggestions. What are money ideas of your family?

HOME CRAFTS

You might like to make an inventory of the talents of your family in making things. Are there other crafts that some family members would like to learn? There are many books of instruction available today and there are classes or individual instruction offered in needlework or other departments in department stores or in schools. An older person in the neighborhood may be pleased to teach you.

The Hawaiians and the Japanese make lovely oshibana cards which may also be used for notepaper or framed. Flowers, weeds, leaves, and other materials are dried and arranged artistically. A seaweed called *Ogō* by the Japanese and *Imu* by the Hawaiians is used for food, but the knobby sections are discarded and can be used for making interesting designs.

These oshibana cards can be used for messages at holiday times or to write to friends or relatives. They make pleasing gifts.

Every member of the family may enjoy some type of needlework. If a husky, professional, offensive football player like Roosevelt Grier does needlepoint and writes a book about it, he has done much to dispel the idea that needlework is only feminine. In addition to needlepoint, crocheting, knitting, embroidery, macrame, or quilting, the craft of needle weaving is easy and attractive.

You will need yarn for weaving. Begin a collection of colors and textures by buying single balls of yarn on sale, or using leftovers you may find at home or discards of friends and neighbors. Old sweaters may be unravelled. Strips may be cut from leftover fabrics or from old clothes. Remnants of fabric from upholstery shops give texture and body to your weaving. The possibilities are endless if you use your imagination.

The loom can be made by yourself. Take a piece of cardboard, one ring of an embroidery hoop, a plastic meat tray (not the transparent variety), or a piece of Masonite, and cut slits with scissors or a sharp knife at ¼ inch intervals at both ends. The size may vary from a small 4 by 4 card to one that is 12 by 18 inches.

To warp the loom (set in the threads that serve as a basis for the weaving) use strong and unstretchable carpet warp or linen string. Knot the end of the cord and pull the cord through the first slit from the back. Bring the cord across the face of the loom to the slit at the bottom and then back up to the next slit at the top. Continue until you have completed all the slits. For the last one, tie a knot at the back to hold it securely.

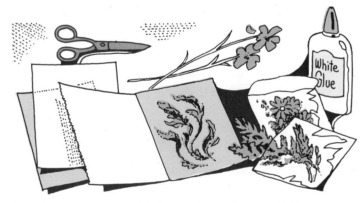

The arrangement might be made on thin colored paper and then covered with rice paper that has a white glue on the surface facing the arrangement. The paper also protects the arrangement and adds to the attractiveness of the result.

These two sheets then in turn may be pasted onto notepaper made from a good quality typing paper or it may be pasted on a plain white card, single or folded. If it is made into notepaper, buy or make envelopes to match.

For the weaving you will need a bent needle with a large eye. You can make one by bending it with a pliers.

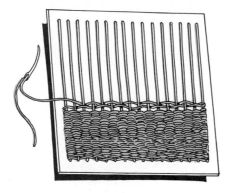

After you have threaded your needle you are ready to start. Do not use too long a weaving thread because it becomes frayed and worn.

Anchor your weaving thread with a knot on the first warp thread. Practice first on plain weaving and experiment later with other weaves. Place your needle over and under every other warp thread and when you return to the other side weave under the threads that you went over and over the threads that you went under.

When you come to the end and reverse directions, make your weaving stronger by wrapping your weaving thread around the last warp thread twice.

Use a large tooth comb to brush your thread up to the top of the loom after going across each time, to make your weaving firm.

Sew together your woven squares or rectangles into pillows, scarves, tote bags, rugs, wall hangings, or other articles that your imagination may concoct. When you feel comfortable weaving, try other kinds of weaves, mix fabrics, yarns, and colors; add feathers or bright colored small sticks; or string some beads on the yarn or fabric you use. With the embroidery hoop one way is to place only a few warp threads and then anchor other warp threads to the ones attached to the hoop. This gives an airy look. You may weave strips that are placed together in some interesting fashion. Your family can become famous for original ideas.

Other craft ideas will occur to you, using other materials for your medium, such as wood, papier mâché, string, collages of almost any material imaginable, plastic, paper, and others. All of these crafts can be used to make your home more attractive, to give as gifts, or to sell.

THINKING IT OVER

1. Choose a family ritual in your own or someone else's family. Trace its history if you can. What started it and what kept it going?
2. What was the nicest gift you ever received? Why was it nice? What in your estimation was the nicest gift you ever gave to someone? Why?

THINGS TO DO

1. Suppose you had fifty cents to buy a gift for a friend. Look in local stores and little shops for suggestions. Could you buy something with the money and then make a gift by adding something to give a unique touch?
2. Make a survey of the family customs or money customs of several families who may be willing to be interviewed. How did they compare with your own family? Which ones did you especially like?
3. Visit a craft museum or a craft show. What ideas did you gain that you could use?

area eight

Looking Ahead

34 Work and careers

Do you realize that you will probably spend at least 40 years of your life working? You will devote approximately a third of a day for four to five days a week to a job for these years. Wouldn't it be a good idea to spend a little time thinking about something that will have such a dominant role in your life?

INFLUENCES OF WORK

One of the first influences of a job is the effect it has on your time schedule. You may have to forego some activities because of your job. Mealtimes may change. The amount of money you earn affects your spending habits. Some jobs give you more recognition with your friends than others. At your age, you may be limited in the kind of work you can do because of labor laws and for other reasons. But you can be alert to opportunities for the future.

MEANINGS OF WORK

What does work really mean to you? For several days listen to the comments people make about work. Do you hear statements like these? "It's Monday morning, I hate to go back to work." "Thank goodness, it's Friday night." "I wish I had a vacation beginning tomorrow." "I wish I could stay home today." Analyze what you overheard. Were more statements positive than negative? What did the people talk about? What were your conclusions? Did you agree or disagree with their viewpoints?

How does your family regard work? Do family members encourage you to get an education or have special preparation for a job so that you can find work more easily, can receive better pay, and have more pleasant work? Do members in your family tend to do the same kind of work and do they expect you to do the same? Do they indicate preferences for some types of jobs and dislike for other types of work? Do you agree with them? What are your family's reasons for liking or disliking certain jobs for you?

How is work regarded in your neighborhood? Is a job a way to earn a living or do some people enjoy their work in addition? How do they label jobs that require strenuous physical exertion? Do your neighbors believe that everyone has the ability to do some kind of work and if sufficiently interested, anyone can find a job? What are the reactions when persons in the community are "laid off" because of a recession or for other reasons? Is work considered more important for a man than for a woman? How does all this relate to your meanings of work?

Can you distinguish clearly between work and play or leisure? Many believe that work is "paid work." Have you ever seen people build a boat, cane a chair, fix a car, cook food over a campfire, or sew a dress and consider it only play? What makes the difference between work and play? What about time for play balancing time for work? How do you regard men and women who "moonlight" or work at other jobs on weekends, holidays, or days off? Under what circumstances should this be done? Could any of this work be called play?

Do you associate unions with work? What do you see as the strengths and shortcomings of unions? Talk to persons belonging to a union. What do they consider the most important benefits? If any of them had previously worked in a non-union situation, what were some of the differences? Talk to a few union leaders or organizers about their viewpoint. Talk to the owner of a non-union shop. Seek their ideas about the purpose of strikes. Summarize your ideas and feelings about these questions and unions.

ATTITUDES TOWARD WORK

What would you consider a good attitude toward work? For example, if you are a delivery person for a drugstore, do you feel that what you are doing contributes to the success of the business? Describe what you would consider a good and a poor attitude in this drugstore job. A famous psychologist believes that attitudes toward work are formed in latter childhood and adolescence— your age. On the next page is a list of attitudes toward work. React to each one. Would you change any of them? Would you hire yourself?

You may be encouraged to stay in school and not drop out so that you can find a better job later.

When is fixing a car work and when is it play?

reasons? Are there jobs you would not like your mother or sister to have? Your father or brother? Are there jobs that you would reject because you believe that they are not appropriate for your sex? Who influences you in these ideas?

You may examine other roles related to work. What kind of person is best suited to be a professional baseball shortstop, a bus driver, a doctor, an airline stewardess, a fashion expert, or a director for a home for the aged?

Other role interpretations are important. Must the father, for example, be the most impor-

Share your findings with your classmates. Do you agree or disagree with them?

INTERPRETING WORK ROLES

Although many jobs are now unisex-oriented, some jobs are still labeled masculine or feminine. Men are now employed as telephone operators, for example, in a field that formerly was occupied solely by women. A few women are welders and "hard hats." Can you cite other examples? Do you feel that certain jobs should be for women only? For men only? What are your

Do you feel you are contributing to the success of the firm you work for by doing your work promptly and well?

Table 34-1

ANALYSIS OF WORKING ATTITUDES			
Attitude Toward	Important	Not Important	Not Sure
1. Punctuality			
2. Interest in the entire business			
3. Courtesy			
4. Pleasantness			
5. Learning to do the job well			
6. Dependability			
7. Enthusiasm			
8. Working only the time required			
9. Care of equipment used			
10. Accuracy			
11. Respect for rules			
12. Thoroughness			

tant provider in the family? In some families the father stays at home and the mother works. Do you believe that wives or mothers should work? How should the decision be made? What should be done with the salary? Do you believe people who are out of work do not want to work?

WHAT IS GOOD ABOUT WORK?

One of the most important satisfactions that some people gain from work is helping others or trying to make the world a little better. When you realize that others are dependent on you or that your job is an important part of an entire organization, you enjoy your work. You have an opportunity to make new friends and you have the companionship of others. The fact that you are making a contribution to our national economy is important. You do this by helping in the processing of a product or in performing services for others. You in turn enjoy the products and services of other workers.

Experts tell us that work has valuable psychological benefits. Maybe you have been lonely and now you will be with others. When you concentrate on work, problems and worries seem less troublesome.

When you are on a job, you usually control yourself more than you do at home. For example, you may be more courteous, less inclined to be silly, or keep down evidences of anger or frustrations to a greater degree. In order to be successful, you have to communicate well, be sensitive to the needs and wishes of your fellow workers, and exchange ideas. All in all, you feel as though you are a part of the world.

If your supervisor praises you for your good work, it makes you feel good about yourself. If you are proud of what you are doing, your feeling of achievement is strengthened. You have proven yourself in a sense. Having other workers interested in you is good for your morale.

Another advantage in working is that you learn to handle yourself well in difficult situations. If a customer complains about the late arrival of goods, by being especially polite, offering a reasonable explanation, and using a touch of humor, you may make her or him pleasant again. What works with this customer may work with others, with appropriate adaptations. You learn to understand people and to test ways of having friendly relations with strangers. This may help you in the future in other jobs.

Gaining an insight about what it is like and securing ideas of the kind of job you might like

in the future provide good experience. And your family may be especially pleased at the way work is helping you grow up.

THINKING ABOUT YOUR CAREER

Although you may have given some thought to your work of the future, you may be undecided about actual directions. First, you may wish to look at yourself and then match your outstanding characteristics to the requirements of the job you desire. On the next page is a 5-point scale on which you might rate yourself. Include other points if you desire.

After you have rated yourself, try to think of actual circumstances when you have demonstrated these characteristics. Do you feel that this rating represents the real you?

In selecting job possibilities, one suggestion is to study the job clusters that have been developed by the U.S. Office of Education. Thousands and thousands of jobs were placed into the following clusters:

Agribusiness and Natural Resources	Humanities
	Hospitality and
Business and Office	Recreation
Consumer Education and Home Economics	Health
	Manufacturing
Construction	Marine Sciences
Communication and Media	Marketing
	Personal Service
Environment	Public Services
Fine Arts and	Transportation

What do you consider appropriate clothes to wear when selling items that you make at home?

359

Table 34-2

ANALYSIS OF PERSONAL CHARACTERISTICS AND ABILITIES

Personal Characteristics	High	Above Average	Average	Below Average	Low
Intelligence					
Activity					
Leadership					
Creativity					
Health					
Critical thinking					
Responsibility					
Maturity					
Stability					
Abilities					
(List your school subjects)					
Communication Skills					
Writing					
Speaking					
Organizing					
Good judgment of others					
Being scientific					
Being artistic					
Having Hand Skills					
Working well with others					
How Do You Like To Work					
Alone					
In noise and confusion					
Actively					
Under pressure					
By planning ahead of time					
With established routine					
Handling details					
Getting immediate results					
Values					
Prestige					
Money					
Getting ahead					
Being well dressed					
Being ethical					

How do your personal characteristics rate?

Select several clusters that have special appeal to you.

Explore the kind of jobs that are available in the clusters that you have selected. Read about these positions—the qualifications, nature of the work, and the like. Talk to persons who are in these jobs, if possible. Try to get some actual in-

formation by visiting a person in the job. Read the want ads in your local newspaper to determine whether any of these jobs are in your community.

One of the best sources of information about jobs is the *Occupational Outlook Handbook* prepared by the Bureau of Labor Statistics of the U.S. Department of Labor. The listing of jobs differs from the 15 clusters mentioned before, but may be more meaningful to you. For each position, there is a discussion of the nature of the work; places of employment; training, qualifications, and advancement; employment outlook; earnings; working conditions; and sources for additional information. Your school library probably has this valuable reference that should be helpful to you.

When you examine the job areas that you especially like, you may encounter some problems. A job that seems great to you has the qualifications of a college degree and that is an uncertainty. Several solutions are possible. You

may prepare yourself for the nonprofessional or paraprofessional levels rather than the professional level. Discuss this situation with your guidance counselor. If you are a superior student and have personal qualities for professional work, scholarships or working you way through college are possibilities. Many students who do not have the finances for four years of college, go to college when they can pay for it and then work in between. Some students study part time and work part time. There are many possibilities. Give some thought to skills that you have for working between college study periods or part time while attending college. Good typing skills are often in great demand. Some students work as full-time or part-time secretaries in the university they are attending and may have tuition-free privileges. You will have to decide how much you want to work in a particular field and how much perseverance you have.

You may feel it is too early for you to be concerned about these matters. Right now you

There are many ways to secure a college education—going to school at night after work, working part time and studying part time, or studying full time for a period and alternating with full-time work. Look at catalogues in the guidance office and see what other possibilities may be available.

can try to improve your school record or grades so that if you want to go to college, you will be admitted. While you are in high school, you will want to plan courses that will be necessary or helpful in your future work. Is science or math necessary? Would some extra art or literature courses be helpful? Otherwise you may find yourself going to summer school to make up prerequisites for your career. You might secure certain kinds of experiences during these years that may give greater confidence on the job later.

Jobs and job requirements change quickly, according to national needs. Keep flexible now and when you are older you may be able to shift into another area or type of position that has higher priority. You have to prepare yourself for jobs that are available, so keep alert to what is needed that you like to do. You may have to have some additional preparation and experience but high schools through continuing education courses usually offer such courses for new-type jobs.

EXPLORE CAREERS THROUGH PART-TIME JOBS

Some of the most valuable experiences you can have for future jobs are through part-time work, volunteer work, and selling your own services. Part-time work may include the following:

 Arranging parties for children
 Baby-sitting
 Conducting a cooking school for
  small children
 Delivering
 Gardening, selling flowers and
  vegetables, or taking care of other
  people's gardens
 Helping with farm harvests
 Girl or Boy Friday—doing odd jobs in
  someone's office
 Mother's helper
 Mowing lawns
 Serving a newspaper route
 Repairing appliances
 Singing or playing in a
  band for entertainment
 Taking care of pets
 Typing
 Tutoring
 Washing and waxing cars
 Making things for sale
 Teaching another language to someone

Taking care of pets may be a way of earning money.

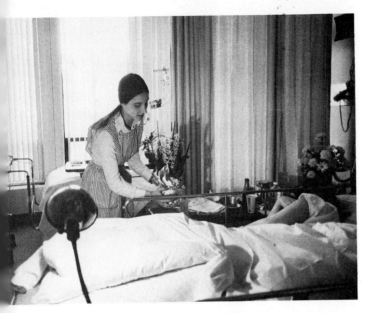

Survey the possibilities for doing volunteer work in your community that would serve as a kind of work experience for you.

Most of these are services you can offer. You might think of a unique business, such as making clever notepaper, memorandum pads, grocery list pads, party favors, place cards, bird houses, place mats, or costume jewelry from materials at hand such as bark, coconut shells, seeds, seed pods, or pressed flowers. You might print a neat card telling about your services and distribute it to potential customers.

Volunteer work, if taken seriously, is equally useful. Think of institutions or agencies in your community that might need help. Being a candy striper in a hospital might involve reading to sick children or other patients, delivering mail or flowers, writing letters for the handicapped, running errands for patients, and the like. Both boys and girls will enjoy these and other work in a hospital. Visiting nursing homes for the aged and performing similar or other duties will be enlightening and useful. Other institutions, such as those for retarded children, orphans, mentally disturbed children, or juvenile offenders, offer possibilities for you to gain valuable experience in working with people.

Community projects for improving the environment, recycling, beautification, litter control, or poverty projects give you an opportunity to help your community and to open up possibilities of careers of this nature. If you live in an area where migrant workers are employed to help with crop harvests, you might help with a playmobile that carries simple play equipment and games that children of these workers might enjoy. There may be an opportunity for you to plan some clever ways of using these materials. You may belong to a family that is political-minded. Joining in such activities as stuffing envelopes, distributing literature, or answering the telephone is a way of learning to work with others. You and your classmates might make a directory of the possibilities of volunteer work in your community. All of these experiences can be recorded on your résumé for future jobs. Other types of interesting jobs may come to your attention. Some of the adults for whom you work may prove to be future employers or they may be willing to give you a character reference when you need one.

CAREERS IN HOME ECONOMICS

Now that you are in a class in home economics you might be interested in some of the careers in this field. The positions available are of three types: nonprofessional, paraprofessional, and professional.

Entry-Level Jobs

Entry-level jobs are considered nonprofessional. Examples are as aides in food service, recreation, interior decoration, housekeeping (hotel, motel, or hospital), or child care in a nursery school or day-care center, cook's helper, counter man or woman, or alteration worker on women's or men's clothing. Positions as a clerk in a furniture, fabric, department, hardware, or carpet store are other possibilities. A worker in a dry-cleaning or laundry plant or in a garment factory are other considerations for nonprofessionals. These positions are available to high-school graduates, dropouts, and adults. Courses in occupational education in high school or through adult education help a person be better prepared for these jobs and increases the likelihood of being hired.

Paraprofessional Jobs

Paraprofessionals have had two years of college preparation. Available positions include food-service supervisors, assistants to dietitians (dietary technicians), nursery school teacher assistants, assistant buyer or fashion coordinator

Paraprofessionals assisting in a day-care center

Home economists with a master's or doctor's degree become college teachers, supervisors, extension specialists, directors of hospital dietary departments, officers in food, textile, pattern, or chain store companies, or administrators at the college level of home economics.

You may find home economists in positions in your own community. Why not talk to them and visit them on the job? Maybe you can do some volunteer work with them and learn more about their work. Talk to your home economics teacher about jobs that appeal to you.

FORMS AND OTHER DETAILS

In addition to all the other planning that has been suggested to you, it is important to become familiar with forms and other details relative to securing a job. Look at application forms to see what they ask so as to inform yourself of the kind of information you will have to supply. You might fill one out for fun to get the feel of it. Now look at it and decide how it would appeal to an employer. Carelessness in answering may give an unfavorable impression of you. Plan a ré-

in retail stores, assistant to a home economist in business, or housekeeper in a hotel, motel, or hospital.

Professional Jobs

Graduates of a four-year college program in home economics or human ecology may become teachers at the elementary or high-school levels, home economists with business firms, advertising agencies, or public-relations firms developing or testing new products or appearing on television or radio programs for homemakers. Being a foods, clothing, home furnishings, equipment, or child care editor for a newspaper or magazine or an editor for a home economics magazine or for a publishing company that publishes home economics textbooks are exciting positions if you are interested in writing. Other positions are as home economists with utility companies to help homemakers with equipment use, energy saving, and other problems; hospital dietitians; or advisers for customers of banks and financial companies to help with budgeting and other money problems. Being an extension worker, a home economics consultant with a welfare agency, a home economics specialist with a teen-age magazine, or a fashion coordinator for a department store or a chain store might interest you.

Write your résumé so that an employer will be impressed.

sumé that gives an overview of your experience, education and training, and personal data. Remember that an employer in looking at a résumé or an application asks the question "How can this applicant help us?" It is a good idea to keep a record of your activities and other information, bearing in mind the points that will impress an employer. In your volunteer work you may have worked a short time on a job under supervision but graduated to independence.

WHAT IS BEST FOR ME?

One of the most serious shortcomings of trying to find the best place for yourself in the world of work is the lack of information about the many opportunities available to you. So be alert to this type of information. Another challenge is to prepare yourself personally to the extent that you will have characteristics that are desirable in an employee.

THINKING IT OVER

1. Think about the job that you would like best. The worst kind of job you could have. What are the differences? Is there a perfect job?
2. How might the interpretation of your role as a worker affect your family? What might be areas of agreement or disagreement? How would you handle them?
3. Describe what you believe is involved in being ethical on the job.

THINGS TO DO

1. In grafitti style or in other ways make short statements on a poster, bulletin board, or other form of communication about some common ideas or feelings about work.
2. Prepare a series of bulletin boards on careers in home economics for the general bulletin board or for the cafeteria so that all students can view them. Place a box near the bulletin board for questions to be answered.
3. Keep track of your activities for a day and label them work or play. Have someone else analyze them. How do you account for differences of opinion?
4. Interview a number of different types of workers in your community about what they like best and what they like least about working. If possible, tape the interviews and be prepared to discuss them in class. Are some of the reactions alike? To what extent do you agree or disagree with the comments?
5. Invite to class a panel of school personnel, such as the school lunch manager, business manager, a department head, or others who have to supervise workers. What do they consider the most serious problems they have with workers in general?

35 The best of your world

There is a saying that "In today walks tomorrow." How are you preparing yourself today so that tomorrow will give you a good life? One way to dramatize your entire lifetime is to devise or sketch a yardstick kind of measurement device that indicates every year of your life until 70 years of age, or for as long as you think you may live. Fill in the highlights of your life to the present and then imagine the rest of your life and its major events, such as first job, high school graduation, marriage and children, and when you hope to reach the peak of your career. Make it unique for you. Take it out periodically and update it. Evaluate your life in terms of the realization of important human desires.

HUMAN DESIRES

Bear in mind that the outside world and other factors will have a strong influence on actual life happenings. Margaret Mead, the noted anthropologist-sociologist, believes that four desires shape our lives. They are (1) the desire to adapt to our environment, (2) the desire to find love and companionship, (3) the desire to relate to something bigger than ourselves, and (4) the desire to work in groups to attain something that cannot be obtained alone. Think about these desires in relation to your future.

DESIRE TO ADAPT TO THE ENVIRONMENT
Physical Environment

How does your environment affect you? Climate, for example, influences your type of home, clothes, and recreation. Inhabitants of warm states, for example, can swim in the ocean or lakes during the winter months but cannot ski in the snow unless they have access to the snow in high mountains. An automobile in the north has to have antifreeze and in the south an air conditioner. These and many other factors will make a difference in family money management and in life-style.

In our physical environment there is a strong desire to eliminate pollution and to improve and save our environment so that our lives will not be threatened. You may be involved in these activities now and the need may become more critical as you grow older.

Economic Environment

Our economic environment has one of the strongest influences on our lives. High prices of fuel, food, and other commodities, the threat of loss of jobs, temporary layoffs, and the lag of incomes to meet basic needs, threaten many individuals and families. This situation is worldwide and threatens the life-style of almost everyone. There is no indication of how or when it will ease. Relief may not come until solutions are found, and in the meantime sacrifices and other ways of living must be explored. The depletion of natural resources, especially oil, will bring many changes. What are some ways that your family is coping with the situation and planning to cope in the future?

If You Are Poor. If you are especially poor, try to find all of the avenues for assistance that are available to you, such as food stamps, free lunches and breakfasts at school, free commodity foods, low-income housing, or summer camps for your younger brothers and sisters. Is there a consumer agency in your community that can help you regain your money from the purchase of goods found to be defective or in tricky sales deals? Try to locate thrift shops, discount houses, and other places where food, clothes, household equipment, or furniture can be secured at reduced cost. What kind of free recreation is available? Can you join or form a cooperative and buy necessities at wholesale prices? Are there dependent children in your family who are eligible for assistance? What provisions are made in your community to assist you with medical and dental costs?

You need not be penniless to get help. City, state, and federal agencies can provide you with the information you need. Welfare is not intended as a dole or money handout. Other services, such as health care advice, counseling on money management, employment counseling, and services to secure child support care, are available.

Other aspects of your physical environment are important, such as adequate and pure water to drink and air to breathe, sewage and garbage

Climate influences the kind of clothes you wear.

367

Are you involved in the prevention of pollution?

DESIRE FOR LOVE AND COMPANIONSHIP

The need for love and companionship will be important throughout your life. Your friends and your family can make a large contribution to fulfilling this need. But the need is not met automatically. You must think about it and work at it. Some families are more loving and companionable than others because this has a higher value to them and they appreciate the importance of family closeness. If each family member is loving and interested in others, the family seems stronger and happier. Think of the ways in which families can demonstrate love and a de-

disposal, transportation, recreational facilities, and many others. What do you feel is lacking in your community? What can you do to improve the situation? On the other hand, what do you feel is good? Do you foresee any changes that will make the living less desirable? Is your community preparing for it?

Free lunches at school will help the family budget.

Plot Your Life—by indicating major events that you imagine

Counseling on various problems is helpful.

What does a friend mean to you?

Working with small children helps you to become acquainted with this age level and with yourself.

and the age when they will take place

1991	1992	1993		1995		2028	2029	2030	2031	2032	2033	
28	(29)	30		(33)		(65)	66	67	68	69	70	

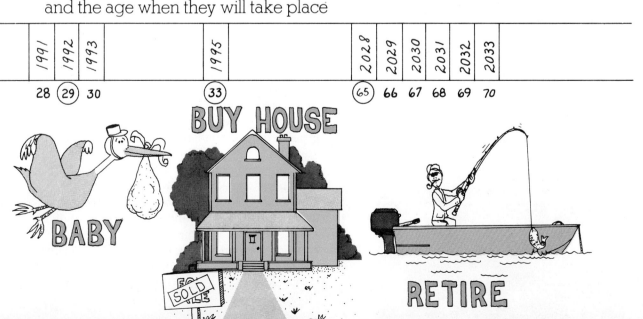

BABY

BUY HOUSE

FOR SOLD SALE

RETIRE

sire for togetherness. Each family develops its own ways. Now think about how you will be a loving parent and try to have a loving family in your future. How will you teach your children to be loving and good companions? Meeting this basic need is one of the most important functions of the family.

Speeches have been made and books have been written about how to make friends. The answer is not simple. Think of the best friends you have now. How did you become friendly? Probably each friendship started in a different way and experiences that cemented your friendship varied. No doubt common interests in the same school subject, sports, music, books and clubs, and personal characteristics that appeal to each other were considerations for starting points. Sharing an important experience together, such as playing on the same team, being in the same play, or having a tragic experience in common, are other possibilities. What do you believe are good ways to make friends? What does a good friend mean to you? How will you make friends with others throughout your life? How will you overcome the problem of unloving family members or not having friends?

Having friends with varied backgrounds has many benefits. If possible, select some of your friends from different national, racial, economic, or religious backgrounds so that you can learn to work together and break down any barriers that may exist. The ideas and experiences of these

4-H Clubs, Girl and Boy Scouts, and FHA are valuable organizations.

friends can broaden and enrich your background.

Do you have friends of different age levels? If you do not have a grandparent, adopt one—someone who does not have grandchildren or whose grandchildren live far away. You will make this person feel young and you will feel more grown-up. There are many other benefits to such a relationship.

Are you friendly with small children? How about being friendly with a baby? This may sound strange to you, but your first child will be a small helpless infant. The baby cannot talk to you and you have to build your own communication system. All of this can be rather frightening if you have not had any experience around a baby. Experiences like these are sometimes called parenting—learning to be parents. But they are enjoyable in themselves. You will also be contributing to the child's development. Love and companionship are powerful forces in helping children and infants grow in many ways.

DESIRE TO RELATE TO SOMETHING BIGGER THAN SELF

The idea of relating to something bigger than yourself may be related to your religion, your philosophy of life, inspiration from noted writers, artists, or musicians, communing with nature, or acquaintance with individuals who broaden your horizons and your thoughts. In those moments when you feel small and somewhat insignificant or troubled, it is rather important to be able to turn to some source that will help to bring peace and harmony to you. Do not neglect this area of your life, because you will want to share it with your children.

DESIRE FOR GROUP MEMBERSHIP

The groups to which you belong now and to which you will belong in the years ahead should be examined for the benefits each group brings to you and in a larger sense what the group contributes to society. The purpose of these varied groups may emphasize recreation, which can contribute to health and companionship; politics, to provide an opportunity to have a part in government; meditation, for spiritual welfare; or community problems of an environmental, educational, or city planning nature. Some individuals feel that they can help the consumer by consumer-action groups. In later life, you may

Food stamps help in making money go further.

clude peace in the world, food for starving children, a better life for orphans, prison reform, conservation of natural resources, civil rights, and relief of poverty. Obviously, you cannot participate in all of them but you can select the one or ones about which you feel strongly. Or, do you believe in causes? In which cause or causes are you interested at present? Why? Think about how much more you can do in a group than alone.

Give some additional thought to how you would like to change the world in which you live. Is the protection of human dignity recognized in programs and projects? What about an old man who pays for his groceries with food stamps and whom everyone in the cashier's line may unconsciously label as poor? A handicapped girl applies for a position for which her counselor and she feel she can qualify but is rejected and wonders if it is because of her handicap. How can we change social attitudes towards these and other groups? How do you suppose these individuals felt in the situations cited?

belong to professional organizations, unions, or other groups for the improvement of working conditions.

There may be a cause about which you are concerned now or will be later. These might in-

These are only two of the many problems that face the world and especially our nation. The challenge is great but not impossible. What you think and do can make a difference.

THINKING IT OVER

1. Describe what "the best of your world" means to you specifically.
2. Consider possible positions that might be taken in regard to a cause, such as the conservation of natural resources. Review facts and ideas of individuals for it, indifferent about it, or opposed. Which arguments do you think are weak? Which are important to you?
3. Project yourself into the parenthood stage. What kind of parenting experiences can you have now to prepare you for the future?
4. Are there other human desires that you would like to add to the list?

THINGS TO DO

1. Make a list of ways that you adapt to your environment. Can you conceive of possible improvements over present ways? Share these ideas with your classmates. Experiment with some of the possibilities and report your results.
2. Make a survey about what people consider the most serious problems of high food prices. How are they meeting these problems? Share your results with others.
3. Could you launch "Make A Friend Week" in your school? What might be done to facilitate friend-making?
4. Have a circle session about what might be done about a serious problem in your community, such as crime, violence, drug or alcohol abuse, or reckless driving. Think about what each of you can do alone and in groups.

index

photo and art credits

PHOTO CREDITS

American Spice Trade Association, 191 (top); B. Anderson from Monkmeyer Press Photo Service, 307; Bruce Anspach/EPA Newsphoto, 368 (left); A. T. & T. Photo Center, 18 (bottom right); Elinor S. Beckwith, 146, 182; John Brandes, 4, 12 (middle left) 20–21, 22, 34, 39 (bottom left and top right), 42–43, 44, 72 (top left), 77 (middle), 80–81, 88, 91, 98, 104, 112, 116 (bottom right), 117 (left), 126–127, 128, 138, 148 (top), 150, 160, 162 (bottom), 172, 176, 180, 183, 188, 189 (top left), 191 (bottom), 193 (bottom left), 196–197, 198, 200 (middle left), 208, 224, 238 (right), 241, 242, 243, 244 (left), 246, 247, 260, 264 (bottom), 274, 286–287, 302, 304 (background), 316 (left), 320, 329, 331 (bottom), 332, 354–355, 361 (bottom right); Campbell Soup Company, 158 (top), 175; Cereal Institute, Inc., 157 (bottom), 217 (left and left bottom); Channel 13 WNET, 50 (right); Bob Combs from Rapho/Photo Researchers, Inc., 6 (top left); Cracker Chatter, Nabisco, Inc., 147; Gene Daniels from Black Star, 38 (left); De Wys, Inc., 18 (top left), 25, 49 (right), 85, 102; Sam Falk from Monkmeyer Press Photo Service, 184, 186; Florida Department of Citrus, 100 (top left), 154 (bottom), 157 (top); Foldes from Monkmeyer Press Photo Service, 117 (right); Mimi Forsyth from Monkmeyer Press Photo Service, 2–3, 6 (middle left and bottom right), 8, 11, 13, 19, 23, 29, 30, 31, 36 (right), 40 (bottom, 51, 53 (bottom right), 70 (top right), 72 (middle right), 73, 77 (right), 82, 86, 99, 101, 108, 110, 115, 119, 121 (bottom left), 153, 167 (bottom left), 168 (top), 170, 173, 177 (bottom), 181, 193 (top right), 194, 199, 200 (middle top), 203, 204, 209, 210, 222 (bottom), 232 (background), 236, 273, 290 (right), 291, 294, 295, 296, 297, 303, 304 (bottom), 305, 306 (top), 308, 309, 325, 331 (top), 334 (bottom), 357, 359, 362, 369, 371; Friesem from Monkmeyer Press Photo Service, 339 (bottom right); Fujihira from Monkmeyer Press Photo Service, 217 (right bottom); General Mills, 152 (left); Margot Granitsas from Rapho/Photo Researchers, Inc., 7; Hays from Monkmeyer Press Photo Service, 59; Michal Heron, 10, 14, 16, 28, 36 (left), 45, 46, 47, 48, 49 (left) 50 (left), 56, 58 (top left), 62, 63, 64 (bottom left, center, and top), 65, 68, 69, 70 (bottom left), 71, 72 (middle left and bottom right), 75, 76, 106, 336; Tana Hoban from dpi, 7, 57; Dean Hollyman from Rapho/Photo Researchers, Inc., 213; Jefferson from Monkmeyer Press Photo Service, 217 (right top); Everett C. Johnson from De Wys, Inc., 24 (bottom right); Freda Leinwand from Monkmeyer Press Photo Service, 89; Lenox China, Inc., 122; Svat Macha from De Wys, Inc., 58 (bottom right); Lynn McLaren from Rapho/Photo Researchers, Inc., 53 (top left); Karl H. Maslowski from Rapho/Photo Researchers, Inc., 322 (top); A. & R. Maucker, 64 (bottom right); The Melamine Council, 116 (top left); Michael Meyerhein, 190, 200 (bottom); Phiz Mezey from dpi, 346; Lynn Millar—UNICEF, 39 (bottom right); Larry Mulvehill, 12 (top left and bottom right), 17, 24 (top left and top right), 32, 52, 60, 84, 100 (middle right and top right), 107, 109, 114, 120, 121 (top right), 124, 139, 140, 162 (top), 166, 167 (top), 168 (bottom), 169, 177 (top), 205, 210 (bottom), 214, 216 (left and right), 217 (center), 221, 222 (top), 226, 228, 229 (bottom left and right), 232, 233, 238 (left), 248 (top), 290 (left), 292, 293, 304 (top), 306 (bottom), 310, 311, 314, 315, 324, 327, 330 (right), 339 (top left), 340 (bottom), 350, 351, 358, 361 (top right and left), 364 (left), 367, 368 (right); The New York Times Studio, 189 (bottom right); Christy Park from Monkmeyer Press Photo Service, 35, 77 (top left); Pepperidge Farm, 100 (bottom right), 148 (bottom); Poultry and Egg National Board, 158 (bottom); Procter & Gamble, 215, 216 (left and right center); Hugh Rogers from Monkmeyer Press Photo Service, 330 (left), 334 (top); Helena Rubinstein, 370; Salton, Inc., 141; O. Schroeppel from dpi, 220; Simplicity Patterns, 38 (bottom right), 248 (bottom), 255, 263; The Singer Company, 244 (right); © Copyright SUVA from dpi, 318, 322 (bottom), 340 (top); Swift & Company, 154 (top left); Sybil Shackman from Monkmeyer Press Photo Service, 264 (top), 316 (right), 326, 363, 364 (right); United Dairy Industry Association, 152 (right), 178, 338; United Fresh Fruit & Vegetable Association, 144; USDA Photo, 40 (top left), 229 (top left); George Whitely from Rapho/Photo Researchers, Inc., 108 (left).

Special thanks to Child Care Center Y.W.C.A. in Ridgewood, New Jersey for permission to take the photographs on pages 45, 46, 47, 48, 49 (left), 50 (left), 56, 58 (top left), 62, 63, 64 (bottom left, center, and top), 65, 68, 69, 70 (bottom left), 71, 72 (middle left and bottom right), 75, 76; the children and teacher, June Riemersma, in the art class of the Reynolds School, Upper Saddle River, New Jersey, 42–43; Threadneedle, Englewood, New Jersey, 264 (bottom).

ART CREDITS

Bob Askey, 36, 88, 89, 90, 91, 142, 143, 185 (bottom right), 213 (left), 241 (left), 242, 243, 244, 245, 293, 298, 304 (bottom right), 309, 310, 330, 333 (top), 349, 351; Librada Castellon, 38, 202, 205, 206, 225 (right), 226, 227, 230 (top), 232, 234, 235, 236 (left), 237, 241 (right), 249, 250, 251, 254, 256 (right), 257 (right), 261 (top left), 262 (middle and bottom), 265 (top left), 266 (top left), 267 (left middle), 270 (top left and bottom), 271, 275, 277 (top right), 278, 279, 280, 281, 282, 283, 284, 331 (bottom right); Tony Giamas, 73, 74, 94, 95, 96, 106, 113, 114 (right), 115, 117, 118, 119, 122, 123, 129, 130, 131, 132, 133, 141, 145, 152, 153, 155, 156, 157, 162, 163, 174, 182, 183, 185 (top left), 190, 192, 200 (right), 201, 212, 213 (right), 215, 218, 219, 220, 225 (left), 228, 230 (bottom), 231, 233, 236 (right), 247, 252, 253, 256 (top and middle), 257 (top left), 261 (bottom right), 262 (top right), 263, 270 (top right), 273, 274, 290, 294, 304 (top left), 305, 314, 315, 318, 319, 323, 331 (bottom), 337, 352, 353; Gary Schuermann, 84, 105, 114 (left), 135, 136, 161, 164, 175, 289, 299, 307, 316, 317, 321, 324, 326, 341, 342, 343, 344, 345, 360, 368, 369; James Walsh, 261 (top right, middle, and bottom left), 265 (top right, middle, and bottom), 266 (middle bottom), 267 (top, right middle, and bottom), 268, 269, 276, 277 (middle and bottom).